From Cultural Rebellion to Counterrevolution:
The Politics of Maurice Barrès

— Où voulez-vous aller, Maurice Barrès ?

— A la Chambre des Députés.

— C'est impossible ! A cause de votre attitude contre l'Exposition de 1900, tous les chemins sont **BARRÉS** !

Anti-Barrès political cartoon from *Paris-Banlieue*, Feb. 22-28, 1896. Courtesy of the Archives de Préfecture de Police, Paris.

From Cultural Rebellion To Counterrevolution: The Politics of Maurice Barrès

C. STEWART DOTY

OHIO UNIVERSITY PRESS
Athens, Ohio

FOR JEAN WITH LOVE

Table of Contents

Introduction 1

CHAPTER ONE: From Cultural Rebellion to
Political Commitment 8

CHAPTER TWO: The Campaign of 1889 in Nancy 36

CHAPTER THREE: Barrès and the Failure of
National Boulangism 70

CHAPTER FOUR: Maurice Barrès, Deputy of Nancy,
1889–1893 100

CHAPTER FIVE: At the Crossroads: Socialism, Nationalism,
or National Socialism, 1893–1896 117

CHAPTER SIX: Nationalism and National-Socialism,
1897–1898 153

CHAPTER SEVEN: Barrès and the Nationalist Leagues,
1899–1903 176

CHAPTER EIGHT: From the "Death of Nationalism" to
the "Nationalist Revival," 1903–1914 211

CHAPTER NINE: The Last Years 237

Notes 251

Bibliography 279

Index 291

Introduction

According to novelist Julien Green, a French writer lecturing at Oxford University once commented that there were three Barrèses, the Barrès of the *Jardin sur l'Oronte*, the Barrès of Charmes, and a third Barrès, which Green could not remember. During the question period after the lecture a student asked, "I would like to know the first names of Barrès' two brothers."[1] For readers of Barrès scholarship three Barrèses all too often seem to be a conservative figure, for he has evoked such a variety of interpretations that he must have been part of a much larger family than that. For some readers he was such a revanchist that he could be seen as the *rossignol du carnage*. Others have seen him as the precurser of fascism, Vichy, *Algérie française*, and even Gaullism. Still others have seen him as the unsung French father of existentialism and the political novel. In early 1974 one commentator even saw him as "a hippie before the word was invented, the pioneer of the spirit of the commune movement," only Barrès' "commune" was Lorraine.[2]

One reason for this confusion in interpretation is that scholars have not given us all of Barrès. Because his novels and political essays took French intellectuals by storm in his own time and later, Barrès scholars have limited themselves to his literary career and political thought. Whether their efforts have been intellectual history, political science, or literary history and criticism, scholars have given generations of readers the impression that Barrès was exclusively a man of letters, an artist and thinker who had little interaction with the "real" world of society and politics. They have not shown us Barrès the follower and leader of political movements, the political journalist and editor, the *engagé* intellectual. This book will examine Barrès the politician.

1

This study began, like many earlier studies of Barrès, as intellectual biography. The intention was to discover how the apolitical Barrès became political and how his politics moved him first toward and then away from a political position resembling later fascism. Questions kept arising, however, which could not be handled within the usual forms of intellectual biography. If Barrès' ideas, particularly those similar to fascism, were as significant as the scholars and his disciples have contended, why did those ideas not catch on and find political success in his own time? After all, French parliamentary democracy seemed about to expire during the Boulanger and Dreyfus crises; it was a time made to order for anti-parliamentary alternatives. Did such threats to parliamentary democracy as Boulangism and anti-Dreyfusard nationalism, like later fascism, have their origins in ideas? Or, did they arise from social and political conditions? If such threats succeeded or failed, was it because of their ideas? Or, was it instead because of the strength or weakness of their political and social bases as well as the nerve, or lack of it, of their establishment foes?

It became increasingly clear that Barrès' life and ideas could not make sense unless social and political questions were asked. Answering them made it necessary to go beyond intellectual history and biography to different sources and method. In sources it meant using more than the usual materials of Barrès' published novels, collected essays, and his literary diary. This study combines those sources with his newspaper writing and speeches, his votes in the Chamber of Deputies, police and newspaper reports of his political activities and electioneering, and social and political data on the electoral constituencies and movements into which he carried his ideas and which, in turn, reshaped those ideas.

This study also required a method different from those used in earlier accounts of Barrès' ideas and career. Geoffrey Barraclough suggests that intellectual historians can trace nazism's origins as far back as the Teutonic forests of Germany to discover an infinite number of reasons why Germany *might* have turned to Hitler; but only by coupling the intellectual origins with social and political analysis, can we learn why Germans *did* bring nazis to power.[3] Barraclough's observation applies to Barrès as well. Certainly Barrès' ideas came to form a good part of the intellectual origins of French fascism, as Robert Soucy's *Fascism in France* (Berkeley, 1973), among other works, has made clear. Although it is important to know how later fascist intellectuals used Barrès' ideas, it is more essential to know exactly what those ideas were for Barrès and why they erupted in him and others at that particular time. It is even more vital to explain why those ideas of Barrès failed to take power when similar ones succeeded later in Germany.

The method for accomplishing these goals required enclosing the intellectual history of Barrès in the matrix of the political and social history of his time and place. Neither his writings nor his political action can be understood without seeing that these two aspects of his life were in symbiosis. Each of his novels must be read as political and intellectual biography. His every political act fed into a novel or essay. Every novel led to new political action or was written to convert readers to his politics of the moment. For Barrès' ideas to make sense, one must examine the origins, composition, success, and failure of the political movements and campaigns of which he was a part. Barrès saw those same movements and campaigns which shaped his ideas, as vehicles for institutionalizing his ideas. Barrès, then, was a politician. His chief weapon of political warfare was literature, and it was forged in the heat of battle.

In combining intellectual with political and social history, this study will do two things. First, it will be an intellectual and political biography of Barrès. It will show that there was an interplay among his art, ideas, and action. Moreover, the ideas and action evolved through stages, often under the influence of key figures and events, in fulfillment of his art.

The study begins as intellectual history because Barrès' decision to enter politics was exclusively an intellectual one: his literary development required a political commitment. Because that need would take him into one political movement after another, this study then begins to mix intellectual history with social and political history. Barrès gave his initial political commitment to Boulangism because its enemies seemed identical to his literary ones. His participation at the extreme Left of the Chamber of Deputies moved him into socialism. His inability to accept the program of socialism and to win victory under a socialist label in two electoral campaigns at Neuilly drove him to try a national-socialist formula on the Nancy working class and petite bourgeoisie in 1898. Defeated at Nancy and faced with a France fractured by the Dreyfus Affair, he converted his nationalism into that doctrine best remembered by later nationalists, a doctrine resembling later fascism. His inability to convince the anti-Dreyfusard leagues of his doctrine, their failure to be victorious, and his own electoral defeat on the doctrine in 1903 finally drove him into nationalist conservatism. With it he finally won election to the French Chamber of Deputies in 1906 and by 1914 reached a cosy conjuncture with the political establishment he had fought throughout his early career.

The fact that Barrès' major writings reflected his participation in these dissimilar political movements further illustrates the need to integrate his intellectual biography with political and social history. The novels of his *Culte du moi* (1888-1891) required the political commitment which took him into Boulangism. His *Ennemi des lois* (1893) was a socialist novel. The three volumes of the "novel of national energy" cycle (1897-1902) were inspired by his disillusionment with socialism as well as by his action in the national-socialist campaign in Nancy and in the anti-Dreyfusard nationalist leagues. His third cycle of novels, "the bastions of the East" (1905–1909), and his *Colline inspirée* (1913) accompanied his shift to conservative nationalism and his compromise with establishment politics. The fourteen volumes of his wartime *Chronique de la Grande Guerre* finally made him a pillar of that establishment.

Second, and just as important, this study will examine the failure of embryonic anti-parliamentary mass movements to win effective support in France before World War I. Barrès' carreer is particularly useful for analyzing their defeat. He was the only significant Frenchman explicitly attached ideologically and organizationally to every major right-wing embryonic mass movement from the 1880s through 1919: Boulangism,

4

the League of Patriots, the League of the Patrie Française, the League of the Action Française, and the Bloc National. He was also the only associate of all of those who had a good relationship with the Anti-Semitic League, the Rochefortists and other such anti-capitalistic nationalists, as well as the Action Liberale. On the two occasions of the Boulanger crisis and the Dreyfus affair, the nationalist movement formed from these bodies threatened to destroy French parliamentary democracy.

Examining this nationalist movement on both the national and local level, this book will show how disgust with the parliamentary republic united certain discontented nationalists, socialists, left-of-center constitutional reformers, and royalists around the charismatic figure of General Boulanger and almost ushered him into the Elysée palace in 1889. It will show how Boulangism fell apart under the government's counter-attack and how its disparate elements passed into eclipse. When the Dreyfus Affair restored a crisis situation in politics, the scattered members of Boulangism rebuilt or created organizations to get what had been denied them earlier. Some of these groups were legal and respectable, like the League of the Patrie Française; others were illegal and paramilitary, like the League of Patriots. Whatever their methods, they failed to unite around, or even to find, a charismatic leader. Forgetting their earlier social program, they went down to defeat. Nationalist organizations of the Boulanger and Dreyfus crises founded movement politics more closely resembling similar mass movements of later times than the party politics of their own time. Unlike their later counterparts in Germany or Italy, however, these organizations ran headlong against a political establishment which refused to lose its nerve.

In short, Barrès characterizes a significant aspect of late nineteenth and twentieth century history. His career represented a search for a mode of political expression which could fulfill the needs of his art and be consistent with it intellectually. The route taken on that search through socialism thrust him into the right-wing mass politics so typical of twentieth-century Europe. His journey made him a prototype of those intellectuals so attracted to such politics. Through him, his ideas, and career, one can come to understand how right-wing mass politics failed to take power in *fin de siècle* France. The understanding of the origins, composition, and beliefs of those politics, and Barrès' role in them, reveal what his ideas meant to him and how they took shape. The failure of those politics at the time also shows how Barrès, doubtless like many others of his persuasion, came to terms intellectually and politically with an establishment he failed to overthrow. Finally, much evidence indicates that few educated Frenchmen arrived at adulthood between 1890 and 1914 without becoming thoroughgoing Barresians. If so, Barrès was a major shaper of the attitudes of French political and cultural leadership in the first half of this century.

Nor is Barrès exclusively a figure of the past. To be sure, his political record of conservatism, anti-Semitism, anti-parliamentarianism and nationalism, plus the persistent denigration of him by such critical literary giants as André Gide and Jean Paul Sartre, drove his reputation into a literary purgatory after his death in 1923. Not until the 1960s did his work return to anything resembling wide circulation. Most of it now appears in the *Livre de poche* collection. Another edition contains admiring introductions by such varied heirs of Barrès as the apolitical Henry de Montherlant, the Gaullist François Mauriac, and French Communist poet, Louis Aragon. Barrès retained an enormous literary influence on these major French writers as well as on others such as the fascist Pierre Drieu La Rochelle and the ex-Stalinist Gaullist André Malraux, as literary historians on both sides of the Atlantic have pointed out.[4] They further suggest that for whatever reasons—political or literary—Barrès' ideas lived on and continue to permeate French politics and culture. In that way he remains a major figure.

* * *

In writing a book like this one an author entails debts to numerous people over several years. My thanks go to Leo Loubère of the State University of New York at Buffalo and to Harold J.

Grimm of the Ohio State University for seeing through to completion my Ph.D. dissertation on Barrès in 1964. The present work would not have been possible without a grant from the Research Funds Committee of the University of Maine, which allowed a summer of archival and library research in Paris and Nancy, France. I also thank my colleagues in the history department at the University of Maine, especially David C. Smith and William J. Baker, for their frequent advice over the years and for reading all or parts of the manuscript. I am likewise indebted to Professor Eugen Weber of the University of California at Los Angeles for his critical reading of the pages dealing with Barrès' association with the Action Française. Special thanks go to Robert J. Soucy of Oberlin College, a friendly critic and fellow Barrès scholar. For years we have debated the Barrès problem in conversation and correspondence. We continue to disagree, but those hours of debate deepened our understanding of Barrès. The reader of this book should also read Soucy's *Fascism in France: The Case of Maurice Barrès* (Berkeley: University of California Press, 1972) and Zeev Sternhell, *Maurice Barrès et le nationalisme français* (Paris: Armand Colin, 1972), which were published while this book was being written. Both Soucy and Sternhell shed much light on the many-faceted Barrès.

CHAPTER ONE

FROM CULTURAL REBELLION
TO POLITICAL COMMITMENT

Maurice Barrès took the train from Lorraine to Paris in 1883. He was twenty-one years old. He came to establish himself on the Left Bank and to make a literary career. He was in a hurry, and within four years he had published a widely-acclaimed first novel. Within two more years he brought out a second novel and won election to the Chamber of Deputies. At the age of twenty-seven, when most young men are just getting a good start, Barrès was a Deputy and an established novelist. Because of his ideas and artistic following, he was hailed as the prince of youth.

Such a meteoric rise would have been exceptional whatever its origins. Barrès' rise was even more remarkable for being rooted in cultural rebellion. His intellectual rebellion against old conventions made his literary reputation. The particulars of this cultural rebellion required a political commitment of a specific kind. Because his entry into politics was so intimately linked to his intellectual formation, even a political biography of Barrès must begin as intellectual history. The years from his arrival in Paris in 1883 to the publication of his first novels and commitment to politics by 1888 are the key to any understanding of Barrès. Those years established him as an *engagé* intellectual. He would remain one for the rest of his life.

Barrès' life before 1883 hardly prepared him for either cultural revolt or political commitment. Rather, his early years were thoroughly conventional. Barrès was born to a good life in 1862. His father was a prosperous civil engineer, married to the daughter of the mayor of his home town, Charmes-sur-Moselle (Vosges). The comfortable home in peaceful, rural Charmes and the bourgeois style of life insulated young Maurice and his class from industrial poverty and discontent. In 1873 his family boarded him at the *collège* in Malgrange, just outside Nancy. Earlier he had spent almost two years separated from his father while his mother took medical treatment in Strasbourg. As a result he arrived at Malgrange somewhat a mama's boy. Throughout his writings he describes his stay there as a time of unrelieved misery. Despising and despised by his peers, bullied, crying himself to sleep at night, he resolved to get even some day. Even this kind of school experience was conventional, at most only peripherally shaping his adult development. Doubtless many another French schoolboy went through the same agonies without ever becoming a famous writer or politician.

From Malgrange Barrès advanced to the *lycée* at Nancy in 1877. There he began to develop intellectually and was imbued with his establishment's almost official philosophy. The revolt against that philosophy would result in his precocious literary achievement and his entry into politics in the 1880s. Part of that philosophy was the positivism of Auguste Comte. Disdaining metaphysics, positivism advocated the scientific or "positive" method of observing facts and ordering them with hypotheses without seeking any ultimate reality or metaphysic behind them. Watered down into popular culture this meant a widespread belief in science as the solution to all human problems. For some, scientists like Louis Pasteur became veritable positivist saints, and the new laboratories and smoking factories became positivist temples. Positivist politicians decried using politics to solve human problems. The apparently inevitable advancement of science and material prosperity would, themselves, bring happiness and remove social inequities. Positivist educators believed that France had suffered defeat in 1870-71 at the hands of the Prussian schoolmaster. If France were to remain a major power or stage a successful *revanche*, it had to be as scientific and practical as Germany.[1] Positivism was a French method for catching up.

Another part of that almost official philosophy was nine-teenth-century German idealism. It, too, was considered a source of German superiority, and French educators made it a fixture of the educational curriculum in the 1880s. Barrès got it from his philosophy teacher, Auguste Burdeau, who would be immortalized as Paul Bouteiller in Barrès' novel, *Les Déra-cinés* (1897). Burdeau made sure his students shared his love for the categorical imperative of Kant, the ego of Fichte, the ego and non-ego of Schelling, and the absolute spirit of Hegel. When the Kantian Burdeau urged his young charges to act as if they were acting for mankind, he gave them a kind of French Protestant ethic, particularly useful for encouraging patrio-tism.

For the Lorraine establishment, nationalism already ran so deep that Burdeau's efforts were hardly necessary. Only by growing up in Lorraine did Barrès' intellectual formation dif-fer from that of other bourgeois French sons of the 1860s and 1870s. Time and time again in his writings, he insisted that seeing German Uhlans march into Charmes in 1870 made him a lifelong nationalist and Germanophobe. No doubt that expe-rience would be difficult for any sensitive child to forget, but his writings and correspondence of the 1880s give little evi-dence that the German occupation was as traumatic as the mature Barrès would have us believe. Rather, his youth gave him a nationalism more as he described it a few weeks before his death in 1923:

> At the *lycée,* at Malgrange, at the University of Nancy every one of the teachers and students was patriotic. All of us from the highest official, rector, dean, headmaster, and *supérieur* to the lowliest students of *dixième,* the sisters at the infirmary, and the waiters put the country above everything.
>
> I never heard expressed, except to refute it, any antipatriotic or apatriotic thought. France was praised continually. It was done not to convince us, but *pour jouer une belle musique.* We found it no more extraordinary than when they invited us to love our mothers.

Barrès added that the first time he was aware that anti-patri-otism existed was when he listened to the *conscious* nationalism of his Kantian philosophy teacher, Burdeau.[2]

10

Lorraine society of Barrès' youth was supercharged with nationalism. According to Louis Marin, a Lorrainer nine years Barrès' junior, schoolteachers did not follow the advice of Léon Gambetta on the loss of Alsace Lorraine, "Speak of it never, think of it always." "On the contrary, they spoke to us about it incessantly" so that "our love for the lost provinces had the allures of a 'cult, of religiosity,' " and only classes in English and German had discipline problems. In their books, students scribbled the cross of Lorraine with the patois motto "C'man po tojo (It is not forever)," but they meant by it Léon Gambetta's formula of trading colonies for the lost provinces.[3] In the 1870s and 1880s Lorraine proliferated with statues to the war dead of 1870-71 and to Adolphe Thiers, whose rapid payment of the peace treaty's indemnity ended the German occupation earlier than anyone had expected. The numerous Alsatian émigrés and the large amount of nationalism worried prefects that nationalistic incidents would accompany the unveiling of every patriotic statue. Newspapers were nationalistic, but quietly so, and there was a sizable, but not so quiet, popular nationalistic literature of dime novels. In all, it was not a patriotism of nationalistic fringe groups. Instead, it was a nationalism of the "respectable" people, who casually took it for granted. Yet, it ran strong and deep in Lorraine, deeper than in any other region of France. It permeated Lorraine life.[4] A boy from Charmes could shake it off only with difficulty; it would remain hidden in him for a while, but it would rise again by the end of the 1880s.

Yet, even this nationalism was establishmentarian in its Lorraine context. In only one respect did Barrès begin to rebel against the establishment during his school days. He began to reject the positivist faith in science and the idealistic Kantian universals. He did so in the name of symbolism, which more than anything else in his intellectual formation, would take him into the anti-positivist cultural revolt and lead him into political rebellion against the establishment values of his youth.

The elements which would lead Barrès to symbolism came early. As a child his mother read him the romantic novels of Walter Scott and he never forgot them. While Burdeau intro-

11

duced him to Kant, one of Barrès' *lycèe* schoolmates, poet Stanislas de Guaita, initiated him into the mysteries of Théophile Gautier, Madame Ackermann, Leconte de Lisle, Baudelaire, and other nineteenth-century poets. De Guaita's influence would be lasting, and the memory of *Emaux et Camées* and *Les Fleurs du mal* was especially strong. He also read the romantic republicans: Edgar Quinet's *Le Génie des religions*, Jules Michelet's popular patriotism and love of the people, and Victor Hugo as symbol of the *patrie*. Their pessimism, reinforced by the introduction of Schopenhauer after 1870, attracted Barrès as it did the major writers of the 1870s, like Ferdinand Brunetière, Jules Lemaître, Anatole France, Zola and the naturalists, as well as Ernest Renan and Hippolyte Taine. As a budding man of letters Barrès was influenced by them as well.[5]

Even with these beginnings of rebellion, it was still hard for him to make the break. Under parental pressures to make him a lawyer he registered, in 1880, at the University of Nancy, where he remained two years. His attendance at lectures was irregular, and he hated his studies. He spent most of his time reading and writing. His first literary efforts were unsuccessful. An early rejection slip from a literary competition shows that his style and thought were far from perfected. "The work," the anonymous critic commented, "is nothing but an incoherent mass of commonplaces and compiled theories. What the author passes off for originality is only eccentricity . . . In this work there is neither style nor ideas."[6] His reading, however, was voracious and profitable. He came to Stendhal and, through him, to a love of Napoleon. He also discovered the German psychologist Hartmann and his theory of the unconscious.

Barrès the writer finally found an audience in 1882 in the pages of *Jeune France*, a fairly prestigious literary magazine. This success won him parental permission to establish himself at Paris in January, 1883. Although his parents sent him there to pursue his law studies at the *Faculté de droit* and the *Ecole des hautes études*, he spent most of his time engaged in the heated literary arguments of the *brasseries*. In an 1887 article Barrès described his typically Latin Quarter Bohemian existence, with its students from the Ecole Polytechnique, Ecole Normale, and law faculty; its restaurants where the students begin "through debauchery or economy the dyspepsia, gastritis, and ulcers which will give them such distinguished-looking appearances by age forty," its streetwalkers "evidently subsidized by families to inspire in their young men a horror of illicit encounters," its cold and lonely lodgings, and in its cafés with the eternal talk condemning a philistine society.[7] With his Latin Quarter friends Jean Moréas, Villiers de l'Isle-Adam, and Charles Le Goffic, Barrès played the role of the dandy and got caught up in the intellectual currents of the day. He met Leconte de Lisle and Paul Bourget. He came under the spell of Anatole France, who introduced him into the brilliant salon of Madame de Loynes. With them he rapidly emerged as a thoroughgoing disciple of symbolism and its struggle against the prevailing naturalism.

To be sure symbolism was hardly clear in the minds of its adherents in these early 1880s. They could not even decide whether to call it decadence or symbolism. When the poet Jean Moréas gave symbolism a capital "S" in his manifesto of 1885, that name stuck, but for a long time symbolist prose continued to be called decadence. Whatever the names, both seemed based on the notion that the exterior world was false, crass, and barbarian. Both held that this so-called reality was only a starting point for exploring the magic of the mysterious, perhaps terrible, inner reality of the ego. Both emphasized the eccentric, satanic, mystic, pessimistic, and dreamy. In style, both showed less interest in a book's unity than in the quality of a single sentence or word. Both wished to brush aside old literary traditions and seek new forms and diction. Influenced heavily by the music of Richard Wagner, both sought, through alliteration and assonance, the music of colors, mood, sounds, and odors which would heighten sensation in reader and writer. The decadent prose accentuated the understanding of the inner self, the meaning of individual existence, and the preference for the inner world of consciousness to that of exterior reality. Both, of course, were in rebellion against current modes of expression—parnassian poetry and naturalistic prose—which were based on positivism and scientism. Both drew heavily on the same sources which were operating on Barrès. By the mid-1880s Baudelaire, Barbey d'Aurevilly, Hartmann, and Wagner were added to them.

While these decadent fires of the Latin Quarter tempered the literary powers of Barrès, they did not give him the audience he wanted to win. His letters to Sorg and de Guaita in these early years in Paris reveal him to be consumed by ambition and driven to find fame.[8] After a year and a half he found a way to get it. In November of 1884 he launched his own monthly review, *Les Taches d'encre*, with an initial printing of 1200 copies. To finance it he needed at least three hundred subscriptions, and he wrote or buttonholed everyone he knew to get them.[9] The review began auspiciously touted by sandwich men whose boards read, "Morin no longer reads *Les Taches d'encre*." In a *cause celèbre*, Morin, who had insulted his fellow deputy, Clovis Hugues, had just been murdered by Madame Hugues. In spite of such morbid ingenuity the review folded after only four of its scheduled twelve issues.

Les Taches d'encre, both written and edited by Barrès, assisted his rapid rise in the symbolist movement by being one of its first periodicals. More than that, however, it tells us something about his intellectual formation and how that intellect would shape his emerging political position. In this regard, its pages show Barrès as a symbolist and decadent rebel against the *fin de siècle* philistine society. He would retain that superindividualism throughout his life. In the very first sentences of *Taches d'encre* he wrote: "It seems to me that the mode of the day sacrifices a little too much the study of superior spirits to that of mean humanity. I gladly esteem with others that there is no drama more interesting than the concourse of ideas in the mind of a sage, artist, or philosopher. . . . All is vain, all is futile aside from what touches our selfhood [moi]." "That great indolent people which cares for nothing aside from the unseizable shadows of its dreams," was not nearly as great an object for artistic concern as the magnification of the sense of selfhood, the discovery and fulfillment of the artist's inner spirit.[10] Here, with symbolism as the catalyst, Barrès separated himself from the current mainstream of French literature and life, but his rebellion was only an artistic one, almost indulgent toward a society which he believed would eventually see the error of its ways. He felt more distress over the young, however, and attacked the Parisian student organizations because they bred conformity. He believed this conformity was encouraged by the *lycées*, where the positivist ideas of Littré and the Kantian ones of Renouvier had recently become official doctrine. They, more than the student associations, thwarted individualism and were products of "this Jacobinism which everywhere sacrifices the individual to the mass."[11]

Second, *Les Taches d'encre* showed none of Barrès' later chauvinistic nationalism. His review of Victor Tissot's *Voyage au pays des milliards* revealed a deep attachment to Germany, which comes as a particular surprise to those who think of Barrès as an uncompromising hater of the Teuton. In criticizing Tissot for fanning the flames of French resentment of the 1870 defeat and for calling the German spirit totally materialistic and beneath French contempt, Barrès exhibited no trauma over the events of 1870. Memory of those events, as Claude Digeon points out, remained hidden by the "vague fog" of his youth.[12] This was in sharp contrast to Barrès' mature attitude, generally accepted at face value, that the memory of the Bavarian Uhlans indelibly marked him with a lifelong Germanophobia. To be sure, he called for a readjustment of the frontier:

> All the military fanfare draws us to the conquered territory; the fluttering of the flag seems like a distant call to the exiles; our fists close . . . . Our special task as young men is to retake the lost territory, to reconstitute the French ideal which comes as much from the Protestant genius of Strasbourg as from the brilliant facility of the Midi. Our fathers failed, but they left us a task of honor . . . It requires only a little blood and some greatness of soul.[13]

The bulk of the article, however, was hardly "the habitual language of revanchard patriots."[14] His criticism of Tissot's handling of the German spirit singled out for special consideration Paul Déroulède, head of the most revanchist organization, the League of Patriots, and poet of the *Chants du soldat*. "We hardly love the warlike poems of M. Déroulède," Barrès wrote, but only because they are bad poetry.

> Nevertheless, we feel there is sincerity behind them. Devotion to an ideal, whatever it be, merits our respect. It is a weakness in us to laugh at him. And if his chauvinism appears cumbersome to some, if his League of Patriots seems a little too noisy to others, no one can doubt his disinterestedness . . . . He has sung of France and he believes enough in it not to underestimate the enemy. We go farther than that. We say great France and great Germany as well. Moreover, regardless of the politics of the day three peoples guide civilization in this century: France, Great Britain, and Germany. It would be an irreparable loss for everyone if any of these flames were extinguished. Humanity would stagger . . . . We have intellectual fathers in all countries. Kant, Goethe, and Hegel are equal to our own intellectual leaders.[15]

Very early, then, Barrès distinguished between the intellectual and the political.

He showed the same ability to discriminate in his letters to Sorg and de Guaita, describing his admiration for the autobiographical novels of Jules Vallès. It was not the politics of that old Communard, member of the Socialist International and editor of the socialistic *Cri du peuple* nor his naturalistic style and social protest that captured the imagination of Barrès. He mentioned those not at all. What fascinated him was the indomitable ego, the personal suffering and *élan* of Vallès' protagonist against society and a hostile world.

Les Taches d'encre may not have been a financial success, but it launched its editor's literary career. Barrès' short-lived journal allowed him to be "discovered." Although his allowance was cut off when his family realized that it had lost a lawyer only to gain a bohemian writer, he now found steady employment in a Paris abounding in reviews and daily newspapers.

In the years immediately following the demise of *Les Taches d'encre*, Barrès continued developing its themes of patriotism and decadent reaction to existing society in various Parisian journals, notably the very sophisticated and republican daily, *Le Voltaire*. In his literary criticism, reviews, obituaries, and

16

analyses of exhibitions for that newspaper Barrès continued his admiration for German idealism, adding a growing apprehension of German politics. Caught up in the veritable Wagner cult which made such a great impact on the symbolists and inspired a *Revue wagnérienne*, Barrès even journeyed to Bayreuth in 1886 and 1887. In writing of his 1887 trip, he concluded that German animosity toward France was far deeper than it had been the previous year. "In recent years," he wrote, "I found a sentiment I would describe as made up of envy and *bonhomie* rather than of hate. Today all that has changed. I am assured, however, that a Frenchman is still able to travel to Bavaria without vexations; I admit that, but according to the mood I saw, most of Germany has become impossible for us."[16] Hardly revanchist, this would have been the observation of almost any traveler in the aftermath of the Schnaebelé affair, the war scare in 1887, arising from the German arrest of a French border official and go-between for French spies in Alsace-Lorraine.

Yet, these articles reflected no overwrought nationalism. They exhibited a fairly conventional patriotism, consistent with the republican policy of *Le Voltaire*. To be sure, they reflected an admiration for Napoleon I, an admiration gained from reading Stendhal.[17] Such a respect was solely patriotic; it no more converted Barrès into a political Bonapartist, a party still strong in France, than a trip to the Invalides would convert the average tourist. Nor did his articles reflect the anti-Semitism which marked so much of French nationalism. For example, Barrès regretted the death of banker James de Rothschild and the passing of his salon.[18]

Generally Barrès' articles merely served as springboards into literary criticism. In one of them he displayed his lack of excitement for the rising Dostoyevsky cult, saying that Dostoyevsky had simply read his Stendhal.[19] In this article, Barrès combined his patriotic theme with his decadent one to attack naturalism. He urged French writers to stop aping the Russian novelists and return to the spirit of Stendhal and Balzac, as Dostoyevsky did, and look inside their characters. In another article Barrès contended that the "historians of the scientific method," such as Taine, Sorel, and Ernest Lavisse, "will better

17

serve the reawakening of the national spirit than will the efforts of our showiest patriots" [*nos patriotes les plus affichés*].[20] On another occasion he called for international cooperation.[21] Here was little enthusiasm for the professional patriot which so marks nationalism.

Other articles of the same period, however, indicate how Barrès' patriotism could be directed toward the nationalism which marked his entry into politics. In spite of his intellectual sensibilities and disdain for the "barbarian" mob, he displayed a love of country geared to the irrational and emotional. The sentimental pap which the *Marseillaise* passes off for patriotism, he wrote on Bastille Day in 1886, becomes real patriotism simply because it stirs the crowd who sings it. It does that just as "words of love, which each day become more banal and prostituted, appear sublime to lovers if they say them with accents of sincerity."[22] In another article Barrès was repelled by the bad verse of a patriotic music hall song. In spite of its saccharine flavor, however, he was moved by its effect on a rapt soldier audience. The whole episode caused him to toast the army and forget the tinsel atmosphere of the song and cabaret.[23]

These two articles show Barrès' exhilaration when caught up in the mob. Such a feeling explains how two years later this ivory-tower intellectual could go before the "barbaric" working class at Nancy to win their votes for an anti-intellectual nationalistic movement. Barrès later recalled that at the time of his first plunge into politics, he had "profoundly enjoyed the instinctive pleasure of being in a herd."[24] These examples illustrate the relation of decadence to his politics. The shallowness of those patriotic songs was only a surface reality. Their inner meaning, their true reality, was expressed in the way they fulfilled the consciousness of the mob. Perhaps Barrès saw that he could vicariously magnify his own ego, could heighten his own sensations, by empathizing with this barbarian crowd.

Although his newspaper writing gave him employment and a vehicle for some of his ideas, it did not help him to resolve the emerging crisis of his life. That crisis climaxed in 1887-1888 with the writing of his first novel. The crisis was so basic that he portrayed it again and again in his novels. At least until

18

1914 his effort to resolve its problems dominated his life and dictated the direction of his art. That effort also brought about his plunge into politics and his concern for the ways that politics would be expressed. For those reasons, no event in Barrès' career was to be more significant for him or for the understanding of his work.

The crisis was created out of personal elements. A positivist and neo-Kantian education had uprooted him from his Lorraine values and taken him to Paris, but the values supplied by his education did not equip him to put down new roots there. Adrift in Paris, he found no trustworthy guides toward his self-fulfillment. Instead, he fell into a nihilistic rebellion against all the conventions of his origins, education, and society. The individualistic rebellion of symbolism, which captured him, neither prepared him for solving the problems raised by the rebellion nor for winning acceptance as an artist. His efforts to establish a review failed; his literary criticism earned him only a bare existence; he had yet to write the novel which would give him the acclaim he craved. Moreover, by 1887 the symbolist movement which nourished him was under wide attack in almost all the press and the literary journals. The campaign was led by such worthies as Jules Lemaître, Ferdinand Brunetière, and Anatole France. The attack was particularly vicious in *La Revue bleue* and had greatly offended Barrès and other symbolists. Critics increased their ire when symbolists wrote in prose which was universally denounced for its incomprehensibility and obscurity, its gnarled diction and syntax, and its ivory-tower disdain for the crowd. Barrès himself was named as one of a group with "the same objective: a refined and sickly incoherence which causes one to fear for their reason if they linger in their ways."[25] On top of this was Barrès' feeling that he was being crushed by the entire world of barbarians, that world of businessmen, politicians, and thinkers who made up the crass, herdlike society the symbolists rejected. In a letter to Léon Sorg in November 1887, which describes both his state of mind and that of the protagonist of the novel he was writing, he wrote "that all men appear like brutes to sensitive souls like me."[26]

With all those frustrations and disappointments bearing in

on him at one time in the winter of 1887–1888, his exhaustion and depression drove him first to Lorraine and then to Venice. Under the therapeutic Italian sun Barrès completed his first novel, the first volume in a trilogy to be called the *Culte du moi*, the cult of selfhood.

Nothing shows the joining of Barrès' life and art more than his writing of the three novels of the *Culte du moi*. The first novel appeared in early 1888, and thanks to a well-placed favorable review by the influential Paul Bourget, it made Barrès' literary fortune. With the appearance of the second in 1889, he became the toast of the Latin Quarter. The publication of the final volume in the trilogy, in 1891, completed the intellectual biography of Barrès and the generation of young intellectuals he influenced. At least it brought for Barrès, as Pierre de Boisdeffre puts it, that "moment when the caterpillar becomes the chrysalis"[27] if not the moth. The trilogy describes Barrès' personal crisis of cultural rootlessness and personal alienation. It charts the path to its resolution—personal involvement and commitment. That path would be long; its many twists and crossroads would require choices. As it turned out, the *Culte du moi* not only put Barrès on the path toward resolving his crisis. It also determined how the choices would be made.

The first novel of the trilogy, *Sous l'oeil des barbares* (1888), tells of Philippe's quest "from the awakening . . . to conscious life, first in the milieu of his books, then among his first brutalities in Paris"[28] to find for himself the meaning of life and to end his alienation from himself and his world. He learns from the beginning that "our morality, our religion, our sentiment of nationalities are all crumbling . . . and we cannot borrow rules of life from them. Until our masters remake certainties for us, we hold to the one reality, our sense of selfhood [moi]."[29] By removing his pre-cognitive certainties, his early education leaves him in worse condition than he was before. He is cast adrift. "Tired and hopeless in losing his innocence, he detested life and did not know any precise way to build a permanent universe for himself."[30]

Now rootless, he rushes off to Paris to find the answers. Instead, he finds himself "under the eye of the barbarians," those "beings who possess a dream of life opposed to the one he has," "outsiders [*étrangers*] and adversaries."[31] They are beings who wish to substitute their personhoods for his, and they run everything:

> We are the barbarians . . . we are the convinced. We have given to everything its name; we know the time to laugh and the time to be serious . . . We have the value system, the country, and every office in our pockets. We have created the notion of ridicule (against those who are *different*) and the model of the good fellow (so admirable is the depth of our soul).[32]

Initially, Philippe conforms to the attitudes their personhoods wish to impose on him: irony, dandyism, positivism, scepticism, worldly success, and ivory tower intellectuality.

Philippe soon learns, however, that he has to give them up, not only because they represent the entire positivist world the symbolists attacked, but because none of those worlds is his own.

> There is only one thing that we know and that really exists among all the false religions that they propose, among all the cries of the heart with which they pretend to rebuild in you the idea of the fatherland, to communicate to you social concern and to indicate to you a moral direction. This single tangible reality is our selfhood, and the universe is only a fresco that it makes beautiful or ugly.
> Let us attach ourselves to our selfhood, let us protect it against outsiders, against the barbarians.[33]

Philippe has discovered, as Delmore Schwartz said of existentialism, that no one can take a bath for you. "The first thing is to exist."[34] But Philippe's recognition of this fact has taken away his former energy and violent sensibility and left him lifeless and with a "dolorous torpor." The book ends with him crying out for some "axiom, religion or prince of men" to help him find his own absolute, his own destiny.[35]

Saying that a man could find reality and fulfillment only in himself and not in the crowd was one thing, doing it was another. The novel raised more problems than it solved, both for Philippe and for Barrès. As Barrès wrote, he discovered that

21

detachment from the world proved to be an intellectual dead end. One's personhood must be fully developed, but it alone could not provide enough nourishment for its growth. "It is not enough that personhood exists; because it is a living thing, one must cultivate it and act on it mechanically (study, curiosity, travel)."[36]

Barrès took that path in the next novel of the cycle, *Un Homme libre* (1889). In it Philippe, to end "the anemia of [his] soul" and to discover "energy" and "enthusiasm," retires from Paris with a friend to a "laboratory of enthusiasm." There, they systematically cultivate their selfhoods by following a mechanical program of study, analysis, and meditation on the lives of great self-fulfilled "intercessors," "famous persons who had spirituality."[37] Unfortunately, these meditations ultimately yield up only a "great barrenness." Therefore, Philippe says later,

> worn out from reaping from my *intercessors* only notions of my sensibility without arriving at ways to improve it, I sought in [my native] Lorraine the law of my development . . . When the barbarians have deformed us, nothing is better for rediscovering ourselves than reflecting on our past. I was right to seek where the instinct of my ancestors grew; the individual is guided by the same law as his race.[38]

His study of Lorraine's history makes him see that "individuals, no matter how perfect one imagines them to be, are only fragments of a more complex system which is the race, itself a fragment of God."[39] It also reveals to him that both he and Lorraine, "weary from clashing with outsiders . . . abandoned our free development in order to adopt the tone of the majority."[40]

While Lorraine makes him aware of his origins and deepens within him "the impression which forms [my] anguish: the sense of the provisional,"[41] its failure to defeat the barbarians offers no solution to Philippe's crisis. Only Venice shows his future possibilities.

> Venice, I said to myself, was built on lagoons by a group of men anxious to preserve their independence. She always kept her pride of being free. Her politics, mores, and arts never submit-

ted to outsiders. In the same way the foremost act of my intellectual life is to avoid the barbarians, the outsiders; and the
perpetual basis of my virtue is my desire to be a free man.[42]

Unlike Lorraine, Venice protected herself from outsiders without renouncing the world. That example provides the key to
Philippe's quest for the meaning of life and a way to restore
the energy so necessary for his self-fulfillment. "Tired of soli-
tude, contemplative dilettantism and so many petty experiences . . . Philippe accepts action,"[43] but in acts which "have no
importance in themselves. They merit only the interpretation
given them by the soul which orders them."[44] Any kind of action
will do so long as it feeds a sense of selfhood still hungry after
the mechanical cultivation of study and travel.

The last volume of the *Culte du moi* illustrates that dilettantism and action for action's sake are not enough. In the *Jardin de
Bérénice* (1891), Philippe learns that "to reconcile the practices
of interior life with the necessities of practical life"[45] one's self,
surrounded by barbarians, must become part of a greater self,
as in Hartmann's unconscious. Already in *Un Homme libre* Philippe had decided that his personhood had to identify with
something greater than itself, or it would become sterile. To
grow, the self had to feed on a race or locale. While Lorraine
and Venice made him realize "the moment I represented in the
development of my race" and "that I was only an instant in a
long culture, one of a thousand signs of a force which preceded
me and which would follow me,"[46] they were too narrow and left
his selfhood parochial and unsatisfied. His quest had been too
conscious, too rational, too cerebral.

Now, in *Le Jardin de Bérénice* he finds the answer. At last he
realizes that "our reason, perpetually misled, is in essence absolutely incapable of either surmising or resulting in that superior being we are in the middle of becoming. It is instinct, far
superior to analysis, which makes our future."[47]

In the end this revelation comes to Philippe from two
sources. One is by going to the people in an election campaign:
"Only the masses put me in touch with the very well-springs of
humanity . . . The people revealed to me the substance of humanity and, better than that, creative energy, the life force of

the world, the unconscious."[48] By drawing their instinctual power and energy to himself, he can at last shake off the lassitude which prevented him from fulfilling his personhood. By losing himself in the people, he can find himself. Second, this realization comes not so much from the people themselves as through his love for the "completely spontaneous" Bérénice. Thanks to her submission to instinct rather than to reason, she is "harmonized with her world." "She is the very incarnation and personification of the popular soul, the religious soul, instinctive and, like a little girl, filled with a past of which she is unconscious."[49] The peace and energy which flow from her instinctual nature at last give Philippe the energy to reach out to the people, instinctive like her, to end his isolation.

The instinctual power of Bérénice and the people give Philippe the energy to stand up to and reject the barbarians without abandoning what is distinctive in his own sense of selfhood. The barbarians are personified by Charles Martin, his political opponent who

> ignores the culture of selfhood: Men and things do not appear to him as emotions to be assimilated so that they might multiply. He is only preoccupied with condemning them for straying from the image he has improvised of the universe. In the life striving for community he is a sectarian. In the life seeking universal understanding, he is a specialist. For him multiplicity is subversive. He does not grasp the truth released by the unity which subversiveness forms. At each minute and in all aspects he is the Adversary.[50]

But while Philippe despises Martin as he loves Bérénice, he knows that it is too late for him to throw over completely his rationalism, a rationalism he shares with his fellow intellectual Charles Martin. At best he can but combine their two methods:

> I saw this universe as it is in the soul of Bérénice: the very dear and obscure appearance she gave it through intuition and the religious emotion with which she timidly enveloped it. I also see it as it is in the mind of the "Adversary:" a collection of arid little details which forms a great touching picture he cannot see for the brushstrokes. I recognize both views. I am in-

24

stinctive like Bérénice. I have a distinct view of all the parts and I know how to make a unity of them, for I understand the role of each in the ensemble . . . I have spontaneous emotions, but I cultivate them with a method which surpasses even the method of Charles Martin.[51]

This ambivalence in Philippe between the two methods, an ambivalence rooted in his devouring self-love, causes him to limit his love for Bérénice and to turn her over to the tender mercies of Charles Martin in a marriage which kills her. That devouring self-love would always be present in Barrès, too, just as there would always be within his quest for individual fulfillment an eternal struggle between the method of Bérénice and that of Charles Martin, between the need for instinctive energy and cold intellectuality. But in all this there was a far more important element for the future of Barrès. Although sensibility and instinct, as taught to Philippe by the masses and by Bérénice, may be altogether adequate for an artist's perception of life and knowledge of his world, they are very dangerous for a politician, as Barrès would discover by the mid-1890s.

For now, however, a yearning to recover a lost energy in his drive for selfhood was probably the only impulse which could have propelled that ivory-tower decadent into politics. It is here that the *Culte du moi* as intellectual biography becomes politics. Between the formulation of his intellectual problem in *Sous l'oeil des barbares* and *Un Homme libre* (1887–1888) and his "answer" to that problem in *Le Jardin de Bérénice* (1891), the formerly apolitical Barrès became a politician. In short, at the very time his intellectual and artistic development demanded involvement and action, a political movement came along which perfectly suited his needs: the politics of *le brav' général*, Georges Ernest Boulanger.

To understand how the apolitical Barrès could become political, to see how the intellectual problem of the first two novels of the *Culte du moi* could be given the political answer of the third novel of the trilogy, and to make clear how Boulangism and not some other form of politics could fulfill the needs of Barrès' quest for selfhood, it is necessary to trace the progress of Boulangism and Barrès' conversion to it.

25

The 1885 legislative elections had thrust General Boulanger into politics. These elections had so weakened the massive Opportunist and Left Republican majority that a coalition with the Radicals was essential to form a stable government. Naming Boulanger war minister in 1886 was part of the price for Radical cooperation. As war minister, Boulanger proved trustworthy to his Radical friends. He transferred a cavalry brigade for holding ardently royalist views and relieved seven officers of royal blood from their commands. When a royalist suggested to him that the army would object to such actions, Boulanger replied, "As long as I am its head, the army will not judge; it will obey."[52] When he sent troops to the strike at Décazeville in 1886, he told the soldiers to take no side in the dispute but to share their soup and bread with the strikers. "On that day," Barrès wrote years later, "it appeared that General Boulanger had spoken like a true Frenchman."[53] Through his dramatization of the reforms initiated by his predecessors, such as the reduction of the length of service, a more generous leave policy, and improved weaponry, the army recovered its confidence and morale. For the first time since Sedan, said one observer, the troops felt bold enough to wear their kepis cocked over one eye.

The activities of the minister soon became disturbing, however. At the Bastille Day review of 1886, Boulanger proved to be more popular with the troops and crowds than the president of the republic. Music hall composers wrote songs celebrating the *brav' général*. Early in 1887 Bismarck attacked Boulanger in the Reichstag for being too revanchist. With his demand for immediate mobilization during the Schnaebelé affair, against the wishes of the premier, Boulanger convinced French chauvinists that he was the only Frenchman who would stand up to the German chancellor. The music halls now sang of General *Revanche*. Maurice Barrès, returning from Italy through Nancy, was caught up enough in the fervor engendered by Boulanger to write, "Everyone talks only of Bismarck and Boulanger. The sentiment rises daily in everyone that France is sworn to master her fate."[54]

Boulanger's popularity, insubordination, and warlike threats convinced the Opportunists to get rid of him. To do so, they struck an alliance with the royalists, and the new war minister transferred Boulanger to Clermont-Ferrand. On July 8, 1887, a mob chanting "Vive Boulanger!" and "We must prevent the exile of the general" halted rail traffic for hours at the Gare de Lyon in an attempt to prevent him from leaving Paris.[55] The Bonapartist character of this demonstration, coupled with the discovery of a fawning letter from Boulanger to the Duc d'Aumale in 1880, convinced Clemenceau and most of his Radicals that Boulanger was a dangerous "man on horseback." They abandoned him.

Instead of finishing Boulanger, these developments created Boulangism or, as Adrien Dansette points out, a "multiplicity of Boulangisms."[56] The Boulangism of Boulanger was very simple: he would use any political friend and almost any means to regain the war ministry. For the other Boulangisms, it was a more complex story.

One of these Boulangisms was originated by Henri de Rochefort, a Second Empire Jacobin, Communard, Blanquist, and violent opponent of the Opportunists, a term he coined. His Jacobin nationalism and Blanquist revolution-for-revolution's sake made him see Boulanger, the protector of strikers and enemy of royalists and Bismarck, as the vehicle for a nationalist social revolution. Rochefort publicized the general's chauvinism and working-class sympathies in his widely-read personal journal, *l'Intransigéant*, and was one of the key figures in the demonstration when Boulanger left Paris.

The German war scare of 1887 created another Boulangism, led by Paul Déroulède. In 1882 he had founded the League of Patriots to revive the dying revanchist spirit in France through military and patriotic education and the consolidation of all patriots, regardless of party. When Boulanger became war minister in 1886, Déroulède threw his nation-wide league behind the general's army reforms and the tough responses to Bismarck which, Déroulède believed, made a *revanche* really possible. The League of Patriots played a major role in the demonstration for Boulanger at the Bastille Day review in 1886.

A third Boulangism consisted of those men of the extreme

Left and Radicalism, who refused to follow Clemenceau's abandonment of the general. One of them, Alfred Naquet, whose Radicalism had caused him to sponsor the divorce law and to turn against Gambetta for being too conservative, believed that the Third Republic was finished. No régime since 1789 had lasted longer than eighteen years. To him the 1885 elections and the Wilson Scandal, the influence-peddling of President Grévy's son-in-law and chief aide, were symptomatic of decline. Naquet's solution was to use Boulanger to provoke a political and constitutional crisis that could transform France into a republic on the American model. Other Radicals, many of whom sat at the extreme Left of the Chamber of Deputies as a *groupe ouvrier*, concluded after the 1885 elections that Radicalism's credo of anti-clericalism, social reforms, and suppression of the Senate would never triumph through strictly parliamentary means. This conclusion led several deputies to break with Clemenceau and join Boulanger: Georges Laguerre, the fiery defense attorney for leftist causes; Charles Laisant, whose anti-parliamentarianism would eventually make him an anarchist; Jean Baptiste Saint-Martin, a biographer of both Mirabeau and Raspail; and Jean Turigny, an old victim of Louis Bonaparte's 1852 *coup d'état* and a fighter of forty years standing for a Radical republic. The group also included Francis Laur, whose book *La Mine aux mineurs* made him the parliamentary champion of mine reforms, and René Le Hérissé, an ex-royalist now at the extreme Left of the Radical party. Less socialistic than Rochefort and the Blanquist-Boulangists and more socialistic than Déroulède, these Radicals rallied to Boulanger as the only instrument capable of instituting a social republic. Constitutional change under Boulanger would be the medium.

Each of these "Boulangisms" saw the General as an agent for achieving its ambitions. By 1888 all of them adopted similar platforms, melting into a single movement. Built on the clientele of these disparate groups and the general's popularity, this united Boulangism stood for dissolution of the parliament, constitutional revision through a constituent assembly to establish an American-style presidential republic, sweeping social reforms, and a vigorous foreign policy.

The movement's method was to run Boulanger in one parliamentary by-election after another. With money from an old friend, Count Dillon, and a Paris newspaper, *La Cocarde*, Boulanger got out of the army and after several defeats, won election in the Aisne in March, 1888. He won again in rural Dordogne and industrial Nord, both previously Opportunist strongholds. Boulangism was born.

These surprising by-election victories brought a fourth group to Boulangism, the royalists. Realizing that two-thirds of Boulanger's votes in these by-elections had been royalist votes in 1885 and that their alliance with the Opportunists had been ended by the Wilson Scandal, the royalists considered: A renewed alliance with the Opportunists and Boulanger's defeat would permanently consolidate the republic; Boulanger's victory without them would insure that conservatives made no gains. Seeing no alternative, they joined Boulangism, hoping Boulanger would restore the throne or at least establish a strong Catholic and authoritarian régime. Boulanger seemed amenable to these aims. He secretly met with the parliamentary leader of the royalists and the Bonapartist pretender. He took enormous amounts of royalist money, but kept it secret from his republican rank and file. Never, however, did royalists replace the Radical Boulangists at the head of his party organization.

The success of the by-election campaign coincided with Barrès' formal conversion to Boulangism. In an article sent from Venice to *La Revue indépendante*, the principal organ of the symbolists, Barrès made a frank appeal to the younger generation of writers to join him in rejecting the parliamentary republic and embracing Boulangism:

> I would have a great effect if I could unite others with the France of tomorrow, a France which impatiently endures the parliamentary tumult and hopes to find the vigorous man who will open the windows, hurl the praters from them, and air out the place.[57]

Like all "honest men," Barrès hoped for "the man elected by popular instinct."[58] "Since Gambetta," he added, "General Boulanger is the only clear-sighted man of all those who have risen to power."[59]

Until the appearance of this article there is, interestingly enough, not one hint in the writings of Barrès that he was attracted to Boulanger. His letters to Sorg and de Guaita discuss neither politics nor the general. Only twice in his newspaper articles did he even mention the existence of Boulanger, once to use a Boulangist song as an excuse to praise the army, and once in discussing the hysteria created by the Schnaebelé affair when Boulanger was still war minister. It is clear from these writings that he did not become a Boulangist for the reasons others did. Never did he give any evidence of espousing the politics of Naquet and Laguerre, the social concerns of Rochefort and the *groupe ouvrier*, the nationalism of Déroulède, or the royalism of the conservative Boulangists. Indeed, his pre-1888 writings show no political or social awareness at all. To be sure, he was patriotic, feared Germany, and was greatly attached to Lorraine, but even in these matters his views were so commonplace that, had they been his motivation for becoming politically engagé, they would have led him into conventional Opportunist or Radical politics.

It was no accident, however, that his formal conversion to Boulangism coincided exactly with the publication of *Sous l'oeil des barbares* and the formulation of *Un Homme libre*, that point in the *Culte du moi* where action was a compelling necessity for him. Boulangism offered action, and it attacked the enemy: the parliamentary agents of the barbarians. "I have confidence," Barrès wrote, "that my country will know how to escape the tide of barbarians which covers and dirties it. Involving ourselves in public affairs is now a prime redemption for us, the young men, pushed aside by the interests and tricks of the vulgar band that exploits our elders and that we will know how to bring down."[60] He saw himself and other young men of his age as "sensitive and disoriented," "in sad isolation," in a world controlled by barbarians and vulgarity. Such a conviction doubtless grew out of both the theme of the *Culte du moi* and the belief that there was a veritable conspiracy against symbolism. The public and politicians had remained indifferent to symbolist poetry, but they objected to symbolist novels, believing that the pessimism and individual isolation of the works were decadent, debilitating rather than reviving the nation.

When Barrès experienced the massive attack on symbolism, accompanied as it was by his emotional and intellectual crisis which gave birth to the *Culte du moi*, he came to one conclusion. The barbarians, buttressed by the establishment literary critics, had behind them a parliamentary regime which attacked the decadents openly and perpetuated the intellectual climate the decadents despised. Thus, for Barrès, an intellectual revolt against the barbarians became a political revolt against the parliamentary regime which supported barbarism and particularly against the parliamentary parties, the Opportunists and Radicals.

It was not enough to chase the rascals out, however, for new rascals would come in. Since 1870, Barrès argued, several hundred "inexhaustible lawyers" and "ridiculous writers" had dominated parliament, forming themselves into a new aristocracy. They used politics to make their fortunes and to perpetuate themselves and their families. They had "hated, maltreated, and proscribed" the intellectual aristocracy.[61] No matter how idealistic a new deputy, he would have to compromise himself when he joined the "villainous men" of the multi-party Chamber of Deputies, its perpetual intrigues, and its continually forming governmental coalitions. Only Boulanger could change that situation; only he was convinced that changes were needed; and only he had the vigor necessary to put such new ideas into circulation.

More than that, Boulanger was sympathetic to artists. Barrès naively assured his fellow decadents that Boulanger was "of our race, in the large sense of that beautiful word." With Boulanger in power "we will forget our years of humiliation and isolation among the obscure circle which guides the stupid freethinkers, bureaucrats, and charlatans."[62] "Boulanger represents the opposition to the parliamentary régime. Through him—who alone is capable of this audacity today—will disappear these barbarians, so decidedly decried by honest Frenchmen of every caste."[63]

More than being an outlet for his intellectual disgust, however, Boulanger and Boulangism might provide the "axiom, religion or prince of men" Barrès cried out for at the end of *Sous l'oeil des barbares*. Years later he revealed that motivation in his novel on the Boulangist movement, *L'Appel au soldat* (1900). While most of the "facts" in the novel were twisted to provide lessons for a France in the middle of the Dreyfus affair, some of them square with the events of Barrès' experience of the 1880s. As early as the Schnaebelé affair, Sturel, the character in the novel who most closely resembles Barrès, saw in Boulanger the "rough draft" of his own "heroism."[64] In a brilliant evocation of the instinctive animal-like hysteria of the Gare de Lyon demonstration, "the soul of the masses immediately possessed" Sturel.[65] Later, he "knew the joy of fraternizing with the thousands of unknowns, exalted by the struggle and the signs of victory."[66] For Sturel, like Barrès, the content of Boulangism was not as important initially as was its energy, élan, and excitement.

In short, Barrès' entry into Boulangism had two motives—the revolt against a barbarian establishment decried in the *Culte du moi* and antiparliamentarianism. Nothing he wrote or said at the time indicates anything else. Never in his adherence to Boulangism did he mention the motives of the other Boulangisms in their "multiplicity": neither the nationalism, *revanche*, and yearning for the return of Alsace-Lorraine demanded by Déroulède, nor the social reforms so desired by the leftist Boulangists, nor a royal restoration. His only tie with them was his willingness to agree with Déroulède who wrote, "I am of *the party of the disgusted*, and they are numerous. It is with this rubric that we can line up all of France."[67]

For Barrès in 1888–1889 Boulanger was merely the charismatic leader who could demolish the barbarians and their parliamentary régime. Sybil of *La Revue bleue* observed that "Boulangism is political decadence and decadence is literary Boulangism; the two phenomena are akin. They are two sicknesses of the contemporary French soul, and M. Maurice Barrès is afflicted with both of them at the same time."[68] Such an observation could be expected from a journal which had carried on an unrelenting campaign against symbolism and which gave to decadence its derogatory connotation. But the linking of Barrès' decadence and his Boulangism was more logical than Sybil imagined. For Barrès Boulangism was indeed decadent—mystical, obscure, irrational, full of élan, rooted in instinct, against conventional political parties. Moreover, Boulangism was attacked by the orthodox politicians of the same barbarian world that was crushing him and the decadents. Because of their mutual enemy, Barrès and Boulangism were made for each other. The *Culte du moi* demanded action; only Boulangism offered action consistent with Barrès' intellectual formation.

To be sure, Barrès would see it differently when he wrote of Boulangism later. Barrès scholars have usually found their principal source for understanding his Boulangism in his novel about the movement, *L'Appel au soldat*, which emphasized Boulangism's nationalism. The novel and its nationalistic message were to guide the welter of nationalist leagues spawned by the Dreyfus affair. Barrès' view of Boulangism in 1888–1889, however, was different. It was tuned exclusively to the world of the *Culte du moi*.

If Barrès intended his appeal to touch off a rush of artists into the arms of Boulanger, he could not have been more disappointed. Paul Adam, a novelist whose literary and intellectual development paralleled that of Barrès in the 1880s and who had been swept off his feet by the masses at the Gare de Lyon, was the only significant writer to espouse the General.[69] Although Boulanger became increasingly a frequenter of the salons, the intellectual aristocracy remained aloof from him and continued to consider him more anti-intellectual than the barbarians Barrès despised. The intellectuals doubtless felt like Francis Magnard of *Le Figaro*, who hardly expected Boulanger to make a pilgrimage to Bayreuth to hear *Parsifal* or read Verlaine just to please Barrès. The General's artistic tastes were too ordinary for that. Indeed, said Magnard, Boulanger was flattered by the support Barrès gave him in *La Revue indépendante*, but he did not understand the article. According to a story making the rounds, someone offered to have Barrès explain it. "No," replied the general, "it is enough that M. Barrès admires me. I will dispense with his reasons for it." Magnard thought that the story was false, but that Barrès' failure to see through the general's intellectual shallowness illustrated "the sunstroke afflicting so many of the men who support *le brav' général*."[70] Almost a year later another writer remarked that Barrès' appeal "was coldly welcomed by the 'rising generation,' " which felt that Boulanger was more interested in winning the votes of the multitude than the votes of artists and that his military background put him against art and intellectualism.[71] Barrès' article did perhaps contribute to a large student demonstration for and against Boulanger on April 21, shortly after the appearance of "M. le général Boulanger et la nouvelle génération." The group most involved was the *Association générale des étudiants*, whose members were almost two to one against the general.[72] For Barrès, taking everything in stride, the motivation of the anti-Boulangist students was simple. "They dream of settling themselves some day at the *bosom* of the parliament and do not want that *vache* driven to the slaughterhouse."[73]

Even though his adherence to Boulangism was largely ignored by the audience he addressed, Barrès was welcomed into the Boulangist movement. Until its very end, Boulangism accepted all comers, and Barrès was no exception. He joined the staff of *La Presse*, the official newspaper of the movement, and wrote literary criticism for it similar to his writings for *Le Voltaire*, where he was no longer wanted. By December, 1888, his rise in the movement allowed him to speak briefly at a Boulangist banquet in Nevers honoring the Deputy, Jean Turigny.[74]

It soon appeared, however, that Barrès had joined Boulangism just as the movement began to decline. On June 4 Boulanger was almost drowned out by interruptions in the Chamber of Deputies when he presented his program: a revision of the constitution to provide for the popular election of the president, a single-chamber legislature with commissions, separation of powers, and the referendum. Even the general's magic with the voters appeared to be losing its touch when he was defeated in an Ardèche by-election. In spite of victories in three later by-elections, conservatives began to have serious second thoughts about their alliance with the Boulangists. Despite the protestations of Boulanger and Count Dillon, they became increasingly sceptical of capturing the Boulangist movement or profiting from it.

This decline and threatened breakup of the Boulangist alliance was prevented by calling a by-election in Paris, the most republican part of France. Boulanger had never won in an ardently republican constituency, and he was up against a candidate who was backed by every shade of anti-Boulangist opinion from Radical to Opportunist. Yet, the government's determination to stop Boulangism at Paris could not have been more unwise. Elsewhere Boulanger had won through royalist money and the coalition of disgruntled conservatives and Radicals. But in Paris and only in Paris, Boulangists had real organization. Drawing on the organizations of Déroulède, Rochefort, Laguerre, and Le Hérissé and the Bonapartist organs, they established an efficient electoral machine even on the *arrondissement* and *quartier* level. The machine had behind it the not inconsiderable Boulangist press and 500,000 francs of royalist money. Paris was the only place in France where the republican Boulangists were strong, and they delivered the votes—245,236 for Boulanger against 162,875 for Edouard Jacques, the principal opponent. On election night, January 27, 1889, with an enormous Boulangist mob surging around the café where its leaders celebrated, it looked as if victory in the fall legislative elections of 1889 would be certain and France would become Boulangist.

Barrès was not in Paris for the celebration. A month earlier he had gone home to Nancy to launch a Boulangist movement there which would carry him to victory in those legislative elections of 1889. The returning prodigal, however, was vastly different from the person he had been even one year earlier. The quest of his *Culte du moi* to discover and fulfill his individuality had demanded political action. Boulangism was the appropriate action because its enemies, the barbarians, were his enemies. With his selfhood now energized, Barrès entered his first political campaign.

CHAPTER TWO

THE CAMPAIGN OF 1889 IN NANCY

If Barrès' commitment to Boulangism in 1888 had little effect on his fellow intellectuals, it did take him into the Boulangist movement. In turn, the progress of Boulangism made him decide to carry its cause to Nancy where he founded a Boulangist newspaper and electoral committee in December, 1888. It was hardly an auspicious beginning. He was so unknown in that city that the first police report called him M. Barèze. Although they soon got his name straight, they still said that he was "without influence" as late as March, 1889.[1] Yet, by October he had accepted without question the ready-made program of the national and Nancy Boulangists and had conducted a successful campaign for a seat in the Chamber of Deputies. In this enterprise the twenty-seven year old Barrès was hardly an original political thinker or leader, but it did make him a politician, and a successful one at that. More important for his future intellectual and political development, however, the experience at Nancy brought him into working-class politics and to the brink of socialism.

Boulangism at Nancy was already under way by the time Barrès arrived there. It dated from the Schnaebelé affair, which had so greatly agitated Barrès on his 1887 visit. Anti-German excitement was given no chance to abate during 1888. Some observers feared that German troop movements around Nancy would provoke frontier incidents. *Le Progrès de l'Est*, Nancy's principal Opportunist newspaper, discounted the importance of these troops, but they agitated *Le Figaro* enough to run an entire series in August, 1888, on the military situation around Nancy. The very reluctance of the Opportunist press to support revanchism at such a time probably encouraged patriots to extremes. Such feelings manifested themselves as Boulangism as early as March, 1888, when twelve to fifteen demonstrators shouted "vive Boulanger" and "à bas Carnot" in front of the offices of *Le Progrès de l'Est*.[2] On April 26 anti-Boulangist students at the University of Nancy, following the lead of their fellows in Paris, organized a demonstration against Boulanger. Its last-minute cancellation came too late to head off three nights of pro-Boulangist demonstrations. By the last night, April 28, the demonstration, swollen to five to six thousand Boulangists, turned into a riot, spread over most of the city, and went on well into the night before the police put it down. Fifty-one Boulangists were arrested. Their occupations—printers, bakers, steel workers, shoe workers, enginemen, etc.—indicated the social composition of Nancy's Boulangist movement.[3] The young working class was pitted against the students, the future leaders of Nancy politics and property. One anti-Boulangist student leader, for example, was the son of the head of the Republican Alliance, the local Opportunist organization of Nancy's legal, university, and business establishment.

By the time of Barrès' arrival in Nancy, the young, middle-class leaders of this demonstration—a twenty-one year old medical student, a thirty-seven year old traveling salesman, and a twenty-seven year old clerk—came together with two other groups to form the local Boulangist movement. One group was the League of Patriots, an organization dating from 1884 with a membership of over one hundred in Nancy, which was presided over by a very proper attorney, Victor Courtois. Socially its members probably matched those of nearby Frouard's thirty members, described by the police as the "principal notables of the locality."[4] All they seemed to want was something done about Alsace-Lorraine and the foreign workers, but that changed when Déroulède tried to turn the league into a Boulangist troop in April, 1888. By July Courtois had led the members out of the league and into a non-political *Union*

37

patriotique de l'Est. This left a rump Boulangist League of Patriots in the hands of a dealer in artist's paints, Alphonse Victor Bouttier. Bouttier shared the typical leaguer's interest in rifle and physical fitness clubs, and as president of Nancy's boating club, he had a wide following. His politics remained consistent, too. By 1898 he was head of Nancy's Anti-Semitic League, but in 1888 his leaguers, with the April demonstrators and a third group, provided the personnel for Nancy Boulangism.[5]

The third group was Nancy's Left. Its leader was Alfred Gabriel, a forty year old bachelor, former bookkeeper, journalist of Blanquist leanings, and shabby owner of an ill-kept beard. His role was to be decisive in Barrès' success in Nancy politics. Gabriel had written for *Le Cri du peuple* and had run the *Patriote de l'Est* and the *Reveil democratique de l'Est.* An early police report describes him as "absolutely without fortune; well-informed enough; live and fertile imagination; imbued with socialist doctrines . . . man of action."[6] He had run on the defeated 1885 Radical list with its program of constitutional revision, progressive income and corporation taxes, separation of church and state, and working class reforms.[7] In 1888 he still headed the organization of that party, which was at the extreme Left politically and working class socially. Like other Radical committees which joined Boulangism, Nancy Radicals had become disgusted with the failure of their party to deliver on its platform or to do more in Nancy than assure Opportunist victories against conservatives.

Throughout the 1889 campaign, in arguments which Barrès would take as his own, Gabriel insisted that although France had been a republic for twenty years, the necessary reforms had not materialized. Parliamentarianism, established by the monarchist framers of the 1875 constitution, had become only a pretext for booty and corruption.[8] For years reformers had felt that success would follow the abolition of the undemocratic Senate, but the leaders of this struggle for revision, Clemenceau's Radicals, had abandoned this struggle in spite of their promises.[9] Feeling this way, Gabriel turned to revolution: The people "has been eternally oppressed and duped by all the revolutions, and in spite of that it believes in the revolution and wants it. That is why the people are Boulangist. The destruction of the oppressor is the dream of the proletarian, the hungry and exploited of humanity."[10]

Paul Adam, the novelist friend of Barrès who campaigned with him at Nancy, later felt that Gabriel came to Boulangism because of its principle of federalist reconciliation; that is, if there were local autonomy, leftist strongholds could pass social reforms without having to wait for France as a whole to be converted to reformism. Adam also held that Gabriel, with his program and following, almost single-handedly brought over to Boulanger the workers of Frouard, Champigneulles, and Dombasle, the main working-class centers of Nancy.[11] For an extreme leftist like Gabriel to be taken in by Boulangism was not unusual. Even Paul Lafargue, the son-in-law of Karl Marx, leaned toward Boulangism for a while until Friedrich Engels set him straight.[12]

In large part the social and economic conditions of Nancy aided the political efforts of Gabriel and Boulangism. A virtual explosion of industrialization had followed the Treaty of Frankfurt (1871), which brought in many factories from Alsace-Lorraine and gave Nancy the fastest economic growth rate in France. In 1870, for example, Nancy had only five hosiery factories; by 1890 it had twenty-two, and the domestic system had been ended. The same years saw the number of shoe factories, whose workers were a major source for Boulangist militants, rise from ten to thirty-two. Other industries experienced similar growth so that Nancy was a center for tanning, brewing, textiles, clothing, pottery, and glass. The key to Nancy's industrial economy was mining. The Nancy iron ore basin, the area containing the constituency Gabriel won in 1889, produced 52,460 tons of steel in 1888. The introduction of the Thomas-Gilchrist process in that year shot production up to 227,886 tons by 1893. At the southern edge of Nancy, the area containing the constituency Barrès would win in 1889, was a major salt producing district which produced 400,000 tons in 1892. This rapid growth had given Nancy a population of 213,364 by 1891, with about an equal number of *patrons* and *ouvriers*, by census classification. The rapid industrial growth, however, had also necessitated considerable importation of workers so that the city had 29,788 foreigners, mostly Belgian, Luxemburger, and Italian workers. With thirty-four parishes, Nancy was overwhelmingly Catholic, but there was also one Protestant congregation and six Jewish clergymen, a fact Barrès was not to let the voters forget.[13]

While the economy boomed, social reforms, working-class organization, and wages lagged. For example, only 1,546 students attended tuition secondary schools, compared with the 66,957 in the free elementary ones. This lag also marked the trade union movement. According to the prefect, membership in the key metal workers union had increased only from seventy to eighty in its five year life. Its activity was next to nothing, and membership in the long-established shoe workers union had fallen from seventy-eight to forty-eight. Indeed, in 1889 no local trade union had more than one hundred members in spite of the large work force.[14] Nor, aside from Gabriel's Radicals, was there anything resembling a working-class political movement. The lag was also seen in wages. A national inquiry in 1890 figured that with three hundred twelve-hour work days a year a Nancy worker would earn nine hundred francs and his wife would get two hundred. If that family had no unemployment or sickness its minimum yearly expenses would be 120 francs less than the total wages, but few families could make ends meet. Such low wages were due, of course, to under-unionization, the placement of factories in neighboring agricultural villages with their cheap labor, and to the employment of foreign workers. The sub-prefect of Briey reported to the prefect in 1885 that "large industry employs a great many foreigners who are a kind of guarantee against strikes."[15] Little wonder that Barrès and Gabriel struck a responsive chord among the workers with their attacks on foreign workers during the 1889 campaign. In these ways industrial growth had made Nancy a fertile field for a reformist political movement. The city's large foreign element and proximity to Germany, coupled with the anti-German resentment of Alsatian employers and working-class resentment against Belgian and Italian workers, had made it nationalistic. The nationalism and re-formism of left-wing Boulangism was made to order for such a situation.

In this political and social milieu the various elements came together with Barrès to form a Boulangist organization by the end of 1888. As late as October the prefect reported that Bou-langism was only in "a latent state," being "neither organized nor in the way of becoming so," without any money, and with only the leaders of the April demonstrations and Bouttier's League of Patriots as members.[16] By November they were joined by Gabriel who presided at an appearance by Maurice Vergoin, a left-wing Boulangist Deputy charged with organizing pro-vincial Boulangist committees. The same month saw the "re-visionists"—everything from Boulangists in all but name to a Radical-Republican who ran against Barrès in 1889—break off from the Opportunist-dominated Republican Alliance.[17] On December 17, accompanied by speeches from Vergoin and Charles Laisant, the Boulangists of these revisionists formally organized a committee.[18]

A few days later Barrès arrived from Paris with his friend and fellow novelist, Paul Adam. Adam later described the ar-rival in his novel about the Nancy campaign, *Le Mystère des foules*. According to it the fictional Barrès (Coesarès) had been sent to Nancy by Boulanger to organize a campaign, and the fictional Adam (Dessling) came because he had an influential relative in the area. Both, along with a fictional Stanislas de Guaita, were already left-wing and nationalistic. De Guaita and the lawyer-director of the review, *La Lorraine artiste*, intro-duced them to the leaders of the base: the fictional Bouttier (Desreaux) and Gabriel (Liverdun). In their first contact with him, the ugly, somewhat bohemian Gabriel "accused every-one" because the old Radical committee had no newspaper or money.[19]

That was soon remedied when the newly formed committee purchased the failing *Courrier de Meurthe et Moselle* with 21,000 francs furnished by the Orleanist-Boulangist Prince Edmond de Polignac on behalf of the Boulangist National Committee. The idea was to convert the newspaper's already revisionist

41

policy to open Boulangism with articles by Barrès and Adam, but legal problems and balky stockholders prevented this from happening. Instead the old *Courrier* quit publication and on January 22, 1889, reappeared as *Le Courrier de l'Est*, a "revisionist republican journal," with Barrès as editor-in-chief.[20] He proposed to serve the Boulangist cause with it throughout eastern France, including Edmond de Polignac's projected campaign against Jules Ferry in the Vosges. By March, circulation failure forced Barrès to turn his ambitious journalistic endeavor into a weekly almost exclusively put together by him, Adam, and Gabriel.

It was on this base—a newspaper and Gabriel's organization —that Barrès would take Boulangism to the voters of Nancy on two occasions in 1889: the cantonal elections of July 28 and the legislative ones of September 22 and October 6. This effort, begun with the establishment of a Boulangist committee and newspaper, reveals two important features: the conversion of the formerly apolitical Barrès into a left-wing reformer, and the fact that Nancy Boulangism, like much of national Boulangism, was built on a working-class and left-wing base.

Of these two features the most surprising was the conversion of Barrès, in great contrast to his earlier and subsequent career, into a bona fide leftist. Given the fact that the *Culte du moi* demanded the fulfillment of his ego through politics, his adherence to Boulangism had logically grown out of his resentment of the "barbarians" and the Opportunist republic which reinforced them. His political thinking included only the conviction that Boulanger could rid France of the parliamentary Opportunist republic and, by doing so, end "barbarism." Certainly that kind of straight political Boulangism was sufficient for the "involvement" his quest for selfhood needed, and that is the variety he had expressed in the *Revue indépendante* article of 1888 and continued in the early issues of the *Courrier de l'Est*.

Barrès set this theme in bold-face type as early as February 1, 1889—"Opportunists: Financial society organized for the exploitation of France under the Third Republic."[21] The Opportunist republic was also permanently immobilized, for in a remarkable feat it had established a system which institutionalized immobility. Thus, any party which, like the Radicals, supported the parliamentary constitution also helped perpetuate Opportunism no matter how reformist its rhetoric. In such a way the *Courrier* could label the Nancy Republican Alliance of Radicals and Opportunists as the "Ferryist Alliance" and the party of "liars and false republicans."[22] Moreover, the deputies of this parliamentary republic knew about the Wilson scandal for years and did nothing.[23] Barrès asked a rally at Frouard, " 'What is a deputy? It is today a man whose impotence and immobility would astonish the cripple himself.' (All the audience is delighted.)"[24] Periodically the *Courrier* published a facetious "letter from an Opportunist," which bore the stamp of Barrès' ironic sense. One of these letters, objecting to the contention of the *Courrier* that the Opportunist deputies from Meurthe-et-Moselle were dishonest, argued that they were good family men, against sin, and so on. In another, the "Opportunist" insisted that deputies only appeared to be immobile, for they required two years of legislative apprenticeship:

> In arriving you are *as much as lost in the Chamber*. You get lost in the corridors. You do not know where the tap-room is. You are the laughingstock of the door-keepers who direct you to the water-closet when you ask them where the *cabinet* is. That happened in 1885 to our poor Cordier [a local Opportunist deputy] the first day of his arrival at the Palais Bourbon. And, as an apprentice, he had to do in the first two years a thousand disagreeable things, as do the errand girls in Parisian shops. He made himself useful in making up the commissions. He was able to carry to the sharpener the knives his colleagues would apply [to the current cabinet]. He accompanied debate with uproar and heckling. He prepared black coffee.[25]

The implication of this line of attack was obvious: Only Boulangism could bring reform; only it would cut through the institutionalized immobility by ending parliamentarianism.

Barrès' initial attack on Opportunism was hardly unexpected considering his reasons for joining Boulangism, but the early issues of *Le Courrier de l'Est* revealed a surprisingly new Barrès—the ivory-tower decadent had become working class oriented. "The workers are clearly revisionist," Barrès wrote in the very first issue, because their patriotism and demands for reforms have not been met by a parliament "absorbed in petty intrigues."[26] And again, "The small shopkeepers, the workers, the peasants are not pleased that [parliament] has done nothing for them? That life is difficult for them. We bring them the means to drive out the parliamentarians, who have argued with sterility for twelve years, and to directly take power for themselves."[27] He insisted that "social reforms ought to be generously dispensed to the workers," but he made no effort to spell them out.[28] Hardly an issue of the *Courrier* went by without a story about workers somewhere in France supporting Boulanger and suggesting that France awaited the decision of Nancy workers. He constantly reiterated, even throughout the subsequent campaign, that parliamentary government was unwilling and incapable of helping the workers. This same tone expressed itself in the initial rallies the Nancy Boulangists held in January and February to get the campaign going. On January 26, with a so-called "revisionist committee" only a month old, Gabriel drew an audience of three hundred fifty through the appeal that Boulanger was the only hope of the proletariat.[29] On February 10, in keeping with his determination to serve more than Nancy, Barrès shared a rostrum at Saint-Dié with Edmond de Polignac. It was the last time Barrès would venture from the Nancy area during 1889, and Polignac retired from the scene within a month.

Barrès' sudden working-class orientation was the result of three things. Revealing one of them in an article written several months after the 1889 campaign, he implied that his discussions with his "dear workers," in their "sad working class sections," as they "fraternally smoked their cigars," seemed to draw him into an almost existential involvement with the "popular soul." "It is impossible," he confessed, "to live for several weeks in the milieu of the disinherited without receiving from them an emotion, a sincere impulse of love." Yet, this contact with the masses not only stirred his pity. The thrill of touching the people and the rough and tumble of the campaign, with the workers defending him from hecklers and rowdies, compelled him to follow up his words with deeds: "It was [during the campaign] that I grasped how to understand and love life as well as the completely laid bare instinct. After that, would I have the ingratitude to neglect the improvements demanded by these brave men who, without knowing me, did not hesitate to love me and who personally bettered me?"[30]

All this sounds remarkably like *Le Jardin de Bérénice. Sous l'oeil des barbares* and *Un Homme libre*, completed after he was converted to Boulangism but before he was caught up in the Nancy campaign, merely called for action. Certainly straight political Boulangism was enough for that, and *Le Jardin de Bérénice* opens with Philippe entering a Boulangist campaign in Provence. But the mood of the novel, published two years after the Nancy campaign, abruptly departs from the self-contained egoism of the first two novels of the *Culte du moi.* "I come into [politics]," says Philippe, "because I am against abuses,"[31] and he is "put into contact with the most generous spirits of the arrondissement, with those who are impatient for change, those who are discontented."[32] "[Political meetings] must bore you a great deal," Philippe's political adversary says to him.

> I assure him that I am more pleased with the workers of the people than I am in a salon in Arles or a café.
> "But what have you in common with a worker?" . . . "You fall into the same error I once did. I once believed that talking with the individual voters of a certain class was merely making a deal with the people. I was wrong. Men united by a common passion create a soul, but each of them is a part of that soul. Each possesses it in himself, but he is not yet aware of it. Only in the atmosphere of a great political rally, in contact with passions which fortify his own, does he forget himself and his small reflections and allow his Unconscious to develop. From the sum of these Unconsciouses the popular soul is born."[33]

"How can I make you believe," says Philippe on another occasion to his friend, "that I prefer these masses with their creative, disinterested and spontaneous spirit to the mediocrity of the salons and the demi-culture of *bacheliers* . . . The people give me a soul, its soul, my soul, humanity's soul."[34]

45

However sincere these post-election pronouncements about the ability of the popular soul to regenerate his sense of self-hood, they were arguments after the fact. The real fact of the matter was that the Boulangist movement in Nancy was a working-class movement. That in itself was reason enough for his sudden orientation toward the unconscious masses. In April, 1890, the Nancy police made a report on each of eighty-nine Boulangist militants.[35] Of these, 76 percent were workers. Another 16 to 17 percent were "white collar" and professional (such as store and office clerks, a dentist, students), and only 8 percent could be classified as bourgeois (wine merchants dominated, not to mention the single dealer in gravestones). While the reported militants were overwhelmingly working class, they heavily represented a "First Industrial Revolution" work force of shoe and leather workers, cabinet makers, and stoneworkers. Boulangist workers from nearby "Second Industrial Revolution" industries of steel, salt, and chemicals were not represented in these reports, apparently because they lived in towns outside the jurisdiction of the Nancy police. These Boulangist militants were not only predominantly working class; they were also young, much younger probably than the members of the Opportunist organization with which the police were not as statistically concerned. Of the Boulangists 74 percent were no older than forty years, and 46 percent were thirty-five years old or under. Indeed, a surprisingly high 21 percent of them were twenty-five years old or under. Moreover, 30 percent of them were born in Alsace-Lorraine with almost half of those being born in Metz and a great number being only recent arrivals to France. Two had been *Communards* in 1871, but the overwhelming majority were described by police as hard workers of good character and high morals. In short, Barrès' fellow Boulangist militants could be characterized as stable, young, nationalistic, and working class. It was only natural for him to identify with them, for they were the *Jardin de Bérénice's* instinctive crowd which could both energize his selfhood and bring political victory.

If any one person in Nancy played the role of Bérénice in

placing Barrès' "self" in contact with the popular soul, it was the champion of the Nancy workers, Alfred Gabriel. At Nancy, Barrès had native roots and a newspaper, but he had no following. Gabriel did have a following, and he introduced Barrès to it in a series of meetings in February.[36] Gabriel could come, in turn, to Barrès because of his stature in the national Boulangist movement and because his newspaper offered Gabriel a forum.

Although Barrès brought to Nancy only his personal entourage and ideas, he came to rely increasingly on Gabriel and, eventually, his well-developed working-class program. Gabriel's program proposed, first of all, that education should be truly open to working-class children. Education was paid for with taxes on the workers, but only bourgeois sons were permitted into secondary and higher education.[37] Second, there should be equalization of taxation with "the end of the tax crushing the little purse in order to enlarge the big one, the end of theft and thieves." "Yes or no, is it just, is it theft," he asked, that workers be taxed indirectly at 20 percent while the *rentier* is taxed 4 1/2 percent.[38] Third, he urged a national program of old age pensions since even "despotic and imperial" Germany had one. "Will France do less? Will our Republic be less democratic and socialist than feudal Germany?"[39] Fourth, the referendum should be used to solve social problems. With it, reforms that might fail in the nation as a whole could be made in local socialist strongholds. At the same time, a national referendum could enact reforms turned down by the Senate. Fifth, there should be equalization of military service so that sons of the wealthy could no longer exempt themselves.[40] Finally, worker and agricultural unions should be allowed to incorporate so that they could own the means of production and establish cooperatives.

At the beginning Barrès was quite cool to Gabriel, his program, and his working-class following. The Paris dandy quite naturally found sophisticates like Adam more to his liking than the often dirty and unkempt Nancy agitator and his workers. The police unsurprisingly noted, for example, that after the first of the February rallies Barrès went off to a café with two local Boulangist men of letters while Gabriel went off "with several workers to sit in a corner of the café."[41] After Gabriel spelled out his reforms at a rally on February 24, Barrès hastened to remind his readers that while he listened "with the most lively curiosity" to "the most advanced socialist dreams" of Gabriel's "very daring spirit," "we hesitate before applying the theories with which his warm eloquence makes us sympathize." Boulanger, he added, "will get for us several reforms—more moderate, I fully believe, than those dreamed of by our friend Gabriel."[42]

By summer, however, it had become a different matter. By then Barrès came to share leadership with Gabriel and adopt his program, at first because he wanted the victory which was possible only through working-class votes. This illustrates the interplay between the thought and action of Barrès. He had joined Boulangism because his thought necessitated action. His constant association with Gabriel on the newspaper and in political rallies exposed him to leftist ideas. His mingling with the worker and shopkeeper Boulangist militants in Nancy eventually made him sensitive to their plight. His awareness of the hold social reforms had on these workers showed him that victory lay in such a program, and the scent of victory was sweet.

The radicalization of Barrès was complete when, on the anniversary of the Tennis Court Oath, he toasted those workers "whose effort with their arms and minds buys the gold which fattens the thieves and men worthy of prison who are our deputies." This dandy and decadent went on to remind them that besides the "worker laborers," there were "bourgeois laborers," obviously himself, who had abandoned their privileges to work for the cause of labor. In pleading for old age pensions, he went so far as to tell his audience that such a reform could not be realized by an "incapable bourgeoisie." "Mindful of the weary worker whose worn-out muscles refuse to toil any longer for his stomach's food," Barrès concluded, "these measures would protect him from the poor-house, from the malevolence of that authority which right now 'walks the streets' under these windows to find out the words of our orators and to gape at our independent citizens."[43]

48

By the end of the legislative campaign in September and October Barrès had advocated Gabriel's reform program before most of the working-class groups of Nancy. Typical of his reformist rhetoric were these words to the workers of Saint-Nicolas-du-Port:

> We will occupy ourselves . . . with creating pensions which will protect old and tired workers from their last years of poverty. In addition, the application of limited liability legislation to labor and agricultural unions will permit these societies to . . . become a real force, instead of being, as they are now, at the caprice of a government able to disperse a union and seize its funds. Only union independence will assure the independence of labor to resist capitalism or give it armor in the economic struggle.[44]

Yet, attractive as this relatively mild program might sound to the workers, Barrès made no attempt until the mid-1890s to buttress it with any theories on property or society. In 1889 he simply accepted the Gabriel program as a formula for victory and as a plan for working-class amelioration.

For both Barrès and Gabriel, as well as for most of the Boulangist movement, social reforms were tied to political ones. For years the Radicals had insisted that social reforms were impossible so long as the Senate exercised its veto; but the Radicals had failed to win the nation. Boulanger, through strong presidential leadership, could galvanize the nation into constitutional change which would guarantee the various reforms desired by his entourage—Radical, nationalist, Blanquist, and even royalist. Often, as in the case of Barrès and Gabriel, the various Boulangist elements came to adopt one another's points of view. Barrès, drawn by Boulangism's promise of national revival through constitutional change, came to accept social reform. Gabriel, drawn to Boulangism by the inability of parliamentarianism to bring social reforms, came to accept Boulangism's offer of national revival. Boulanger was so vague that to his voters and supporters he appeared to accept all the views of his lieutenants. In short, the promise of constitutional revision united the divisions of Boulangism.

Arguing as he did that the Third Republic had institutionalized immobility, Barrès sought to convince his prospective constituents that a Boulangist republic would change all that. Pressed by his opposition to prove that Boulangism had a program as well as a personality cult, Barrès spent much of February and March, 1889, spelling out the details of the proposal for constitutional revision, deposited by Boulanger at the Chamber on June 4, 1888, and ghost-written by Naquet. Since 1789, Barrès held, France had been gripped by political schizophrenia. On the one hand, monarchy had brought unity and continuity at the expense of the liberty and popular sovereignty which a parliamentary republic could bring. Yet, the instability of the parliamentary republic had been unable to bring France unity and continuity. The Boulangist republic alone could bring unity and continuity as well as liberty and popular sovereignty.[45] The parliamentary republic could work if the electorate were homogeneous, impartial, attentive, and disinterested and if a parliament elected by such voters would usher its best members into the ministry.[46] Unfortunately, voters chose deputies on the basis of electoral programs, but they could not force deputies to carry out these programs. Once in the Palais-Bourbon, the politicians distributed themselves into groups and served the interests and ambitions of the group instead of the interests of the nation. Ministers were unable to follow a "suitable and durable" policy, since they were the "servile agents" of the political coalition which supported them. Because they wanted to stay in power, they could not antagonize any faction of the coalition. Thus, they could do nothing. "At the end of several weeks of using [a new ministry], the 'out' coteries recruit several malcontents and become in turn a majority; a new coalition is tied together; the ministry falls; a new ministry is raised in the same conditions to pursue the same destiny."

These conditions could be remedied by establishing a presidential republic with separation of powers: the president would be directly elected by universal suffrage to prevent an electoral college from naming a nonentity. He would appoint the cabinet, which would be approved by but independent of the legislature and responsible to him. He could veto legislation, but the vote of two-thirds of the members of the legislature could override a veto. Indeed, Barrès insisted that the constituent assembly, which would write the constitution, must "find ways to prevent any peril of dictatorship." It could either abolish the Senate or require the direct election of senators. The constitution would also provide for the initiative, referendum, and recall.

Such ideas were certainly not original with Barrès; his expression of them at this stage in his development simply reflected the position of the Boulangist leadership, which formulated them. The form of this constitution had various origins. First of all, and like so much of Boulangism, it lay in the political frustration of the various Boulangist elements, which found themselves unable to achieve their aims through the parliamentary republic. Obviously, Barrès shared this feeling of frustration, especially in his conviction that such a republic perpetuated "barbarism." Second, in rejecting the Third Republic, the Boulangist constitution harked back to the Second Republic; frequently the Boulangist leadership admitted this. Third, foreign republican models influenced the framers of the Boulangist constitution. The American republic, with its checks and balances, provided a formula for preventing both a dictatorial president and an immobile legislature. Boulanger, himself, admitted being impressed with the American experience as a result of his trip to the United States as the French representative to the centennial of the battle of Yorktown. Other Boulangist leaders expressed similar feelings. Swiss use of the initiative, referendum, and recall also made its mark on the Boulangists. On reading Barrès, one gets the feeling that he was drawn to the Boulangist constitution for these reasons and for an additional one, namely the translation into politics of the *Culte du moi* philosophy. The strong president, fulfilling his ego would be above politics but involved in the life of the nation. His example could inspire the renewal of France and, perhaps, the self-renewal of individual Frenchmen, who could find in him sustenance for their own personhoods.

Moreover, through the Boulangist constitution and the "open republic," the factions would be reconciled. The Boulangist republic could finally bring France the unity, continuity, liberty,

51

and reform which parliamentary factionalism prevented. For Barrès, the "open republic" meant that civil rights and civil liberties would be guaranteed for all but those "in irreconcilable and revolutionary opposition to the free institutions accepted by the people."[47] Besides, Boulangism proved its ability to unite factions with its record of electoral victories won by uniting conservatives, patriots, and disgusted Radicals. Barrès scoffed at other alternatives:

> M. Clemenceau, M. Ferry (oh! improbable hypothesis) today will sustain revision, but they will not arrive at it. Their friends today who try to take our program from us will not even get the right to speak from their disgusted voters. Today General Boulanger alone . . . is able to serve France usefully and save the Republic.[48]

In this wide-ranging attack on Opportunism and its republic, Barrès regularly sharpened his jabs by applying his generalities to specific local issues. In such a way he hoped his readers could see the proof of his argument in their own experience. In denouncing the incompetence of the current government, for example, he claimed that a local school official, dead for six months, had just been promoted according to the *Bulletin administratif*.[49] In attacking the anti-clericalism of the Opportunist government and its decision to get the nuns out of hospitals, Barrès alleged that Nancy hospital nuns cost the government nine hundred francs a year while lay personnel would cost two thousand francs. Worse yet, he felt (and he was sure his readers would agree from their own experience) that the sisters were more dedicated to their vocation.[50] In trying to prove Ferry the national villain and to label the Republican Alliance the *"alliance ferryiste,"* Barrès on more than one occasion reminded the workers that the "Ferry of Saint-Dié," an industrial town in neighboring Meurthe, had called the workers "mud."[51] Of course, this Ferry was Albert, not Jules, and he had been defeated for re-election as mayor; but if the workers confused him with Jules, no harm was done.

Related to this was Barrès' anti-Semitism. In 1889 it fitted perfectly with his labeling of Boulangism's entire opposition as "Opportunist." The *Courrier de l'Est* reported that at the second meeting of the Boulangist committee, "Barrès gave the flunkeys and menials of the Jewish High Bank the tongue lashing they deserve for imprisoning the liberty of Fràncе in the name of Opportunism."[52] Late in the campaign he argued that everyone in eastern France distrusted the Jew:

> I say distrust, I do not dare write that they hate the Jew . . . We distrust the Jew: we refuse to hate him. We belong to the party of conciliation . . . We accept all sons of the Revolution as a reality . . . . We do not say: war to the Jew! But it would be stupid for a son of the French soil not to defend himself.

Then he launched into an attack on the High-Bank, Jewish control of the cattle trade in eastern France and its legal cheating of the peasant. He contended he heard one Jew say, "We will run over the Christians in twenty years!" He went so far as to believe that the Jews of eastern Europe probably deserved the pogroms. Jewish "usurpation" had even been protested in the French parliament where "Jews and Opportunists consolidate."[53]

It is difficult to determine how much of Barrès' anti-Semitism derived from his own attitude and how much was due to political expediency. His writings of the 1880s, rather than expressing the racism of his later career, evidence no anti-Semitism. He had numerous Jewish literary friends, and one of the principal Boulangist lieutenants, Naquet, was Jewish. On the other hand, Lorraine, like Alsace, was anti-Semitic at the most popular level. It had been so for centuries, and it would remain so. Nancy had a relatively large Jewish population. In the 1890s it would have one of the most active Anti-Semitic Leagues outside of Paris. In the 1898 election, with all the survivors of the first round of balloting anti-Semites, Barrès would be beaten by a candidate who was even more anti-Semitic than he was. Nationally, popular anti-Semitism was the stock in trade for almost every persuasion at the extremes of the political spectrum. For example, the principal socialist organ, *La Revue socialiste*, and Edouard Drumont's rightist mass circulation *La Libre Parole* were anti-Semitic, and both hated Boulangism. Boulangists like the staff members of *La Cocarde*, Francis Laur, and Maurice Vergoin, who had been so instrumental in founding the Nancy Boulangist committee, were quite anti-Semitic. On the other hand, General Boulanger and his chief advisers criticized that tendency in the movement.[54]

What emerges from Barrès' experience in Nancy, then, is that his thought became leftist as he involved himself more and more in politics and that the Boulangist program in Nancy was sharply republican, democratic, socially reformist, and no more anti-Semitic than most socialists of that day. But more than that the campaign in Nancy, because it was Boulangism in microcosm, throws a good bit of light on what Boulangism was and why it deserved the fate it received.

When Barrès came to Nancy, a successful Boulangist campaign in the fall elections seemed more certain than it would later. All he would have to do would be to duplicate in Nancy the tactics used by Boulanger elsewhere: provide lots of propaganda in an American-style campaign, put the general at the top of the Boulangist department-wide list of candidates in the multi-member constituency, and let the other Boulangist candidates ride to victory on his coat-tails. But the victory that seemed so sure after Boulanger's election in Paris soon became less certain. Between February and July, 1889, the interior minister, Ernest Constans, foiled the Boulangist tactics by pushing through laws ending multi-member constituencies and multiple candidatures. Barrès called these actions "exceptional laws," put through by the "caesarians" of parliament to help "a little group of the privileged."[55] He conceded that they would hurt Boulangism nationally but that they might help in Nancy, where Alfred Mézière's popularity had carried the entire Opportunist slate to power in 1885.[56]

Such optimism was whistling in the dark. In March the government broke up the League of Patriots, that highly effective vote-getting Boulangist troop, by arguing it was a secret society threatening the state. "It is very evident," remarked Barrès, "that if our leaguers adored Ferry, [the government] would not dream of breaking into their tills."[57] The arrest of the leaguers lent credence to rumors that Boulanger was next. On

April 1 he fled the country, soon followed by Rochefort and Dillon.

The *Courrier* tried to explain away Boulanger's apparent cowardice by saying, "it is on the *formal injunction* of the [National] Committee that the General, after a long resistance, decided to leave."[58] Barrès argued that Boulanger could not have allowed himself to be imprisoned, because his jailors would not have let him communicate with his followers. Such communication was necessary, for Boulanger's personal popularity alone would bring victory for his lieutenants and their program.[59] On April 28 Barrès returned from a meeting at Brussels with Boulanger where the Boulangist high command decided to capitalize on the "martyrdom" of Boulanger, hoping that his magnetism would transfer to them at the elections and praying that the voters would not view the flight as cowardice. Barrès reflected the consensus of the Brussels meeting when he admitted that single-member constituencies would make it difficult for the parliamentary candidates.[60] This difficulty was all the more real since the anti-Boulangists were now able to face the parliamentary elections with Boulanger gone, his lieutenants on the defensive, their principal organization in disrepair, and electoral machinery changed to prevent Boulanger's personal popularity from rubbing off on his followers.

It was not much different in Nancy. There as elsewhere the anti-Boulangist opposition was a coalition of Opportunists and those Radicals who had not followed Gabriel into Boulangism. That coalition, with the Opportunists as the senior partners, had dominated Nancy politics for years. In the 1885 legislative elections, the first place Opportunists combined with the third place Radicals to defeat the conservatives in the run-off election. This was the normal electoral pattern, and thanks to it the Opportunists controlled the mayoralty, the municipal council, and the deputation to the Chamber of Deputies.[61] Everything was decided by the Republican Alliance, dominated by Nancy's power elite of university professors, chief attorneys, and businessmen. In turn, the Opportunists, with the conservatives, controlled Nancy's press.[62]

Such was the opposition—formidable and typical of the

opposition Boulangists faced everywhere in France. Given its working-class sociology, Nancy Boulangism had inherited the following of the third place Radicals of 1885. To convert that following into a majority at the legislative elections, Barrès and Gabriel, like Boulangists generally, could either ally with another party or remain independent and convert enough voters from the other two parties to win victory. Elsewhere in the provinces most Boulangists would win in 1889 either by utilizing the electoral machines of incumbent converts to Boulangism, or by building an alliance of disgusted Radicals and conservatives, or by taking advantage of earlier by-election victories of General Boulanger himself. Only in Nancy and Bordeaux,[63] where Henri Aimel and Albert Chiché played a role similar to that of Barrès and Gabriel, did provincial Boulangists build a movement from scratch on a leftist base and win by cutting into Opportunist and conservative strength without allying with either.

At first, Nancy Boulangism was weak enough that its major problem was to defend itself from the attacks of the Republican Alliance in rallies, its press, and in heckling at Boulangist rallies. From January to the end of the campaign, Alliance speakers, writers, and hecklers labeled the Boulangists "false democrats" and the "clerical party" because of the financial support of the royalists, the Boulangist toleration of all religious opinion, and the caesarist threat of Boulangist anti-parliamentarianism and war-mongering.

While Barrès and Gabriel could laugh off most of these charges, the eternal question of "where does the money come from," persistently cried by anti-Boulangist hecklers as they turned out their pockets, was another matter. Who had any proof that Boulanger or Barrès were financed by royalist coffers? When the Opportunist press asserted that he had received a check from Mackau, the royalist treasurer, Barrès made an unanswered challenge that the issue be settled by arbitration with the loser giving one thousand francs to charity.[64] Barrès and the Nancy Boulangists certainly got money from the Boulangist national committee to finance the newspaper and picked up some by charging admission to rallies, but the rest is a little cloudy. Paul Adam later claimed that they got nothing more than a bundle of posters and "several louis" with which to paste them up. An exposé of Boulangism by Terrail-Mermeix, a disillusioned insider, held that Barrès won without outside help, "without any other trumps than those in his hands." But the claim of the equally disillusioned Vergoin, whose activity made him more knowledgeable of those areas where Boulangist candidates were leftist, is more credible. He insisted that every candidate got five thousand five hundred francs from the National Committee, although the royalist origin of the money remained a secret. In addition, Barrès raised over nine hundred francs by writing, with the help of André Vervoort of *l'Intransigéant*, a continued story for the Boulangist *Presse*. The protagonist of this potboiler, *Docteur Douche*, fulfilled his selfhood as an American-trained practitioner of magnetism-hypnotism by taking advantage of the *jolies femmes* who required his treatment.[65]

Of course, Republican Alliance hecklers could always be fended off with cries of "down with the Opportunists!" but Barrès did have to take the charge of royalism seriously after Boulanger spoke at Tours on March 17, 1889. The volume of written and spoken words on this issue testifies to its effect on the thoroughly republican Nancians who adhered to Boulanger. At Tours, the General set at rest whatever doubts the royalists had entertained toward him, or at least that was the reaction of the anti-Boulangist press.[66] Although he reminded the royalists that the people were against the corrupt republic, not republicanism, he offered them a referendum on the church-state question, the repudiation of "Jacobin" anti-clericalism, and its replacement by an open republic, tolerant of all religious beliefs.

Barrès tried to still the uneasiness raised in republican hearts by the Tours speech by repeating the "official" explanation, designed to attract conservatives without antagonizing republicans. The apostles of monarchy or empire were joining Boulangism because they saw that the liberty-loving people were opposed to any kind of restoration. Yet, Boulanger could reconcile authority and liberty, a conservative principle. In ad-

57

dition, the Bonapartists could embrace Boulanger, for while he condemned the hereditary principle, he upheld that of the plebiscite; the royalists, who had argued that only a king could unify France's factions, could find in Boulanger a man who would unify France against a unitary Germany.[67] But these conservative adhesions did not threaten the republic, for even the Bonapartist *Autorité* admitted that Boulanger unfortunately would not bring a restoration. "Never," concluded Barrès, "has General Boulanger missed an occasion to explain himself unequivocally. He wishes a Republic fortified by the adhesion of all honest Frenchmen and by the expulsion of Wilson and Constans; but he believes firmly that the republican form is definitive in France."[68] At one of the Boulangist rallies Barrès answered a vigorously applauded criticism of Opportunism by a royalist:

> It is not at the side of monarchy that this country wants to go; it is attached to the republican form. The enormous effort of a right-thinking portion of republicans goes to give us a purified republic: a republic where all honest men can live, where the scoundrels will be unveiled, where the interests of the workers finally will be taken to heart. At the present time only General Boulanger is able, without reversing the Republic, so justly dear to the masses, to give France an honest government, as only he has known how to cry to all: Down with the thieves![69]

On the anniversary of the Tennis Court Oath, Gabriel echoed this theme. According to Gabriel, the people had to overthrow the aristocracy to get a new constitution in 1789; to get one in 1889, the people had to "coalesce against the bourgeois oligarchy whose emblem is parliamentarianism and the Senate." The opposition claimed, said Gabriel, that the Boulangists were the party of the 16th of May; but the republic was hardly in danger from men like Rochefort, who overthrew the Second Empire, or Laisant, who in protest resigned his commission in its army: "The Republic of the National Party is in the hands of men animated with a great spirit of justice. And if General Boulanger ever breaks the promises he solemnly made, these men will turn against him while his adversaries of today will offer him their services."[70] On another occasion Gabriel admitted, "The hatred of Opportunism is the beginning of wisdom. But the love of monarchy is the worst of follies." The monarchists had rallied to the Boulangist republic by necessity, he added, but the original Boulangists were republicans by conviction and had spent a long time fighting for that conviction. While he, like Barrès, welcomed the conversions of the monarchists, he saw no danger of their capturing the movement.[71]

These charges and counter-charges heated up as the electoral campaign reached its climax between July and October, 1889. Here, and only here, was the real test of the Boulangist campaign and program which the inexperienced Barrès and the so-far unsuccessful Gabriel had conducted for several months. They met the challenge and emerged victorious from the cantonal elections of July 28 and the legislative ones of September and October. As it turned out, the two elections were part of the same campaign, for the cantonal ones were but the preliminary bout for the main event, the legislative elections, and in Nancy the Boulangists were running scared. Not to present a candidate would be a mark of cowardice, but in a day without opinion polls there was no way of evaluating Boulangist strength. Barrès seemed particularly worried, and the optimism of police reports would seem to justify his apprehension.[72] Certainly the meteoric rise of Boulangism imparted to its followers a feeling of desperation which only successive victories could dispel. For this reason Barrès and Gabriel felt compelled to enter the cantonal lists, although they believed that defeat would be ruinous. Faced with this prospect, they had already brought in some of the biggest names in Boulangism to speak at rallies in June. Having no guarantee that either of them could defeat any of the Alliance candidates, they submitted the name of Boulanger himself at Nancy-Ouest, the most solidly working-class canton, against Larcher, the incumbent and mildly reformist president of the bar association. Then they embarked on a dedicated smear campaign to discredit the general's opponent.

Anti-Semitism was one club with which to beat Larcher. Jews, Barrès contended, were the most ardent anti-Boulangists and would vote for Larcher *en masse*, for he would uphold the parliamentary republic that refused to crack down on the influence of Jewish bankers. How to prove it? Just look at the Nancy press which supported Larcher, said Barrès, for all of it was in the hands of the Jews.[73] At least the *Dépêche de l'Est* was. Of course, what this national issue had to do with a campaign for local office was beside the point in a battle which was obviously being waged only for the propaganda value it would provide for the national elections in September.

"Guilt by association" could be carried into other areas, too. Larcher was not a "dishonest man," but he was chairman of the Republican Alliance which supported Grévy, Wilson, and Opportunism. "Thus, M. Larcher is the representative of [Constans], and defends him and does not want him to leave the ministry any more than formerly he defended Wilson and did not want the Grévy family to leave the Elysée."[74] As in so many of Barrès' attacks, there was the artful shift from moderation to extremism. The article began by calling Larcher honest, then attached him to the Opportunists, and finally made him appear the direct supporter of Wilson, Grévy, and Constans. Bad as Barrès was, however, the Alliance and its allies in the prefecture showed that Boulangism had no monopoly in Nancy politics on innuendo, mudslinging, and intimidation. Rallies of both sides were invaded by hecklers and hoodlums. Gabriel and Barrès came in for their share of name-calling. In both this campaign and the legislative one, officials refused the Boulangists meeting-halls, apparently in the interest of public order, and employers fired and threatened to fire Boulangist workers. More than one pro-Boulangist Alsatian was deported.

The sharpness of the campaign was probably unnecessary, for the Boulangists had more support than they had anticipated, and Larcher turned out to be a weak candidate. Earlier in the year he had spoken in favor of the foreign workers of Nancy, mostly Italians, who unlike French workers were willing to work on Sundays and had a lower absentee rate.[75] Nothing could less endear a candidate to a working-class constituency than that. Barrès and Gabriel added the charge, far from substantiated, that Larcher also believed in the laissez-faire dictum that employers alone could determine worker salaries. Had Larcher been born in a worker section of Nancy, said Gabriel, he would not so vigorously support Sunday work and "capitalist exploitation."[76] With that, Boulanger had no trouble defeating Larcher on the first ballot in a district whose voters were quite sensitive to low wages and job security.

The result in the neighboring canton of Nancy-Est, however, provided another dimension to the electoral problem of Barrès and the Boulangists. There, the first ballot necessitated a run-off election between an Alliance candidate and a monarchist in what was normal Nancy politics. The conservative had gotten neither support nor coverage in Le Courrier de l'Est before the first ballot, but now his candidacy had implications for the legislative elections to be held later. Boulanger's victory in Nancy-Ouest was not so impressive that Boulangist candidates in the legislative elections could do without conservative help. Boulangist-conservative coalition slates were already being worked up by the National Committee, in spite of the objections of left-wing Boulangists; Nancy was included in those plans. So, between the efforts of the National Committee and their own ambitions, both Barrès and Gabriel, with tortured logic, "proved" the conservative to be a republican and gave him a qualified endorsement.[77]

The planned coalition was to take form in the legislative elections, with Barrès and Gabriel taking two of the working-class districts of Nancy and in the third supporting the conservative Welche, who had been prefect in the 1870s and who was now one of the powers behind the conservative Journal de la Meurthe. According to Vergoin, the scheme was sponsored in the National Committee by Count Dillon over Vergoin's vigorous objections. It fell through largely because of the objections of Paul Adam who insisted on having a place on the ticket. Even then, said Vergoin, Welche remained the "occult candidate of the Committee."[78] Barrès, Gabriel, and Adam duly received letters of investiture from General Boulanger, couched in vague terms, which proclaimed that a vote for so-and-so was a vote for Boulanger.[79]

For its part the Republican Alliance could not find candidates until just before the election. Thanks to the Larcher defeat, only one incumbent chose to run, and not until September 8, fifteen days before the election, did the alliance hold a congress which was broadened to include some workers. The candidates suggested by the workers got nowhere, however, and the Alliance put up the incumbent, Noblet, against Gabriel in the first *circonscription*. In the second, against Adam, went Pierre Albert Papelier, a businessman and moderate member of the municipal council. Against Barrès in the third *circonscription* went Albert Colson, a professor and member of the municipal council. He was enough of a Radical-Revisionist that Gabriel had approached him in December, 1888, and the Opportunists had little love for him. Indeed, throughout the campaign Barrès showed considerable concern that Colson would take the Radical-Revisionist vote away from him. Unable to find anything like the Larcher "foreign worker" issue, Barrès had to admit that Colson was a good man. Only when Colson hedged that his demand for constitutional revision "will be for later," did Barrès find an opening.[80] Now Barrès could associate him with the party of Opportunism, the party of Ferry, Larcher, and Constans.

Throughout September the central thrust of the Boulangists at Nancy was to convince the voters that the Republican Alliance would bring no new ideas, only new faces with the same ideas held by the incumbent deputies who did not dare to run again. The arguments which Barrès and Gabriel battered home all year continued to be repeated: the offers of social reform and revision made by the Alliance candidates were empty promises. The new Alliance was the same as the 1885 one, still committed to the immobility of the parliamentary system, its bankruptcy proved by multi-party ministerial instability. The new candidates were the representatives, in spite of their professions, of the same old "Nancian Opportunism, offender of the workers and sustained by Jews."[81]

All of it was enough to alarm the prefecture. Less than two weeks before the election the prefect predicted that the Alliance candidates would lead on the first round but that the final outcome would be in doubt, thanks to a probable Boulangist-conservative alliance. Interestingly enough, he commented that the *"parti ouvrier"* was now the Boulangist party, and in his predictions put it in third place behind the Opportunists and conservatives, just like its forebears, the Radicals of 1885.[82] The prediction was as inaccurate as usual, but for the first time since Barrès and Boulangism arrived on the scene, the prefecture took them seriously.

It is difficult to evaluate Barrès' effectiveness as a politician and campaigner in 1889. He was constantly criticized by the Nancy Alliance for being a political dilettante. At the height of the campaign an opportunity came to reply to that charge which would plague him throughout his political career. Paul Buquet, a writer for *La Voix* of Millerand, wrote in *Parti ouvrier* that Barrès was one of "those detached from politics who have created a literary and political party." Buquet argued that Barrès entered politics, not to secure a program nor to pursue a political career, but only to experience something new, to satisfy a momentary urge of his ego. Thus, men like him were deluding the voters, were using the voters to serve their solely literary self-interest. They had jumped on the Boulanger bandwagon because "they are at bottom *adorers of the fait accompli*." Because they have no real commitment to their man or program, they will just as readily "accept the collapse of Boulanger."[83] Seizing this opportunity to reply to the attacks of the Alliance, Barrès admitted to loving the *fait accompli*. In explaining why, he again revealed his attitude toward politics. "I am a lover of real force," he wrote, "that is to say, I intend to march always with the *live force* of the nation. Compared with the great popular current, politics is only a dispute, mediocre arguments without any consequences." In other words Barrès could find self-fulfillment in Boulangism because it was an embryonic mass movement rather than a political party. Unlike political parties, Boulangism was of the "great popular current" which demanded national strength, serious social reforms, and conciliation of all parties. By attaching himself to Boulangism, Barrès could finally get out of himself and into the *"live force* of the nation" where he could fulfil his selfhood.

63

Thus, he was not, nor did he claim to be, a politician in the strict sense of that term. He was attached to a movement that sought control of the state more in the manner of twentieth-century mass movements than in the orthodox pattern of party politics.

As to his campaigning ability the *Courrier* unwittingly gave an interesting insight. Describing Barrès' performance at a rally, a reporter wrote that he was not "a fiery orator like Gabriel, an indignant demolisher." Rather, he "has all the gravity of a savant, of an economist discussing with the voters the principles of better administration, possible ameliorations, and indispensible reforms. He is . . . a delicate and refined spirit that the press of the entire world recently has come to call one of the foremost thinkers of the age." When Gabriel spoke, he went on, the workers and hecklers responded with great enthusiasm, but not while Barrès spoke.[84] As they listened quietly, were these workers and peasants in awe of the *grand seigneur?* Reading this, one gets the feeling that its author was trying to convince the Nancy workers that Barrès was every bit as good as Gabriel. No, Barrès was not fiery like Gabriel, and that was what the workers liked and expected. As a "savant" Barrès might bore them to death, but they were privileged to be offered this "foremost thinker."

Barrès' lack of warm rapport with his voters would always mark his political style. "He performed with strict correctness and almost with ritual his role as deputy," wrote a later eyewitness who accompanied him to his post-1906 constituency, "except that he turned as little as possible to public rallies where he felt inferior. He did a great many small services and shook hands with everyone, but with the air of a king of France touching his subjects in order to cure their scrofula."[85] Barrès' vivid newspaper writing, his stature in the national party, and Gabriel's support could command the respect of the earthy, impressionable and loyal Nancy workers, but his performance at the tribune left them cold.

Barrès' assets, however, outweighed his liabilities. The vote of September 22, 1889, gave him 6,241, Colson 5,090, and Renard, the conservative attorney, 2,667.[86] Although the conservatives retired in favor of the three Boulangist candidates, one of the two conservative newspapers counseled abstention on the second round.[87] Either conservatives, believing Barrès too radical, split their votes on the second round, or the electorate reshuffled itself to give Barrès 7,183 votes to Colson's 6,108.[88] Gabriel also was victorious, but Paul Adam lost. The campaign had been so hard fought that even in victory the Nancy Boulangists were bitter. Adam insisted, with the usual shibboleths, that the Jews had financed the anti-Boulangist campaign.[89] Barrès still had harsh words for Colson and the employers who had fired Boulangist workers. He felt a double duty of living up to his program in the Chamber and healing the scars left by the campaign.[90] He felt that one way would be for the employers to accept the election results and hire back the discharged workers. By the end of October the victory was sealed with the fusion of the Nancy Boulangist and Radical committees. Many members of the latter had already supported the Boulangists in the election.

In their personal victories Barrès and Gabriel were part of a national defeat for Boulangism. Only about thirty republican Boulangists were elected. Aside from Meurthe-et-Moselle, victories were restricted to Paris, the Northwest, the Gironde, and the departments of Ille-et-Vilaine and Nièvre where the electoral machines of Le Hérissé and Turigny operated. When Barrès began the Nancy campaign at the time of Boulanger's brilliant victory in Paris in January, 1889, it was obvious to everyone that Boulangism would sweep the nation in the September legislative elections. Without question, the charismatic Boulanger, coupled with the Boulangist movement, was the best-financed, talented, and organized threat to French parliamentary republicanism between the establishment of the Third Republic and the advent of Charles de Gaulle in 1958. Neither the anti-Dreyfusards nor the fascists of the 1930s had Boulangism's purse, talent, or organization. Certainly none of them had a charismatic leader like Boulanger. How was it that Barrès, rather than marching with "the *force vive* of the nation," had signed on with the crew of a sinking ship?

65

On the surface the defeat was the direct result of Boulanger's flight which dissipated the thrust of the general's earlier victories.[91] His uncourageous flight might have lost considerable votes; certainly his lieutenants constantly urged his return, to prison or martyrdom if necessary. Yet, Rochefort, whose career testified to his bravery, also fled. Ten years later Emile Zola, in the aftermath of his *J'Accuse*, also fled without losing support. The flight seemed to do no damage to Boulanger in the Paris constituency he won handily in September, 1889.

The real source of Boulangism's defeat lay elsewhere, in two inter-connected causes. The principal one was the change in the election laws. Had they not been changed, Boulanger would have run in every department at the head of a department-wide list of Boulangist candidates. Although he could only serve one department, all the candidates swept in on his coattails could have served. His ability to win by-elections in every conceivable kind of constituency showed that the technique could easily have given Boulangism a two-thirds majority in the Chamber of Deputies and, with that, the overturning of parliamentary republicanism which had to await defeat in World War II and Algeria. The unsung hero of the Boulangist crisis, then, remains Ernest Constans, in every other respect a mediocre and shoddy politician. When he ended multiple candidatures and multi-member constituencies and began proceedings against the League of Patriots and the exiled Boulanger and Rochefort, the Boulangists had neither organization nor candidates to substitute for the earlier technique.

Faced with the change in the election laws, Boulangists almost overnight had to build a party organization down to the local level. Their failure to do that constituted the other cause of their defeat. In the 1888 by-election campaign the Boulangists had only an improvised organization. The first full-scale one emerged for the Paris election of January, 1889. It centered around three groups: the League of Patriots with committees in every *arrondissement*, those few Radicals who believed that the Radical party had reneged on its promises, and those socialist committees which followed Rochefort into Boulangism. The Boulangist leaders mistakenly viewed the Paris election as a popular groundswell. Although fifty to sixty thousand conservatives voted for Boulanger in that election, his principal support came from republicans, and it was organization which had delivered their votes. In the months which followed, the Boulangist lieutenants spent their time seeking headlines from their Chamber oratory rather than mobilizing and organizing the Radical and nationalist discontent in the hustings.

Party organizations capable of victory were built in those areas where the League of Patriots was strong, such as in the northwest, southwest, and in Nancy. It was also possible where organizations remained from Boulanger's by-election victories in 1888 and in departments where long-established deputies could bring their constituents to Boulangism. But it was bound to be risky, compared with the opportunities offered before the electoral changes. For example, Vaucluse in 1885 had elected three men—Naquet, Laguerre, and Saint-Martin—who were high in Boulangist circles. Yet, they deserted Vaucluse in 1889 to serve Paris, where Boulangism was better organized and had sufficient clientele to insure success.

The success of Barrès and Gabriel in Nancy fits neatly into this picture. Barrès arrived at Nancy virtually unknown only nine months before the election. Within two months he had a newspaper and had joined forces with Gabriel, whose party had been denied earlier victories because of the system of multi-member constituencies. Gabriel's discontented Radical committees, the local League of Patriots, and a handful of revisionist republicans-cum-Boulangists formed an embryo of an organization. With the newspaper, innumerable rallies, and a program of real appeal to workers came several months of intensive campaigning on the voters' home ground. By election time, having already tested their organization and popularity in the cantonal elections, their organization and support were strong enough to carry them to victory and to almost carry the equally unknown Paul Adam. Most of all, they had done it by themselves, without appreciable help from

Boulanger, his treasury, or his lieutenants. Two political unknowns had cracked an Opportunist stronghold through organization, unrelenting effort, and an appealing program.

Where such local organization was impossible, another
alternative appeared to the Boulangist National Committee.
In spite of the misgivings of some of its members, it saw that
a coalition with the Right was imperative for any victory for
constitutional revision. By election time the Right did have
respectable candidates for almost every district, with money
and organization to back them up, while the republican Boulangists were short of candidates and without organization.
For example, *Le Figaro* told of a man who just walked in off the
street and volunteered his services. Because he had been a
naval surgeon, he was offered the Senegal candidature. The
same reporter believed that Barrès had been chosen for Nancy
in the same way, simply because no one else presented himself.[92] To save their skins, the Boulangist powerhouses ran in
Paris, their only well-organized stronghold. The provinces got
either conservatives or left-overs. The National Committee's
support of Welche's conservative candidacy in Nancy in
preference to the republican Adam was repeated time and
again in its conviction that only a coalition with the Right could
save Boulangism. Déroulède, Vergoin, and others with more
insight into the political realities vainly protested that there
were many fiery republicans of the League of Patriots or Radical committees with strong local support, but the Boulangist
high command consistently turned them down in favor of the
untrustworthy conservative allies. With these developments
the alliance with the Right became inevitable.

In the aftermath of the election it was obvious to the Boulangist leadership that it would not sweep the nation, that its
coalition with the Right had been built on sand, and that its
base was narrower than suspected but at least defined by the
election results. It was just as obvious that Boulangism still
had a considerable appeal as a protest movement to large
numbers of workers not yet attracted by regular socialism.
This clientele had elected some thirty deputies. The job for
this nucleus, certainly one far larger than that of the original

Five who had opposed Louis Napoleon, was to conquer the nation.

Unsuccessful as the elections had been for national Boulangism, they were extremely important for Barrès. His quest for selfhood had found concrete reality in the Nancy campaign. More important than that to the development of his political ideas, the campaign had given him a leftist political orientation. The understanding of that and how it came about is critical for comprehending his subsequent career and ideas. With the election over, the arena for his further development along these lines would be as part of the Boulangist bloc in the Chamber of Deputies; the weapons would be socialism and nationalism.

CHAPTER THREE

BARRÈS AND THE FAILURE OF
NATIONAL BOULANGISM

Soon after the French legislative elections of 1889, the critic Jules Lemaître predicted that in the first vote of the new Chamber of Deputies the Boulangists would become either monarchists or Radicals; that by the spring of 1890 Boulanger would get an offer to be an agent for a London life insurance company; and that then the only remaining Boulangist would be Maurice Barrès, and he would be one only "for exclusively literary reasons understood by himself alone." Most of Lemaître's readers doubtless agreed that historians a hundred years later would consider Boulangism of little importance in spite of its noise. In a time of republican weakness, it had been able to unite all the malcontents simply through "hatreds and negations."[1] In October, 1889, it certainly looked as if Boulangism and Boulanger were finished.

The elections had been a crushing defeat for them. The monarchists, seeing that Boulanger could not muster a majority in the Chamber, let alone bring restoration or an authoritarian "open republic," melted away as soon as the election results came in. Yet, when the Chamber did convene, there were still some thirty deputies who persisted in calling themselves Boulangists and who hoped to rebuild their party by winning the Paris municipal elections in 1890 through a program of sweeping social reforms. Although the plan to rebuild the party failed by 1890, the reformist program, which many a Boulangist called socialism, continued throughout the life of the Chamber

70

elected in 1889. An examination of the parliamentary activity of the Boulangists after 1889 shows that they did not die or return to their origins. Rather, they continued as a major parliamentary bloc. With considerable solidarity they voted on social reforms with as radical a bent as that of the anti-Boulangist socialists and on foreign and colonial issues with as much nationalism as the most conservative deputy. Yet, in spite of all this the Boulangists failed as a distinct movement.

Although Barrès was really a minor figure in Boulangism's failure as a party and a parliamentary bloc, a look at the course of its failure is absolutely essential to understand his intellectual and political development. As a member of the bloc he would have to vote for proposed legislation which would have practical effect. This new "action" was bound to develop his political selfhood in ways far more concrete than either the *Culte du moi* or the 1889 campaign could have. Just as his experience in national Boulangism would develop his political point of view, the failure of Boulangism obviously would limit his future political options, and his options would parallel those of Boulangists in general. Finally, the subsequent efforts of Barrès to build a new mass movement from the debris of Boulangism would be influenced by the friendships, lessons, and ideas he had found as a minor figure in national Boulangism.

To understand why the Boulangists could call themselves socialists at all it is necessary, first of all, to look at the men who made up the Boulangist remnant.[2] One group came from socialism. Bordeaux and Paris were its centers. At Bordeaux, Albert Chiché, a lawyer and biographer of Louis Blanc, led to victory two other socialists: Henri Aimel, a contributor to the undoctrinaire *Revue socialiste*, and Antoine Jourde, an old Communard and member of Jules Guesde's Marxists. At Paris there were the lieutenants of the Blanquist-Boulangist, Henri Rochefort: Ernest Granger and Ernest Roche. And there were others. Eugène Farcy had fought in the siege of the Commune and sat on the extreme Left of the Chamber ever since. Emile Revest was mayor of the left-wing Paris suburb of Saint-Denis. Georges Le Veillé, a Limoges attorney, ran as a socialist republican under the aegis of Boulanger. Jean Baptiste Argeliès was active in

71

the cooperative movement and as the municipal councilor of Juvisy. Francis Laur championed a "mine to the miners" socialism. These men were genuine socialists before they became Boulangists and had always visualized Boulangism as a vehicle for social revolution, even if it had to be made in cooperation with non-socialists and, indeed, with royalists. Rochefort, for example, was a recognized leader of the Blanquists, and Jourde was a favorite of Paul Lafargue, the son-in-law of Marx and a leader of French Marxists.[3] Moreover, socialists such as these had been among the first adherents to Boulangism and now remained with it after the royalists, who had joined at the eleventh hour, had deserted.

Another group came from Radical-Socialism. It included former Radical or Radical-Socialist deputies like Georges Laguerre, Alfred Naquet, Charles Laisant, René Le Hérissé, Jean Baptiste Saint-Martin, Léon Borie, and Jean Turigny and Gaston Laporte from Nevers, many of whom had gotten their starts at the side of Clemenceau. Even before Boulangism some of them, such as Laguerre and Laisant, were moving toward socialism as members of the *groupe ouvrier* in the Chamber. This group also included new men like Louis de Belleval, whose negative answer in his *Sommes-nous en République?* brought his dismissal from a government post; Alfred Martineau, formerly of the Paris prefecture and leader of the League of Republican Action; Jean Pontois, a former judge in Tunis whose disagreement with colonial policy drove him to Laguerre; and Dieudonné Terrail-Mermeix, a writer for the Boulangist *La Cocarde* and *La Presse*.

A third group came from the League of Patriots, founded in 1882 as a non-partisan nationalistic movement but converted into a Boulangist electoral organization, or the kind of nationalism it expressed. Led for the most part by the League's president, Paul Déroulède, elected at Angoulême, most of these men went to the voters as virtual unknowns and won. From Paris came Jean Boudeau, the "fiery right arm" of Déroulède; Emile Goussot, a league publicist and former bureaucrat; Charles Le Senne, an unknown attorney specializing in literary properties; César Paulin-Méry, a doctor whose presidency of

the League in his *arrondissement* gave him victory over the socialist Emile Basly; and Pierre Richard, secretary-general of the
League. From Aisne came André Castelin and Jean Marie
Dumonteil. These men had been, and remained, thoroughgoing republicans and more than once had taken alarm that the
royalists were capturing Boulangism. Like the Boulangist Radicals and socialists, they had been among the original Boulangists and were now also in the remnant.

Another group came from those monarchists who had not
reverted to their former ties. The monarchists had been the last
to join Boulangism and the first to leave. Among the remaining
royalists in Boulangism only Lucien Millevoye, a Bonapartist
rentier whose League of Patriots ties involved him in the by-
election campaign of Boulanger in 1888, accepted the post-
1889 Boulangist program completely. However, other conservative Boulangists who at least attended or adhered to a
post-election meeting of the parliamentary bloc, held at Jersey
with Boulanger were: Marius Martin, a Bonapartist and Parisian municipal councilor; Albert Gauthier de Clagny, a
Bonapartist from Sèvres; Charles Lalou, a journalist on the
Boulangist national committee; Robert Mitchell, a Bonapartist
who won at Bordeaux with the aid of Chiché; Jules Delahaye;
and Raoul du Saussay.[4]

Since over two-thirds of these remaining Boulangists had
left-wing pasts, they naturally reverted to their left-wing program when their broader one of 1889 failed to win a majority
in France; most of the remaining third went along because they
had been elected from working-class districts. In Paris, for example, the Boulangist vote was heaviest in the newer lower-
class and poor *arrondissements* on the northern and southern
edges of the city. Boulangists got 54 to 60 percent of the vote
in the fifteenth, seventeenth, eighteenth, and nineteenth *arrondissements* and swept every seat in the lower-class Paris suburbs
of the Seine department, except the one for Charenton.[5] Indeed,
a map of Boulangist strength in Paris would coincide almost
exactly with Bertillon's census map of Parisian working-class
districts for 1891.[6] Here, as elsewhere, the Boulangist voters
were mainly workers, lower middle class, petty civil servants,

73

pensioners, and anti-Ferry ex-soldiers. The Boulangist working-class voter appears to have worked in large stores or factories, such as the Villette slaughterhouses of Paris. As a case in point, the workers in the small shops of the Saint-Antoine and Marais districts were not Boulangist.[7] Generally, Boulangist workers had either no union or a weak one. Boulangism could win over the unorganized workers of Dunqerque, but not the Nord coal miners organized by Jules Guesde. Alfred Gabriel wailed that no "serious union" existed in Nancy, but had there been unions he and Barrès would have had less chance of victory.[8] Usually these voters were mobilized by Boulangist committees formed out of earlier League of Patriots and dissident Radical or socialist organizations. The Paris Boulangists, especially, formed organizations out of such groups, as did Chiché at Bordeaux and Barrès and Gabriel at Nancy.

Barrès, himself, became one of the chief publicists for explaining this new left-wing Boulangist program. On the first anniversary of the January, 1889, victory of Boulanger in Paris, he announced that Boulangism had become a socialist party. Boulangism of early 1889 had only a negative program. Boulanger was simply more popular than "the other republican chiefs." " 'Dissolution' was only a battle cry. 'Revision, Constituent Assembly, Referendum' were excellent indications, but too abstract, unable to satisfy for long the heart of profound France." Barrès argued that Boulangism had always been concerned with the "disinherited." For Boulangists of Radical-Socialist or socialist persuasion such a concern had always been evident. For others, it was an extension of the principle of reconciliation in Boulangism. For Boulanger, it flowed from his "instinctive love of the commander for his soldiers."[9]

Throughout 1889, however, this concern for social reform had been dulled by other Boulangist planks which Barrès believed would have facilitated social reform: "the cult of the American constitution" achievable through a constituent assembly, the abandonment of anti-clericalism, the "defenestration of parliamentarianism," as well as patriotism, *revanche*, and a Russian alliance. The defeat of these planks in the autumn of 1889 told Barrès that these "better hammers are crushed in our hands" and should be abandoned. This defeat showed that the Boulangist political program was incapable of victory and, because of that, unable to bring social reforms. By 1890 the desires of the people for the amelioration of their misery "alone still impassions them." It now appeared to Barrès that it was socialism which had driven the voters—at least a majority of them—to elect those deputies who remained Boulangist. Because most of these deputies had been left-wing anyway, held Barrès, the evolution of Boulangism to socialism was not "contrived," nor did it come from the "dexterity" which Boulangists were so often accused of having. Instead, "necessity created this wisdom for us." Socialism provided a base on which to restore the National Party; perhaps the base would be strong enough to bring victory. The defeat at the 1889 elections made it appear that Boulangism would perish, Barrès concluded, "but we rediscovered ourselves on this hospitable shore of socialism. It is a fair abode which necessity created for us. For us, our Jersey is socialism." He credited his own surprising victory at the polls to his left-wing program and the help of Gabriel. His election and that of his fellow Boulangists had revealed the instinctive desires of the nation, had shown what really moved the people:

> The word of the day is not politics. It is neither EMPIRE nor MONARCHY; the republican form satisfies us. It is no longer an appeal to *GLOIRE* . . . our workers are little preoccupied with foreign complications. The deep concern of the people is only in demanding social reforms. SOCIALISM is the dictum where contemporary France has put its hope.[10]

If the position described by Barrès was socialism, it had a peculiarly Boulangist tinge to it. For example, Barrès insisted that socialism could triumph only through the leadership of a strong president. Writing in the Boulangist *La Presse*, he took the view that socialism was necessary to "re-establish the free equilibrium between the downtrodden masses and a few egoistic monopolies." Such free equilibrium could not come of itself, because "the little world of capitalists" controlled both the economy and the parliament. "Liberty of commerce, all this pretended liberalism is only a fiction: the contest is not equal between the workers and their exploiters. It is necessary that a force intervene in favor of the former to re-establish equality." That force, he believed, was the strong leadership only a Boulangist presidential republic could provide. He thought how ironic it was that the authoritarian Wilhelm II of Germany, for whom Barrès could not find harsh enough words, had just commemorated the 1881 workmen's compensation law, identical to one just introduced in the Chamber by Laisant and the Boulangists, while the French government engaged in "shabby quarrels."[11]

Another example of the Boulangist nature of this "socialism," be it merely social reform, was its continuing concern for the reconciliation of all parties. The royalists' break with Boulanger found Barrès increasingly sceptical of the old alliance being renewed, but expediency still demanded that Boulangism "sup with the conservatives and vote with the people."[12] The efforts of Leo XIII might motivate the conservatives, through their sense of peril or charity, to accept the force of socialist ideas. Success, of course, depended on the willingness of the conservatives to follow Saint-Just's dictum that the "makers of half-way revolutions only dig their own graves," just as it depended on the willingness of the masses to renounce anti-clericalism. These concerns caused Barrès to demand the *"suture of Old Régime France and democracy in socialism, the forgetting of shabby anti-clerical quibbling, the acceptance and completion of the Revolution of '89.* And it is necessary to avow that the election of last September and October in Meurthe-et-Moselle created the first lines of this new mental state in France."[13] Barrès would recruit a revolutionary personnel by appealing through reason and education to the privileged like himself and through Christian love to the conservative Catholic.

The Boulangist evolution to what Barrès called socialism was soon complete. By February, 1890, the *Courrier de l'Est* proclaimed that "today the National Party is composed only of socialists" and proudly attributed this development to Barrès' articles "which made great noise declaring that the politics of the National Party ought to be entirely socialist."[14] In a widely reported speech at Reims in November, 1889, Gabriel declared that the republic would be "democratic and social," that it was necessary to "relieve the lot of the small and humble, and to protect labor against the financial syndicates."[15] At Ivry-Port, to an enthusiastic crowd for de Belleval, who had been anything but a socialist, the ex-Guesdist Antoine Jourde, speaking "in the name of the revolutionary socialists of Bordeaux," compared the exile of Blanqui to that of Boulanger and boasted that "our chief," Boulanger, would lead the National Party to social reforms. "If wanting the republic and social reforms makes one a member of 'the rabble,' " he concluded, "then I am of 'the rabble.' "[16] At the Pére Lachaise cemetery on the anniversary of the death of Blanqui, Granger revealed that the Boulangists followed the politics of Blanqui.[17] On the anniversary of the Paris Commune, Ernest Roche paid his respects to Boulanger by saying that France removed "a general who has never done but his duty, while a Gallifet [the crusher of the Commune] is covered with honors."[18]

Of course, few of these Boulangists interpreted socialism as public ownership of the means of production; by socialism most of them merely meant advanced social reform. Yet, social reform in this period was widely interpreted, except by genuine socialists, as socialism. Jules Huret, writing in *Le Figaro* in 1896, put his finger on this mood:

> The pope is a socialist. Wilhelm II is a socialist. Maurice Barrès is a socialist. . . .The more securities one has, the more idle one is, the more poker one plays, the more one goes to cocktail parties, the more one is tailored by Redfern, the more one has her hair done by Lenthéric, the more one is a socialist.[19]

Indeed, not all Boulangists craved a socialist label even under this definition. Laguerre's *La Presse*, for example, listed the fifty-six deputies who refused to vote for the government after objections to the government reprisals against the May Day demonstrators of 1890 but carefully distinguished the socialists and Radicals from the "revisionist-republicans" or Boulangists.[20]

For non-Boulangists it was amazing enough for Boulangism

to be turning socialistic, but for Barrès to be its chief publicist was beyond belief. The ability of this effete celebrator of "selfhood" even to be elected had been shock enough; for him to be a socialist was simply inconceivable. This mood of incredibility was captured by this parody of the opening session of the new Chamber:

> The session begins at two o'clock. The president gives the floor to M. Maurice Barrès to question the minister of interior concerning the working classes.
>
> M. MAURICE BARRÈS—Gentlemen, I come before you to plead the sacred cause of the worker, the proletarian. It is our role to grasp the guileless victory of suppressing the shadows. Thus, the worker is in the shadow of the manager [la personnalité dirigéante]. (Murmurs from the Center: Explain yourself. We do not understand.)
>
> THE PRESIDENT—I invite the speaker to clarify his thought.
>
> M. BARRÈS—Poor worker. Let us better his lot. (Agreement from the Left: We have understood.) Let him come to us, into our arms (Protests from several benches) and in our arms dreams smile. . . . The worker need not renounce nor construct in a dream evil or ugliness. He needs only to desire that beautiful and good things be born.
>
> M. CONSTANS [minister of interior] (To his bench).—It will be difficult to reply to the previous speaker.
>
> M. DÉROULÈDE—I understand him. That is enough. . .
>
> M. BARRÈS—I continue and I present a motion conceived in this way (Movement of attentiveness): "The Chamber, delivered from the hymn of renouncement regarding those who, bearing a life scarcely worth living, turning aside from reformers and other fine souls as sterile sensualists [voluptueuses] who gesticulate at the crossroads, and, abandoning the hymns, will ignore all martyrs [all this is quoted directly from *Sous l'oeil des barbares*], returns to the day's agenda."
>
> M. CONSTANS—The minister declines to reply. He feels overwhelmed. He asks the pure and simple return to the agenda. (Yes, pure and simple, from a great number of benches).
>
> The government's motion, having the priority, was voted by a colossal majority.
>
> Those voting against: M. Barrès and M. Déroulède, who asked M. Barrès for permission to put his speech into verse.
>
> "My speech? No," replied M. Barrès, "but the text of my motion, yes."
>
> If that is not modesty, I do not know what it is.[21]

The opening session of the new Chamber, meeting from November, 1889, through July, 1890, showed that Barrès and the Boulangists did, indeed, stand for their brand of "socialism" and revealed which deputies really were Boulangist. Although the verification of the latter is made difficult by the multi-party system in which the Boulangists were almost always forced to ally on particular issues with other parties and blocs, two kinds of evidence help us reconstruct the membership of the post-1889 Boulangist bloc. One was the caucus held at Jersey with Boulanger on November 7, 1889, which listed the names of twenty attending deputies and thirteen more excused ones.

In turn, this list of the Jersey caucus can be correlated to parliamentary activity, since the first session of the 1889 Chamber contained two proposals on which the Boulangists stood by themselves against the rest of the Chamber. The first of these came on May 13, 1890, when the Chamber verified the by-election victory of Auguste Delpeuch for a seat won in 1889 by a Boulangist whose election had been invalidated by the Chamber. In the first months of the session conservatives and Boulangists had voted together against all invalidations, but by the time of this vote only 33 Boulangist die-hards, including Barrès, claiming to be upholding the infallibility of universal suffrage, could be found to oppose the seating of Delpeuch.[22] The second time in the first session when the Boulangists stood completely alone was in opposing new duties on sugar. Such issues usually invited the support of the Radicals or the dozen non-Boulangist socialists. On July 26, however, only 31 Boulangists, including Barrès, were found to vote for the proposal of Francis Laur to eliminate all indirect taxes on sugar destined for the table. Laur, speaking for the Boulangist brand of socialism, argued that revenue should be raised by progressive income and corporation taxes rather than by indirect taxes affecting food prices. "We are," he concluded, ". . . of that socialist school (Exclamations from diverse benches) which thinks that the worker ought to be favored principally by augmenting the purchasing power of his wage in the basic necessities of life rather than by giving him laws on hygiene and inspection which, in reality, have no influence on his well-being."[23]

A comparison of these two votes, neither of which won the support of the sometime allies of Boulangism, shows that Barrès and 27 other deputies voted alone together on both occasions.[24] Three additional conservative Boulangists—Marius Martin, Raoul du Saussay, and Gauthier de Clagny—voted only against Delpeuch, while two Blanquist-Boulangists—Granger and Ernest Roche—voted only for the Laur proposal. These five, especially the last two, could be relied upon in most Boulangist votes. Add to these the thoroughly Boulangist Déroulède and Laporte, who were absent from the Chamber on one or both of these votes, and one gets a bloc of 30–32 Boulangists.

By following the votes of these men on the issues which commanded a multi-party vote in the Chamber, one can discover that the program of Barrès and the Boulangists was twofold.[25] Socially, it stood for sweeping working-class and petit bourgeois ameliorations; politically, it demanded a program of constitutional revision and nationalism.

The first session of the new Chamber soon showed that on social questions Barrès and the Boulangists were side by side with the socialists and, less often, the left-wing Radicals.[26] For example, on November 23, 1889, they comprised 33 of the 74 votes in favor of the proposal of the socialist Jean Baptiste Dumay for a minimum wage in match factories to be established by workers and municipal councilors.[27] On November 25, 1889, Barrès and the same number supported socialist Joseph Ferroul's proposed financial assistance and amnesty for Nord strikers.[28] On March 28, 1890, they and Barrès composed 34 of the 50 votes in favor of immediate consideration of the Granger-Paulin Méry proposal to aid slaughterhouse and tanning workers, unemployed as a result of a hoof and mouth epidemic.[29] They made up 31 of the 44 votes favoring Le Veillé's amendment to the trade union bill which would allow an indemnity of sixteen days pay to a worker whose employer had prevented his employee from joining a union.[30] In the debate of May 19, 1890, on the mine inspection bill which would have allowed workers to elect a fellow worker as a mine inspector, Roche was the principal speaker for a Ferroul amendment to create full-time inspectors, but the Chamber beat down the 111 vote minority of Boulangists, socialists, Radical-Socialists, Radicals, and Barrès. Other amendments to put teeth in the bill and provide for inspector independence were supported by Barrès and the Boulangists and defeated by similar majorities.[31] The debates of July 5–8, 1890, on the Senate child and female labor bill saw Barrès and the Boulangists supporting every amendment—many sponsored by Roche, Granger, Chiché, and Gabriel—to strengthen it. Most were defeated with the minority made up of Boulangists, Radicals, Radical-Socialists, and socialists. Others, with the help of de Mun, commanded larger minorities or were even victorious. The lure of de Mun defined the differences between the socialists and Boulangists. A de Mun amendment on July 7 to make Sundays and holy days the required days of rest for women and children even mustered 22 Boulangist votes, including that of Barrès, with only 9 remaining true to socialist anti-clericalism.[32] In addition to voting for those social reforms which reached the floor, Boulangists introduced several proposals in the first session which promptly died in the commissions. Laguerre sought to unify all pension funds; Le Veillé to lower the price of ordinary tobacco while raising that of deluxe; and Laisant, Gabriel, and Laguerre to establish old age pensions for workers through an elaborate tax scheme against gas and railroad companies.[33]

Although the Boulangists and Barrès almost always voted with their fellow blocs of the extreme Left in the Chamber on social questions, their record was more complex on political questions. On some, Barrès and the Boulangists still cooperated with the Left. They were 35 strong for the proposal of the Radical Adolphe Maujan, turned down 345 to 123 on November 19, 1889, to revise the constitution immediately.[34] They overwhelmingly supported the amnesties of Emile Moreau, defeated 317 to 180 on February 24, 1890, and that of Joseph Ferroul, defeated 305 to 134 on June 5, 1890.[35] On June 14, 1890, they comprised 27 of the 45 deputies who refused to vote with the government after Valentin Couturier's objection to the use of troops to crush a Lyon strike of glass-workers earlier in the year.[36] Barrès voted with the Boulangists on all these issues.

Other issues put Barrès and the Boulangists on the side of the conservatives against the Left. The vote of the Chamber on January 25, 1890, to annul the election of Jules Delahaye, who had deserted his former Boulangist friends, found Barrès and the Boulangists unanimously on the side of the defeated Right in objecting to all invalidations.[37] On February 10, 1890, only Boudeau, Granger, and Roche refused to follow the support of Barrès and the Boulangists for the conservative proposal to repeal the 1886 law against the entry to France of members of former ruling houses.[38] In so voting, the Boulangist press described itself not as "authoritarian Jacobins," but as partisans of the "open republic."[39] On March 25, 1890, when the Boulangist de Belleval proposed that the Paris municipal council be based on proportional representation of the parties, Barrès and the Boulangists won support from the Right instead of the Left.[40] The strangeness of the sometime Boulangist cooperation with the Right was illustrated in the proposal of the Baron de Mackau on June 16, 1890, allowing city governments to use the referendum. Naquet, speaking for the Boulangists, made an eloquent speech in favor of a kind of Swiss federalism, arguing that only the referendum could really implement universal suffrage in the French republic. Although Naquet criticized the undemocratic features of the de Mackau bill, particularly its concurrent majorities principle of voting by tax groupings without the secret ballot, he nonetheless led Barrès and the Boulangists in unanimous opposition to the government's attempt to kill it.[41]

In short, the first session of the new Chamber of Deputies saw Barrès and the Boulangists seeking allies on any side of the house to carry out their program. In demanding sweeping social reforms, Barrès and the Boulangists regularly voted with the Left. In hope of carrying out at least part of the Boulangist political program of the "open republic" and whatever remained of "Dissolution, Revision, and Constituent Assembly," Barrès and the Boulangists voted with both Left and Right. No other bloc in the Chamber followed this Boulangist voting pattern.

The Boulangists could not be content with being a parliamentary bloc, however. Their central thrust had been to conquer France for their constitution. Their alliance with the Right had been a mistake; the 1889 elections had been a great loss, but the Boulangists were so caught up in the mystique of their movement that they would not abandon their cause. As Laguerre pointed out in the opening days of the new Chamber, the National Party would rebuild itself on socialism, find revenge in the Paris municipal elections of 1890, and go on to capture France.[42]

Early in 1890 the Boulangist National Republican Party, as it called itself, still had several factors which augured well for its future. Its some thirty deputies were the most disciplined bloc of the extreme Left and, in many ways, the most left-wing. By comparison, the dozen socialists were disunified and so minute in numbers that they created scarcely a stir. The National Party had a substantial press, headed by *La Presse* and *l'Intransigéant*; the potential of formidable leadership in men like Laguerre, Naquet, Laisant, Déroulède, and Rochefort; well-established electoral committees at least in Paris, Nancy, and Bordeaux; and the national organization of the League of Patriots. The latter, as in 1888 and 1889, constituted at least fifteen thousand members with seven thousand in the twenty Paris chapters and eight thousand in the provincial ones. While these numbers were far short of the one hundred thousand figure Déroulède claimed, their "singularly active, resolved and ardent" middle-class militants reached out and influenced great numbers of workers, through gymnastic and rifle clubs, businessmen, teachers, traveling salesmen, and former military officers.[43] With such assets as these, it was not for nothing that Déroulède could tell his supporters at Angoulème, "The Boulangist group is to the Chamber what the flame is to the candle."[44]

On the other hand, there also was a built-in instability in the National Party. With Boulanger in exile, too many "indians" wanted to be "chief." As early as November, 1889, the police noted a "deep disaccord" between Laguerre and his *attentistes* and Déroulède and his "party of action." While Déroulède had the better grass-roots organization, the party press was in the hands of Laguerre's men and was kept somewhat closed to Déroulède.[45] As time went on, the apparent voting discipline in the Chamber was but a thin veneer hiding the poorly joined segments of the party. This factionalism tended to dissipate the leadership potential, split the local organizations, and prevent the party from pursuing a united policy.

The common peril at the beginning of the new Chamber nonetheless held the factions together. The most immediate danger, it appeared to Barrès and his fellows, was the Chamber's invalidations of the elections of several Boulangist deputies.[46] As the invalidated candidates stood for re-election, their rallies reflected the unity of the National Party, as intraparty rivals shared platform after platform together. The effort was successful for Paris and its suburbs, where the invalidated deputies were easily re-elected, but it did not prevent defeats in the provinces. The elections showed that Boulangism remained a protest vote of those urban workers and lower middle class who had lost faith in the Radicals but not yet turned to the socialists. In contrast, the 1889 victories had been achieved in the provinces through the help of conservatives.[47] In short, the voters were returning to their old loyalties, and Boulangism could no longer link Left and Right.

One of these by-elections again raised the issue of Boulangist anti-Semitism. A rally on January 18 for the invalidated Francis Laur, attended by the usual wide spectrum of Boulangist leadership, also included Laur's anti-Semitic friends Edouard Drumont and the Marquis de Morès, who spouted their usual shibboleths about the "Jewish financial coalition." The violence of their arguments bothered many Boulangists, especially as two of their leaders, Naquet and Elié May, were Jews. At the rally, Laisant agreed that it was all right to shout "down with the Jews" so long as one added all those who lived on the labor of others. Déroulède hedged by saying, "Naquet is not a Jew; he is a *philosophe*, a patriot, and a French republican."[48] Laisant repeated his formula two days later at a rally for the invalidated Naquet, and at the Boulangist anniversary banquet of January 27, 1890, attended by Barrès, a letter came from Boulanger saying, "I wish liberty of conscience for all, for the Jews and for Catholics, Protestants, and even Moslems."[49]

This anti-Semitic furor in Boulangism gave Barrès, as the respectable *Figaro*'s resident Boulangist, an opportunity to cast his own anti-Semitism in a theoretical framework for the first time. Following Laisant's formula, he saw anti-Semitism merely as a technique for leading the voters to socialism. "The crowd has always needed a battle cry to be rallied; it wants some cry of passion which will make abstract ideas concrete." "Hatred . . . is one of the more vigorous sentiments which produced our civilization" and anti-Semitism happens to be the most popular hatred of the time. When it goes out of style, find another. Barrès argued that anti-Semitism, unlike that of Drumont and his ilk, had to become more than just hatred of Jews. "Down with the Jews!" had to be converted into "down with social inequality!" At present, Jews personified to the public the chief perpetrators of these inequalities. As such, anti-Semitism was a useful tool for leading various non-socialists— Catholics ruined in the *Union générale* crash, patriots hating German Jews, bourgeois and peasant debtors—to socialism. "State socialism," he concluded, "is the indispensible corrective of the anti-Jewish formula." State socialism under a strong man would be able to reconcile classes and end the injustices which Drumont simply labeled "Jew."[50]

A year later Barrès saw what he thought proved his argument. According to him, Drumont's *Testament d'un antisémite*, which favorably mentioned Marxist Jules Guesde and *La Revue socialiste*'s Benoit Malon more than any other writers, sold one hundred thousand copies. If each copy had thirty readers, three million Frenchmen were exposed to Drumont's socialistic, as well as anti-Semitic, ideas and made receptive to the socialist cause. Since these three million had to come from the old parties, the promise of Boulangism to bring working-class reforms by reconciling and "declassing the parties" was possible through anti-Semitism.[51]

These statements, like those he made in the Nancy campaign, are remarkable in contrast to the anti-Semitism of the later Barrès, as well as for what they say of his view of politics. There is no racism here as there would be in his thought later on. Neither these two articles nor his earlier career show any personal animosity toward Jews on any grounds. They are not described as "un-French," although they would be later on. He had no Christian hostility against Jews, because at this time religion was largely meaningless to him. He made no reference to nineteenth-century pseudo-scientific racial theories, Darwinian or otherwise, although he would later on. Rather, anti-Semitism for him was no more than a device for winning over classes, other than already converted workers, to socialism.

In some ways such a motive is even more base than one rooted in some deeply-held but wrong-headed principle. Instead, it was purely demogogic, appealing to the emotions and non-reason. Even though orthodox French socialism would not get anti-Semitism out of its system until the Dreyfus affair, the nature of socialism requires its adherents to be rational and analytical, not irrational. Even socialists may require a "battle cry" or a "cry of passion to make abstract ideas concrete," but those cries usually are positive ones of love or justice, not "hatred." Even when "hatred" becomes a "battle cry," it has always been better integrated with socialist analysis for being only class hatred, not religious or ethnic. Neither was the case for Barrès. Not only was hatred necessary for him; any hatred would do, even anti-Semitism, just as for the *Culte du moi* any action would do. Indeed, his anti-Semitism was an outgrowth of the theme of the trilogy; anti-Semitism was an emotion or instinct which could energize the collective sense of personhood where reason and analysis would fail.

Nor was this recognition of the efficacy of hatred a passing thing, a phase he would outgrow politically. His collection of essays, *Du Sang, de la volupté et de la mort* (1894), is full of the notion. He found it reinforced by his first visit to Spain in 1892 where he discerned that "man becomes man again: he had the desire to bite, to claw!" Barrès already saw, as Robert Soucy has pointed out,

> hatred was the most powerful emotion of all, overriding all other emotions, tapping our deepest resources and moving us to accomplish the most extraordinary acts. Barrès illustrated this principle by telling the story of a Spanish noblewoman who had taken it upon herself to marry an uncouth brigand who had

previously raped her because she needed him to avenge her father's death. "Hatred carries all else before it," Barrès proclaimed, "it is the queen of the soul, an absolute monarch."[52]

At this point in his political career, such cultivation of irrational political means was no problem, because Boulangism, itself, was irrational. The problem would arise with great severity only when Barrès turned in the 1890s to socialism, a rational political persuasion.

As Barrès addressed himself to anti-Semitism, however, Boulangism still seemed to be a vital movement. Two developments in 1890 would begin to eliminate that option for him. One was the Paris municipal elections of April and May, 1890. There, where the party was best organized and had its biggest vote, Boulangism would find revenge for the defeat of 1889. Instead of revenge, it got rout. Not even another meeting of the Boulangist high command at Jersey, designed to devise a common slate of candidates, could heal the splits in the party.[53] In spite of an official slate, most quarters found at least two Boulangists on the ballot, usually representing the Laguerre and Déroulède factions. At Clignancourt, for example, the "official" candidate and the one of the quarter's Boulangist committee so wore themselves out in weeks of mutual recrimination that neither won in this most ardently Boulangist quarter.[54] The electoral program contained so few local issues that it was national Boulangism warmed over, an obvious attempt to win national power for the National Party.[55]

By election night, April 27, the Boulangist dream of capturing the nation through the Paris Hotel de Ville was shattered. Only one Boulangist was elected; another made it in the May 4 run-off. Had Boulangism had single candidates, they might have won in the seven other quarters where Boulangist majorities had been split up among as many as four candidates on the first ballot.[56] By the second ballot the feuding had so broken Boulangist *élan* that even these quarters failed to give the single remaining Boulangist a majority. Of course, the other parties, particularly the Radicals, had organizational problems, but Boulangism could not afford them. With its platform of national reconciliation, it was supposed to be above

87

faction, and unlike the other parties, it could no longer make deals on the second ballot, its socialism alienating the Right and its authoritarianism repelling the Left. Yet, even with better organization and less factionalism, the Boulangists still could never have won more than ten seats. Charles Chincholle pointed out that Paris had given Boulanger 247,000 votes in January, 1889. In 1890 this same total was split between Boulangists (127,000) and their conservative allies of 1889 (120,000). The old alliance no longer worked.[57]

Naquet, speaking for the National Committee, now wrote the General that all was finished unless he returned, that being the only way to keep the people worked up. Otherwise, continued agitation would only keep the anti-Boulangists united. Boulanger wrote Laisant, now chairman of the National Committee, that he would not return, that further fighting was sterile, and that the elections proved he no longer needed the National Committee as intermediary between himself and the people.[58] Within a week the committee was dissolved.

All this is to show how unreal were the dreams of Barrès and his fellows. Barrès spent the summer advising his workers how to form trade unions and consoling himself with the fact that there still were thirty Boulangists to agitate in the Chamber of Deputies. Even this crashed down with the revelations in the conservative La Figaro of the "Coulisses du Boulangisme" by a mysterious "X."[59] Installment after installment of this vibrant exposé, too accurately detailed to be written by anyone other than a Boulangist insider, revealed among other things that the Boulangists had planned a coup d'état for the night of the Paris election of January, 1889; had negotiated with and taken money from the royalists; and had seen to it that Boulanger, himself, secretly met with the Pretenders.

After initial shocked disbelief, the Boulangist press guardedly admitted the authenticity of the "Coulisses." Barrès, typical of the Boulangist apologists, pointed out that even "X" admitted that Boulanger refused to adhere to the coup d'état because of his republican attachments. Thirty years of military service under civilian control, however, had ill-prepared him for politics; it had conditioned him to accept without question his civilian political lieutenants, who had thrust themselves on him and who were not all good men. From the bad ones, the ones urging victory at any cost, came the "thousand shameless, absurd steps of Boulangism," especially the willingness to accept a *coup d'état* and a royalist alliance when republican means had failed. Although the Boulangists had the "best intentions in the world, they made stupid blunders: too many politickers and questionable meetings with reactionaries."[60]

By September Laguerre admitted that he had permitted Mermeix to write the "Coulisses," not knowing they would tell so much.[61] The old National Committee revived itself long enough to force Mermeix (now being called "Merdmeix") out of the party and to pledge continued dedication to constitutional revision for a "liberal, democratic, and socialist Republic."[62] Then its members ran for cover. Not until the end of September did they brave their voters and then only to claim, as did de Belleval, that they followed the Boulangist program without becoming "infeudated" to the general or paid by royalist gold.[63] Belleval could only hope that his voters had forgotten his expensive American-style campaign of 1889. Rallies, such as the one for Laguerre which Barrès attended, were almost broken up with chants of "Resign."[64] But the worst was yet to come.

At his "trial," Mermeix, who was not an insider of Boulangism until after the 1889 legislative elections, said his information had come from monarchists and "republican friends." Who were they, and why did they allow Mermeix to tell all? Fingers pointed to Naquet and, especially, Laguerre. To the party faithful at a rally on October 31, Laguerre appeared to abandon Boulanger when he said that Boulangism was finished and no more than a "fact of history." The nation needed "peace and repose," and revisionism should "look to the future and go forward" without Boulanger. On November 9, Déroulède accused Laguerre of being behind the "Coulisses" as a way of getting back into favor with the governmental parties: "M. Laguerre . . . pleaded the cause of General Boulanger with so much talent; now that this cause appears lost to him, he abandons it for a new client. Who? . . . Is it

M. Constans?"[65] November ran its course with a series of duels between Laguerre and his faction and Déroulède and his.

These feuds so broke the National Party's unity that by December the Boulangist bloc in the Chamber was down to twenty-four members, having lost Radicals or radical-revisionists like Naquet, Laguerre, Le Hérissé, Pontois, Turigny, Borie, and Laporte and conservative revisionists like Martin and du Saussay. This figure was revealed by the votes on seven issues in the first three months of the session, which began in October. Although many of these transactions were supported by other blocs of the Left or Right, these twenty-four Boulangists supported all of them. These seven issues also showed just what Barrès and Boulangism stood for by the end of 1890. With two dozen others of the extreme Left and an handful of rightists, they supported a series of Boulangist budget amendments demanding governmental efficiency and economy.[66] They were joined by fifteen other deputies in a de Belleval proposal to reduce the Justice Ministry's budget until judges, presently "the creatures of M. Wilson," were popularly elected.[67] With a handful from Left and Right, they supported de Belleval's nationalistic proposal for old age pensions to be financed principally by taxes on the Bourse and resident aliens.[68] A handful of socialists joined the Boulangists behind Paulin-Méry's proposal to submit to a referendum—that populist plank in Boulangism—a proposed conversion of outstanding short term bonds into long term ones, a conversion that both socialists and Boulangists believed constituted a new bond issue.[69] They were the bulk of the socialist, Boulangist, and rightist 53 votes against the budget of 1891. Speaking on behalf of "twenty-seven irreconcilables," Déroulède said they would serve the Third Republic like the *Cinq* served the Second Empire, by voting against the budget as a way of voting against the ministerial republic and for the Boulangist tolerant, open, presidential republic.[70] Barrès and Gabriel later claimed, more practically, that they voted against the budget because it was unbalanced and its new taxes fell on the poor instead of the rich.[71] In his "twenty-seven irreconcilables," Déroulède optimistically included Borie, Laporte, and Turigny who had joined the opposition with Laguerre and Naquet. They did not join the twenty-four Boulangists, including Barrès, against the validation of Lavy for Boulanger's Clignancourt seat, although they were joined by eight conservatives, six of whom had voted for the budget.[72] The same twenty-four were alone in their opposition to a credit for Sudanese flood relief.[73] Their nationalism meant taxes on foreigners, a vigorous European military and diplomatic posture, but an intransigent anti-colonialism.

Although the Boulangists were fewer in number, they still continued to show considerable solidarity in the Chamber. Yet, they were only a parliamentary bloc and no longer a party. As a bloc, they kept their reformist stance, still as left-wing as that of the socialists. For example, with Barrès they sought to strengthen the Senate child and female labor bill, even to strongly supporting de Mun's efforts to make holy days the required days of rest.[74] They and Barrès were joined by socialists and Radical-Socialists when Francis Laur proposed the extension of the twelve hour day to all workers.[75]

As a party, however, their leadership, press, and organization split or disappeared. As soon as the Laguerre-Mermeix authorship of the *Coulisses* became obvious, Déroulède sought permission from Boulanger to take command of the parliamentary party. Boulanger, ambiguous as ever, granted it so long as the Boulangist deputies agreed. According to police reports in July and August, 1891, Déroulède succeeded in winning over Pierre Richard, Boudeau, Castelin, Dumonteil, Goussot, Laisant, and "several others," while Paulin-Méry and Pierre Denis remained with Boulanger, and Le Veillé and Millevoye sat on the fence. These Boulangists whose origins lay in socialism were unhappy that Déroulède stood up for the soldiers who "followed orders" in shooting down the May Day demonstrators at Fourmies in 1891. They looked to Rochefort for leadership. Barrès publicly refused to accept the leadership of either Déroulède or Rochefort.[76] With this development it was obvious that only Boulanger could unite the disparate factions, but he was so absorbed with his dying mistress that he refused to return to France or direct the party from abroad, even after her death in the summer of 1891. The party press

91

also disappeared with the withdrawal of the Laguerre faction, except for the readerless *La Voix du peuple* of Pierre Denis, the last remaining confidant of the General. The comment of *Le Figaro* not only summarized the state of the Boulangist press but that of the party as a whole:

> Sign of the times:
> The *Courrier du Soir* called *La Presse* a "Boulangist journal." *La Presse* objects to this label.[77]

Whatever illusions Boulangism had about preserving its separate identity were dispelled at the end of September, 1891, when General Boulanger shot himself on the grave of his mistress in the Brussels cemetery of Ixelles. At first old Boulangists, who trooped to his funeral, saw this as an opportunity to renew their solidarity. The group of Le Veillé, Paulin-Méry, and Denis issued a manifesto that they would remain true to the Boulangist program, and Henri de Rochefort told the London *Daily Telegraph* that the suicide would reunite the Boulangists.[78]

But most Boulangists knew, in Barrès' words, that "the faded carnations they had worn as boutonnieres and thrown into the open tomb at Ixelles were the last flowers of the Boulangist bouquet."[79] *Le Temps* told them that by themselves they were nothing and probably could not effect "the alliance with the Radicals which they seek."[80] Francis Magnard also told them they were finished. Without press, leadership, or program they would return to their origins. Some might remain successful in areas where Boulangism was strictly anti-capitalist and anti-bourgeois, but it was all over in the provinces.[81] Barrès knew it, too. He polled the Boulangists and decided that some would continue to challenge and debate the government for their own ends—Laur to ruin Constans, Déroulède to champion patriotism. Naquet, the philosopher of Boulangism, would philosophize on his new condition. Although Laguerre would become a member of the governmental bloc, Barrès could not: "When I take a place at the theatre, it is not in the claque."[82] He saw that the Boulangists might sentimentally remember their days of near glory but that "without doubt they will follow—such is my intention at least—the program and temperament of the voters they represent, and differences will be accentuated among them."[83] He sympathized most with Laisant, who argued that parliamentary agitation by individual deputies or in a bloc was now sterile. The scene of combat was now outside parliament; the effort would be to mobilize public opinion in favor of nationalism, reconciliation, and social reform and to wait until the public became thoroughly disgusted with the Opportunist Republic. "Let us never forget," concluded Laisant, "that the Republic is only a word if it does not signify social justice and grandeur of the fatherland."[84] To his voters, Barrès identified himself several times with the views of Laisant.[85]

As long as Boulanger had been alive, there had always been the possibility that he might return, galvanize his forces, and again threaten the *status quo.* His death both allowed the republican extreme Left to cooperate openly with the Boulangists without fearing the downfall of the republican form and swept up the Boulangists, left adrift, into the more orthodox socialist movements which readily accepted them. Barrès welcomed both developments. By November, 1891, he thought he saw the emergence of an anti-governmental leftist bloc in the Chamber, extending from the Radicals to the Boulangists and socialists. Of course, such a bloc was still negative in character, since its members could not agree on a positive program. Its future was bright, nonetheless, for the nation was moving leftward, as shown by the recent election of Paul Lafargue, the socialist son-in-law of Karl Marx.[86] Lafargue's speech at the Chamber on December 8, 1891, for an amnesty, co-sponsored with Lafargue by other socialists and the Boulangists Aimel and Jourde, seemed to Barrès to bear out the possibility of this coalition. According to Lafargue,

> The Boulangist crisis has been only the shrill manifestation of a sick society. Today, Boulanger is dead and Boulangism is finished; but the causes which gave it birth still persist and each day continue to create a considerably larger number of malcontents. These malcontents formerly grouped themselves behind General Boulanger; now they are beginning to group themselves behind the socialists.[87]

93

Barrès particularly applauded Lafargue's unsuccessful appeal to de Mun for a coalition of Left and Right for social reform, but cautioned that such a coalition hinged on the abandonment of the religious question and had to include the question of national defense.[88] He further showed his growing tolerance of the members of this new bloc by attacking those who claimed that proletarian socialist leaders were "soured by extreme poverty" or that opportunistic and bourgeois socialists were declassed. Quite the contrary, argued Barrès. Benoît Malon of *La Revue socialiste* was a "noble and gentle man," Jules Guesde of the *Parti ouvrier* an "obstinate logician," Lafargue a "very adorned mind," and Paul Brousse of the Possibilist-socialists an "acknowledged great man."[89]

Ever since 1889, of course, socialists and Boulangists had voted together on social reforms; by early 1891 they cooperated in getting sufficient signatures for roll call demands in the Chamber; and by late 1891 a thoroughgoing alliance existed between them. With Barrès, they formed the basis for the 38 votes cast on December 15, 1891, against the total budget.[90] On social reforms, such as the Pierre Richard minimum wage proposal of February 16, 1892, and amendments to strengthen the conciliation and arbitration law of December 27, 1892, the deputies of the Left, be they socialist or Boulangist like Barrès, also could agree.[91] On other legislation, notably the various laws dealing with the anarchist outrages of 1892, the parties of the Left of every stripe split in every possible direction.[92] The only issue which continued to distinguish the Boulangist from the socialist was nationalism, most marked in votes on colonial appropriations. In the most extreme example, Barrès and seventeen other left-wing Boulangists voted alone against the Chamber on the supplementary credit for colonialism of July 4, 1892, while another seven of their group abstained.[93] It is interesting that all but one of the Boulangists who voted with the most orthodox socialists on the anti-anarchist vote of July 2 voted as part of these eighteen anti-colonialists.

Even Boulangist flirtation with conservatives, which had long distinguished Boulangists from other leftist republicans, increasingly lessened, particularly on the clerical issue. The

94

votes in favor of the perennial proposal to end the embassy to the Vatican saw the Boulangists becoming increasingly anticlerical. When the issue was raised in 1893, only three of the remaining twenty-five Boulangists could be found to vote against it, and Barrès for the first time abstained instead of voting against it.[94] Of course, no Boulangist could support the proposal of October 28, 1891, for separation of Church and State, since it came from the *"israélite"* Camile Dreyfus. The proposal was a response to the French clergy's objection to the government's recent condemnation of anti-Italian French pilgrims to Rome. Yet, when a similar proposal was made by Hubbard on December 12, after the clergy's criticism of the government had become more heated, no Boulangist, including Barrès, could vote against it.[95]

Déroulède had tried to get control of the Chamber's Boulangists after the death of Boulanger, but by December his only remaining supporters were Millevoye, Castelin, and Pierre Richard. The rest, including many former members of the League of Patriots, were flying into the arms of the socialists, and not just as part of a parliamentary alliance.[96] On March 2, 1892, socialists like Joseph Ferroul, Valentin Couturier, Paul Lafargue, and Gustave Cluseret, and Radical-Socialists like Girodet and Louis Théron joined eighteen Boulangists, including Barrès and even Castelin and Richard, in a meeting to declare they would stop their obstructionism in the Chamber as a way to help pass several pending social reforms.[97] In early July similar men held a rally at the Cirque d'Hiver in Paris, chaired by Cluseret, to demand amnesty for the Boulangist Rochefort and Marxist Culine, a leader of the May Day demonstration at Fourmies in 1891, and to hear Gabriel condemn Lavy and Dumay.[98] If Francis Magnard of *Le Figaro* was right in believing the rally had "a Boulangist scent whose nature is not able to excite republican and, above all, governmental sympathies," socialists were becoming Boulangist rather than the other way around.[99] Indeed, Friedrich Engels had already taken alarm at the March meeting and had warned Lafargue that just such a result might come from an alliance with the numerically superior Boulangists.[100]

95

If any event was likely to fulfill Engel's fears it was the Panama scandal, whose proportions made the Wilson scandal pale in comparison. Panama was just the kind of incident to rekindle the dying embers of Boulangism rather than to drive its members into socialism. The scandal should have revived the public disgust with the parliamentary republic—the lifeblood of Boulangism in 1889. The scandal first broke in the Chamber on November 19, 1892, in mild interpellations by the Boulangist, or some-time Boulangist, Argeliès, Gauthier de Clagny, and Jules Delahaye.[101] When Delahaye, amid general tumult and shouts of "give the names," charged on November 21 that more than one hundred deputies received checks from the agents of the Panama Canal Company, Baron de Reinach and Cornelius Herz, and that the government knew who they were, there was no turning back.[102]

From then on rightists and Boulangists (notably Millevoye, Déroulède, Paulin-Méry, Gabriel, Le Veillé, Argeliès, Martin, and Chiché) kept up a steady barrage against the government and commission of inquiry, named by the Chamber to investigate the charges. Indeed, they colored with the stain of Panama almost every issue debated in the Chamber until the spring of 1893. In return, the Chamber, which had almost forgotten the Boulangist past of these gentlemen, now turned that past on them again and again. On one occasion Maurice Rouvier, a member of the cabinet, replied to a vicious Boulangist attack by admitting that he had taken money from Reinach only to save the republic from Boulanger. Déroulède came back with the argument that taking French royalist money was preferable to taking German Panamist money. He continued with one of the most brilliant, unrepentant, and concise statements of the Boulangist republic, a reborn Second Republic with a re-electable president.[103]

As the Panama scandal wore on, however, Déroulède and his followers, principally those who led the anti-Panama debates, increasingly used it more to ruin their enemies than to bring down the republic. In doing so, they forestalled the scandal's ability to coalesce all the revisionist parties—Boulangists, socialists, Radicals, and rightists—to topple the Constitution of 1875. Again and again the Déroulèdists almost single-mindedly attacked Clemenceau, who had deserted his one-time protégé Boulanger and had led the anti-Boulangist opposition in 1889. Now, according to Barrès who was a second in Déroulède's duel with Clemenceau, Clemenceau was cooperating with the government while appearing not to and taking money from the Panama Company.[104]

The Déroulèdists continued to pursue Clemenceau even after the scandal was over and the Chamber had exonerated all the accused deputies save the one who had the incredible folly to confess. By June, 1893, Déroulède and Millevoye came upon some letters purportedly from the British ambassador to France, which held that Clemenceau and the Blanquist-Boulangist Rochefort were in English pay. Even though the foreign minister convinced him that the papers were forgeries, Déroulède agreed to have Millevoye use them against Clemenceau, but not against Rochefort. Indeed, in January Déroulède and the Marquis de Morès had visited Rochefort in London to form an electoral alliance.[105]

Millevoye questioned the government about the papers on June 22, hoping to duplicate Delahaye's success at withholding the names while getting the Chamber to appoint an investigating commission. However, when the Chamber kept shouting, "the papers, read the papers," Millevoye lost his head and read the papers dealing with both Clemenceau and Rochefort. The foreign minister revealed that Millevoye was the victim of a hoax; Déroulède resigned his seat in disgust and left, but Millevoye read on and on. With the entire Chamber hooting the ludicrous performance, Boulangists Castelin and Barrès told Millevoye to resign like Déroulède. Ernest Roche, the lieutenant of Rochefort, pounced on him for besmirching Rochefort's patriotism. Castelin and Barrès swore that the Boulangists would abstain, out of friendship, on the motion censuring Millevoye, but the smear of Rochefort drove seven Boulangists to vote for the censure.[106]

The farce played out by Millevoye, preceded by the irresponsible Déroulèdist treatment of the entire Panama scandal, forestalled any possibility of Boulangism to capitalize on the scandal. Instead of bringing socialists into Boulangism, the scandal moved Boulangists into socialism. In January, 1893, amid snow and cold, Boulangists like Granger, Turigny, Jourde, Roche, Laporte, and Chiché, joined by socialists and Radical-Socialists as varied as Alexandre Millerand, Désiré Barodet, and Lafargue, held a rally for six thousand at the Tivoli-Vauxhall in Paris to demand the creation of a social republic through an anti-Panama, anti-Fourmies revision of the constitution by a constituent assembly. Both Cluseret, the chairman, and Millerand called for all socialists, even Boulangists, to join hands for the upcoming parliamentary elections.[107] Only days before, Chiché argued that a demand being debated for dissolution of a Chamber corrupted by the Panama scandal was not enough. Instead, "it is necessary to dissolve both chambers and throw the bastard constitution of 1875 into the fire." His plan to let the parliament remain to legislate a budget while a constituent assembly sat concurrently was repulsed 320 to 187 Radicals, rightists, socialists, and Boulangists.[108]

The Tivoli-Vauxhall rally, coupled with the Déroulèdist use of the Panama scandal, was followed by a flight of Boulangists into socialist ranks. By spring, Gaston Laporte became a charter member of the Federation of Independent Socialists, the Millerand group.[109] The Boulangist Henri Aimel attended the *Revue socialiste* banquet in July, 1893. He had already been welcomed back into that journal's pages in May, 1892, and soon became a regular contributor of apologies for Boulanger.[110] Antoine Jourde returned to the Guesdist *Parti ouvrier*, from which he had entered Boulangism, became a delegate to its 1893 congress, and was elected a member of its national committee.[111] Socialist journalists like the Blanquist Victor Jaclard and the Guesdist Hugues Thiercellet came not to care whether a man had been a Boulangist or not, so long as he was now a socialist.[112]

If Boulangists had any reservations about socialism, they were removed when Déroulède and Millevoye followed up their absurdities on Clemenceau and Rochefort with still another. Their questioning of French socialist patriotism for accepting campaign money from German socialists brought the wrath even of the tolerant Lafargue.[113] *La Revue socialiste* condemned their chauvinism as one of the most ridiculous features of Boulangism, having nothing in common with socialist patriotism.[114] Most Boulangist deputies agreed and chose to run in the upcoming parliamentary elections as Radical-Revisionists or socialists, but only ten of their thirty members won re-election. The May 1, 1892, municipal elections had already shown that Boulangism had little chance with the voters.[115] Panama turned them even farther away. By 1893 socialism was not just a Jersey for Boulangism. It appeared to be a permanent home.

The parliamentary activity of Barrès and Boulangism after 1889, with their leftist program and voting record on social issues and their relationship with the anti-Boulangist socialist parties, poses several problems. It tends to undermine the picture of Boulangism, with its advocacy of authoritarianism and its ties with the royalists, as a party of the Right; if the activity of Barrès and the Boulangists makes them leftist instead of rightist, their thirty members make Boulangists, not the dozen anti-Boulangist socialists of 1889, the major bloc of the extreme Left. Moreover, if these leftist Boulangists and socialists are combined, they comprise a bloc almost as radical and large as the fifty-member socialist bloc elected in 1893, the election generally assumed to mark the first major parliamentary advance of French socialism. In short, the usual categories of Left and Right do not work very well for the post-1889 Boulangists and Barrès any more than they do for various twentieth-century groups, as Professor Weber has shown.[116] Perhaps a neater classification for them would be his term, "national socialist"— leftist on social issues, ardently nationalistic on political ones, respectful of ideology, and attached to movement rather than to party. Yet, Barrès and his fellow Boulangists had no "national socialist" term for themselves and lacked many of the other qualities of more recent national socialists. Instead, in the vagueness of French socialism of the 1880s and early 1890s, Boulangists tended to think of themselves as socialists pure and simple and were just as easily accepted on that basis by more orthodox socialists. The same would be increasingly true for Barrès.

CHAPTER FOUR

MAURICE BARRÈS, DEPUTY OF NANCY, 1889–1893

Boulangism had elected Barrès, but with its rapid decline it certainly was not going to re-elect him. The failure of national Boulangism, obvious as early as 1890, convinced Barrès that in building a political career for himself he was strictly on his own. His political fortunes were dependent on building a personal electoral machine. The years 1889-1893 would see him attempt to do so, first at Nancy and, when he failed there, in the Paris suburb of Neuilly. Moreover, if his experience in national parliamentary Boulangism moved him in the direction of socialism, or at least "national socialism," that of Nancy and Neuilly would do so even more. At least it would cause him to test that water with a toe.

Barrès' attempt to build a personal electoral machine in Nancy, separate from national Boulangism, did not begin until 1890 because in 1889 Boulangism still looked like a national force. That appearance of power fused the Boulangists and the Nancy Radical committee, many of whose members had supported the Boulangists in the run-off election, into a socialist-revisionist committee in October, 1889.[1] The theme of Boulangist national power and Barrès' role in shaping the movement's socialism marked several rallies he held in April, 1890.[2] After the defeat in Paris and the admitted desertion of some Nancy Boulangists, Barrès tried a new approach. He sought to renew his direct contact with the voters by circulating questionnaires, ostensibly to buttress his legislative program, to discover, for example, the number of foreign workers at Nancy, the number of unemployed French workers replaced by them, and the household budgets of a typical working-class family.[3] Concentrating increasingly on building up his Nancy following, he and Gabriel held another series of rallies in May, June, and July and filled the summer issues of the *Courrier de l'Est* with articles to educate the voters in consumer self-help and social reform through political action. He discussed with them the nature of borrowing and profits and ways to form trade unions, cooperatives, and a more equitable tax structure. In particular, Barrès offered his assistance in achieving the formation of trade unions at Saint-Nicolas-du-Port and Dombasle.[4]

Throughout 1890 and 1891 these early initiatives developed into a full-scale effort to build trade union and socialist movements capable of making the voice of the Nancy working class effective and of sustaining the electoral careers of Barrès and Gabriel. Trade unionism, which had amounted to nothing in 1889, expanded greatly in 1890 and 1891, largely under their initiative. Six new trade unions were formed in 1890 alone, notably in tobacco and leather and shoes. By 1891 Boulangists controlled most of the trade union movement with the exception of the five-hundred member tobacco workers' union, and Barrès and Gabriel spoke frequently at trade union meetings. The aims of the unions, like those of any newly-formed trade union movement, were largely in the direction of self-help rather than militant preparation for strikes.[5] In a big trade union rally on April 19, 1891, Barrès linked this trade union activity with socialist politics by viewing unions as pressure groups able to force the parliament to enact working-class reforms.[6] Barrès' political tendency was reflected by the masthead of *Le Courrier de l'Est* which changed on February 7, 1891, from "Revisionist Republican Journal" to "Socialist Republican Journal" with the sub-heading, "The aims of all social institutions should be the amelioration of the moral, intellectual and physical condition of the most poor and numerous class." May Day observances at Nancy also indicated rising working-class confidence and its linkage with the politics of Barrès and Gabriel. In 1890 the workers were so

101

unorganized and so threatened by the possibility of being replaced by foreign workers that they followed Barrès' advice
to remain "calm and silent" instead of engaging in a "useless
and dangerous manifestation."[7] In 1891 one thousand two
hundred trade unionists attended an after-work rally presided
over by Gabriel and Boulangist trade union leaders.[8]

The same period saw the Nancy anti-Boulangists function
in the national framework. The Paris *Coulisses du boulangisme*
brought local imitations by the *Est Républicain* and *Progrès de
l'Est*. They revived the charges that Barrès and Gabriel had
received royalist money in 1889, curried favor with the bishop
of Nancy, supported conservatives in the cantonal elections of
1889, and made an electoral deal with the Nancy conservatives to steal the 1889 elections.[9] Through the *Courrier de l'Est*
and a series of rallies, Barrès and Gabriel successfully blunted
the attack by pointing to their impeccably republican and
reformist voting record.[10] "My program and my votes are republican and anti-Opportunist," said Barrès. "They demand
reforms always repressed by the band of Ferry and Rouvier.
If men belonging to the clerical party prefer to fortify the
cause of the workers more than that of the exploiters, we are
not at all surprised."[11] Even though many disreputable politicians hid in its shadows, Boulangism "had been a revolutionary instant of the great revisionist movement" and had
won Nancy to socialism. "For my part," Barrès added, "I
could resign out of disgust with those Opportunists and
mediocrities of all colors on the benches of the Palais Bour-
bon who sicken me, but the belches of our Opportunist Alliance will not sound my retreat."[12]

In spite of their failure to capitalize on the *Coulisses*, the anti-
Boulangists did discover a line of attack which ultimately
destroyed Nancy Boulangism. By 1891 the followers of Pierre
Albert Papelier launched a campaign to convince the workers
that their votes were wasted on socialists who could make
noise but not realize their program. The governmental parties,
on the other hand, could and would give the workers more
than would the Boulangists and socialists. In 1889 Papelier, a
grain merchant and founder-director of an organization for

agricultural development, had beaten Paul Adam for election to the Chamber of Deputies on a program of protectionism, conciliation of all parties, and such social reforms as old age pensions, workmen's compensation, rural public assistance, and reform of apprenticeship contracts.[13] With the later addition of planks for a Nancy *Bourse du travail*, tax reform, miner delegates, regulation of child and woman labor, and measures against the *livret* and foreign workers, he had all the Boulangist program except constitutional revision and Boulanger.[14] He also headed a commission in the Chamber which had just favorably reported an old age pension bill. Against Gabriel at a trade union meeting at Pont-Saint-Vincent, he successfully debated his thesis that the governmental parties would bring those reforms and that the socialists were incapable of them. He followed up by getting behind a series of worker-oriented conferences. By 1891 Papelier's thesis became the basis of the anti-Boulangist attack on Barrès and Gabriel.

So effective was this new assault on Boulangism that throughout 1891 and 1892 almost the entire Nancy Boulangist movement and propaganda, including virtually every issue of *Le Courrier de l'Est*, were directed against what Gabriel dubbed "Papelierism": the technique of falsely appearing reformist to win over the workers while really remaining in favor of the *status quo* and employers. Gabriel argued that the success of Boulangism had finally forced the Nancy Republican Alliance to become worker-oriented. Yet, the Alliance's Papelierism was just a ruse to delude the workers, for Papelier and his fellows knew that his pension bill would fail in the Senate. His real views could be discerned from his votes, such as his support for age twelve, rather than age thirteen, as the minimum age for a ten hour day.[15] Barrès added that the Papelier program was too little and too late and only the result of the public being conditioned to social reform by years of socialist propaganda.[16] With the entry of Papelierism coinciding with the Chamber's consideration of the Senate bill on hours for women and children, Gabriel sponsored several amendments to it.[17] The *Courrier* took great delight in pointing out that although the Meurthe-et-Moselle deputies voted for the Gabriel amendment, which required miners to be fourteen years old, their Nancy newspapers opposed it.[18] Another *Courrier* writer commented that while the Papelierists posed as the friends of trade unions in the Chamber and in rallies, their employer-clientele prevented the formation of unions in their factories and even blacklisted a stonecutter who tried to form a union. Barrès and Gabriel protested this, the writer claimed, but they were powerless since the trade union law of 1884 did not prevent employer reprisals.[19] Papelierism also colored the Barrès-Gabriel rally of April 12, their first confrontation with the voters since October, 1890, where Gabriel contrasted his and Barrès' votes against those of Papelier.[20] The same was true of a "non-political" meeting on April 19, chaired by the president of the carpenters union and called to have the three Nancy deputies explain the trade union law. Papelier bowed out at the last minute, and at the meeting one of Gabriel's lieutenants pushed through a vote censuring him.[21]

In spite of this meeting and their many words telling the workers not to be taken in by the governmental parties, Papelierism had a telling effect on the efforts of Barrès and Gabriel to hold their working-class clientele. Nancy workers gave every indication of becoming more and more oriented toward purely economic action, and their lack of militancy is reflected in the reports of the prefect. By 1896 he could say that the political situation "has rarely been more tranquil,"[22] and in 1898 he attributed their lack of interest in strike activity to the efforts of Papelier.[23] Working-class lack of interest in the politics of Barrès and Gabriel was reflected in the falling off of attendance at their political meetings. Both newspapers and police reports note that, save for the big trade union rallies which still drew one thousand to one thousand five hundred people as in the electoral campaign of 1889, attendance at Boulangist political meetings by 1891 ran at one hundred to two hundred people, even though it was common to send out two thousand invitations.[24] Some Nancy socialists even split with the Boulangists, formed their own organization, and controlled the large tobacco workers union; one group of them even won four seats on the city council of Malzéville, a Nancy suburb.[25]

The opportunity for Papelierism to test its political strength against Nancy Boulangism, which no longer had the glamor of Boulanger nor the prospect of a national Boulangist victory, came with the calling of municipal elections for May 1, 1892. For that May Day, Barrès and Gabriel urged the workers to confine their demonstration to the ballot box. "A fragment of the future is in your hands," Barrès told them. "Each ballot lies heavily on the destinies of the working class. If you want tomorrow to resemble today, abstain or vote for the Opportunists [i.e., to Barrès, the followers of Papelier were still Opportunists]. If you are malcontented today, vote for the party of reforms."[26] Gabriel told the workers that socialism was not strong enough to win a national election, but that by winning municipalities "the socialists will attain the government."[27]

Before long, however, Nancy Boulangists, renamed Revisionist Socialists, saw that such strategy required new tactics. Gabriel admitted that before 1889 Nancy politics had been split three ways among Opportunists, conservatives, and "the socialist party, which then was called the Radical party." In order to prevent conservative victories, the socialists had always supported the Opportunist candidates, but when the latter were elected, they did not repay the socialists with social reforms. The socialists had broken out of this impasse in 1889 with the complete victory of Barrès and Gabriel, who were socialists disguised as Boulangists.[28] By 1892, however, with Boulanger dead and Papelierism on the rise, socialists were again in the minority at Nancy, just as they were in the nation as a whole. As a result, they had to settle for a partial victory or none at all.

To get this partial victory, twelve socialist candidates formed a common slate with seventeen Independent Republicans, whose platform was only slightly to the right of the socialist one, and six conservatives.[29] Victory for this proportional representation slate over Papelier's Central Republican Committee, the renamed Republican Alliance, would mean that twelve socialist city councilmen could urge enactment of the socialist platform—council sessions at night to allow working-class participation, no foreign workers on either the city payroll or jobs contracted by the city, a minimum wage for city employees, employment of trade unionists on city jobs, establishment of a municipal pharmacy, a free technical school, and a *Bourse du travail*, as well as improvement of the hospital, the fire and police departments, and street lighting.[30]

Barrès and Gabriel had some justification for believing that part of their program could be realized, even in coalition with the other two parties. At the beginning of April the bishop of Nancy, newly converted to reform by the *Rerum Novarum* of Pope Leo XIII, had begun a series of conferences in the cathedral on working-class problems. At the first meeting the bishop began by supporting trade unions, "work and saving," and "entente, union, and complete peace" rather than socialism and class struggle which would "destroy society." With that, his working-class audience started throwing chairs and shouting "Long live the republic" and "You are not a worker." Order was restored only by turning out the lights.[31] At the time, Barrès and Gabriel were skeptical of the bishop's new concern for the worker and fearful that his views would lure some workers from socialism.[32]

The opportunity never arose to test whether or not the Nancy conservatives had joined Leo XIII, for only one candidate of the proportional representation slate survived the first ballot on May 1.[33] The election was a clear victory for the Republican Alliance, as reshaped by Papelier, who helped produce a platform little different from the proportional representation one and who was even brave enough to pronounce his views at a meeting of the Boulangist shoeworkers union on election eve.[34] The voters had obviously rejected the lure of partial victory under proportional representation in favor of the promise that Papelierism would produce real results.

If that defeat damaged the political fortunes of Barrès and Gabriel, 1892 saw things go from bad to worse. In a rally as early as February, Barrès had barely survived criticism of his abstention on the Chamber's passage of the Méline tariff. His vote had been recorded as being for it while Gabriel's had been against it, and his voters had been conditioned by the cries of the *Courrier de l'Est* that protectionists were "starvers of the people," "ignoble exploiters," and "imbeciles." He explained it away sufficiently by changing the record of his vote after the rally, by pointing out his free-trade position in preliminary votes on consumer goods duties, and by enlisting the support of Gabriel.[35] In June both deputies "had been received by shouts which were not very sympathetic" as they participated in President Sadi Carnot's visit to Nancy.[36] Shortly afterwards they retired as political directors of the *Courrier de l'Est*, claiming their Parisian affairs kept them too busy.

The end came within a month. The appointment of a Barrès supporter, Paul Didier, to the Saint Cyr faculty was withdrawn upon pressure from Albert Colson, a faculty member of the *Ecole Polytechnique* and the Republican Alliance candidate against Barrès in 1889. Seizing upon this apparent act of spite to halt his slipping political fortunes, Barrès swung into a full-scale campaign to elect Didier to Colson's seat as municipal councilor of Saint-Nicolas in the elections of July 31. It was a complete mistake. Didier was an incredibly weak candidate, nothing more than a proxy for Barrès' act of spite against a former opponent. When the Republican Alliance substituted a Papelier moderate for Colson, Didier was swamped at the polls.[37] After the election the *Courrier de l'Est* tried to discount the ordinarily sympathetic *Impartial*'s charge that this was a "personal defeat" for Barrès, just as Gabriel had suffered a set-back with the failure of his chief protégé in May.[38] Yet, the defeat was complete. Before August was over the *Courrier de l'Est* ended publication, and Barrès retired from the Nancy political arena.

After the defeat of Didier, Barrès deserted Nancy, traveled in Spain, established himself in the Paris suburb of Neuilly, renewed his critical writing for various newspapers and reviews, and limited his political activity to the Chamber and his political writing to the Panama scandal. Not until the legislative campaign of 1893 did he again actively throw himself into politics. When he did, the scene of his political action was not at Nancy, but at the fourth *circonscription* of Saint-Denis, the seat for Neuilly deserted by the Boulangist Francis Laur. Gabriel also abandoned Nancy for a neighboring district in St. Denis.

They moved to the old Boulangist fief of Saint-Denis for the obvious reason that Papelier's forces had won over their electoral clientele and promised reformist candidates. No longer was Nancy a bastion of Boulangism. Papelier had rallied around his organization all malcontents, be they moderate, conservative, or socialist, because he was moderate, conciliatory, and constitutional. Success for Barrès at Neuilly, however, was far from certain.[39] The enormous Laur majority of 1889 had melted away by 1892. In the municipal elections of that year the Boulangist slate, led by an *Intransigéant* writer, garnered only 500 votes against the 3,700 split between moderate and Radical candidates.[40] The Radical victor, Louis-Victor Lefoulon, became municipal councilor and was now the candidate against Barrès.

More important, however, was the marked difference between Barrès' Neuilly program and the one he had been espousing. Under Gabriel's influence at Nancy, he had gradually moved to where he could call himself and his newspaper "socialist," but at Neuilly he asked for victory only "to aid in the formation of a party in favor of honest and intelligent government."[41] Moreover, he admitted to an interviewer that he wanted only his 1889 program—"constitutional revision, complete application of universal suffrage, respect for religious liberty, and three or four more specific reforms such as a national pension fund for workers and the protection of national workers against foreigners."

Although he told the interviewer that "it was the workers who made me enter political life to serve their just interests," the only "just interests" he felt deeply enough to comment upon was the foreign workers issue. His argument favoring it made it unclear whether his prime concern was nationalism or socialism:

> In the next political campaign I intend to insist very much on the great national theme of France for the French, which certainly gains ground more and more and impassions the workers. In philosophy, modern evolution is nationalist. In the practical order, there is reason to state that protectionism introduces the notion of fatherland into political economy.

> The exclusion of foreign workers is the necessary corrective
> of protectionism. Since industrial and agricultural owners are
> protected by tariffs against foreign products . . . it is just that
> workers, who have only their labor and their arms, also be pro-
> tected against competition of foreign labor and arms . . . .
> This question is a meeting point of anti-Semitism, socialism,
> and the patriotic current.[42]

He ended by admitting that it would be difficult to find a
widely-supported formula for achieving this. Such hesitation
resulted from the Chamber debates of May 6, 1893, on proposals for strengthening a bill requiring registration of foreign
workers. The debate had once and for all separated the old
Boulangists into two camps—nationalist and socialist. The nationalists wanted some kind of tax on the employers of foreign
workers; socialists saw the answer in requiring foreign workers to be paid at the same rate as Frenchmen. Although both
formulae failed, the votes on the taxes found Barrès on the
nationalist side with twelve other Boulangists of the Déroulède
variety, the Right, and a handful of socialists, including Jean
Jaurès. Twelve other old Boulangists, including Gabriel, took
the position of most of the socialists.[43]

This foreign worker issue became the principal plank in
Barrès' 1893 platform. In a series of articles in *Le Figaro*, published as an electoral pamphlet entitled *Contre les étrangers*,
Barrès spelled out his views. He admitted that France should
be hospitable, but that the 1,300,000 resident aliens posed a
threat to French workers. Foreign workers came to France because of the promise of good jobs and no military service.
Because they lived like animals, they accepted lower pay than
French workers demanded. Using reasons he would later re-
develop, Barrès went on to dismiss the arguments made by
the opponents of anti-foreign workers legislation: in spite of
what the liberal Léon Say and Marxist Jules Guesde said,
the world was not a single economic unit, but a collection
of national units; in spite of the internationalist aspect of the
Declaration of the Rights of Man and of Citizen, the French
Revolution encouraged nationalism, which now ruled the universe. Just as Frenchmen would not stand for military conquest

of France, neither should they stand for economic conquest, either from cheap goods or cheap labor. To keep cheap foreign labor from preventing full employment in France, Barrès proposed the following: tax employers at 10 percent of the salaries they pay foreign workers; subject foreigners to the same military obligations owed by Frenchmen; exclude foreign workers from military construction; deport all foreigners who go on public relief; apply the American formula of excluding paupers, the insane and diseased, and contract laborers from entering France; and exclude foreign workers from projects undertaken, subsidized, or contracted by governmental units.[44]

With this program Barrès threw himself into a heated campaign at Neuilly in which he faced a vigorous opposition. His growing nationalism and his Boulangist background, both used to identify him with the Right, focused on him the attacks of the Left. On August 18 anarchists who saw him as a reactionary entered his Neuilly headquarters, beat up his secretary, and left his house placarded with anarchist posters.[45] Barrès was certain the police put them up to it but was perfectly delighted when his supporters formed a body guard for him.[46] A socialist candidate, Francis de Pressensé, used such anti-Barrès posters that Barrès challenged him to a duel, fought without result on September 4.[47] For the Radicals and moderates, Barrès was too much of a socialist and Boulangist. For the universally hostile local press he was a doubtful republican who was supported only by the reactionary *Autorité*, *Gaulois* and *Libre Parole*. His claim of being only a *former* Boulangist and his fence-straddling made his candidacy difficult for even his electoral committee to swallow; he was an outsider and "exotic" who came to Neuilly only because he was finished at Nancy, as if a Paris seat were created just for his convenience.[48]

The nature of the Neuilly-Boulogne constituency does much to explain both the ambivalence of Barrès' program in 1893 and the charges leveled against him. To win in the district's three legislative elections between 1893 and 1896, a candidate, whatever his real label, had to pose as a moderate reformer and build a majority from the moderate Neuilly voters and the more leftist Boulogne ones. Even a single socialist candidate running on a real socialist platform could not hope for more than 2,500 votes, far short of a majority. Boulangism had been able to broaden that base for Francis Laur in 1889, but now it was dead. To win, Barrès, like any other candidate, had to appear as a moderate reformer. That meant toning down the socialist stance he had been taking in Nancy. He was able to do that sufficiently on the first round on August 20—to get 3,264 votes to his Radical opponent's 2,556 with another 2,089 going to a moderate and 1,642 being split between two socialists.[49] That lead was enough to win the belated endorsement of the conservative *Figaro*, which applauded his "tolerant opinions and program of practical reforms."[50] The same was true for the socialist *Intransigéant*. With two other socialists running against him, it gave him neither coverage nor endorsement until the very eve of the election when it added his name to its approved list of socialist candidates.[51] From the beginning it had given both to Gabriel, who did not survive the first round, and to other ex-Boulangist socialists. Both influential newspapers, one calling him a moderate and the other a socialist, seemed to have endorsed him only because he appeared to have the election in the bag. The newly-founded *Petite République*, the organ of the *Union socialiste*, would not go even that far. Although it endorsed some former Boulangists, it made no endorsement on either round in Barrès' constituency and referred to him only as a "revisionist."[52]

But victory was not to be Barrès'. With the other candidates out and 607 fewer voters on the second round of September 3, there were 2,186 moderate and socialist votes for Barrès and Lefoulon to split between them. Barrès picked up only 661 of them while his opponent gained 1,597 to beat him 4,153 to 3,925.[53]

The defeat of Boulangism in France and of Barrès in Nancy and Neuilly, both of which brought to a close the first phase of his career, raises the question, what had it all meant for him? Specifically, was he an effective deputy and politician? In what ways had the legislative and political experience changed the ideas he had held at the time of his decision to enter politics?

111

In answer to the first question, Barrès was not an effective deputy, except for his respectable voting record. He spoke but five times and hardly ever engaged in the fine art of interrupting which so marked his Boulangist fellow deputies. A notable exception was during an interpellation on the July, 1893, Paris student uprising when he told Prime Minister Charles Dupuy, "You are the parrot of the police."[54]

Generally, Barrès' speeches before the Chamber give every appearance of having been read from a prepared text, and in almost every case they concerned themselves with government censorship. On October 23, 1890, he questioned the government on the Hachette monopoly of book sales in railroad stations. According to Barrès, Hachette established a *de facto* censorship by refusing to sell books it considered immoral, such as works by Emile Zola, Guy de Maupassant, and Catulle Mendès, or detrimental to "social order," such as books on socialism and anti-Semitism, and even a work by Yves Guyot, the minister of public works whom Barrès questioned. The Chamber rejected his motion for giving bookselling concessions to the highest bidder.[55] Barrès also spoke when members of the Chamber contested the government's closing of Francisque Sarcey's play, *Thermidor*, which cast an unfavorable light on the French Revolution and, particularly, on the grandfather of President Sadi Carnot. Although the debate brought forth the leaders of each bloc to give their historical interpretations of the French Revolution, Barrès limited his remarks to a summary of the play's plot and theme and a plea for free artistic expression.[56] On March 17, 1892, he challenged the government for deporting a Nancy Boulangist of Alsatian birth.[57] On March 6, 1893, he questioned government on its closing of Paul Adam's *Automne*, a play of working-class sympathies which climaxed in a strike scene. "It is necessary that political passions maintain art," Barrès argued. "Shall we permit one of those who cuts such a figure in this Chamber, a Chamber which is more particularly a theater of political tragedy, to ban a competition on the part of those who aspire to [make the Chamber] nothing more than a theater for political comedy."[58]

In all these speeches Barrès came off badly, faced with inattention or interruptions.[59] Those who replied to his charges and those who interrupted invariably won their points at his expense with ironic references to "selfhood," "psychology," the "ivory tower," and "barbarians." He was so unskilled in debating that he could not reply in kind. He came off just as badly as far as legislation went. Seldom did his ideas reach the floor. Once he did co-sponsor with Gabriel an amendment to a bill setting up labor arbitration boards which would allow the boards to act on work rules, but Gabriel did the talking.[60] Coming as it did on the eve of the Nancy municipal elections, the amendment was little more than electoral propaganda.

As a debater and legislator in the Chamber, then, Barrès was a failure, but it may be unjust to judge him by these criteria. When he first went to the Chamber he wrote:

> At the Chamber there are 560 interesting physiognomies. They are there under diverse titles, but one could prepare an interesting catalog of them. And, by reducing these varied characters to thirty types, one will get a kind of illustrated guide composed of little likenesses with descriptive legends underneath them. Such a guide would be suitable for posting in city halls and analogous to those I have seen in grammar schools in the country entitled: *Illustrated Guide of Harmful Insects*.[61]

Indeed, throughout his years as a deputy Barrès seemed to see himself as a student looking at an illustrated guide of harmful insects. Given his frame of reference—the sterility of Chamber business, the endless debate about nothing, the impossibility of pursuing his program, which forced him to act like the rest of the deputies and do nothing—there was no choice but to play the part of the student and chronicler of a Chamber not famed for its creativity or probity.[62] In this role Barrès' power was more than adequate. It was certainly evident by the time of his descriptions in *Le Journal* and *Le Figaro* of the Panama scandal debates, many of which were incorporated into his novel, *Leurs figures*. It was also visible at the beginning. Witness this succinct analysis of a politician who typified the dynamic of the Opportunist Republic: "Charles

113

Floquet, [an Opportunist prime minister] is the navel of the Chamber, the flower of the parliamentary belly—of that Center which costs France so much. He is the spot where the governmentals of Radicalism and Opportunism can contemplate each other and be reconciled."[63]

Yet, Barrès could have accomplished his role of student and chronicler of the Chamber as well from the press gallery as from the benches. It was not a record on which to build a political career. His inability or refusal to meet the criteria usually prescribed for deputies caused him to be dogged with charges of dilettantism, of being in politics simply to magnify his ego and literary horizons. "M. Maurice Barrès," wrote Henri Beranger, "seems to make of politics the occasion of a game and of his legislative mandate a literary curiosity . . . . When he came to sit in the parliament he was still a dilettante and ironist. The connection between his obscure fever of energy and reality did not reveal itself until much later, around 1893 and 1894. When it did, his voters sent him back to literature."[64] Théodore Duret, the art critic, told Edmond de Goncourt that Barrès "is very wrong to become a socialist politician since he has an *aristocratic* air never favored in politics, since he is not even a journalist of those benches, since he is too literary, too refined, too metaphysical."[65]

In his interview with Barrès, Jules Huret asked if his political involvement was motivated by "dilettantism, curiosity, and the need for emotion." Barrès as much as confessed to the charges. In entering politics, he said, "I simply wanted to participate in the passions of my epoch, to put myself in their service." He added that it was necessary to get on a "ground of truth, to be fixed on it solidly and intimately." Politics provided a "ground of truth" for him to be a "publicist," that combination of man of letters and man of affairs in the tradition of Chateaubriand, Constant, Lamartine, and Disraeli. Moreover, Barrès was confident his voters would agree that such a "publicist" was not a dilettante.[66]

He touched on Huret's charges again during the campaign of 1893. Only by communicating his dreams to the masses,

114

Barrès said, could a thinker realize his dreams, even though he might prefer the solitary dreaming in the Bibliotèque Nationale reading room. He added that what really excited him in politics was not the hobnobbing with fellow deputies, most of whom were mediocrities, but the electoral campaign. Only there did he really touch the people.[67] Imagine this being written during the heat of a campaign by a man supposedly fighting to get elected to serve his constituents in the Chamber!

In a letter to Emile Zola on June 6, 1893, Barrès wrote much the same. "The Chamber is only one part of a whole. It gives me a sense of realities, truths, the sentiment of what is common to all men . . . . You remark that my role has been null. I think that it has not begun." He saw his *"raison d'être* more as an observer . . . than as an actor." But it was not just that. Even though he was "attached to a vanquished party and isolated even in that party," his effort in that party had been to transform individual and collective property "to the profit of the masses." Most of all, he wanted to make permanent "the idea of fatherland." Through his participation he could educate "a new generation" to throw out the "parliamentary personnel" and usher in these "socialist, nationalist, and dictatorial" aims through a "dictatorship of a man or an assembly."[68]

In short, legislative and political experience had given Barrès the "ground of truth" the *Culte du moi* had called for but not provided. He was a different man in 1893 from the one he had been in 1889. The Nancy record shows that. No longer did he create dreams out of thin air. The mere contact with the workers in rallies and interviews made him aware of their plight more than any book could have done. Seeing at first hand the difficulties of forming trade unions forced him to think more concretely on solutions. The failure to build political victories from an almost solely working-class base required him to seek a broader base. That requirement drew him closer to nationalism and anti-Semitism, a bridge able to span the gulf between the socialist Left and the Catholic Right.

The day by day participation in the Chamber of Deputies convinced him of the Opportunist Republic's uncreativity in a way Boulangist polemics never had done in 1887 and 1888.

In these ways the four years in the Chamber and Boulangist politics had left their mark on Barrès. His job now was to put his ideas and experiences into a synthesis which could win where Boulangism had failed. Without press, leadership, party, local following, or a seat in the Chamber, however, where was he to go?

CHAPTER FIVE

AT THE CROSSROADS: SOCIALISM, NATIONALISM, OR NATIONAL-SOCIALISM, 1893–1896

Without question Maurice Barrès eventually became a politician of the Right, but for awhile in the mid-1890s it looked as if he would end up at the opposite end of the political spectrum. To be sure, he had entered politics as a political innocent for the literary and psychological needs of his individualism. Under the impact of Nancy and parliamentary politics, he had turned from his original acceptance of the ready-made Boulangist solutions to a radical working-class orientation and program. Vague though his Neuilly-Boulogne program was, he had been the candidate of socialist committees. By the mid-1890s he seemed to be traveling a road to socialism, working to systematize and unify his individualism, socialism, and nationalism, seeking to convert the French socialist movement to those ideas, and trying to win under the socialist banner that elective office from which he could put his ideas into action. "In truth, Barrès was at the crossroads," recalled Joseph Paul-Boncour, a socialist of sorts, "it would have taken little to change his direction," to take the fork to the Left permanently into socialism.[1] Not until 1897 did Barrès really reach that crossroads. By then socialism had rejected his brand of socialism and had refused him electoral support. That rejection and, more importantly, the very style of his socialism made him veer down the fork to the Right.

117

Strange as it may seem from his later career, socialism certainly did seem to be an option for Barrès in 1893. One reason for this was his Boulangist record in the Chamber, where as early as 1890 he and his twenty-nine to thirty-one fellow Boulangists thought of themselves as socialists. Indeed, in that year they and Barrès were closer to socialism than were the still unconverted future leaders of the movement, Jean Jaurès and Alexandre Millerand. One-third of the thirty to thirty-two Boulangists had even come out of socialist backgrounds, and the entire group had formed one of the largest blocs of the extreme Left. By 1893 as many as a dozen of them had been welcomed into socialist ranks, had adhered to the Tivoli-Vauxhall manifesto, or had cooperated with socialists in the 1893 elections. By 1894 seven out of the ten Boulangists re-elected in 1893 joined the *Union socialiste*, the parliamentary group organized "to unify and direct the activities of the socialist deputies."[2] Barrès' beliefs made it quite logical for him to follow their example.

Yet another reason was the willingness of socialists to accept their former enemies, the Boulangists. This willingness was due to the fragmentation and weakness of the French socialist movement in 1893–1894. Just as there had been a "multiplicity of Boulangisms," there was a division of socialism into five major groups: the nationalistic and revolutionary Blanquists, themselves sometimes split between the followers of Rochefort and Edouard Vaillant; the Marxist followers of Jules Guesde of the *Parti ouvrier*, whose charter had been approved by Marx himself; the gradualist Possibilists, Marxist like the Guesdists, but differing from them in their willingness to accept bourgeois support and refusal to be part of a centralized party; the Allemanists, who rejected both Possibilist reformism and Guesdist revolution in favor of trade union activity; and the Independent Socialists, re-emphasizers of the humanitarian elements of "utopian socialism" and seekers of some doctrinal and tactical common ground among the various socialist factions. In such a diverse socialist world it was not impossible to think of Boulangists as socialists.

While this factionalism made socialism weak, so did voter

reluctance. In the 1889 legislative elections, for example, much of the potential socialist vote had gone either to Boulangist candidates or, because of socialist determination to beat Boulanger at any cost, to anti-Boulangist republican candidates of Radical-Socialist orientation. Hardly more than a dozen socialists reached the Chamber of Deputies as pure socialists. Later, just as the failure of Boulangism drove the Boulangist socialists closer to their socialist allies in the Chamber, the failure of the Chamber to pass sweeping social reforms drove the socialist deputies away from their 1889 allies, the anti-Boulangist republicans, and closer to the Boulangist socialists. This socialist willingness to cooperate with Boulangism marked Lafargue's speech for an amnesty on December 8, 1891. By 1893 Victor Jaclard, reflecting a widespread socialist attitude, argued that there was no longer any need for republican concentration against Boulangism. The need now was for a new concentration of socialists, ex-Boulangists, and Radical-Socialists to achieve a social republic against the "new Boulangism," the alliance of the Center and Right in the Chamber.[3] Finally, the spectacular gains made by socialism in the 1893 elections can be explained largely by the continued dissatisfaction of the voters with center governments, the ability of the socialists finally to cooperate among themselves electorally, and the absence of Boulangism. Of course, the gains were not so dramatic if one remembers that the extreme Left of thirty to thirty-two Boulangist socialists and a dozen socialists in the 1889 Chamber was not much smaller than the approximately fifty members of the *Union socialiste* of the 1893 Chamber.

All this is to say that in its weakness and fragmented diversity, French socialism of 1893 was willing to accept all comers, even Barrès. Out of expediency and the need for parliamentary and electoral cooperation in a time of weakness, a wide divergence of socialist views was tolerated. Even many Radical Socialists and Boulangists could be considered comrades. In turn, his voting record and public statements as a deputy could cause Barrès to consider himself a socialist so long as socialism had no precisely defined program or single party. With the Blanquists he shared the view that the proletariat needed the leadership of an elite of advanced bourgeoisie and a concern for nationalism. With the Guesdists he shared the Marxist view of history and the need to be "scientific." He loved to quote Marx's dictum, especially in evaluating the corruption of the Panamists, "In history there is no place for choler."[4] With the Independent Socialists he shared a willingness to work with all reformers of good will and to laud the ability of Jean Jaurès to bring to the Chamber both socialism and "the preferences of a philosopher."[5] With the Possibilists he believed in the efficacy of reformism—not revolution—and localism—not centralization. As long as socialism retained an armed truce among its followers and a willingness to respect one another's doctrinal differences, Barrès could remain a socialist. Should it ever resolve its differences and, in particular, reject nationalism, Barrès and the Boulangist socialists would be driven away. Yet, that moment seemed far in the future.

Until 1894 Barrès simply stayed on the fringes of socialism, but in September, 1894, he became political director of the Paris daily, La Cocarde, turned it into a socialist newspaper, and plunged into socialism. In his brief direction of La Cocarde, he showed the kind of contribution he could make to socialism. His literary prestige made the newspaper perhaps the liveliest member of the socialist press. It also brought to socialist readers a wide variety of writers, who were certain to influence young intellectuals.

La Cocarde had had a chequered past. Founded as a Boulangist newspaper, it declined and passed from hand to hand until it was bought by a paper merchant who thought that Barrès' literary prestige could make the newspaper prosper. The "new" Cocarde, as it called itself, disclaimed any connection with the old. It asserted that its only past was Maurice Barrès, twice the candidate of "socialist committees." Its future would be dedicated to "republican opposition where socialists and intellectuals will group themselves" and to Barrès' principles of "patriotism and social solidarity."[6] The newspaper was a tabloid in both size and style, with lurid headlines, and an almost daily lead editorial by Barrès, patterned on Francis Magnard's "Echoes" in *Le Figaro*.[7] While *La Cocarde* sought rapid news release with several editions, its news coverage was so thin that it made its mark mainly as a journal of opinion.

La Cocarde's readers would have agreed with the newspaper's characterization of itself as socialist, intellectual, and devoted to Barrès' views of social solidarity. In short, they would have seen it as a socialist newspaper aimed at young intellectuals. With few exceptions, however, those who have written about Barrès' association with *La Cocarde* have not seen it that way at all. Rather than seeing it and Barrès as socialist, they have viewed it as presaging Barrès' right-wing nationalism of a few years later. They have done so for two reasons.

For one thing they have taken the word of Henri Clouard, the newspaper's biographer.[8] Writing in 1910 as a member of the extreme right-wing Action Française, Clouard found a useable past in *La Cocarde*. He made it appear as the harbinger of the Action Française's concern for nationalism and social order. With great selectivity he extensively quoted *La Cocarde* articles by Barrès and others which would show the appropriate Action Française blending of "nationalism" and "socialism" into a kind of proto-fascism. He pointed out that *La Cocarde*'s writers came almost equally from the Left and Right, without indicating that the political commentary came from the Left while the literary criticism came from the Right. He contended that nationalist and socialist meetings regularly were announced side by side, although such parallel announcements or any publicity for nationalist meetings occured most infrequently. He claimed that the thrust of Barrès' writings was toward nationalism, not socialism, disregarding Barrès' socialist writings and the fact that every issue was filled with one socialist article after another by *La Cocarde*'s other writers.

After his career did become rightist, Barrès carefully disavowed his *La Cocarde* socialism and, in doing so, reinforced Clouard's interpretation. When Barrès selected newspaper articles for inclusion in books, he chose only those which continued to have relevance for the later nationalist movement. This was even true of the collection of essays, drawn both from *La Cocarde* and *Le Journal* of 1894–1895, which appeared as *De Hegel aux cantines du Nord* (1904). This was also in keeping with the Barrès comment, made about the same time: "In *La Cocarde* I traced all my program of nationalism."[9]

With the exception of Zeev Sternhell,[10] most writers have followed the judgement of Clouard and Barrès. For Eugen Weber, Barrès' *Cocarde* "first gave nationalism and socialism the chance to meet in print" through the efforts of "such unlikely companions as René Boylesve, Charles Maurras, Frédéric Amouretti, Camille Mauclair, and extreme syndicalists like Augustin Hamon and Fernand Pelloutier."[11] For Barrès' chief living French disciple, Pierre de Boisdeffre, *La Cocarde* was "a little nationalist and anti-Semitic newspaper which announces the Action Française" and which mixes "socialist themes and a Hegelian sensibility that one will find fifteen years later among Georges Sorel and his school."[12] For Robert Soucy there was "conservative ballast underlying Barrès' socialism" in the "superpatriotic" *Cocarde* which was much closer to the "socialism" of later fascism than it was to French socialism of the 1890s.[13]

These views of Barrès and *La Cocarde* are correct, of course, if one reads history from back to front. Because Barrès did become a rightist, there are bound to be connections between his writings in *La Cocarde* and that end of the political spectrum. On the other hand, if all one knew about Barrès was what he said and wrote from the early 1880s to the end of his editorship of *La Cocarde* in 1895, and if one was thoroughly grounded in what recognized French socialists believed in 1895, one could only conclude that Barrès and *La Cocarde* were socialist in 1894–1895. The fact that Barrès abandoned socialism for right-wing nationalism, however, both presents the major Barrès problem, so often overlooked, and makes an understanding of his thought and influence difficult. It means that one has to establish that he was a socialist in 1894–1895. Then, one has to explain why he gave socialism up for nationalism and the Right.

122

The difficulties of understanding *La Cocarde* can be removed if one analyzes three aspects of the newspaper described in its credo: intellectual stance, politics, and Barrès. As Clouard and those who followed him maintained, the newspaper's writers spread completely across the political spectrum, but the right-wingers like Hugues Rebell, Charles Maurras, and Georges Bonnamour wrote almost exclusively on literary themes. Although Maurras rarely wrote a political article on decentralization, a count of *La Cocarde* writers by article content should demonstrate to any reader that its right-wingers were literary men, not political ones. Only in the arts did *La Cocarde*'s writers see a wedding of Left and Right, and fully a third of the newspaper's daily fare covered them. Aside from Bonnamour, Maurras, and Camille Mauclair, no single contributors stand out quantitatively, but the newspaper's galaxy of symbolist poets, novelists, and critics included, in addition to those already named, Paul Bourget, Lucien Muhlfeld, and Gustave Kahn. The inclusion of the last two makes it difficult to charge *La Cocarde* with anti-Semitism. Put together, all these intellectuals, be they Left or Right politically, made the newspaper one of the liveliest literary journals in the decline of symbolism.

If one also counts the political articles, looks at their ideological content, and observes who wrote them, it becomes obvious that the newspaper's political articles, with hardly any exception, were socialist. Daily, *La Cocarde*'s readers were presented with several political articles, in addition to Barrès' political editorial. The most frequent contributors included the future editor of *La Revue socialiste* and author of a volume in Jaurès' *Histoire socialiste*, Eugène Fournière; Barrès' old friends from Boulangism like Pierre Denis and Alfred Gabriel; the "poet socialist" Deputy from Paris and sometime Boulangist, Clovis Hugues; longtime follower of Guesde and Vaillant and women's rights militant, Paule Minck; Barrès' apparent protégé, Paul Pascal; and follower of Malonist Independent Socialism, Paul Lagarde. During their stay at *La Cocarde*, Fournière, Hugues, and Minck contributed the same kind of articles to *La Petite République* of Jaurès and Millerand. Numerous other

123

socialists contributed to *La Cocarde* less frequently, and no less a personage than Fernand Pelloutier, founder of the *Confédération générale du travail*, covered the trade union congress of Nantes (1894) in several articles. While there may be doubts as to what kind of socialism Barrès, Gabriel, and Denis had, Fournière, Minck, and Pelloutier had the genuine article.

Even if *La Cocarde*'s political writers were socialists personally, can the content of their articles and the whole newspaper, itself, be given the same label? Given that the "multiplicity" of French socialism of 1894–1895 was reflected in *La Cocarde*'s writers, what definite and specifically socialist tenets did the newspaper contain? To be a socialist, whether Marxist or otherwise, one has to hold certain minimum beliefs: one has to have some kind of class analysis of society, however vague it be; one has to believe economics and property relationships are the keys to restructuring society, whether that rebuilding be collectivist or cooperativist; and finally one has to have a vision of a just future order as an alternative to the existing unjust capitalist one, although varied tactics can be used to reach it.

Individually and collectively these political articles of *La Cocarde* held to these basic socialist beliefs. They were completely clear that the problems of injustice lay with capitalism and its parliamentary system. To be sure, the ex-Boulangists were more hostile to parliamentarianism than were the socialists, but all were critical of the capitalistic system. They were as unclear as socialism generally on whether the solution would bring centralism and collectivism or decentralization and cooperatives, although the latter method, especially consumer cooperatives, had the edge in support. All, however, advocated the immediate collectivization of mines, railroads, and banks. All supported progressive income and corporation taxes. All opposed "machinism" and the dehumanization brought by machine society.

While *La Cocarde*'s political writers agreed on basic socialist principles, they presented their readers with a lively variety and vitality. Fournière, for example, could be suspicious of producer cooperatives, because of the large capital outlay needed to establish them. Consumer cooperatives, on the other hand, could rapidly ease the lot of workers with very little capital, "and we must not omit anything which can lighten the misery of the workers."[14] Gabriel could call for the replacement of a salaried class by a "more and more collectivist general workers association" even though "this evolution will be for the future."[15] Socialism would be achieved, he wrote on another occasion, "only after a violent upheaval. Universal suffrage is a worn out instrument."[16] Pierre Denis could condemn those collectivists who believed that industrialization had brought indispensible social progress. "The progress realized is pauperism, bankruptcies, unemployment, servile labor, and misery. It seems to me that humanity can do very well without all that progress."[17] No one personified the infinite variety of *La Cocarde* better than Fournière, however, when he wrote:

> I am collectivist when I see factories, mines and railroads in use, produced by armies of workers and exploited by grasping capitalists . . . I am a cooperativist because the State does not seem to me to be completely cleansed of the taint which centuries of authoritarian abuse have given it . . . I am individualistic for the engraver, the writer . . . I am communalist because I find it absurd not to be able to set up a gas lamp at the corner of a street without the approval of the State . . . I am centralist because I do not want the absolute political and judicial autonomy of the provinces imposing its inequities.[18]

That may be ideologically confused, but it is socialism—at least French socialism of the 1890s. It typifies the politics of *La Cocarde*, both totally and day by day, and Fournière's authorship of it further testifies to its ideologically correct position. In short, *La Cocarde*'s content was neither "national-socialist," proto-fascist, corporativist, or "reformist." It was socialist, but open and tolerant to all socialist schools.

Barrès' ability to fill the pages of *La Cocarde* with views of such a varied group of political and literary writers resulted, first of all, from his capacity to recruit old Boulangists, like Denis and Gabriel, whose views were no longer welcome at any other newspaper. Second, there was Barrès' faculty for recruiting socialists untainted by Boulangism, like Fournière. This came from the enormous stature Barrès had attained by the 1890s with young intellectuals of both Left and Right. During the Paris student uprising of July, 1893, for example, a group of students seeking parliamentary help for their cause addressed an appeal to Barrès as "the most eminent representative of intelligent youth."[19] Alexandre Zévaès, the future Guesdist, described Barrès as the most influential and popular writer among the students of the Latin Quarter in the early 1890s, lauded his socialist articles of 1890 in *Le Figaro*, spoke warmly of *La Cocarde*, and concluded that "Maurice Barrès drew me out of the Latin Quarter."[20] Joseph Paul-Boncour wrote that Barrès' "influence on us was incontestable," especially through his writings in *La Cocarde* and his socialist campaign at Neuilly in 1896.[21] Léon Blum, a frequent visitor to Barrès' home in the 1890s, recalled, "I am sure that [Barrès] had for me a true fondness, a solicitude of an older brother . . . He was for me, as for most of my associates, not only the master, but the guide. We formed around him a school, almost a court."[22]

Many of these men had been drawn to Barrès as a result of the doctrine of the *Culte du moi*, the need for individual fulfillment outside oneself, expressed, of course, in the novels, but also in frequent newspaper articles as early as 1889.[23] In them Barrès attacked the educational system for isolating the student from the working class. Boarding schools, with their valets and maids, made it difficult for the student to fit into his post-graduate economic status. Either way, the schools and their hot-house atmosphere did not prepare students for real life. More than that, the schools and student organizations bred conformity. In associations, students conformed to a standard of mediocrity and vulgarity. Added to this was their increasing difficulty of finding jobs after graduation. "Bohemians of yesterday, déclassés of today, only pitiful people in frock coats: a *proletariat des bacheliers*," they formed "an enormous revolutionary force."[24] Barrès urged young men to break out of this isolation and conformist mediocrity, to search for individual fulfillment by getting out of themselves and into, first, Boulangism and, later, socialism. Doubtless, Zévaès, Blum, and Paul-Boncour had agreed, as had many of *La Cocarde*'s writers.

On his part, Barrès could welcome the diversity of his writers because he valued them as intellectuals, giving them that very name. An intellectual, he wrote in contrast to his condemnation of the intellectuals of the Dreyfus affair, is "a man who has had the good fortune to receive an integral education" and who, because of his concern "to lift all humanity to intellectuality," seeks a social transformation.[25] He later wrote that the young intellectuals of *La Cocarde* were men who "came quite naturally to carry the curiosities and moral uneasiness" of earlier "psychologues" and "analysts," like the Goncourts, Taine, and Renan, "into dreams of social transformation. One saw it clearly at *La Cocarde*, where numerous young men were impassioned with sociology."[26] At any rate this approach certainly made *La Cocarde* lively reading and added to Barrès' stature and influence.

If the political content of *La Cocarde* was socialist and written by socialists while its coverage of the arts was done by writers of both Left and Right, what about the third part of the newspaper's credo, its dedication to the ideas of Barrès? Certainly the newspaper's major importance was as a vehicle for his ideas, shared in part by all his writers. These ideas revealed a second stage in the ideological growth of Barrès—his attempt to formulate systematically a personal socialism of his own.

In the early issues of *La Cocarde*, Barrès first stated what any ideology, be it socialist or not, had to proclaim if it were to win his support. "Free and profound individualism," he wrote, "social solidarity, there are the two concerns of our ideal." This was, of course, hardly a new idea in his thought. In simpler form it had been the central notion in the *Culte du moi*, just as it would be the unifying principle in all his writings: individualism through anarchy was not fulfilling; full individuality could not come from one's self alone; true selfhood resulted from identifying oneself with society.

By individualism Barrès now meant "total liberation" [*affranchissement*, his favorite term in *La Cocarde*] which would

127

satisfy not only the economic and bodily needs of the individual. Each person also had to bring all his powers into action, recognize his vocation, "single out his likings, conform himself to his destiny."[27] As if echoing the young Marx's concern with alienation, he agreed with Marx that for the individual fulfillment of the worker, at least, economic liberation was necessary. Yet, Barrès felt the Marxist analysis fell short of explaining why the economically privileged young bourgeois could not find self fulfillment. Had he been familiar with the young Marx's writings on alienation, of course, he would have known that Marx, too, was concerned with bourgeois alienation and held that it, too, was rooted in capitalism. Instead, Barrès viewed the problem of individual liberation as double, necessitating economic emancipation for the worker and educational liberation for the bourgeois. The latter needed deliverance from a hide-bound educational system which bred conformity and isolation and which poorly prepared him for the struggles of life.[28]

All this sounds as if Barrès had come under some Marxian influence, and indeed he had. The source doubtless was a book by G. Platon, probably *Le Droit de propriété dans la société franque et en Germanie*, published at Paris in 1890. Barrès was enough taken by this book to recommend it wholeheartedly and write two articles on it. He summarized Platon's position as follows: from the earliest warfare of tribe against tribe there has been a hierarchical social structure with class struggle. With the French Revolution the capitalist class conquered the state. "In place of the culture and philosophy of the Church, it substituted its philosophy, the culture of the State. At the same time it took possession of other social functions: justice, police, administration. All that is the property of the capitalist class." During the nineteenth century with its "division of labor resting on science," the capitalist class became all important, all powerful, and international in operation, using all its power to exploit the workers. Yet, the workers had the potential to end capitalist exploitation by following the capitalist example of invoking the revolutionary heritage, which included the vote, and by organizing themselves as effectively as international capital.[29] While Barrès could accept, at this point of his career, Marxian class analysis of society and the primacy of property relationships in determining social structure, Marxism would always conflict with that first part of his ideal, individualism.

That conflict would also shape the second part of his stated ideal, social solidarity. By social solidarity Barrès meant the corporate determination to create the conditions capable of emancipating the individual. His discussion of it marked a considerably further development of the *Culte du moi*, and would seem to place him either into Radical or socialist politics. Indeed, in several articles, published separately much later as *De Hegel aux cantines du Nord*, he discussed the ability of these two parties to solve the problem he had set forth. As to an immediate program he found himself in agreement with both René Goblet of the Radicals and with Jaurès. Like them he stood for nationalization of mines, railroads, and the Bank of France and tax reform.[30] Yet, that was as close as he could come to Radicalism. Its legislative program was perfectly acceptable, but it had no view of the ideal society toward which the legislation would lead and toward which the party would educate the voters.[31] Any party which wanted Barrès' support had to have such an ideal.

In contrast, socialism did have such an ideal, Barrès thought—the transformation of society. What Barrès said he learned from Taine, as Jaurès had learned from Marx, was that "our epoch is a moment of an evolution which, under the pressure of the same causes which produced capitalism, conducts us toward a situation that Marx calls collectivism." Because of that, Barrès was convinced that the people supported the Radical and socialist legislative program only because it was the indispensable station "on the path to the ideal." "The people wants to be presented with complete social perfection . . . What impassions us is not the introduction of a little harmony into the world, it is the journey toward complete justice, liberty, and harmony." Barrès then made the interesting observation that many so-called socialists, at heart only advanced Radicals, would be horrified by "the immediate and complete application of the doctrine which they sanction. What pleases them in socialism . . . is its ability to give them an important role in the

129

history of the universe; it permits them to consider themselves as a moment in a sublime evolution, as workers for the great and final social harmony: it keeps them nearer the ideal." In spite of the contradiction, socialists were wise to champion the people's ideal. In so doing, it was necessary to operate on two fronts: legislate for the present intermediate stage; then educate the people for the final stage of social perfection.[32] This was purely practical, Barrès believed, in that the people's desire for an ideal had all the aspects of a religious faith. Because voting was "more a movement of faith than one of personal reflection," socialists had to put themselves with the people by "embracing large hopes."[33]

In his discussion of the need for an ideal and the incapacity of the Radicals to formulate such an ideal, Barrès showed himself heavily under the influence of Jean Jaurès, even to imagining a debate between Jaurès and Goblet, willingly making the former the obvious victor in the argument. But the ideal Barrès embraced was not collectivism.[34] Much as he was willing to be convinced by the "verbal force, fluency, and evident conviction" of Jaurès that collectivism would not "crush us under a uniform dictatorship," Jaurès could not allay Barrès' fears of "this immense dictatorial infinity that Marxism was able to be."[35] Barrès could accept the Marxist interpretation of history, but not its plan for the future. "The Marxists," he wrote, "are not content with the forceful analysis of the successive forms of property: they pretend to formulate what will be the future and to bring us under this formula."[36] This did not mean, however, that Barrès was ready to go to war against collectivism. To be sure, collectivism, for him, was only one "hypothesis" of social transformation, just as Darwin's theory was a hypothesis for biological transformation, supported by the "collectivist socialists" of *La Petite République*. Yet, he still wanted to cooperate with the collectivists as well as with the Radicals. "On the ideal," as he put it, "each of us has his views, the sincere expression of his temperament. It is necessary to let the future ferment in our brains. But on the immediate work . . . it is necessary that we take a common view of the first stage."[37]

130

If, in Barrès' mind, Radicalism lacked an ideal, anarchism negated solidarity, and collectivism destroyed the individual, what could achieve individualism and solidarity? For an answer, Barrès apparently had turned first to the French Utopians Fourier and Saint Simon—if we are to believe his socialist novel of 1892, *L'Ennemi des lois*—but by the time of *La Cocarde* he had come to Proudhon. Proudhon did have an ideal, one which Barrès saw as a Hegelian synthesis of Marx's collectivist thesis of solidarity and Bakunin's anarchist antithesis of individualism. In Proudhon's desire for "federalism and contract" lay the solution. "It is federalism," Barrès wrote, "which best respects the diversities and disagreements of the physical and moral universe. It is contract [i.e. the voluntary and free association of man with other men] which permits the 'self' to arrange tolerable relations with other 'selves.' "[38] Barrès never tired of quoting Proudhon's dictum: "Who says republic and does not say federation says nothing; who says liberty and does not say federation says nothing; who says socialism and does not say federation still says nothing."

Barrès further believed that federalism was thoroughly rooted in French tradition. Federalism had been supported by the Girondins, many of whose ideas were incorporated into the Jacobin constitution of the Year II; by the 1871 Commune movements in Paris, Lyon, and Marseille; by moderate leaders such as Léon Say, Aynard, and Deschanel; by Radicals in their support of municipal autonomy; by socialists like Millerand and Abel Hovelacque, who proposed in 1890 to divide France into eighteen regions; and by a variety of literary men as varied as the Provençal poet Frédéric Mistral and Hippolyte Taine.[39] Yet, Barrès believed, Proudhon always remained the master of it.

In what can only be described as federalist socialism, Barrès held that the "inevitable social transformation" would not come from some scientific authority, but "in multiplying the fields of experiences, in restoring autonomy to moral and geographical groups." Such groups would adhere to both individualism and solidarity: "The individual who follows to the end his instinct of expansion has a tendency to assemble and join in solidarity with others according to his electoral affinities, his needs, his aptitudes, and his kinships in a social body, and thus to become a unity in a larger individuality, in a hundred individualities, local and moral groups."[40] On the one hand, society would organize itself into local or geographical groups according to communes, regions, nations, and so on: "Families of individuals, there are the communes; family of communes, there is the region; family of regions, there is the nation; family of nations, socialist citizens, there is the federal humanity." These regional groups would recognize national unity, national constitutional guarantees to the individual, and national control of war and peace, tariffs, national bonds, and regulation of nationwide business enterprise. The commune, on the other hand, would have the right "to buy, sell, borrow, decree, and vote its budget by itself without authorization, to provide for its poor and its roads, and to finance and direct its schools without governmental intervention."[41] Barrès was not clear on the size or location of these regions, but he did insist that they be viable units with a realistic common bond in economics, tradition, and culture. Marseille, for example, filled the bill to be the center of all Provence. Whatever their size or location, these regions would finance themselves through direct taxes on incomes and profits, thus facilitating long overdue tax reform, while leaving indirect taxation with the national government. Regions would also have local legislative assemblies and utilize the referendum to keep the people closer to governmental decisions.[42]

Barrès was less specific with respect to another aspect of decentralization, the moral groups. His discussion of them was limited to some variation of this passage:

> Federation and contract! Geographic groups (regions, communes), moral groups (*agrégations professionnelles ou* [sometimes *et*] *de tous ordres*), are dependent only on themselves in a federation and are directed internally through contracts analogous to transactions and exchanges.

That passage was always followed by the comment that such an arrangement would prevent restraint, combine liberty and socialism, or allow "that free play which we insist on for the essential social precaution."[43] Again, reference was always paid to Proudhon's ideas on the same subject. Apparently, Barrès simply accepted the Proudhonian scheme of "free contract." At any rate, the whole point of the moral groups, as well as the regional ones, was to restore man's ability to cooperate with others in a society based on free association. This would be possible, Barrès believed, if the moral groups were simply allowed to exist and to be strong. As it was, laws prevented strong moral groups from emerging. Although Barrès did not bring it up in these articles, one gets the feeling that his ideas were predicated on what he learned at Nancy, where the unions were weak because they were forbidden by law to own the means of production. Remove such barriers and society would no longer be an "artificial creation." Instead, it would be based on "the spontaneous instinct of the individuals composing it," those who had regained their "faculties of cohesion" through free association.[44] In this plan, Barrès believed, "I go farther than the Marxist dream. With great good fortune I catch a glimpse of that spontaneous organization of society as Proudhon saw it, conforming itself to harmony through the simple play of natural necessities rather than under the pressure of laws."[45]

Convinced as he was that the socialist ideal would arrive in stages, Barrès believed that his federalistic socialism was the best and fastest path to an ideal society in which man could fulfill his highest individual potential in harmony with others. Yet, Barrès was just as convinced that man was still unprepared for that ideal state. Man had to relearn the cooperation he had forgotten, and he could not relearn it in the mass, in a national framework. Because localities knew their needs better than central authority ever would, because the members of the localities were close to each other and to the immediate situation, there was the logical place to relearn cooperation.[46] In such a way, the communes and regions would act as "laboratories of sociology:"

> It is there that we will have political and economic experiences, tried in modest proportions, then generalized, not by acts of decree or mass laws, but through the spontaneous imitation of

133

neighboring cities and regions, witnesses of the good or bad effects obtained here or there.[47]

In other words, peculiar local conditions and problems would have peculiar local solutions, and more varied solutions could be tested with fewer risks of big mistakes. Regional groups might formulate plans for unemployment compensation and old age pensions, perhaps on the Swiss model of employee-employer contributions.[48] With the same reasoning, he supported the unsuccessful attempt at Roubaix to create a municipal pharmacy.[49] Moreover, these sociological laboratories would more firmly root the ideal end in ideal means. Barrès was aware that teaching harmony and cooperation would be a struggle, but he was also convinced that community could be restored only if social solutions were arrived at spontaneously by the people involved. It was far easier, he believed, to learn cooperation with a close neighbor than with a distant one, far easier to support community and corporate solutions than ones imposed from the outside.

To bring this about, Barrès also visualized a *Parti national et social*. The party would galvanize France to decentralize political institutions. It would also renew society by encouraging existing "multiple organisms" to modify themselves "according to their needs and their aptitudes." These could do so if they were freed from central authority.[50] Again, this seems to recall the situation in Nancy where Gabriel had argued in 1892 that local socialist majorities could effect social reforms even when the national majority was anti-socialist. Even national legislation for national problems, such as the joint legislative program of the Radicals and socialists, would serve both as immediate social amelioration and long-range education toward the ideal society.

One cannot but be struck by the enormous influence of Proudhon on this program. The very vagueness in the discussion of the moral groups, particularly, indicates that Barrès assumed that his readers would know he accepted the Proudhonist scheme completely. Admittedly drawn to Proudhon through Taine's concern for the breakdown of reciprocity,

134

Barrès shared the Proudhonist regard for individualism, its aim to achieve justice rather than collectivism, its opposition to the centralized state and parliamentary government, its fascination with contradictions (such as the tension between the individual and society), its belief that such contradictions were the very stuff of life and should not be abolished, its petit bourgeois orientation in which peasants and shopkeepers were the leaders of the proletariat, its desire for associations to preserve rather than abolish individual freedom, and its concern for the utilization of Rousseauian sentiment rather than reason to bring justice. At the same time, Barrès showed little affinity for the Proudhonist idealization of the family. Rather, the moral group itself would be the basic unit. Nor did he utilize Proudhon's credit system. Rather, Barrès believed that the right to incorporate and to own property was all the associations needed. Finally, he saw Proudhon not as an anarchist, but as a socialist.[51]

Even though Barrès called his program socialistic, its details and closeness to Proudhon made it appear closer to the corporative schemes of the 1890s than to socialism. Yet, one can look in vain for such influences. Once he used the term "corporation," but in this period he never mentioned the major corporative theorists such as René de La Tour du Pin, Albert de Mun, Jean Paul Mazaroz, Emile Durkheim, or Léon Duguit.[52] For Barrès in his newspaper articles, speeches, and *Mes Cahiers*, the journal he kept from 1896 on, the master was always Proudhon. The social Catholic corporativists were suspect because they distrusted individualism. Nor did Barrès couch his ideas in their religious terms. The aim of the moral and geographical groups was to liberate the free expansion of the individual, not to promote Christian brotherhood.

Apparently the only corporative thinker to have influenced Barrès at all was Frédéric Le Play. A *Cocarde* writer said that its staff agreed with Le Play on decentralization, on "the necessity to favor individual initiative, and on several details on the conditions of the workers."[53] Yet, Le Play was too much the darling of liberal critics of socialism for Barrès to be committed to him. Indeed, he vigorously attacked a series of lectures for

135

university youth by a Committee of Defense and Social Progress, sponsored by the liberal Anatole Leroy-Beaulieu, Albert
Gigot, Georges Picot, and Paul Desjardins, which had adapted
the laissez faire features of Le Play into a paternalistic phi-
lanthropy as the answer to socialism.[54]

If *La Cocarde's* long range purpose was to serve as the medium
of Barrès' political and social ideas, its immediate purpose was
to convince the public to get rid of the existing parliamentary
regime. For Barrès, political reconstruction was the first step to
social reconstruction. He started out with only the anti-Panama argument that the parliament was run by that "filthy band"
of bribe-takers. From then on his attacks on the day by day
conduct of the government were couched in anti-parliamentary tirades. The deputies were "ignorant, malicious, basely
docile, mediocre, without ideas or conscience, sometimes cun-
ning."[55] They were a "band of lawyers" forming the "putrification
and mediocrity of that parliament which depresses everything," a "despised assembly . . . composed of nullities and
scoundrels."[56] "The system is rotten, the regime has fallen to
the ground. Long live the republic! Parliamentarianism is no
more than a game for the Assizes. Its stall is reserved at Noumea."[57] He regularly attacked the Dupuy ministry and the
Casimir-Perier presidency, insisting that the former had his
"gang" while the latter his "society" but that both were part of
the Wilson-Grévy-Panama band. *La Cocarde* greeted the resignation of Casimir-Perier with the observation that he "had been
chosen by the entire reactionary syndicate" and had come "to
be the instrument of supreme resistance against the ideas of
social renovation and against the manifestations of public contempt merited by a regime and a personnel sunk in scandal and
shame."[58] In early 1895 Barrès hotly pursued the parliamentary
inquest of the railway conventions of 1883, seeing in it a new
Panama scandal in which the railroad companies had bribed
politicians and newspapers to withhold the terms of the government guarantees of the company bonds.[59] "I swear to you
that if a Boulanger reappeared," he wrote on the exposure of
the railroad conventions, "our 'republican aristocracy' would
no longer find anyone to defend it. Neither bandits, nor brave
men."[60] With such men in power, the only way to bring about

social reconstruction was to cleanse the parliament of all the corruption since the days of Gambetta, whom Barrès very much admired. This could be done either by the real application of universal suffrage, through the elimination of the Senate's "veto," or through the rise of a new Boulanger. Turn out the parliamentary clique who claimed to be the followers of Gambetta, but who were really traitors to him and the true followers of Morny and republicanized Orleanists.[61] "The end is *social transformation*; the method is *everything through universal suffrage*; the immediate way is cleansing."[62]

Unfortunately socialists did not have the majority necessary to effect the cleansing. To get the necessary majority, Barrès sought an alliance as broad as Boulangism and extending from socialists of all schools through those Radical-Socialists who were not tainted with Opportuno-Radicalism to nationalists and anti-Semites. Thus, he could praise Rochefort, Millerand, Jaurès, and Ernest Roche as "voices of spirit, justice, and independence."[63] At the same time, he could welcome an alliance between Millerand and the Radical Goblet, "an honest man execrated by his dishonored colleagues."[64] He could also claim Déroulède as one of his "masters" (along with Proudhon, Quinet, and Michelet) and a man of valor, honesty, and eloquence.[65] He could also praise the decentralization league of the Radical deputies Charles Beauquier and Maurice Faure as being a start in the right direction.[66] At the reception for the amnestied Rochefort, Barrès stood with Jaurès, Viviani, and Millerand to hear the old Communard and Boulangist praise *La Cocarde*.[67] Within the next few days, *La Cocarde* also sent representatives to welcome the return of the Allemanist Jules Breton, and Barrès, himself, headed a delegation honoring the returning anti-Semitic Drumont, "the untiring struggler against the Panamists, the intriguers of parliament, and financial speculators."[68] While Barrès consistently praised the leadership of Jaurès, given a choice his loyalties remained with those socialists of a Boulangist past. Typically, he and *La Cocarde* supported an old Boulangist at a Paris parliamentary by-election in December, 1894, but rallied to Léon Gérault-Richard, the *Union socialiste* candidate, in the run-off.[69]

Immediately after Barrès left *La Cocarde* in March, 1895, after arguing with the newspaper's financer, his ideas of federalistic socialism appeared to be taking him completely into the socialist movement. In 1895, some of his followers founded a National Republican League of Decentralization, headed by Deshayes de Marcère, the foremost writer in the decentralization campaign of *La Nouvelle Revue*. The new organization was very much under the influence of Barrès' ideas.[70] Through it and local organizations, Barrès made two major speeches, summarizing his *Cocarde* writings, at Bordeaux on June 29, 1895, and Marseille on October 1, 1895. In reviewing the Bordeaux speech, *Assainissement et fédéralisme*, Paul Lagarde described it as *"une belle conférence"* and identified Barrès with all the socialist decentralizers like Paul Pascal, Paul Brousse, and Georges Renard.[71] When *La Revue socialiste* reprinted the speech in pamphlet form, Adrien Veber agreed that Barrès was motivated by socialism when he desired economic justice through federalism, even though there were other motives as well: federalism would provide a vehicle for reconciling patriots with the socialist internationalists, a way to achieve political cleansing, and a path to individualism.[72] That verdict was not unanimous. Charles Maurras, who accompanied Barrès to Marseille, recalled that the speech before a largely socialist audience had been greeted with little enthusiasm because Barrès was too much the aristocrat.[73]

Even so, the overall effect of the speeches was to advance Barrès' ideas. With the speeches and *La Cocarde* as a base, Barrès co-sponsored with the Portuguese socialist Sebastian Magalhaēs-Lima a federalist and internationalist conference in Paris on November 5, 1895. It was attended by such varied French socialists and non-socialist decentralizers as Paule Minck, Victor Jaclard, Rodolphe Simon, Paul Lagarde, Camile Mauclair, Marcel Sembat, Leopold Lacour, Charles Maurras, and Frédéric Amouretti. Georges Renard, director of *La Revue socialiste*, adhered to the conference.[74] Such a varied group of French and international delegates could not even agree, however, on whether federalism was to be among nations, such as a Balkan or Iberian federation, or within a nation, such as a French federation. Nor could they agree whether internationalism meant an alliance of nations or the destruction of nationalities.[75] At any rate, this activity prompted one observer to say, "Maurice Barrès, Independent Socialist, makes at this time an active campaign for federalism."[76]

Yet, it was not to be. Barrès' tendency to draw ever closer to the socialist movement reached its zenith in the 1894—1895 campaign of *La Cocarde* and the federalist conferences. His political activity in 1896 and the socialist movement's reaction to it would make that patently obvious. The fact remains, however, that even as he approached socialism there were elements in his thought which made it impossible for him ever to be a real socialist for long.

What made it difficult if not impossible for Barrès to accept real socialism and for it to accept him was that he, like Sartre's Hugo Barine in *Dirty Hands*, got into it "by the wrong door." He joined the socialist movement, as Hugo joined communism, "so that all men, secretaries or not, could have the right to respect themselves some day."[77] To be sure he had joined by a somewhat more circuitous route than Hugo, the route described in the *Culte du moi*: rootlessness demanded commitment, fulfillment of the self required reaching out to the masses, and socialism would set both them and him (as well as rootless young bourgeois intellectuals like him) free. Barrès' individualism, like Hugo's, demanded a pure ideal to give him the energy to fulfill the self, and socialism had such an ideal. These are both bad and dangerous reasons for going into socialism, as Hoederer told Hugo:

> Purity is an idea for a yogi or a monk. You intellectuals and bourgeois anarchists use it as a pretext for doing nothing. To do nothing, to remain motionless, arms at your sides, wearing kid gloves. Well, I have dirty hands. Right up to the elbows. I've plunged them in filth and blood . . . . Your purity resembles death. The revolution you dream of is not ours. You don't want to change the world, you want to blow it up . . . An intellectual is never a real revolutionary; just good enough to make an assassin.[78]

Barrès, like Hugo, had come to socialism not because he was hungry and oppressed but because it was the fashionable thing to do: it was an intellectual exercise.

Just the same, there was always the possibility that Barrès, despite his wrong reasons for joining socialism, could develop the right ones. Many intellectuals did. That Barrès could not do so was due, most of all, to his way of knowing things. He did not come to socialism by way of rational analysis, but through sensitivity, sensibility, feelings, Bérénice's intuition, the creative energy and life force of the masses. Reason was not to be trusted. The trouble with that, as Alasdair MacIntyre said in criticising Herbert Marcuse, is that "a man may be rational who holds many false beliefs and a man may have true beliefs and yet be irrational. What is crucial is that the former has the possibility of progressing toward truth, while the second not only has no grounds for asserting what he believes, even though it is true, but is continually likely to acquire false beliefs."[79] The irrational individualism of the *Culte du moi* could take Barrès and the youth who idolized him into socialism, but it could just as easily take them anywhere. Barrésian individualism was a life style and not an ideology. Its way of knowing things was a perilous one if it drew its holder into a rationalist ideology. Socialism, whether its economic and social analysis was Marxist or not, was just such a rationalist ideology. For Barrès or the Barrésians to stay in socialism for long, they would have to shuck off their earlier methodology.

Nothing presaged the inevitable conflict between socialism and Barrès' reasons for becoming a socialist like his novel, *L'Ennemi des lois* (1892). It was his first and last socialist novel, and coming as it did a year after *Le Jardin de Bérénice*, it is a complete extension of the *Culte du moi*. The protagonist and *porte parole* of Barrès is no longer Philippe, but André Maltère, a teacher at the Ecole des Hautes Etudes and editor of a socialist newspaper. Caught up in arrests following an anarchist bombing, he defends himself by describing his socialism and his role in it. Rather than encouraging revolution he sees that revolution "blows us away like chaff."[80]

> Violence is useless and reprehensible. Reprehensible because there is no place for molesting men, guilty only of holding as truth principles which became outdated twenty-four hours ago. Useless, since the same people recommending [violence] do not believe that dynamiting a "bourgeois" will destroy the so-

cial condition which created him. Their bombs only serve as signaling shots for calling their ideas to the attention of a thousand persons of whom five or six will be converted. Rather, good conferences, clear brochures, and debate itself seem to me to be more effective means of propaganda.[81]

To that point the Barrès-Maltère view seems to be sound socialism, somewhat defensive about the anarchist outrages, but Barrès' way of knowing things increasingly gets in the way. As early as the introduction he wrote, "It is not systems that we need, but energy: energy to conform our ways of doing things to our ways of feeling."[82] To the court, Maltère applies the dictum to himself in words almost identical to Philippe's in the *Culte du moi*. He is a socialist because he wants "the free flight of all [his] faculties and to give its complete sense to the word 'exist.' " This desire to be a "free man" makes him, he admits, an "egoist." To succeed at selfhood, however, he believes it necessary to put himself in harmony "with other men and with their dreams," to "use the intelligence and education that I received against society," and "to associate them with the efforts of all men."[83]

Convicted just the same, this notoriety gained from his trial makes Maltère, if not the toast of Paris, at least the darling of two remarkably dissimilar young ladies. A well-born professor's daughter desires to learn socialism from him at first hand, while a Russian princess yearns only for his love. After giving the former a brief course in the ideas of Saint Simon, Proudhon, and Fourier, apparently drawn from commentaries, Maltère typically fulfills his "self" by reclining in the arms of the latter lady amid the sensual beauties of Venice. He returns to Paris and marries the professor's daughter while maintaining the other relationship.

The honeymooners rush off to Germany to study German socialism in the land of its birth. The lesson in Lassalle is very simple. Maltère merely shows the young lady a photograph of the socialist. "She recoils in horror. He had, in effect, a bad appearance, ghastly and envious, of a Jewish banker and marked with all the signs of a disputer with neither expansiveness nor generous movement."[84] It takes them considerably longer with

141

Marx, but he is ultimately dismissed because he was a Jew. Jews, thanks to their persecution, never developed "the notion of the point of honor or that of justice." They think only as logicians, though excellent ones, and only "calculate forces." As a result, Marx hung all his thought on economic forces to the exclusion of "pity, justice, enthusiasm," and judged "the appeal to the heart hardly compatible with pure reason, the expression of economic forces."[85] For Maltère, as for Barrès, the Marxists were concerned only with the material world. They had to be tempered with the socialists of the French school who went beyond materialism "to give our sensibility the psychic satisfactions that they demand" and "a complete mental reform."[86]

If that were not bad enough, Maltère-Barrès finds more inspiration in that great German cultivator of "selfhood" King Ludwig II than in the German socialists. Moreover, "the people" never appear in this "socialistic" novel except as personified by a dog, Velu II, who ends up as a laboratory animal, barely escaping with what is left of his life. Although that made Barrès an honorary member of the antivivisection society, Velu II was a strange literary device for a democrat. Maltère, like Barrès, craves his selfhood more than socialism, and socialism is no more important to it than the love of an exotic Russian princess, the pleasures of Venice, the example of Ludwig II, and the rescue of a shaggy dog from the vivisectionist's knife. At least one reviewer of the book, a real socialist, saw through the socialism of Barrès:

> The intellectual education of Maurice Barrès is without system. He selects like a delicate and very bourgeois spiritual idler. Intellectual cosmopolitanism constitutes one of his attributes and selection without serious inquiry one of the deficiencies of M. Barrès.
>
> Is he a socialist? In the sense I give to that word he cannot be called one. Will he become one? I doubt it, for he is not one of those that work attracts and that action captivates. With him the heart masks a respectable inertia.
>
> He will come to us as a momentary political ally and some day he will be astonished to see that we are not psychophobes.[87]

142

If his way of knowing was the most serious flaw in Barrès' path to socialism, it was the most difficult for his contemporary socialists to detect. With *La Cocarde* and his federalist campaign, his other flaws became much easier to see. One was his nationalism, which was at one with his federalistic socialism. Indeed, Barrès even claimed his federalism was derived from his nationalism, for through federalism "each of us is more completely bound to his birthplace, to all that surrounds it."[88] It would make men more patriotic and unify "national energy." Rather than compromising the fatherland, it would make the fatherland "one and indivisible," even though liberty had been given to groups. Federalism would strengthen patriotism by making men masters of their local economy and intellectual life rather than subjects without a real stake in their nation. It would unify national energy if the rest of France shared the economic, cultural, and political spotlight with Paris. The Franco-Prussian War, he argued, saw the defeat of a centralized state, for with the fall of Paris, the seat of the centralized regime, the nation collapsed. On the other hand, it had been the provinces which had saved Spain in 1808.[89]

This nationalistic urge of Barrès added another dimension to his criticism of Marx. The Marxist notion that workers were *"sans patrie"* was every bit as bad as Léon Say's liberal notion of "the planet is a workshop."[90] Barrès argued that history showed just the opposite, that since the sixteenth century, history had moved toward the national state and away from internationalism. Although the ideology of the French Revolution might have been international, its effect only sped the development of the nation. Nationalism, by which he meant common "language and legends," did not need to assert itself by chauvinism. "The socialism really respectful of historical laws and the directions of humanity will limit its effort to the maintenance of harmony in Europe as in each nation." For Barrès, it was as necessary to prevent one nation from crushing another as it was to keep one class from oppressing another within a nation.[91] "Here is our response," he insisted, "to all the objections raised against us by the patriot, for whom only the German problem exists, or the internationalist, who wants to efface all nuances of races: federalism permits us to love the nation without forcing us to hate the foreigner."[92] Although such a view did not preclude some cooperation with the socialist parties of other nations, Barrès was distrustful of any permanent internationalist union of socialists, especially a proposed international congress of socialist parliamentary members.[93]

If Barrès' nationalism was not a flaw to open the eyes of the socialists, his belief that solidarity could come from the utilization of heroes and the "glorification of energy" should have been. Men are won to socialism, not by rational analysis, but by the self-discovery of their own destiny through self-education and solidarity with their fellow-man, region, and nation. One needs "energy" for this and can get it by recognizing his own hero as the "designated intercessor" of his life.[94] By seeking out and following the legends of great men, one can rise to heights not possible otherwise, just as by following a saint the faithful are raised to God. "Great men," Barrès wrote, "are the heroic moments of history, its vivid aspects. We agree that they do not determine events, but are determined by them . . . . But on the imagination, who can deny their victorious power? Sublime educators! Each of us must choose among them his guide, his director, the chief of his breed. They are the intercessors between each of us and our personal ideal."[95] Barrès was convinced that the "flabbiness of public spirit in our epoch," the incapacity of the poor to create a "strong movement," and the tendency for students to become "a collection of aspiring functionaries" were due to a lack of "energy, will, enthusiasm."[96] The cure lay in seeking out a great man to follow in order to integrate individual selfhood with the larger selfhood of the region and nation.[97] Barrès' personal choices were clear; his guides were Napoleon and Loyola, not for their political and religious ideas, but because of their "genius," the "force of their souls," their "interior force."[98] Barrès had no notion of a *führerprinzip* here. He merely meant that socialism needed to rely on more than rationality to win. While a pat on the head and a bone would suffice for Velu II, real voters required socialism to use "exciters of the soul," be they religion or great men.[99]

Considering the vagueness of Barrès' ideas, with their almost

equal parts of federalist-socialism, nationalism, and anti-parliamentarianism, his irrationalist way of knowing, and his willingness to consort with such diverse and antagonistic types as
socialists, Radicals, Boulangists, anti-Semites, and nationalists,
he was not what we customarily call socialist. Yet, all his ideas
were founded on basic principles which can only be called socialist. With the socialists of *La Cocarde*, Barrès did believe in a
class analysis of society, that capitalism alienated both worker
and bourgeois intellectual. He knew that the key to restructuring society was economics and property relationships, although he was perhaps equally convinced that "glorification of
energy" was also helpful. Certainly, his federalistic socialism
was a vision of a just future order to replace the present unjust
capitalistic one. For many a contemporary socialist those facts
were enough to convince them that Barrès was, indeed, a socialist.

Thanks to the strange elements in his socialism, however,
some of his socialist friends began to doubt him by 1895. Although Georges Renard, the editor of *La Revue socialiste*, could
still "salute him as a companion in arms," he warned Barrès to
give up the "perilous ironies of the artist" in his politics and to
sharpen his perception.[100] Eugène Fournière went outside the
pages of *La Cocarde* long enough to caution Barrès that he was
too impatient, too willing to seek a new Boulanger, too distrustful of the people and to hope that Barrès would shed
these views and become a real socialist.[101] Yet, even the tone of
their criticism indicated that no matter how deviant Barrès'
ideas were, they were still subsumed under a socialist rubric.

As it turned out, however, his tendency to draw ever closer to
socialism reached its climax in the 1894—1895 campaign of *La
Cocarde* and the federalist conferences. Events of the following
year, 1896, truly would put Barrès at the crossroads, would
force him to choose the socialist path or some other one. Until
then there was always the possibility that he could outgrow his
irrationalism and the nationalistic debris of his Boulangism
and stay in socialism. Two events of 1896 would demand that
he give up his "purity," as Sartre's Hoederer called it, and get
"dirty hands" if he were to continue in socialism. One was the

CULTURAL REBELLION TO COUNTERREVOLUTION

attempt by French socialists to clarify their ideological position so that the movement could be unified. That clarification would run against certain deeply-held principles of Barrès. The other event of 1896, which like the first would prevent Barrès from staying on the road to socialism, was a political campaign in which the socialist movement opposed him.

The second event of 1896 not only came first in time, but the trauma of it would prepare Barrès to reject the socialist ideology accomplished by the first. In February, 1896, he posed his candidature in a by-election at Neuilly-Boulogne once again. In a field of four serious candidates, Barrès ran against two other socialists. Except for the Blanquist candidate, all had left-of-center programs mild enough to attract Neuilly's moderate majority and radical enough to win Boulogne's socialist vote. Since Barrès had been the principal socialist candidate in 1893, he felt fairly confident of victory, and initial police reports agreed with his judgment.[102] His program seemed designed to meet the electoral mix of the constituency; he proposed graduated taxes other than an income tax detrimental to those residing in high cost-of-living Paris, judicial reform so that the poor could receive justice, abolition of the Senate and individual rather than collective ministerial responsibility, a tax on the employers of foreign workers, separation of Church and State, lukewarm support for consumer cooperatives, and an offer to join the *Union socialiste* if elected. All manner of old Boulangist-cum-socialists and occasional real ones, such as Chassaing and Cluseret, came into the district to campaign for him.[103]

As the campaign unfolded, however, his chances diminished. All the candidates resurrected all the old charges against him: he was a Nancian, the conservative and clerical darling of *Le Figaro*, *Le Siècle*, *Le Libre Parole* and *Le Petit Caporal*, a dilettante, an exotic, and a poor campaigner and silent deputy. Most could be dismissed, but the most telling charge was his opposition to the extremely popular proposed Exposition of 1900, which he had attacked in *Le Figaro* of September 23, 1895 in the name of federalism. Try as he might to claim he merely wanted the exposition neighboring his district in either Auteuil or Courbevoie, this seemingly minor charge was such a hot local issue that it constituted one of the two major factors in his defeat.[104]

The other factor was the introduction into the campaign of a *Union socialiste* candidate, Louis Sautumier, whereas there had been none in 1893. Sautumier was, remarkably, a carbon copy of Barrès. A rich lawyer of conservative background, he had rapidly moved left when he saw the future lay with it, and he unsuccessfully offered himself to various leftist parties before landing on the staff of *La Petite République*. He was a young, dynamic speaker and campaigner, in stark contrast to Barrès, and according to a socialist critic, the only available *Union socialiste* militant moderate enough to stand a chance in Neuilly-Boulogne. In effect, like Barrès, he ran as a Radical in Neuilly and as a socialist in Boulogne. Their platforms were almost identical even on the foreign worker question. Thanks, however, to his strong campaign (with the help of Rouanet, Viviani, and Jaurès) and the row over the exposition, he convinced a number of voters that only the naive would mistake Barrès for a socialist instead of the clerical he really was. One supporter of Sautumier even questioned Barrès' patriotism, because he published in *Le Figaro*, a newspaper defending Dreyfus "who gave away our war secrets."[105]

By election eve the police were divided on whether Barrès or Sautumier would survive the first round, but when the ballots were counted on February 23, Barrès' 1,899 votes put him in third place behind a moderate republican's 4,090 and Sautumier's 2,345.[106] Barrès admitted that he knew he was beaten as early as eight days before the election, because his socialism was only his own. The socialist committees wanted only the socialism of the *Union socialiste*, and Barrès felt that he could not reduce his integrity to accept subservience to it. As a result, he got only the unorganized socialist vote.[107] Yet, he maintained socialist unity and withdrew in favor of Sautumier, who won in the run-off on March 8.[108] He even chaired a victory dinner for Sautumier, but in toasting the *Union socialiste* he could not resist admonishing it for seeking inspiration in a Germany which knew only authoritarianism.[109]

The defeat at Neuilly brought a marked change in Barrès.

147

His tolerance of all socialist schools, save the Guesdists, and respect for all socialist leaders rapidly disappeared. This change was rooted in two things: a resentment over his failure to receive the support of socialist leadership in the Neuilly campaign and a growing opposition to the emerging socialist stand on internationalism. These two developments created a gulf between him and socialism which grew even wider throughout 1896.

Barrès showed this growing bitterness in his journal entries. On February 28 it was a "painful impression" to find his socialist friends desert him after the Neuilly defeat, throw their support to Sautumier, and make excuses for their earlier support for Barrès. But, he added with indulgence, "It is just. In doing battle for myself I harmed them."[110] As the year wore on, he brooded on his failure to get support from organized socialism, and by August he wanted revenge.[111]

By that time it had become difficult for him and other old Boulangists to accept organized socialism at all. Tactical cooperation with the socialists in the 1893 elections and in the parliament which followed had been easy enough. In 1896, however, a real attempt was made to find a common socialist program capable of uniting the factions. The sweeping socialist gains in the May, 1896, municipal elections, which gave the socialists 1,400,000 votes and majorities on one hundred and fifty municipal councils, occasioned this attempt, the so-called Saint-Mandé banquet of May 30, 1896. There, with old Boulangists Jourde and Argeliès at the speaker's table, the socialist leadership gathered to hear Millerand set forth a minimum program: the progressive collectivization of the means of production beginning with banks, transport, and mines and adding other industries as they became ripe for socialization; the triumph of socialism through the ballot box rather than through the barricade, through seeking socialist majorities in commune, department, and national governments; and the recognition that socialists could be both internationalists and patriots, could maintain an "international entente of the workers" without destroying the "French fatherland."[112] A few days later, the *Union socialiste* accepted this "minimum program" as the basis of what French socialism really stood for. After much soul-searching, the Guesdists and Blanquists were able to soften their stand on revolution, accept the new program, and come together with the Independent Socialists.

For most of the old Boulangists and Barrès, however, this meant the parting of the ways. As long as they had only to accept the collectivization of mines, banks, and transport with the future being open-ended, they could think of themselves as socialists. But the worst was its dilution of the homeland. The Saint-Mandé program, with its stand on collectivization and, especially, internationalism, drove out Barrès and the other old Boulangists.

The opportunity for Barrès to find revenge for socialist rejection of him at Neuilly-Boulogne and the adoption of a socialism antithetical to his own came at the funeral of the Marquis de Morès. Morès' advocacy of the strenuous life had carried the well-to-do aristocrat into an unsuccessful venture in Montana cattle ranching, the building of a viciously anti-Semitic and socially radical organization of butchers in the Paris district of La Villette, and murder at the hands of North African tribesmen. Barrès had worshipped this cultivator of selfhood from afar. He ran a verbatim report of a Morès speech in La Cocarde, indicating that more would follow.[113] None did. Police reports never list Barrès as a Morès friend in the 1894–1896 period, although they list many of Barrès' associates like the Boulangist Millevoye and Belleval, Pierre Denis of La Cocarde, and the sometime socialist, Clovis Hugues.[114] The socialists of La Petite République and even L'Intransigéant ignored the funeral, claiming Morès was not worth their time one way or the other.[115] The only socialists to show up were those like the old Boulangist Paulin-Méry, who like Barrès, had refused to accept Saint-Mandé. They joined with the anti-Semites Jules Guérin and Edouard Drumont, a few other ex-Boulangists, the abbé Lemire, and Barrès.

In his funeral oration for Morès, Barrès spoke of him as a genuine socialist, wanting "the economic transformation and the alteration of personnel in our society," as well as a nationalist. "Certain socialists," however, were attached to interna-

149

tionalism, which they erroneously thought was a consequence of the French Revolution. That belief was false and only a socialist inheritance from the Radicals. While the *philosophes* and the Declaration of the Rights of Man and of Citizens did claim cosmopolitanism, the Revolution did not act to make a single state. Quite the contrary, it "posed the principle of the right of peoples to govern themselves."[116]

In a later article Barrès insisted that the error of the socialists in believing that internationalism was the consequence of the French Revolution was compounded by their acceptance of Marx's idea that history determined the triumph of internationalism. Quite the contrary, argued Barrès. In the Middle Ages, dominated by the Holy Roman Empire and the papacy, there was universalism, but with the emerging monarchies of the sixteenth century and since the French Revolution, "Europe organized itself according to the principle of nationalities." Yet, while this was the greatest error, it was not the only one. *La Petite République*, the main organ of the *Union socialiste*, had not only swallowed the internationalist arguments, but "it had failed . . . to show the fatal, inevitable character of collectivism" and had fallen into the additional error of trying "to define and to specify the future."[117]

The final trauma, a Barrès break with socialism, came with the suicide of Louis Sautumier in November, 1896. In paying his respects to the family of his twenty-seven year old opponent at Neuilly-Boulogne, Barrès recalled how, in the very same room, he had congratulated Sautumier on his victory in the spring. "While I was alone with him, I had seen his hand open telegrams and more telegrams. I listened to the silences of his conversation, created by the reading of these telegrams of congratulation. He told me the names, and they were my friends who congratulated him." And now, the father was reading telegrams and more telegrams.[118] These entries at the time of Sautumier's suicide show both a keen sense of loss over the death of the young man and a great gratitude that Sautumier, in his victory at Neuilly, had released Barrès from the illusion that he could really be accepted by French socialism. By snatching away the victory Barrès felt was rightfully his, Sautumier had ended Barrès' youth, had awakened him to the realities of his illusory tie with socialism.[119] Because he felt he had been so personally involved with and changed by Sautumier, Barrès dismissed the funeral oration of Jean Jaurès, who before the Neuilly election had enjoyed Barrès' admiration, as "sonorous vanities" and "intellectual poverty."[120] When the funeral was over and the cortege moved to the train station, Barrès found himself surrounded by the same "circle of liars" who had icily greeted his withdrawal in Sautumier's favor at the spring election.[121] Sautumier's funeral convinced Barrès that socialism had disowned him.

Barrès' growing bitterness toward socialist leaders he had formerly admired was even more apparent in the campaign for Sautumier's seat. Although he initially entered the race and held rallies, he never had a chance. Most of the socialist committees of the district chose André Lefèvre of *La Petite République*.[122] Barrès withdrew from the race with posters charging that the *Union socialiste*'s "hate" for his revisionist past and "ingratitude" for his contribution to the district's socialist cause "would be capable of destroying socialism in Neuilly-Boulogne."[123] The newspaper of the Radical victor agreed that only Barrès' socialism was moderate and patriotic enough to get the support of all the socialist committees and appeal to the peculiar electorate of the district.[124] "What folly," Barrès wrote in his *Cahiers*, "is this *ex cathedra* socialism which requires adhesions to slogans, which rejects living men."[125] He increasingly believed that it was the refusal of Marcel Sembat and Jaurès, specifically, to accept divergent views that had been most responsible for his Neuilly defeat, but "Jaurès will use himself up. Our turn will come again."[126] And again: "I have reconsidered the tragic inside circumstances of my defeat at Neuilly. It was not from having been betrayed by my friends. After all, I never made a real conjuncture with this Jaurès and what is a Sembat? They are waiters selling wine at the establishment where I drink my liqueur."[127]

In the minds of the socialist leaders attempting to give socialism integrity by purging its hangers-on, the opposition to Barrès was clear. For Jaurès, as for so many socialists, Barrès simply was untrustworthy. He was too ineffective as a campaigner and speaker; he could not really rouse the voters. Moreover, he had too many politically strange friends like Drumont, Morès, *Le Figaro*, and royalists. "To decentralize without transforming property," Jaurès wrote in a review of Barrès' novel, *Les Déracinés*, "is to re-establish the supremacy of the old landholder influences and to return to the past."[128] Barrès was too bourgeois and too willing to compromise with reactionary decentralizers.

For Barrès, then, 1896 marked the turning point. The Neuilly election and the Saint-Mandé program convinced him that he could never accept or be accepted by the French socialist movement. In *La Cocarde* and the federalist campaign he had attempted to blend a federalist socialism with nationalism. As he saw it in 1896, the *Union socialiste* refused to tolerate either position.

In reality he had over-reacted. Saint-Mandé had made neither organizational or ideological unity all that firm. Real unity would await the Congress of Amsterdam in 1905. Even then the ideological commitment to internationalism and a collectivist future was never very deep in French socialism. The eternal reformism and accommodation with the establishment, from Jaurès' association with the Dreyfusard ministries to the present, and the stampede of socialists to vote for war in 1914 should be evidence enough that the commitment to collectivism and internationalism was shallow at best. All Saint-Mandé and Neuilly-Boulogne politics required of Barrès was that he get ideological and organizational "dirty hands," to play ball with the *Union socialiste* establishment as did other patriotic anti-collectivists such as Millerand.

Instead, his demand for "purity" put Barrès at the crossroads. He had to opt for either nationalism or socialism. The choice was really between nationalism with a little socialism or socialism with a little nationalism. The year 1897 found Barrès yet undecided, although the scales were tipping toward nationalism. By 1898, however, he would go all the way toward nationalism as a new element entered French politics—the Dreyfus affair.

152

CHAPTER SIX

NATIONALISM AND NATIONAL-SOCIALISM, 1897–1898

If there was ever a rootless intellectual it was Barrès. Like Philippe in *Sous l'oeil des barbares* he constantly needed an "axiom, religion or prince of men" to give life meaning. Perhaps because fame had come too early and too easily for him, because his character had not been "strengthened" by struggling for artistic recognition, he could not find such an axiom in himself. Instead he traveled restlessly to find answers in Italy, Spain, and elsewhere and sought axioms outside himself. Boulangism briefly had been one. That experience had led to socialism, as Barrès himself pointed out, because it had an "ideal." By 1896 that axiom was finished for him. What would he substitute for it? The answer was, of course, nationalism, which had been a part of Barrès' thought for some time, but always subsumed under Boulangism or socialism. With the publication of *Les Déracinés* in 1897, his first novel in four years and his most successful one, his nationalism came into its own, becoming central to his thought and action thereafter. By 1898 it also became for him a nationalism of combat in the Dreyfus Affair and in his national-socialist campaign for a parliamentary seat from Nancy. The problem is to see how he came to nationalism as a new "axiom, religion" and what it meant for him as thought and action.

There can be debate on how much of a nationalist Barrès was before 1897. At the least his nationalism was merely a sideshow for his individualism, Boulangism, or federalist socialism. At most, as Jean Touchard points out, it was "very fluid," a "negative and critical" nationalism and not a doctrine.[1] In *Un Homme libre*, for example, bits of earth like Lorraine and Venice are merely mechanisms for discovering the well-springs of individualism, and the description of Lorraine was insulting to many a Lorrainer. The same was true of his essays on Spain and Italy, written in the 1890s, which appeared as *Du sang, de la volupté et de la mort* (1894) and *Notes sur Italie* (1929). When Barrès reached out to the masses, he did not personify them with nationalism, but through such devices as Bérénice and Velu. His federalism and regionalism, individualism and solidarity, anti-parliamentarianism, "glorification of energy and heroes," were directed by socialism, not nationalism.

With the publication of *Les Déracinés*, the first volume of his "novel of national energy" trilogy in 1897, all of that changes. From that point on, Barrès' thought was cast in a doctrinal nationalism. Nationalism, far better than socialism, was able to unify the various threads of his thought of the 1890s, and unlike socialism, nationalism was an ideology completely in accord with his way of knowing things.

When Barrès began *Les Déracinés* in 1894, it was to be a socialist sequel to *l'Ennemi des lois*, which ended with the characters entering a phalanstery. The novel was to answer the question, "How is a society without constraint possible."[2] By 1896, however, Barrès' notes for the unfinished novel posed different questions. "What strikes me . . . is the non-coordination of things in France. It is a sign of the general paralysis among individuals" and "among the ruling classes." The answer? "I reflect. There is a *national consciousness* and then *energy*. Having a national conscience, the sentiment that a country has a past, the inclination to belong to that past closest at hand."[3] "In a word," he added a few weeks later at the funeral of Morès, "a creature is viable only in the measure where he is transformed according to his character and hereditary ways. This historic sense, this high naturalist sentiment, this acceptance of determinism is what we mean by nationalism."[4]

To show these themes in *Les Déracinés*, Barrès proceeded to rewrite, in a much more conventional manner, the first novel of the *Culte du moi*. Although the action remains set in the 1880s, it is reinterpreted by Barrès' ideas of the 1890s. While the need for energy formerly had taken Philippe into socialism, it now takes the new protagonist and principal *porte-parole* of Barrès, Sturel, into nationalism. While the rootlessness of both Philippe and Sturel necessitated group action, Sturel's group is not Philippe's workers or masses, but his fellow Lorrainers.

In brief, *Les Déracinés* takes seven young bourgeois and petit bourgeois Lorrainers from their last year at the *lycée* of Nancy in 1879 through their establishment in Paris and success or failure in 1885. At Nancy they are uprooted from their Lorraine souls both by the unreal and artificial world of the boarding school and the Kantianism of their teacher, Paul Bouteiller, an *Ecole Normale*-educated son of Lille workers. With his dictum, "Always I ought to act in such a way that my action serves universal law,"[5] Bouteiller's teachings act "to uproot these youngsters, to detach them from the soil and the social group where they are entirely connected in order to put them outside their prejudices into abstract reason."[6] "If this education suppressed their national conscience, . . . it developed their energy,"[7] and multiplied it to the extent that they can cry, "à bas Nancy, vive Paris!" By the end of 1882 they have all arrived at the city of light to fulfill their egos, but instead of putting down new roots to replace their uprooted Lorraine ones, they drift. Two of the poorest, Suret-Lefort and Renaudin, become careerists in law and journalism with Gambettist politics. In his insatiable quest for energizing new experiences, Sturel takes "the poisoned cup," the "dangerous foreign elements" of the beautiful pearled and turquoised Armenian, Astiné Aravian, and only further uproots his "disordered organism."[8] Saint-Phlin returns occasionally to Lorraine to put himself in accord "with the homeland, whose fields vaguely teach him historical laws." Roemerspacher falls under the influence of Tainian "scientific research, not only to indulge deep curiosity or amplify general well-being, but to satisfy [his] need for harmony and . . . the divine."[9]

The first tentative move toward re-rooting comes by combining "two contradictory ethics," that of individual action,

155

which Sturel learns from Napoleon, "the professor of energy," and that of acceptance of determinism and group action, which Roemerspacher gets from Taine. The seven Lorrainers opt for group action, but the group is not the workers or the masses of the *Culte du moi*. It is themselves alone, bound together not by class or opinion but by the common Lorraine experience. "All our theories are excellent," says Sturel as if he had just served on the staff of *La Cocarde*, "if each of us finds his motive for action."[10] Indeed, their group action takes the form of collaboration on a newspaper, *La Vraie République*, financed with the inheritance of one of the band, Racadot. Within a year, however, they fall out among themselves, Racadot exhausts his inheritance and every other means for continuing the newspaper, and he and Mouchefrin atrociously murder Astiné for her money.

Racadot is caught, convicted and guillotined; and only the testimony of Sturel, Astiné's former lover, can break Mouchefrin's alibi. While Sturel is disgusted by the particularly ugly murder, he is racked by ethical indecision. Only as he participates in the funeral of Victor Hugo "among the surging masses and receives excitation from them" does he reach a decision.

> Through his acts, he said to himself, each of these men belongs to the isolated life and perhaps to a strongly villainous life. But through his life force [*sève*] each one belongs to the common life. The national life force today is in emotion and now all these individuals think generously . . . . There are ignoble instants, but their sum makes a noble eternity. Hugo made me sense it with so much spirit so that I knew passion, disgust, and contempt. Just when I needed it, his work and this multitude strongly summon up in me the mysterious unity of all of life's manifestations. Let us accept our role and the roles our neighbors play. Would to nature that we were conditioned at birth for good and that nothing foreign came strongly to tempt our free will. Let us keep together as best we can as we are carried down stream. Let us move with the tide of our contemporaries. Our existence and theirs is only an instant of a more general heroic action on any of us.
>
> . . . .

> In following all the ceremonies of [Hugo's] funeral, I had been led to think that if one wanted to transform humanity, for example, to walk with young Lorrainers, the children of tradition, citizens of the universe, and men of pure reason, such an operation entailed risks. A potter or glass maker loses in the making a certain percent of his pieces and the percentage is increased when he is concerned to turn out very beautiful pieces. In the attempt of our little band to raise ourselves up, there was bound to be some waste. Racadot and Mouchefrin are our ransom, the price of our improvement. I hate their crime, but I persist in holding them, in regard to me, as sacrificed. That is why I have refused to testify against the two scoundrels.[11]

In short, Sturel (and Barrès) recognized that there were "diverse groups of energy" in France: governmental administration, the religions of revelation and scientific method, prospering agricultural, industrial, and commercial enterprises, and trade unions "born of a movement hating the existing social form and struggling to destroy it while the administration seeks to crush them." Unfortunately they were so uncoordinated and worked against each other so much that France was *dissociée*, disunited and dissociated.[12] Even worse, the real problem was that France was *décérébrée*, drifting and directionless, unable "to remake the injured national substance . . . to restore the sections of the country, or . . . to organize this anarchy."[13]

Sturel's banding together of the seven Lorrainers was but the first halting step of the "instinct of the sick" to heal a disunited France. Entire regions and the entire nation must band together in cultural rootedness, even with the Racadots and Mouchefrins. They must unite against those foreign to the fatherland or to the achievement of one's selfhood, be they Astiné, "the German spirit," or Jews like the Reinachs of Panama. The social glue was no longer class or similarity of opinion, but the emotional tug of a common "soil and dead," as expressed in the irrational bond for one another held by the countless participants in Hugo's funeral ceremonies. As a result, the greater good demanded that none of the participants could be sacrificed to abstract justice just because they murdered a "perfumed Turk." At last Barrès had found that long

sought for "axiom, religion, or prince of men" capable of energizing his quest for selfhood. Moreover, the new "axiom,"
unlike socialism, was in keeping with his irrational way of
knowing things.

Nor was this fact lost on the rationalist and socialist review-
ers of the book. "What becomes of [Barrès'] theory of selfhood
and individualism?" asked Léon Blum. "Nothing violates or
diminishes energy like such groups as the family and commune. These are the most dangerous collectivities."[14] "M.
Barrès laments," wrote Jean Jaurès, "that his young men of
Lorraine come to Paris instead of awakening the dormant re-
sources of their province." Rather, he and his fellows should
recognize "that the centralization they complain about is an effect of the economic order . . . If the young men of M. Barrès
had wanted to sink mine shafts in Lorraine, they would have
had to beg from Parisian capitalists . . . To decentralize without transforming property is to re-establish the supremacy of
old landed influences and return to the past."[15] Although *Les
Déracinés* shared many of socialism's enemies, wrote *La Revue
socialiste*, the novel did not have "the same foundation" as
socialist criticism. The reviewer was wrong in seeing the
novel's theme as "the crushing of proletarian intellectuals and
the harmonious evolution of rich ones." The seven Lorraine
intellectuals were all bourgeois or petit bourgeois, with one of
the two poorest having "harmonious evolution" and one of the
richest being "crushed." He was right, however, in seeing no
socialist criticism in the novel.[16]

The publication of *Les Déracinés* in 1897, with the new Barrésian "axiom" of nationalism, coincided with Barrès' return to the
Dreyfus affair. His reaction in 1894–1895 to the original conviction of Alfred Dreyfus for selling secrets to a foreign power
was to see him as one illustration of the venality of the parliamentary republic. Barrès' fear then was not that the Jews
were selling out the nation, but that Dreyfus would not get
his just deserts. Dreyfus' motive "was neither hate, nor ambition, nor love, nor gambling losses;" it was nothing more
than "thirty pieces of silver." Barrès had been afraid that,
just as those bribed by the Panama Canal Company had re-

gained their political fortunes, Dreyfus would be a captain of uhlans within three years.[17] By the autumn of 1897, however, this situation began to change radically, and by the spring of 1898 Captain Dreyfus' cause forced Barrès to complete his break with his intellectual friends of the Left and to engage in an electoral campaign highly colored by anti-Semitism.

What brought about the change in his views was the growing belief that Dreyfus was innocent. To Barrès and the public, however, the innocence was far from certain in 1897. Much of the case, part of which continues to be cloaked in mystery, was still known only to a few members of the General Staff, the Government, and the real traitor or traitors.[18] What was known was that in March, 1896, the intelligence section of the French General Staff intercepted a *petit bleu* from the German embassy to a Major Ferdinand Walsin-Esterhazy. Colonel Georges Picquart, head of intelligence, trying to discover why secrets were still being sold to Germany even after the conviction of Dreyfus, noticed the similarity between Esterhazy's handwriting and that of the *bordereau*, the principal evidence against Dreyfus. After unsuccessfully attempting to convince the War Office of the innocence of Dreyfus, Picquart revealed his discovery to his attorney who, in turn, told a sympathetic senator, Auguste Scheurer-Kestner. The Dreyfus family had come independently to the same conclusion when, after a facsimile of the *bordereau* had been published, Esterhazy's banker had told them of the similarity of Esterhazy's handwriting to that of the *bordereau*. By 1897 these varied Dreyfusard forces had united to accuse Esterhazy, who was tried and acquitted in January, 1898. Throughout all this, the Government and the War Office for various reasons, not the least of which was the fact that not even Esterhazy's guilt could now erase all the fabricated or assumed evidence against Dreyfus, continued to declare Dreyfus guilty.

It was only when the above revelations were made in the autumn of 1897 that Barrès returned to the Dreyfus case. As early as November, he expressed his fear that the publicity of the case was destroying faith in the army.[19] By December, he set forth the position he would hold throughout the Affair.

159

"If I believe the individual guilty, it is because the exceptional people who are informed, through knowing the seven members of the court martial and several documents of the first inquest, have declared and still declare that he had deserved to be stripped completely." Barrès could understand the family's desire for revision, but unfortunately its cause had won adherents and had divided France into two parties. He was convinced that the Dreyfusard party, an alliance of Jews like Joseph Reinach and Protestants like Scheurer-Kestner, had seized upon the Dreyfus case to regain Jewish prestige lost under the anti-Semitic attacks on Jewish high finance and internationalism, or to head off the growing nationalistic resentment against anti-clericalism. Their efforts, common only in that they had a mutual enemy, only served to weaken and divide France against foreign attack. Faced with this possibility, Barrès asked the government to clear the air once and for all, to declare Dreyfus definitely guilty or innocent, and then keep quiet so that France would be reunited.[20]

At this point Barrès' position on the guilt of Dreyfus was not entirely unfounded, for very little of the case was known to the public. It was mainly a choice of whose word one wished to believe—that of Dreyfus, an isolated and convicted traitor, and the handful of journalists, politicians, and socialists who believed in him, or that of the respected generals, the bulwark of national defense. The evidence that the *bordereau* was the work of Esterhazy was no more substantial than the evidence that it belonged to Dreyfus. Both arguments hinged on the testimony of graphologists, highly inexact scientists; and the most prestigious graphologist, Alphonse Bertillon, wrongly believed Dreyfus guilty. When the evidence in favor of Dreyfus was not overwhelming as far as the public was concerned, and especially when Esterhazy was acquitted, it was easy to distrust the advocates of Dreyfus, especially if there were reasons for distrusting anything they said. For example, Reinach and Scheurer-Kestner were too identified with the parliamentary republic Barrès hated for him ever to believe them.

A similar prejudice prevented him from accepting the Dreyfusard testimony of Emile Zola. Barrès had never gotten along well with Zola, whose "scientific" novels stood for the literary and philosophic traditions of naturalism and positivism Barrès rejected. Yet, this antagonism did not prevent the two from coming together, with other intellectuals Zola tried to line up, through several meetings in 1897.[21] This armed truce ended when Zola in *J'Accuse!* specifically denounced the government and various officers for falsely convicting Dreyfus and of preventing the necessary revision. Soon, Zola's courage inspired three thousand intellectuals and artists to sign a petition in support of Dreyfus, and Léon Blum went to get Barrès' signature. "Zola has courage. He is a man," Barrès admitted to Blum, but in recalling his attendance at the degradation of Dreyfus and his anti-Dreyfusard articles for *Le Journal*, he added:

> *Eh Bien!* I ask myself if I was not mistaken. I realize that each of the attitudes . . . that interpreted [Dreyfus] as the sign of a total, perfect villainy also allowed the opposite conclusion. Was Dreyfus the villain? Was he a stoic, a martyr? I no longer know anything about it.[22]

He sent Blum away with the promise that he would think about it and send his decision by letter. A few days later he wrote Blum that the Dreyfusards had not convinced him, that the omissions in their arguments disquieted and irritated him. His refusal to sign the manifesto hit Blum hard: "One of the avenues of my youth had been closed."

Blum's shock was carried to other leftist intellectuals, who had drunk deep of the *Culte du moi*, when Barrès published an article directly against those intellectuals, as the press described them, who signed the Zola manifesto. In it, Barrès argued that the Dreyfusard intellectuals were not the cultivated individuals they believed themselves to be; instead, they were part of a "demi-culture," which "destroys the instinct without substituting for it a conscience." Moreover, intellectuality had no relevance to the Dreyfus Affair, for

> we do not possess all the elements for a real knowledge, but only some elements. We are able to construct only hypotheses.

161

How are you, man of culture, man of method, able to under-take the resolution of a problem when you do not at all have all the data!

As a result, Barrès believed, an "intellectual" was "an individual who is persuaded that society ought to be founded on logic and who fails to recognize that it, in fact, rests on necessities anterior to and perhaps foreign to individual reason."[23]

The motive in this for Barrès was clear. Zola's *J'Accuse!* forced him and others to make the choice between Dreyfus and the army. So many charges had been fabricated against Dreyfus by Major Henry and others of the intelligence service that Esterhazy's authorship of the *bordereau* was no longer sufficient to dispel them. The army and the government insisted, wrongly, that these charges were genuine. Hence, Zola and the other Dreyfusards, frustrated in pinning the blame on Esterhazy, could only attack the army, and this Barrès could not tolerate. Blum saw the choice of Barrès in this way:

> He came to feel that his choice would decide the rest of his life. Until then, he had succeeded in reconciling the Boulangist Barrès with the Barrès of *Sous l'oeil des barbares* and *Un Homme libre*. From this time he chose; he chose with the same stroke between his literary public, from whom he cut himself off, and his companions of the political struggle . . . . Boulangist solidarity swept him away, even him . . . . Political action had not at all been for Barrès, as I had believed, an exercise, a pastime, nearly a game.[24]

Dreyfus might be innocent, although Barrès doubted it. Even if he were, the innocence could be proved now only by destroying the army. In the years which followed, Barrès regularly supported the formula of Déroulède: "There is not any likelihood that Dreyfus is innocent, but it is absolutely certain that France is innocent."[25] In such a situation, Dreyfus had to be guilty.

As Blum suggested it was, Barrès' article proved to be a declaration of war against the intellectual community when it was answered by Lucien Herr, the librarian of the *Ecole Normale*. Just as Barrès had led the young intellectuals to the

162

quest for selfhood, Herr almost singlehandedly had brought an entire generation of them into socialism. His eloquence struck away the support Barrès once enjoyed from the young men of the Left. Against Barrès, Herr wrote:

> The young men whose demi-culture you deride know that in fact they possess all the truth no more than you do. But they have in themselves something which is perfect, the faith in a humane ideal, and this naive force of generous action will sweep away the absurd hatreds which excite the crafty. Look out! You believe yourself in accord with the nation. Instead, you have with you only that coarse, noisy, fluctuating, and changing fraction of the nation which disappointed you at the time of Boulangism, and it is not a force. You also have with you the men of parliament who disgust you, the satisfied interests, the crowd, Jewish and Christian capitalism, and the *Semaines religieuses* of all of France. All that, you know, is weak. At the same time you have against you the real people and the men of good will . . . that majority of men who know how to put law and the ideal of justice before their persons, their natural instincts, and their group loyalties.[26]

With Herr's article, Barrès' contact with the men of the Left was finished. His entries in *Mes Cahiers* of 1897 show that he could still meet with men of the Left like Herr, France, and Zola. With 1898 there are no more such entries. Barrès, who had sought in Boulangism, *La Cocarde*, and the federalist campaign to bridge the gulf between Left and Right, had now lost the orthodox Left. Before the Dreyfus Affair was over he would also lose the young men of the Right. Even his ability to retain the disgusted, unorthodox Left and Right was precarious, as seen when he again went to the voters in the campaign of 1898.

Against this background of the outbreak of the Dreyfus affair, Barrès conducted another electoral campaign, this time for a legislative seat at Nancy in the general elections of 1898. The campaign saw him formulate a new political program of nationalism which united his varied concerns for social reform, national strength against the weakening influence of a generation of parliamentary corruption and inaction, and the reconciliation of classes within a kind of republican corporativism.

163

Also, although it had little effect on the campaign elsewhere in France, the Dreyfus affair entered the Nancy campaign in its most vicious anti-Semitic form. Barrès had to face up to that issue and put to the test the anti-Dreyfusard credentials he had established in the winter of 1897–1898.

The anguish of two successive defeats at Neuilly made Barrès debate with himself at length before deciding to enter the 1898 campaign.[27] Yet, the situation at Nancy seemed much improved for him over that of 1893. Papelier's coat tails were no longer long enough to carry other candidates. Nancy trade unionists, not yet having moved into orthodox socialism, were still capable of being organized by Barrès' brand. Although the old League of Patriots and Boulangist organizations had collapsed, many of their members continued similar work in the Anti-Semitic League, and its national leader, Jules Guérin, had spoken in Nancy as recently as February, 1898.[28] In March and April, 1898, Barrès formed the Boulangist debris of these trade unionist and nationalist organizations into a new electoral committee, the Nationalist-Socialist Republican Committee of Meurthe-et-Moselle, whose first resolution demanded a new prosecution of Zola, "insulter of the army and defender of the traitor Dreyfus."[29] Barrès even won the support of the local *Union socialiste*.[30]

The fact that Barrès could not pass muster as a socialist in Neuilly-Boulogne did not mean that he would have the same experience in Nancy, thanks to the nature of the Nancy working class. In following the election returns in the socialist *Petite République* and in reading the emerging volumes of Jean Maîtron's masterful *Dictionnaire biographique du mouvement ouvrier français*, one is struck by the absence of any significant socialist movement or leadership in Meurthe-et-Moselle before the turn of the century. Given the Nancy basin's importance as an iron and steel producer, this late emergence of socialism there comes as a surprise. Nancy workers had been Boulangist until the collapse of the movement in 1892, but neither socialism nor nationalism immediately replaced it. By 1896 the Prefect could happily report that the political situation "rarely has been more tranquil."[31] Although the importation of doubtlessly socialist miners from the St. Etienne region to meet the expansion of Nancy basin production did bring the formation of a miners union, the Prefect could report in 1898 that the one hundred eighty member union and its socialism were unattractive to local miners. Rather, thanks to moderate republicans like Papelier, workers were nice and quiet. Only a minority wanted to make strikes or radical politics. The rest were interested in mutual aid and consumer cooperative self-help. Not until the end of 1898, after a year of rapid expansion, would the Prefect be alarmed by the socialist miners union, whose membership had quadrupled and whose strike fund was three to four times larger than its mutual aid fund.[32]

Weak in membership, with an ephemeral press and little influence in getting the Republican Congress to nominate even middle-class reformers, Nancy socialism could easily accept Barrès' half a loaf over going hungry. After a series of meetings with local socialist and trade union leaders, Barrès brought the working class of Nancy to his cause.[33] In the absence of a strong socialist or trade union movement, or in a region with only an embryonic working class, Barrès' brand of "national socialism" could still make sense to large numbers of workers not yet pre-empted by real socialist politics.[34]

The first issues of a revived *Courrier de l'Est* were devoted to the program Barrès would develop through the campaign[35]— a program which was a natural outgrowth of Boulangist revisionism, the Proudhonist socialism of *La Cocarde*, and the nationalism of Barrès' attacks on the *Union socialiste* and Dreyfus. Barrès may have described it and his committee as nationalist-socialist, but it was neither the chauvinism so often identified with nationalism nor the public ownership of the means of production identified with socialism. Instead, in a politicalization of the theme of *Les Déracinés*, Barrès saw nationalism as the touchstone for uniting all classes as well as the Left and Right around a purely domestic program of social reforms and national strength.

The first job of this nationalism was to bring France political security. "We are nationalists," Barrès asserted, because "for twenty years the Opportunist system has favored the Jew,

165

the foreigner, and the cosmopolite." The army, ministries, courts, and administration were riddled with them and served their interests. The result was a generation of Reinachs, Cornelius Herzs, and Alfred Dreyfuses. Although the Jews had once been persecuted, they had been liberated by the French Revolution and "have become dominators," Barrès wrote. He believed that political balance had to be restored. Jewish influence should be proportionate only to its population of seventy thousand. The influence of foreigners had to be reduced by making military service a pre-requisite for naturalization and by allowing the naturalized to have only civil rights of a private nature, with the vote going only to second-generation Frenchmen.

The second job of nationalism was to protect France against "economic insecurity." In this regard Barrès believed that "nationalism necessarily engendered socialism," which he still described as "the material and moral amelioration of the largest and poorest class." Such a definition, of course, would not obligate Barrès to a program of collectivism but would direct his attention to working-class insecurities: The retired worker endured hunger, while the young suffered the insecurity of unemployment. Foreign workers depressed wages. Machinery subjected the worker to a "military discipline" and to the arbitrariness of the employer in establishing work rules. "Certain economic organizations turn man into a virtual slave." The shopkeeper class shared the same economic insecurities: The bourgeoisie bought from the large store, but the worker, be he white collar or blue collar, dealt with the small merchant who gave him credit when he was unemployed. In a long period of unemployment this extension of credit exposed the shopkeeper to ruin, just as it created so many hardships for the worker. In addition, the shopkeeper paid higher prices than his large competitor did. The farmer also had insecurities. He was at the mercy of world grain prices, driven down by large American and Indian harvests. This was only partially offset by the tariff, which Barrès considered a socialist measure, because grain speculators absorbed too much of the profits from the tariff. Finally, even the bourgeoisie had economic insecurities; it was "menaced by international financial feudalism which turns securities into dry leaves." Although the little investor furnished the capital for French industry, this capital was controlled by a "financial general staff," made up of no more than one thousand five hundred persons who, in turn, were controlled, through interlocking directorates, by several dozen former Genevan Protestant bankers and Jews. These feudal financial lords had become "the veritable masters of modern society." They controlled industry, because they decided where investments were to be made. They also controlled the dividends of investors and wages of workers, because they manipulated the profits of industry.

To remedy these economic insecurities, Barrès recommended a wide program. He would require foreign workers to fulfill a military obligation. They would also be ineligible for employment on public works. He would overcome the barrier to the establishment of a national, state-controlled old-age pension plan by finding a reasonable way to finance the scheme. He would replace indirect taxation with a progressive tax on income and the profits from bonds and French investments abroad. He would improve and decentralize agricultural credit with funds from the *Caisses d'Epargne* and guarantee minimum grain prices to the producer, since too many of the benefits of the Méline tariff went to the grain speculators. He would extend limited liability legislation to trade unions and agricultural unions so that they could raise capital and own factories. In that way workers could emancipate themselves through voluntary associations, modeled on the Albi glassworks which still had to operate illegally, rather than through collectivization. He would encourage the association of little investors so that they could retain control over the capital they created. In such a way "the modern corporative movement" could combat the financial aristocracy just as the "commune movement of the twelfth century" battled feudal tyranny. He would extend vocational education in public schools to "permit all national aptitudes and dispositions to be developed." He would revise the constitution to widen the effect of universal suffrage, particularly through the proposal of "our friend Argeliès," an old

167

Boulangist, to allow municipal referendums on economic and administrative matters. He would extend limited liability legislation to communes so that they could try new solutions to social problems. He would support the Georges Berry proposal to require large stores to have a fixed and proportional license for every line of goods they sold, thereby making their prices more competitive with those of the small shopkeeper. He would support the re-establishment of the right of *bouilleurs de cru*.[36]

The striking features of this program were its continuities, and lack of them, with the past. First of all, Barrès played down the Boulangist strain in his past. He made no mention of constitutional revision in favor of a presidential republic, although he continued to hold such views privately. Perhaps because he sought a major office of the parliamentary system, he now saw the political solution in the federalist program of decentralization, in the increase of communal powers.

Second, Barrès even modified his former position on decentralization. He adhered to statist solutions for pensions and agricultural credit, programs which were supported by nearly all the parties of the Left, minimum grain prices, and legislation against foreign workers. He would have argued, of course, that in his federalist framework these were national problems requiring national solutions. Yet, the fact that these were more central to his program than was the advocacy of voluntary solutions by geographical and moral groups, modeled on the Albi glassworks, showed that he had modified his position in the face of political exigencies—national amelioration in these areas simply was easier to achieve, although decentralization remained the long-range goal.

Third, the 1898 program was thoroughly couched in nationalism. The program was to reconcile classes and to create the social justice, economic security, and political strength necessary to make France strong. Even his electoral committee carried the nationalist label. The emphasis of this nationalism was almost solely domestic, however. Foreign affairs was noticably absent in a campaign fought out only three months before Fashoda would re-ignite nationalist fires on the foreign

situation. For Barrès in 1898, the "foreign" threat in his nationalism lay almost exclusively in the internal machinations
of the Reinachs and Dreyfuses.

In a normal election year this program might have been sufficient to bring victory for Barrès, considering the mood of
Nancy. As the campaign unfolded, however, a surprise awaited
all the candidates. Anti-Semitism, engendered by a Dreyfus affair still in its earliest stages, was far deeper in Nancy than any
of the candidates suspected.[37] Anti-Semitism first showed itself
with the original republican candidate. The Republican Congress, formerly the Republican Alliance, met on April 17 and
chose a Radical, Eugène Nicolas.[38] Since the incumbent, a protégé of Papelier whose magic with the voters had ruined Barrès
and Gabriel in 1893, refused to stand for re-election, a progressive candidate like Nicolas certainly seemed the logical choice.

Within days, however, an indication came that this was no
ordinary campaign. On April 23 all the candidates held a joint
meeting. Besides Barrès and Nicolas there was also Ludovic
Gervaize, formerly a *rallié* and now an anti-Semite. Barrès
was fairly-well received, and Gervaize, who impassively
insisted he was only against government bureaucracy and in
favor of freedom of conscience, was largely ignored, except
that the audience objected to being addressed as *messieurs* rather
than as *citoyens*. On the other hand, Nicolas was almost hooted
from the hall.[39] The case against Nicolas was this: he was a
Dreyfusard. In particular, he had helped finance a socialist
and Dreyfusard newspaper in Nancy. As his ill-received campaign unfolded, the Republican Congress discovered that he
was also too radical for its tastes, reconvened, and chose a
new candidate, this time an anti-Dreyfusard businessman, Demenge-Cremel.[40]

The difficulties of Nicolas should have signaled the importance
of anti-Semitism as an issue. To be sure, both Demenge-Cremel
and Barrès struck at Nicolas for that reason. Demenge-Cremel
contended that he would never support Nicolas in a run-off
because of Nicolas' support for Nancy's Left and Dreyfus and his alleged manipulation of the Republican Congress.[41]
On his part, Barrès consistently repeated his charges against

169

Dreyfus and Jewish control of finance.[42] Usually, as in a speech at Dombasle on April 14, he lumped the two together:

> It suffices me to cite this pitiful history of Captain Dreyfus, condemned by his peers. His defenders, instruments of an occult financial power, condemn themselves for insults to the army, and to justify their criminal intrigues reach to obtain the annulment of the verdict. Is that not a challenge which financial feudalism hurls at the French nation? And what kind of reaction against this Jewish feudalism can be made by Opportunism which, even at Nancy, is penetrated, dominated by the Jewish world?[43]

In particular, Barrès used this theme against Nicolas, just as the *Progrès de l'Est* daily attacked, without giving quarter, his involvement with the Nancy Dreyfusard newspaper. Yet, except for their mutual denunciation of Nicolas, neither Barrès nor Demenge-Cremel exploited anti-Semitism. Indeed, both dismissed the candidature of Gervaize who made anti-Semitism virtually his whole campaign. The *Courrier de l'Est* never mentioned Gervaize, and *Le Progrès* simply considered his candidature a laughingstock, with anti-Semitism his only appeal—an appeal incapable of ever coming close to victory. When the votes were counted on May 8, however, Barrès and Demenge-Cremel discovered how poorly they had gauged the difficulties Nicolas posed.

With anti-Semitism as such a side issue, Barrès and Demenge-Cremel simply wore themselves out in mutual personal attacks. The campaign had to be fought on such a level, for in specific proposals the program of Demenge-Cremel was almost identical with that of Barrès: decentralization, respect for the army, solidarity between labor and capital, and legislation against foreign workers.[44] They were separated only by the labels of "national socialist" and "republican congress" and the electoral clienteles which went with them. To Barrès, Demenge-Cremel was inept, incompetent, senile, possibly corrupt, and the representative of the Opportunist-Progressist forces which had always opposed Barrès. Barrès' opposition quoted him out of context to make him appear to hate Lorraine, harped on his undistinguished parliamentary career, poked fun at his "feeble constitution," "pale, hatchet-faced figure," and poor speaking ability, recalled his Neuilly campaigns and Paris residence to call him a foreigner and exotic, and quoted every socialist it could find who would denounce his socialism.[45]

It was a tumultuous campaign. Police reports tell of systematic heckling by Barrès supporters forcing cancellation of Nicolas rallies.[46] Barrès got it back in kind, even though generally he stayed close to the working-class strongholds of Nancy, Dombasle, and Champigneuilles, which had been his strength in 1889–1893. Even at Dombasle, on April 14, a heckler who shouted that Barrès' arguments were "words, words" almost broke up the meeting and did prevent the voting of a resolution of endorsement.[47] At Saint Nicolas cries of "Drown the renegade," "Down with the black horse," and "liar" forced him to quit.[48] His worst experience was at the village of Champenoux on May 2, where an unruly audience, egged on by the chairman, hurled at Barrès local elaborations of every fantastic anti-Barrès story, including a most fascinating one that he had sought to run in anti-Semitic Constantine, Algeria, and marry a *moukère*, the daughter of the Bey of Tunis. In the middle of the meeting, suddenly the lights went out. The mob set upon Barrès and his lieutenant with canes and fists. The two escaped out a back door only to find their carriage a block away. The mob beat them all the way to the carriage, knocking Barrès to the ground several times.[49]

In spite of it all, the May 8 election came and found Barrès ahead, but without a majority. Long upset since his poor showing at Neuilly in 1896, Barrès was now ecstatic: "With a vigorous shove with a shoulder I finally had unmoored the ship; it glided on the water; luck had returned, we were going to sail."[50] However, his elation was premature. Gervaize followed the 5,100 votes of Barrès with 5,052, while Demenge-Cremel garnered 3,139 to the 1,808 of Nicolas. Everyone was surprised at Gervaize's showing, including the candidate himself. All were convinced that the priests had created an electoral success that no one could have foreseen. The anti-Semitic feeling, signaled by the reaction to Nicolas, was far stronger than anyone had realized, for Gervaize ran on a program a Barrès man called "death to the Jews" and a Demenge-Cremel supporter termed "racial hatreds."[51]

The unexpected anti-Semitic surge worked to the disadvantage of Barrès. Before the campaign he and his agents tried to get the withdrawal of Gervaize, whose chief supporter was the former League of Patriots leader and Boulangist, Bouttier. Barrès and his men argued that the programs of both candidates were close to each other on nationalism and Dreyfus, that Barrès, as a former deputy, had priority.[52] Although these several efforts had failed, Barrès undoubtedly believed that Gervaize would make a poor showing and throw his votes to Barrès on the run-off ballot, just as the conservative Renard had done in 1889. Probably for that reason Barrès had not attacked Gervaize in the first ballot campaign, but with only 50 votes separating him from Barrès, Gervaize was not about to withdraw.

Compared to Gervaize, Barrès was a paragon of brotherliness. Ludovic Gervaize had been a "Friend of Morès," had brought the marquis to Nancy for a speech in 1894, and had moved on to be one of the guiding spirits of Nancy's chapter of Guérin's Anti-Semitic League. His electoral newspaper, *l'Indépendant: journal républicain antijuif*, was one of the more vicious anti-Semitic sheets of the period and regularly attacked Barrès for not being anti-Semitic enough. One of his campaign posters read:

> The Jews have taken our MONEY! The *Sans-patrie* have wanted to wipe out our HONOR! Both have betrayed us. Have they not defamed our Generals and Army? Have they not joined with the Foreigner and Zola? . . . PATRIOTS whose motto is HONOR and HOMELAND! vote for the *anti-Jewish protest* candidate . . . Long live France for the French! Long live the Republic! Long live the Army! Death to Traitors![53]

While his program was as nationalist as Barrès' and supported pensions if not worker-owned enterprises, its clericalism commended him to well-placed reactionary Catholic laymen, who regularly accompanied him at rallies, and priests.[54] With the backing of the conservative *Journal de la Meurthe-et-Moselle* and *La Croix de l'Est*, he was riding a conservative groundswell in the East which had brought victory for a conservative on the first ballot in Nancy's first *circonscription*. He also convinced many conservative republicans of his republicanism, including newspapers like *l'Impartial* and the *Est Républicain*, whose editor in 1899 would be one of the adherents to the anti-Dreyfusard League of the Patrie Française.

With Gervaize remaining in the race after the first ballot, Barrès had to do two things to win. He had to pick up republican votes from Nicolas, who retired, and Demenge-Cremel, who stayed in the race to prevent the triumph of both Barrès' "caesarism of the saber" and Gervaize's "caesarism of the aspersorium."[55] To do so, Barrès and his newspaper argued that votes for Demenge-Cremel would bring, if he lost to Gervaize, the triumph of a new, local 16th of May to Nancy, put Nancy in the hands of "a coterie of reactionaries," and "compromise the republic." If Demenge won, the voters would leave power in the hands of the Opportunists who had favored Jews for twenty-five years.[56] To pick up Nicolas' voters, Barrès billed himself as a thoroughgoing republican and reformer. He again summed up his "socialist" reform program. As if to prove his sincerity, he insisted that, though the opposition called him a "millionaire," he wanted his proposed income tax to begin with him.[57]

Barrès also had to keep his voters from switching to Gervaize, whose chance for victory seemed no longer impossible, and to win voters away from him. Anti-Semite that he was, Barrès now made it quite clear that his variety of anti-Semitism was solely political and patriotic, not racial or religious. That of Gervaize, on the other hand, was of "clerical fanaticism" just as that of Drumont was of "religious enthusiasm."[58] Gervaize, unlike the moderate Barrès, shouted "Death to the Jews" in place of advocating "serious reforms."[59] Indeed, said the *Courrier*, Barrès was so moderate that his refusal to demand that Jews be strung up on the nearest lamp-post caused the *Est Républicain* to accuse him of "surface anti-Semitism."[60] The newspaper also took pains to show how extreme Gervaize's position was. It suggested that he was running in the third *circoncision*, instead of the third *circonscription*, and repeated a tale that Gervaize had clubbed a Jewish client and invited his friends over to dine on the corpse. The menu of "this fraternal *agape*" included *"omelette aux bouts coupés d'asperge, hors d'oeuvre et prépuces d'Algérie* [Drumont had just won an election in Algiers], *filet de Juif grillé 'Inquisition,' langue hebraique fumée aux lentilles d'Esau, desserts de Sahara,"* and the wines included *"Sang juif en carafons, Lacryma Christi."*[61] Both the *Progrès de l'Est* and Barrès argued that Gervaize was using anti-Semitism to create a "republic of priests," which Barrès wanted no more than he wanted a "republic against priests," and to parlay this victory into control of the municipal and cantonal elections.[62] The *Est Républicain* had become so clerical and monarchist that it was virtually an *Est Jésuitique*.

To buttress his anti-Semitic and nationalist credentials in the run-off election, Barrès reprinted articles from Drumont's *Libre Parole* and statements from the *Jeunesse antisemite et nationaliste* urging Gervaize to retire in favor of him. He also brought in Déroulède and his lieutenant, Marcel Habert, for a series of rallies in every village in the district. Déroulède urged the voters to abandon the "false anti-Jew" and "remain faithful to republican discipline," because Gervaize was using anti-Semitism to bring clericalism.[63]

Yet, it did not work out as Barrès planned. Gervaize ended with 6005 votes to the 5786 of Barrès. Demenge-Cremel, with 3140, came in a poor third. In the district Barrès carried only the working-class section of Nancy-Est.[64] He was somewhat right to believe that his defeat resulted from his failure to get Gervaize's withdrawal before the campaign, to repair the damage of that failure, and to overcome the strength of clericalism.[65] What he did not recognize was that "national socialism" was not a salable commodity in France in 1898. Instead of uniting disgusted voters of Left and Right as Boulangism had done, it attracted only the Left and a peculiarly nationalistic and pre-Marxian Nancy Left at that. The Right found all the nationalism and anti-Semitism that it could use in Gervaize, with clericalism and social conservatism to boot. It wanted no part of a "capricious socialist," as Gervaize called Barrès, let alone one aided by an anti-clerical populist like Déroulède.[66] How could Barrès build a vehicle capable of bringing victory for "national socialism," if he wanted to call it that, or at least for a nationalist social republic?

CHAPTER SEVEN

BARRÈS AND THE NATIONALIST LEAGUES, 1899–1903

By autumn 1898, when Barrès returned to Paris from a post-election trip to the south of France, the Dreyfus affair was rapidly reaching the crisis stage. Within a year the crisis would breed a welter of nationalist leagues willing to overthrow the parliamentary system if necessary in order to prevent the exoneration of Dreyfus. Barrès would be the only important figure with intimate standing in each of the major leagues: the League of Patriots, the League of the Patrie Française, and the Action Française. Until this time he had been either a follower, as in Boulangism, or a leader of a purely personal or local movement, as in *La Cocarde*, Neuilly-Boulogne, and the Nancy campaign of 1898. Now he was a major national leader.

Because of the power these anti-Dreyfusard leagues were to amass, here was the one great chance in his lifetime for Barrès to have a vehicle for institutionalizing his ideas on social and national regeneration. This means that the years of the nationalist leagues, 1898–1903, were key years for Barrès' ideas and action. Moreover, both his ideas and action were so interrelated that each has to be examined for either to make sense. The Dreyfus affair saw Barrès develop those ideas, especially those most resembling later fascism, which would be remembered throughout the twentieth century as the essential Barrésianism. Only by also examining the context of those ideas—his unsuccessful attempt to win over the nationalist leagues to them and their failure to take power—can one understand how Barrès would later abandon those remarkably fascist ideas in favor of something else.

The Dreyfus affair began heading toward crisis in August, 1898. In that month the General Staff discovered that one of the major documents against Dreyfus, the very one that War Minister Godefroy Cavaignac had read to the Chamber of Deputies in July to "prove" that Dreyfus was guilty, was a forgery. Its author, Major Henry, was arrested and committed suicide in jail on August 31. Key figures in the War Office, including Cavaignac whose Chamber speech was still posted in every commune in France, promptly resigned. Revision now seemed inevitable. The Dreyfusard forces stepped up their campaign with ever more frequent demonstrations, especially when the government moved troops into Paris to put down an outbreak of strikes. The Chamber reconvened in October amid tumultuous demonstrations. The Henri Brisson government was replaced by one headed by Charles Dupuy. On November 28 Raymond Poincaré told the Chamber that in 1894 the government had known only about the *bordereau*, a letter offering military secrets to the German military attaché in Paris. Originally held to have been written by Dreyfus, it was now widely believed to have been written by the shady Major Esterhazy, who had fled the country. By December this announcement by Poincaré had rallied many of his fellow moderates to the cause of Dreyfus, and Jaurès had won over most of the socialists. By early 1899 the government ordered a new court martial for Dreyfus, which was held at Rennes in August and September, 1899.

As these developments unfolded, Barrès was convinced that Dreyfus had become only a symbol for the Dreyfusard leaders to use for their own ends: for moderate Joseph Reinach to strike at anti-Semitism, for socialist Francis de Pressensé to end military justice, and for Jean Jaurès to destroy the army. Even with the declaration of Poincaré, Barrès believed, the innocence of Dreyfus was still only a hypothesis. Guilt or innocence be hanged, national interest was the only criterion, and national interest demanded that the army be upheld.[1] In such a state of mind, Barrès willingly donated to the fund established by *La Libre Parole* to help Madame Henry sue Reinach for accusing her husband of being the real traitor in the Dreyfus case.[2]

Throughout 1899 Barrès persisted in believing Dreyfus guilty and worried that a vast conspiracy was trying to free him. There was not one piece of "evidence" against Dreyfus that Barrès mistrusted nor any testimony in favor of Dreyfus that he accepted. At the court martial in Rennes, which he covered for *Le Journal*, Barrès was completely taken in by the testimony of Bertillon that the *bordereau* was in Dreyfus' handwriting, by that of Lebrun-Renaud that Dreyfus had confessed at his degradation in 1894, and by that of Cernusky that Dreyfus was one of four spies in 1891.[3] At the same time, his blindness to the facts even made him dismiss all the testimony in favor of Dreyfus and believe that a "great plot" had been attempted by the "syndicate," led by Joseph Reinach, to get samples of Esterhazy's handwriting and frame him by getting him a position in the War Office.[4] He was even victimized by the pseudo-scientific racism of his friend Jules Soury, a professor at the Sorbonne who came to Rennes to advise him.[5] Even after Dreyfus was freed, Barrès continued to believe him guilty: he appeared innocent only because the War Office could not reveal all the proofs without risking war. At the same time Dreyfus was only a "pretext" to divide and weaken France, to attack the army.[6] When Dreyfus was finally exonerated in 1906, Barrès told the Chamber of Deputies, "For twelve years Dreyfus has been a traitor through a judicial truth. For twenty-four hours, through a new judicial truth, he is innocent. That is a great lesson, not of scepticism, but of relativism. . . ."[7]

As these events began after the discovery of the forgeries of Major Henry, the anti-Dreyfusards became alarmed. To offset the rising tide in favor of revision, many groups and leagues were formed or revived which would eventually attract Barrès. One of these was the League of Patriots. That old Boulangist troop, which had hung on throughout the 1890s even though its membership fell to one thousand five hundred, was revived by Paul Déroulède in September, 1898. By February, 1899, it had perhaps forty-two thousand members in Paris and the suburbs. To his voters in Charente, who elected him to the Chamber in 1898, and to his leaguers, Déroulède promised a revolution, if necessary, to revise the constitution and stop the Dreyfusards. He assured his followers that "the army will be our ally" to these ends.[8] By October his forces were turning Dreyfusard rallies into riots, and on October 25 when the Chamber reconvened, his forces massed in the Place de la Concorde, with the intention of driving Brisson from office. In this effort Déroulède was accompanied by such old Boulangists as Georges Thiébaud, Lucien Millevoye, Albert Gauthier de Clagny, and César Paulin-Méry.[9] At the Salle Chaynes on the avenue Wagram on December 10, leaguers and anarchists scuffled outside while Déroulède went inside to argue against Anatole France, Francis de Pressensé, and Paul Reclus. By this time the leaguer Henri Galli was convinced that Paris was in a "revolutionary fever," but the army would not go along. Although Barrès participated in none of these activities, he did give them publicity in Le Journal and was considered by the police to be a member.[10] By February, 1899, however, Barrès agreed that the coup d'état which the League of Patriots wanted was possible because the people were really fed up. Yet, he did not think it probable.[11] Moreover, revolution simply did not whet his political appetite, at least not yet.

While few anti-Dreyfusards could agree with the way the League of Patriots sought solutions in the street and in a coup, many like Barrès did see that something was needed. In December, 1898, a "respectable" alternative to the raucous, semi-revolutionary League of Patriots presented itself. Several young teachers, led by Louis Dausset, Gabriel Syveton, and Henri Vaugeois, encouraged Barrès, François Coppée, the poet, and Jules Lemaître, the critic, to organize anti-Dreyfusard intellectuals against the Dreyfusard ones. Out of the discussions came the League of the Patrie Française.[12] These men, like Barrès, had come to their positions, in spite of their attachment to Zola, when the Dreyfusards began attacking the army.[13] By the first week of January, 1899, the new league issued a vague manifesto, eventually signed by several thousand, in support of the army, French traditions, and reconciliation. The point of the new league was to show that the Dreyfusards had no monopoly on intellectuals.[14] Moreover, the league made it quite clear that it was not like Déroulède's organization. Its members were free to act as individuals, however, and that was enough to win the support of Déroulède's leaguers. "It is not a group of revolutionaries," wrote Barrès, "nor is it a herd of sheep which offer their necks to a gang of thieves."[15] Barrès insisted that the members of the new league were "men of good will" and he welcomed all who would come to the league's support of the army.[16]

The first rally of the Patrie Française on January 19 found Barrès sharing the stage with such luminaries as Vincent d'Indy, Albert Sorel, Arthur Meyer, Jean Louis Forain, François Coppée, and Jules Lemaître in front of an audience which, in the words of *Le Gaulois*, was "correct"—no anarchists in caps, no long-haired esthetes; rather a majority wearing the red ribbons of the Legion of Honor.[17] In the chief speech Lemaître insisted that the league believed in justice and would rather see a guilty man at large than an innocent one in jail, but that the nation should support the two courts martial and five war ministers who said Dreyfus was guilty. Lemaître argued that the league was against Dreyfus because it believed him guilty, not because it was anti-Semitic or undemocratic.[18]

Lemaître's speech and the manifesto disquieted Barrès, however. The part supporting the army was all right. As to the part supporting French traditions he asked, with Ernest Lavisse, "What traditions?" If it meant reaction, Barrès would have none of it: "No 'clericalism.' Anti-clerical and militarist is what our government ought to be."[19] The worst of it was that the program of the Patrie Française was so vague. No one would spell out what was meant by tradition and reconciliation.

Although he was one of the founders of the League of the Patrie Française and served on its steering committee, the vagueness of its program caused Barrès to turn to the League of Patriots when events shifted with the death of President Félix Faure in February. Although a *coup d'état* had been in the air for some time, Barrès greeted Faure's death as a time for renewal, not revolution.[20] On the day of the election of a successor to Faure, Barrès wrote:

180

I do not speak of the more ardent who . . . treat the death of M. Faure as a *"coup d'état* by chance" and wish that it be the signal for the nomination of a "provisional government," evidently made up of a general, a popular former war minister, and several men designated by national clamor. I mention this as a sign of the times. I am not stopped by it. But, I confirm the unanimous desire that the future president, in order to put an end to a woeful plot, be a man willing to use the widest powers that the Constitution gives him.[21]

As Barrès wrote those lines, however, Déroulède had decided to use the death of Faure to overthrow the republic, and he won the support of Barrès for his scheme. Barrès had not been an associate of the League of Patriots. He had not been in Paris during the disturbances of the previous autumn when the league had hoped to convince the army that it was its civilian arm. Nor had Barrès attended the big rally of the League of Patriots at Saint-Cloud on January 22.[22] However, he did have a great friendship for Déroulède and supported Déroulède's desire for a presidential republic, if not his willingness to use force to attain that goal. With the death of Faure, Déroulède returned to Paris amid the frenzied cries of his leaguers, "A l'Elysée!" "That says nothing to you?" Georges Thiébaud asked Déroulède. On January 18, after his leaguers had hooted the new President Emile Loubet through the streets of Paris with cries of "Panama," Déroulède promised action for the 23rd, the day of the funeral of Faure.

Déroulède's basic plan was to get the army to lead the League of Patriots to the Elysée and the Hotel de Ville, overthrow the régime, and establish a provisional government. Throughout the fall of 1898, Déroulède had contacted various generals and was convinced that he had the support of at least the royalist General Pellieux and perhaps several members of the Dupuy government.[23] Yet, hardly any of this plan was firm. Placards, in the fashion of December 2, 1851, were printed to proclaim the overthrow of the parliamentary republic, but the place for the official signatures remained blank.[24] A royalist "plot" operated simultaneously, but Marcel Habert, the chief lieutenant of Déroulède, swore that he personally would arrest the Count of Paris if he showed up, while Déroulède

181

insisted that his conspiratorial general had to be a Cromwell, not a Monk.[25] The plot was virtually a public affair with the leaguers being notified of their rendezvous by *cartes pneumatiques*, many of which fell into the hands of the police.[26]

Ill-planned as the plot was, it was firm enough to win the support of Barrès, who believed now that the League of Patriots' action of the past six months had really won the allegiance of the army. After a rally on February 21, the day of the funeral came. Barrès had lunch with Déroulède and his leaguers. Together they went to the Place de la Nation where they were to intercept the troops returning from the Père Lachaise cemetery. As they went, Déroulède assured Barrès that victory would be theirs. "What convinces me to join your attempt," replied Barrès, "is my certainty that if we do not succeed, we will begin it again."[27] When the troops arrived, they were not led by Pellieux, who had had himself replaced, but by General Roget. Déroulède, still flanked by Barrès and others, grabbed the bridle of the general's horse and unsuccessfully tried to engage him in the "plot." Déroulède and Habert continued to plead with him all the way to the barracks on the Rue de Reuilly where the gates were closed behind them and they were arrested. Other groups, both republican and royalist, waited throughout Paris for the never-to-materialize *coup*, hoping to take advantage of it for their own ends. Even Gervaize, the opponent of Barrès at Nancy in 1898, waited with old Boulangists Millevoye and Le Senne.[28] By May, Déroulède and Habert were tried and acquitted. They remained the toast of Parisian nationalists and continued into the summer hatching new plots.

In his public statements in 1899 Barrès saw that the League of the Patrie Française and the League of Patriots were to play a complementary role. The Patrie Française was "to analyse the deep causes of this anarchy [i.e. the split in France which had created so many Dreyfusards], to dissipate that which mingles gloom with the ardor of patriots, to restore complete nobility and intellectual force to that spiritual state which the simple-minded (yes, the pedants of the demi-culture) flout under the name of chauvinism, and finally to double the enthusiasm of the masses through the affirmation of these principles." The Patrie Française was not to engage in politics or in street action. That was to be the role of the League of Patriots. The League of Patriots, wrote Barrès, "has an excellent political program which pursues the fortification of the executive through its popular election, the renunciation of parliamentarianism while maintaining the representative system, and the willingness to use an expedient [i.e. a coup] for ending the existing anarchy if no regular way is able to draw us into it."[29] The Patrie Française was to reconcile Frenchmen to each other. "After that," wrote Barrès, "it is necessary to proceed through stages. Fortify the executive. Renounce parliamentarianism. Accept an *expedient* (Caesar)."[30]

Privately, however, it was a different matter. Barrès really wanted these two leagues to be complementary agents for his brand of nationalism. The vague pronouncements of the League of the Patrie Française, to which he objected, had given it an enormous and influential membership, the kind of membership he had failed to get in Nancy and Neuilly. For it to be a useful agent, however, its ill-defined anti-Dreyfusardism would have to be converted to the more precise theory of Barrésian nationalism. Then it could provide the support necessary for efforts of the smaller, more militant League of Patriots to end the parliamentary regime with either a coup or popular outcry.

Unfortunately for Barrès, the League of the Patrie Française turned to the only action its amorphous anti-Dreyfusard membership would support, namely anti-ministerialism, when the Dreyfusard ministry of moderate René Waldeck-Rousseau came to power in June, 1899. The members of his mainly Radical party ministry extended from General Gallifet, whose troops had crushed the Paris Commune in 1871, to socialist Alexandre Millerand, and promised to end the Dreyfus affair. The Waldeck-Rousseau ministry secured Dreyfus' pardon after his reconviction in 1899, cracked down on the more militant nationalist leagues like the League of Patriots and the Anti-Semitic League, and put in motion legislation which would ban those violently anti-Dreyfusard religious orders like the Assumptionists from teaching.

As the League of the Patrie Française shifted to anti-ministerialism, Barrès tried to orient it to something more substantial than the desire to replace Waldeck-Rousseau with an anti-Dreyfusard ministry. The Dreyfus affair and the Waldeck-Rousseau ministry showed that France's problems were too deep and severe for anti-ministerialism alone to succeed in restoring the national health. Barrès had begun his development toward such an orientation in *Les Déracinés*, the first volume in the "novel of national energy" trilogy, and the Nancy political campaign of 1898. In both instances, nationalism, formerly an undercurrent, was elevated into a new faith in which rootless intellectuals and the masses could join, nourish each other, and find fulfillment. But *Les Déracinés* merely described the symptoms of France's illness, and the Nancy voters rejected the initial cure. Only with the Dreyfus affair, the triumph of the Dreyfusards in the Waldeck-Rousseau ministry, and the action of the nationalist leagues did Barrès develop these tentatives into a doctrine. He set it forth in the two remaining volumes of the "novel of national energy" and in a collection of essays. With *Les Déracinés* these works came to comprise the Barrésian doctrine which would have lasting political appeal in France. Whenever Frenchmen were politically inspired by Barrès, they ordinarily found their scripture in *Les Déracinés*, *L'Appel au soldat*, *Leurs figures*, and *Scènes et doctrines du nationalisme*.

Unfortunately these works have been taken for something else as well. Because *L'Appel au soldat* (1900) and *Leurs figures* (1902) described Boulangism and the Panama scandal, respectively, and many of the essays in *Scènes et doctrines du nationalisme* (1902) were originally published as newspaper articles in the 1893–1895 period, these writings too often have been seen as the essential expression of Barrès' politics for 1888 to 1902. In reality the politics expressed in these books are the same he held in the Dreyfus affair and wanted the leagues to adopt. *Scènes et doctrines du nationalisme* was a "new" book because Barrès included with his essays on the Dreyfus affair only those essays of the 1890s which would provide appropriate lessons for the League of the Patrie Française. Essays which did not meet that criterion were eliminated from the selection.

This was even more true for *L'Appel au soldat* and *Leurs figures*. They were fictionalized, didactic rewritings of Boulangism and the Panama scandal, intended to provide relevant political lessons for the nationalist leagues. This is easy to perceive if one reads Barrès' political novels in the order of their action rather than in the order of their publication and accepts each novel's protagonist as his *porte-parole*. If one does that, one can but conclude that Barrès miraculously shifted from Sturel's right-wing Boulangism in *L'Appel au soldat* to André Maltère's "infantile leftism" of *L'Ennemi des lois* and right again to Sturel's rightist anti-parliamentarianism of the Panama scandal in *Leurs figures*. There was no hint in *L'Appel au soldat* that Boulangism took Barrès into socialism. The leftist leaders of Boulangism like Laisant and Gabriel who had been so important to Barrès' political education were seldom if ever mentioned. The heroes now became such types as Déroulède, desirous of turning Boulanger's Paris election into an assuredly successful coup d'état, and Delahaye, unrelentingly attacking parliamentary corruption in the Panama scandal. The Boulangist crowds, instead of being "workers" as the Nancy constituents were in reality or as Philippe's constituents were in the fiction of *Le Jardin de Bérénice*, now were called "unknowns," while Boulanger's appeal was to "the little people."[31] Nor was there any suggestion in *Leurs figures* that Boulangists had been side by side with the socialists in their opposition to parliamentary corruption.

These novels make sense not so much as accounts of Boulangism and the Panama scandal, but as the beginnings of a Barrèsian doctrine for France of the Dreyfus affair and after.[32] They began a new Boulangism that was further spelled out with the reprinting as *Scènes et doctrines du nationalisme* of Barrès' account of the Dreyfus case, his reply to the Dreyfusard intellectuals, his paeans to such exciters of energy as Morès and Déroulède, his speeches to various nationalist leagues, and his program of Nancy in 1898. Together they constituted the most extreme form of Barrès' doctrine. What was it?

To be sure, some of Barrès' beliefs from the time of the action of the novels remained; they were still relevant for leagues hoping to take advantage of the Dreyfus affair.

185

Sturel, the hero and political innocent like Barrès, was drawn to Boulangism because of its "national ferment." He was "immediately possessed by the soul of the crowds" and exhilarated by "the pleasure of mingling with the collective sentiment and breathing at the center of national energy." Boulangism "exalted" him "like a traveler arriving at night in an unknown city is intoxicated by the famous spaces he can barely make out." The movement gave "to everyone the right to march beside his adversaries without abandoning his differences with them or having to explain himself."[33] Again, like Barrès, Sturel accepted Boulangism's view that "parliamentarianism destroys the brain like alcoholism, lead poisoning, and syphillis."[34] The Panama scandal, in turn, only reinforced his conviction of "parliamentary prostitution."[35] The suicide of a Panama Company executive illustrated the marriage between private and parliamentary corruption in that the "Baron Jacques de Reinach recalls those huge rats which, having swallowed poison and gone behind the woodwork to die, almost make it necessary to demolish the house because their inflamed cadavers poisoned the poisoners."[36]

Throughout *L'Appel au soldat* and *Leurs figures* Barrès was careful to point out that the cure for the national sickness diagnosed in *Les Déracinés* was not the anti-ministerialism he perceived to be so dear to the League of the Patrie Française nor the anti-parliamentarianism so desired by the League of Patriots. It was not enough to turn the rascals out. *Leurs figures* regularly condemned not only the Opportunists. They stood together with the Radicals, conservatives, and socialists to defend the utter bankruptcy of Panama-stained parliamentarianism. No party or political persuasion willing merely to replace dirty parliamentarians with clean ones could be trusted.

If anti-ministerialism was not enough, neither was anti-parliamentarianism. That was the message of *L'Appel au soldat*, and little wonder that it was dedicated to Jules Lemaître, president of the League of the Patrie Française. The trouble with Boulangism, contended a friend of Sturel, was that it merely adopted the anti-parliamentary stance of Naquetism. "As a result Boulangism, which ought to be the national conscience, is still just a fever."[37] After the victory in

Paris in January, 1889, the movement forgot its role of "exciting the country so that it can find the force to smash systems" and became just another political party. "The muscles it formerly had are filled with fat" and "it rallies to success, not principle."[38] The principle to which it should have rallied was that Naquetism was wrong: "deeply divided" France did not need new constitutions nearly as much as it needed a new spirit, and the nationalist leagues should not repeat that mistake.

Nor was Boulangism's lesson for them and for France of the Dreyfus affair Gabriel's socialism. Rather, it was that nationalism was much stronger than social reform or anti-parliamentarianism. "We have seen that a nation is a territory where men possess common memories, morals, a hereditary ideal."[39] Boulanger should have been seen only as an "expedient," "the great national flag" for rallying men to that view of the nation, for giving them a new élan. If Boulangism failed, "we will find a new Boulangism."[40]

Because the Dreyfus affair, like the Boulanger crisis before it, had put France in a "fever," the opportunity was ripe for a "new Boulangism," and the nationalist leagues could be instruments for it. That "new Boulangism," already suggested in "the novel of national energy," was further delineated in a speech Barrès intended to give before the League of the Patrie Française on March 10, 1899, and in *Scènes et doctrines du nationalisme*, which included the speech among its collection of essays. The doctrine held that the "new Boulangism" could not just tinker with the machinery through anti-ministerialism or anti-parliamentarianism. In Barrès' mind even a political revolution was secondary at this point, and a social revolution was left far behind. France's problems were so formidable that the nation had to be rebuilt from the ground up; France was so uprooted, disoriented, and disunified that its greatest need and prerequisite for all else was the spiritual revolution which Boulangism had promised but not delivered. A new, appropriate "organ of national will" or political system, Barrès believed, "will appear by itself," only when the nation's political spirit had been transformed.[41]

The Dreyfus affair, according to Barrès, made it clear once

and for all that this spiritual rebuilding was necessary if divided France was to be saved. The "Dreyfus affair was not at all produced by chance, but it is the result of our milieu," the continuation of the Wilson and Panama scandals.[42] Because of that, it was necessary to discover "what sickness inside us results from these criminal crises" and "to understand the causes of our decadence."[43] The trouble was that "the triumph of the camp which sustains Dreyfus as a symbol would decidedly put in power men who would *transform France according to their point of view*," wrote Barrès, "while I wish to conserve France. Nationalism's entirety is in this opposition."[44]

Thanks to the members of this camp, Barrès' hated intellectuals, "we have lost sense of the relative and then we have gotten used to using words which have lost their meaning." Such men, for example, "talk about Justice and Truth when every reflective man knows that they ought to be examining whether or not the facts of the case are just for those particular men in that particular time and circumstance. Where does this error held by so many of our professors and most of our major philosophers come from?"[45] It came, of course, from the development of Kantianism into "a state ethic" and "official doctrine" which had so permeated the entire education system that Frenchmen had come to study problems from a position of abstract philosophic systems, even if it meant the destruction of society. Their influence had created deracinated, dissociated, and decerebralized Frenchmen.

To find a cure for France's spiritual sickness of uprootedness, dissociation, and drift, Barrès proceeded to universalize on what he said he found in his own "little garden." He, too, had once believed like his masters that he had "an independent reason" "which allows us to come to truth." Even with it, however, he remained "terrified of [his] dependence, powerless to fulfil [himself]," and still unconvinced by "the best dialectic and the most complete demonstrations." "My heart must be filled spontaneously with a great respect as well as love." "We should not unify ideas by purely rational means. They should be reinforced by sentiment. At the root of everything is sensibility." Truth "is not knowing something intellectually. Rather, it is finding a sure point, a single point and no other one than that where everything appears to us in proper perspective."[46] That point, he admitted, might have been anarchism had he not reflected on his Lorraine roots. Lorrainers had become Catholic and French, not by abstract reason, but by the process of history. Their dukes had repulsed Protestantism but had not preserved independent Lorraine development.

Barrès was convinced that the lesson of his and Lorraine's experience could restore divided France to health. "The problem for the individual and the nation is not at all to create themselves into what they would like to be (oh! impossible job), but to conserve in themselves what the centuries predestined them to be. Nationalism is the acceptance of a determinism."[47] To find this determinism and their own roots, Frenchmen needed to "repudiate philosophic systems and the parties they engender"[48] in favor of history, to seek answers in their peculiar traditions and localities, and to substitute the relative for the abstract.

France, in short, would be restored as a nation when Frenchmen were reconciled with their dead and their soil. By the "dead" Barrès meant the restoration of men's sense of their history, the uniqueness of their nation and its traditions, the recognition that "truth," like everything else, is relative. This last meant that men needed to look for French truth rather than absolute truth or German or English truth. To facilitate this, Barrès asked for stiffer naturalization laws, for only the second or third generation immigrant was rooted enough in the French "dead" to be trusted with full citizenship. By the "soil," Barrès meant a regionalist organization for France. The dead could transmit their heritage only by being rooted in a particular piece of France. A feeling of both ancestry and place was necessary to give men roots. A centralized France had destroyed the ability of localities to do this. A man could never learn loyalty to the nation without first learning a regional loyalty. The regions needed to be strengthened so that men would have some reason to be loyal to them. In particular, Barrès urged enough autonomy for regions to cope with the educational and social problems peculiar to them. He made it quite clear that by regionalism and traditionalism he did not mean the monarchical tradition. He was aware that "the conditions of democratic (alas, plutocratic) and industrial France differ from the conditions of monarchical France".[49] His very need to say such words revealed how rightist his former socialist nationalism had become.

To speak about "dead and soil" is to speak about race, and Barrès was no exception. Basically, he argued that while there existed a French *nation*, "a collectivity of political formation," there was unfortunately no French *race*. Nor were the French, unlike the "Anglo-Saxon and Teutonic collectivities," turning themselves into a race.[50] Yet, the goal of "dead and soil" was to turn the French nation into a race. The goal would be accomplished when all Frenchmen recognized that they were "a product of a collectivity" which spoke through them. By that collectivity Barrès did not mean only some of the dead; he wanted Frenchmen "to live with all their dead." "France of the Consulate, monarchical France, France of 1830, France of 1848, France of the authoritarian Empire and of the liberal Empire," he wrote, "all the Frances . . . are from the same seed and are the fruit of different seasons from the same tree."[51]

Elsewhere, however, Barrès indicates that he really did not mean *all* the French dead at all. The exceptions were Protestants and Jews. "Protestants," he wrote in his private journal, "have no fatherland. They live for an idea, for conceiving life in a religious way."[52] While he never made public statements as strong as this about Protestants, he regularly did so about Jews: "Jews have no fatherland in the sense that we understand it. For us fatherland is the soil and our ancestors, the land of our dead. For them it is the place where they can make the most money. Their 'intellectuals' similarly arrived at their famous definition: 'The fatherland is an idea.' "[53] On occasion Barrès veered toward physical and ethnic racism. "Neither his nose nor his firm and perspicacious eyes seemed Jewish at first," thought Sturel upon meeting Cornelius Herz of the

Panama Company, but the young Lorrainer soon concluded that he and the Jew were "representatives of two different species."[54] Generally, however, Barrès limited himself to attacking Protestants and Jews in terms of cultural racism; they were un-French in the same way that Kantianism was.

Barrès' hope was that the League of the Patrie Française would be the vehicle for converting France to this doctrine, for helping France sense the direction in which history had taken her, and for bringing the various presently warring Frances together again. The first step in this direction, he believed, was reconciliation, which was already at work in the league's own membership, a membership able to bring together men as diverse as the anti-parliamentary republican Déroulède and the conservative and clerical Coppée. He also urged the league to sponsor religious reconciliation and, most particularly, to reconcile Frenchmen with their dead and soil.

Included among those dead and that soil, Barrès told the league in a speech on December 11, 1899, were Alsace and Lorraine. In Alsace-Lorraine, he insisted, there were persistent under-currents of hostility to Germany and love for France. Germany he argued, had had trouble with the pro-French church and deputies elected to the Reichstag. French culture persisted. French continued to be spoken privately and taught to children. However, Barrès' argument was not bellicosely revanchist. He simply urged that France continue to view the lost provinces as part of France so as not to betray their trust in France.[55]

Barrès' efforts to win the Patrie Française to his program, however, came to nothing. Lemaître consistently made the vague pronouncements he had expressed at the initial meeting: the nation needed to be strong, resist internationalism, love the army, crack down on "anarchists" and the "collectivists" in the Waldeck-Rousseau government, stay out of politics, respect dissent and freedom of association, and remain committed to republicanism. He and the league regularly claimed the desire to ameliorate the plight of the workers, but their concern for governmental economics precluded welfare spending and pensions. All they could talk about, instead, was worker self-help.[56] Almost anyone could accept such a program, and the membership, needless to say, extended from the followers of Déroulède and Rochefort to respectable Progressistes. Déroulède looked upon it as a recruiting ground for his own league.[57] The only anti-Dreyfusards the league kept at arm's length were the royalists and the anti-Semites of Guerin and Drumont. Though the abundant royalist coffers spilled out to Guerin, no royalist money flowed to the impeccably republican League of the Patrie Française.[58] The money endlessly flowed in from its republican members, and from 1899 to 1902 it was far and away the richest and largest league.[59]

In spite of the Patrie Française's members and money, the league could not organize and focus on any program, let alone Barrès'. No one should have been surprised at this, given the numerous factions coming under the league's umbrella. With Dausset, Lemaître kept the Mélinist and antiministerial wing of the league dominant over the Déroulèdist faction of Barrès and Syveton. Cavaignac stood somewhere in between.[60] Given the factionalism, only an ill-defined program could find support. A circular to local committees merely urged them to limit their activity to defending patriotism and the army, looking out for "the interference and propaganda of the foreigner," emphasizing republican liberties and freedom of association and instruction, organizing voters for an "honest Republic open to all," and engaging in "national politics" in the "general interest" but not in "party politics." The method should be local electoral alliances and politicking around regular conferences on such subjects as the army and democracy, freedom of association, free masonry, mutual aid societies, cooperatives, alcoholism, obligatory voting, proportional representation, and as an apparent sop to the Déroulèdists, constitutional revision.[61]

With this "program" the Patrie Française proceeded to organize France. Dausset, the league's secretary, succeeded in establishing committees in almost every Paris quarter and Seine commune. Beginning in 1900, Syveton, the league's treasurer, sought to do the same in the provinces. Strong committees were established in some thirty departments with elaborate regional organizations set up around Montpellier, Marseille, Toulon, Nice, and Lyon and other strong movements in Nancy, Lille, Boulogne-sur-Mer, Rouen, and Evreux. In short, the league was strongest in Paris, the Est, Nord, Midi, and Normandy, areas which were both rightist and leftist historically.[62] Barrès participated in this drive by going three times to Lorraine with league luminaries. They were greeted by large crowds, but as elsewhere in France, their nets caught a variety of fish. In the Nancy organization Barrès had to curry the favor of many of his old electoral opponents, conservative and republican. The crowd at Saint Dié cheered both Jules Ferry and Déroulède. There Syveton, who was closer to Barrès' ideas than most of the league's leaders, urged the formation of a nationalist party which would work for a constitutional revision.[63]

Indeed, unexpected successes in the Paris municipal elections of May, 1900, did convert the league into a political party. The 250,000 francs the league spent elevated fifty nationalists to the Paris council against thirty socialists and Radicals. The only disappointment was among the league's leaders who had not bothered to run for fear of defeat.[64] Barrès participated with Lemaître, Rochefort, Drumont, Dausset, Syveton, and Galli in a meeting on May 1, 1901, to draw up a list of candidates for the legislative elections of 1902 at Paris. Barrès was to get the first *arrondissement*, but the list ran from conservatives to Radicals to socialists. It included old Boulangists like Paulin-Méry, Gabriel, Millevoye, and Ernest Roche, but not Goussot or Pierre Richard, two old Boulangists who still represented Parisian constituencies.[65]

Yet, for the most part, Barrès remained silent on this transformation of the League of the Patrie Française into a political party, although it ran so obviously against his original intentions for the league. He grew most exasperated with the lack of nationalist fervor shown by his fellow leaguers. On the way to a league rally at Dombasle, François de Mahy, a very respectable republican deputy on the Patrie Française central committee, said to him, "What I will never forgive in Déroulède is that he was not successful." Yet, an hour later at the rally, he attacked illegal methods. A year later Barrès wrote, "Will it come about that our nationalists will do the same thing as our Opportunists? In fact, my friend Dausset is a Mélinist."[66] The Patrie Française's doctrine was obviously too flabby, and Barrès' efforts to strengthen it had failed. Even Lemaître admitted that the league was united only by sentiment— merely anti-Dreyfusard sentiment at that—and not by a program. If lack of program were not enough to give Barrès pause, royalist infiltration into the league's provincial committees, as noted by numerous police reports, should have been.

Although Barrès remained on the League of the Patrie Française's governing board and spoke at its rallies, he did not suffer his disappointment in silence. He was particularly put out when his conference on the "dead and the soil," scheduled for March 10, 1899, was cancelled. Lemaître argued that the conference was cancelled out of prudence, not timidity.[67] He feared, and police reports agreed, that the government's reprisals after Déroulède's coup would reach all the leagues. For Barrès, however, the cancellation was "the supreme infamy." By caving in to governmental threats, the league would destroy the high expectations of its members and die.[68] "The time is past," said Barrès according to one police report, "when the French can be led with generalities and abstract ideas pronounced with a sonorous voice. Today it is necessary to awaken among our fellow citizens the instincts of their local patriotism, to defend their interests in the corner of the province where they were born, where they live and struggle daily with their political enemies."[69]

Barrès' dismay with the League of the Patrie Française caused him to seek a league where his ideas and leadership would dominate. Initially the Action Française promised to do that. The Action Française originated in the minds of Maurice Pujo and Henri Vaugeois, two *lycée* teachers, as early as 1898. Both men also helped found the League of the Patrie Française, but like Barrès they soon concluded it was too weak. Within two months after the organization of the Patrie Française they formed a group with Barrès, Cavaignac, and

Charles Maurras to force Coppée's resignation, reorganize the league on more actionist lines, and start a newspaper.[70] When these plans were abandoned in favor of establishing a new league, the cautious Barrès drew back and only sporadically participated in the discussions. In May, however, he agreed to become the vice-president of the new league, the Action Française.[71] By June 20 the new league staged its first big public rally for 350–450, chaired by de Mahy of the Patrie Française, but without Barrès. The meeting had all the appearances of a Déroulèdist rally. Vaugeois claimed to want an organization which would be more "active" and "audacious" than the Patrie Française, but this activism and the Déroulèdist quality disquieted de Mahy who soon disowned the new league.[72]

These beginnings and his half-hearted participation in them hardly convinced Barrès that the Action Française would be either Barrésian or effective. He changed his mind only after he published an article in October, 1899, in which he typically called for the creation of a nationalist doctrine and of a propaganda publication, a nationalist counterpart to the Dreyfusard *Revue blanche*. Only by doing this prior to political action, said Barrès, could the nationalist movement avoid the pitfall of Boulangism which had had power but no doctrine.[73] The Action Française immediately offered its fledgling review, financed by the Patrie Française, as the instrument of propaganda. The review would publicize Barrès' doctrine of the "soil and the dead" so that nationalism could unite the individual with society and bring together divergent classes with their differing religious, political, and economic views.[74]

That was enough for Barrès. The Action Française's commitment to his ideas now seemed to offer him the pulpit and organizational base denied him by the League of the Patrie Française. In December, 1899, he agreed to write for the Action Française's review. The review reprinted many of his speeches and writings, and he occasionally wrote a new article for it. In March, 1900, he formed an Action Française front organization, the Nationalist Association of Youth. The association, often with Barrès in attendance, held a series of "evenings of

195

studies" to win over the Latin Quarter students.[75] In 1900 and 1901 the league arranged two dinners, billed as *Appel au soldat* dinners, where speeches by Barrès and others sought to convert other leagues to his doctrine. Barrès also spoke at the second anniversary of the Action Française on June 15, 1901. Throughout, he hoped that the new league would serve as a "laboratory" in nationalist education and studies.[76] Naturally, the study would be in his doctrine and the successful laboratory experiments would be adopted by the nationalist movement.

Although the Action Française's beginning was inspired by Barrès' ideas, it soon became something else. By December, 1900, Charles Maurras, through his *Enquête sur la monarchie*, had won control of the organization and converted it to monarchism. Barrès had feared Maurras' influence from the beginning, and his caution in joining the league resulted from that fear. Throughout 1899 Maurras courted Barrès' adherence to the league. Only when he told Barrès that he had been unable to convert the Action Française to royalism did Barrès agree to be a collaborator of the league's review.[77] By the end of 1900, however, Maurras had won the Action Française leadership for the Pretender.

At first the thought that anyone in modern France could be monarchist puzzled Barrès.[78] Finally, he looked on it as perfectly ridiculous. Maurras, Barrès believed, fell into the same trap that the "intellectuals" and socialists did: they placed their faith in utopian solutions based on abstract reasoning.[79] He wrote this to Maurras in the summer of 1900. He added that there was no royalist pretender who could win the hearts of republican France, nor was there an aristocracy which could sustain a king.[80] When monarchist Bourget remarked to him, "What do we owe France? Nothing. Everything to the Bourbons," Barrès replied: "What do we owe the royal family? Nothing. Everything to France, to its culture."[81]

Before 1900 Maurras had been useful to Barrès in the decentralization campaign of 1894–1895 and in his battle with Lemaître's leadership of the Patrie Française in 1899. When the Action Française turned royalist, however, rising friction between Barrès and Maurras increasingly limited their political cooperation. By 1900 the Action Française republicans in the Nationalist Association of Youth continued their studies under Barrès' leadership and a new name, the Republican Committee of National and Social Studies.[82] Although Barrès admitted that the Action Française was "not at all perfect," he still believed its membership retained enough republicans to warrant his delivering two speeches before the league in 1901.[83] By that time letters between Barrès and Maurras were becoming less cooperative politically. Maurras wanted Barrès to write for the Action Française's review but was unwilling to write for Barrès' journalistic enterprises. Barrès was miffed that Maurras would not combat the royalist efforts to undermine his following in Nancy.[84] After 1902 Barrès no longer contributed to the Action Française's review. The two men's association became increasingly concerned with their literary efforts, their attempts to gain membership in the Academie Française, and the Alsace-Lorraine question. They, especially Barrès, revealed less and less of themselves politically in their letters to each other. In spite of their affection for each other they went their separate political ways, and Maurras' way took some of Barrès' following. That added to the friction. "Maurras is able to convince others," Barrès sadly observed in 1903 as he considered the drift of Barrésians into monarchism. "That does not prove that he has the truth; it only proves that he is persuasive."[85]

Just as his disappointment with the League of the Patrie Française turned him to the Action Française, it also veered him closer to the League of Patriots. At the end of May, 1899, he testified at the trial of Déroulède for his attempted coup at Reuilly, sang his praises after the acquittal, and joined in the victory dinner with members of the League of Patriots, Coppée, and Syveton.[86] When the new Waldeck-Rousseau ministry re-arrested Déroulède in August for continuing his conspiracies and brought him before the Senate as a High Court, Barrès again leaped to his defense. The Senate wanted to send Déroulède to Noumea, Barrès cried, so that the Kaiser could come to the Exposition of 1900 "in all tranquility." "Yes, we are all criminals, and [Déroulède] in the first rank, if it is a crime to affirm our mistrust of parliamentary corruption and our fraternity in the national conscience." "I am not one of those," Barrès concluded, "who will let his name or his task fall."[87] Barrès testified at the second trial of Déroulède and Habert, after which they were exiled along with some royalist leaders. Déroulède and Habert then took up residence at San Sebastian in northern Spain, but the back of the League of Patriots was broken. Barrès continued his praise of the league. He traveled to San Sebastian in August, 1900, and February, 1901, to hear Déroulède denounce the "traitor" Pellieux and the royalists who tried to capture control of the coup.[88] In this last visit Barrès served as a second in a duel between Déroulède and André Buffet, the exiled leader of the royalist conspirators.[89]

By the time of this meeting, Barrès was disgusted enough with the lack of doctrine in the League of the Patrie Française to join the cause of the League of Patriots. His decision accompanied only his latest rift with Lemaître's league. In February, 1901, Barrès unsuccessfully tried to get League of the Patrie Française backing for the candidacy of the notoriously anti-Semitic mayor of Algiers, Max Regis, in a parliamentary by-election. Barrès contributed heavily to Regis' campaign, also backed by Rochefort; but even Barrès' usual ally, Syveton, believed that support for Regis would be a greater calamity for nationalism than would be the loss of Rochefort and the anti-Semites. The league did not get along with the anti-Semitic organizations anyway.[90] Barrès showed his mood in this period: "I have still reflected that in the deepest part of my soul I approved the sinister murderers of 1793. Not at all, great God, for their acts, but for their *élan*. They were not moderates. And when I condemn in our Mélinist party all supporters of parliamentarianism, am I not with Robespierre?"[91]

After that it was easy for Barrès to agree to take over the newspaper of the League of Patriots, *Le Drapeau*, turn it into a daily, and act as its editor-in-chief.[92] He even financed the enterprise along with Edmond Archdeacon, the millionaire Deputy from Paris' first *arrondissement* and long-time League of

Patriots angel.[93] Barrès offered the readers of *Le Drapeau* his usual mixture of Left and Right: old Boulangists like Thiébaud, Le Hérissé, and Dumonteil; Patrie Française people like Coppée and Quesnay de Beaurepaire, who had headed the High Court proceedings against Boulanger and Rochefort in 1889; rightist literary figures like Gyp, Maurice Talmeyr, and Georges d'Esparbes; and nationalistic leftists like Ballière and Foursin.[94] The purpose of *Le Drapeau*, Barrès insisted on several occasions, was to be the "dais" for the twenty-two nationalist municipal councilors of Paris and Déroulède and Habert, and the voice of the League of Patriots, which Barrès called "the fever of France." This fever, he went on, would save France with the anti-parliamentary formula.[95] For the most part, Barrès articles in *Le Drapeau* were only warmed-over versions of his earlier arguments against Dreyfus, parliamentary corruption, and *sans patrie* socialism. They were in favor of stiffer naturalization laws, Alsace-Lorraine, and the plebiscitary and presidential republic.

Although Barrès and Déroulède were as one man on policy, the League of Patriots was not the effective instrument Barrès hoped it would be. To be sure, Déroulède accepted the Barrésian notion that decentralization, with its non-revolutionary and anti-collectivist social transformation, would strengthen French nationalism by giving the people roots.[96] To be sure, Barrès made it quite obvious that he believed the league to be the most effective nationalist troop for rallying the nation to the decentralized presidential republic and greater concern for Alsace-Lorraine, even though he did not formally join the league.[97] Moreover, Barrès could agree with the basic program of Déroulède. The League of Patriots had been established, according to a Déroulède speech, read at a rally in May, 1901, to regain Alsace-Lorraine. It soon appeared that to do that the league first had "to liberate France," and Boulangism's patriotic presidential republic was an instrument for doing so. The abortive coup of Reuilly sought the support of the army, if not the royalists, to chase out the parliamentarians, not to make civil war. Rather than being reactionary, the league wished to put more power directly into the hands of the people by abolishing

199

the Senate's power to reverse the decisions of the popularly-elected Chamber of Deputies, by directly electing all representatives of the people, including the president, and by submitting to referendum any conflict between the proposed popularly-elected president and the parliament.[98]

Yet, the League of Patriots was not really effective. The exile of Déroulède and Habert had left it rudderless. It was so much the personal vehicle for Déroulède that it could not widen its membership and absorb other nationalists, and in exile Déroulède became even more possessive of the league. By 1903 Habert had left him, and Barrès concluded he had developed an "insupportable character."[99] Indeed, *Le Drapeau* had been founded as a daily because Déroulède could not get along with other nationalist leaders who closed their newspapers to him. Lemaître's league was not pleased with either its rival's daily newspaper nor Barrès' association with it. The League of Patriots reciprocated in kind, and Barrès had difficulty preventing *Le Drapeau* from attacking other nationalist leagues.[100] Eventually, it even had to give up its daily edition for lack of readers.[101] The declining appeal of the league was also illustrated by its lack of success in its 1901 Bastille Day march to the Statue of Strasbourg in the Place de la Concorde, certainly the most important annual demonstration of the League of Patriots. In spite of an extra-vigorous appeal through its daily newspaper and rallies, the march was no larger than usual, with only one thousand participants.[102] After that it could no longer even hold its own. By the end of 1902, by police estimates, the League had twenty-one thousand members in Paris, only five thousand of whom attended rallies regularly and five hundred to one thousand of whom would turn out for street action. They had become no more than a "nationalist gendarmerie," able to defend rally speakers against hecklers but unable to threaten the regime. With Déroulède in exile the league had become "a train with neither engineer nor fireman."[103] It was held together only with Archdeacon's money, the hope of Déroulède's triumphal return, and the possibility of luring away disgusted members of the League of the Patrie Française. Small as it was, though, it could be militant. Another police report tells that Barrès squelched a 1901 League of Patriots plot to kidnap the president of the republic.[104]

Throughout 1901 it became obvious to Barrès that the weak and disunified leagues had failed to live up to his expectations. As early as February he had observed that the nationalist involvement in politics, and by implication the League of the Patrie Française in particular, threatened to water down nationalist doctrine and, through ill-timed electoral defeats, destroy the movement's ability to do its proper job in educating the public to nationalism.[105] In June the flabbiness of the nationalist troops was illustrated when three Parisian municipal councilors, elected in 1900 under the auspices of the League of the Patrie Française, broke with their fellow nationalists and abstained in a vote which thrust the socialist Adrien Veber into the council presidency. Barrès, Déroulède, and Lemaître all attacked them as traitors.[106] Yet, the nationalist movement was so patently weak that it needed every possible member, even the faint-hearted; within a month the three "traitors" were back in the fold, sharing the stage at a League of Patriots rally in preparation for the march on July 14, to the Statue of Strasbourg.[107] In July the broadness of membership, which in the mind of Barrès had curtailed the effectiveness of the League of the Patrie Française, was illustrated when Alfred Rambaud, an ex-minister of education who had been writing nationalist articles for *Le Matin*, resigned from the central committee of the League of the Patrie Française because its chapter in Saint Dié had condemned Charles Ferry. Barrès welcomed the withdrawal:

> In great national crises, when the country is divided into two armies in which each obeys its faith and temperament, the voters naturally rally to the more frank and decided men. There are parliamentarians and anti-parliamentarians; there are those who are enchanted with the Constitution of 1875 and those who disown it; there is France and the foreigner.[108]

Barrès concluded that the chapter of Saint Dié had done a real service to true nationalism by prompting the resignation of Rambaud. Another illustration of nationalist disunity was the reception given the plan for constitutional revision set forth by Charles Benoist, a *Progressiste* nationalist, who wanted the three thousand councilors-general to elect the president. Thiébaud, in a position Barrès certainly shared, rejected this kind of fuzzy nationalist thinking as providing no improvement on the existing system.[109] Add to this the poor showing of the League of Patriots on July 14, 1901, the circulation difficulties of *Le Drapeau*, the growing anti-ministerialism of the League of the Patrie Française, and the emerging royalism of the Action Française, and it was obvious that the nationalist movement was without discipline, doctrine, or numbers.

With full knowledge of this, Barrès left Paris for Charmes because of his mother's death, and from Charmes he suddenly announced his retirement from politics. The announcement was not made through the nationalist press, not even *Le Drapeau*, but through *Le Figaro*. In it, Barrès stated that his mother had always opposed his political involvement, and in a time of mourning for her, he had decided to return to his art.[110] Déroulède and Habert were thunderstruck. Déroulède even had to learn of the retirement through *Le Figaro*.[111] Habert argued that the stench of politics drove Barrès out. When *Le Drapeau* was given to Barrès, he added, the League of Patriots thought that it had an "excellent captain" for its ship, "but we had not counted on sea-sickness." Barrès just could not take the storms, the smell of gunpowder, and the pounding noise of cannonades which the "daily navigation" of *Le Drapeau* demanded. "Seduced for an instant by the great spectacles and tragic scenes of national life, which he had related in admirable pages, he experiences dreadful nausea from smelling at too close a range the under-side of politics. . . . He goes to find in the republic of letters the pure air which he can no longer breathe in the republic of men."[112]

The explanations of both Barrès and Habert contained grains of truth.[113] The entries in *Mes Cahiers*, which Barrès wrote on his mother's table, bore out his version. As he thought of her life and influence on him, he got "a vague sentiment of wasting. It was the first glimmer of what my reason a few days later formulated for me: since I was she [i.e. his mother], I did not have the right to waste myself." That sentiment kept recurring: "Since I was she, I did not have the right to waste myself. My retirement. Retirement from politics."[114] On the other hand, events in 1901 and 1902 substantiated Habert's implication that Barrès retired from politics because the nationalist movement was turning sour. The nationalist withdrawals of the summer of 1901 were only a prelude to what was to come. In October when the League of the Patrie Française decided to present candidates for the legislative elections of 1902, Barrès resigned from its central committee. He did so not only because he had wanted that league to serve as a nationalist shaper of public opinion, but because, as evinced by its candidates, the league had abandoned nationalism in favor of antiministerialism. It was fine, Barrès wrote early in 1902, for the league to disown the Waldeck-Millerand-André ministry, but in its desire for a Ribot-Méline ministry it was simply backing "the other side of the same coin." Instead of supporting antiministerials, said Barrès, the league should support only antiparliamentarians.[115]

When the legislative elections of April, 1902, were over and the League of the Patrie Française had, indeed, brought victory under its aegis for over fifty predominately anti-ministerial *Progressistes* and conservatives, Barrès returned to politics with a vigor he had not shown since 1898. It was not enough for so-called nationalists to be anti-ministerial and get rid of Waldeck-Rousseau, Barrès wrote in the first of a series of articles in *La Patrie* of Lucien Millevoye, an old Boulangist. They must also be anti-parliamentary. The proposed prime ministers whom the anti-ministerials preferred were just as bad as Waldeck-Rousseau:

> Nationalists know that Rouvier received Panama Company bribes; that Ribot, after having tried to throttle the bribed Rouvier, nursed him and dressed his wounds; that Méline never had a word to condemn the embezzlers, but only words to attack the accusers. When the beast is mangy, the mange is in all the hairs. Méline, Ribot, Rouvier, and Waldeck-Rousseau are hairs of the same beast. The anti-parliamentary scoffs at the anti-ministerial who wants to sort the hairs.

203

Barrès concluded that the nationalists had to sustain the original flag of nationalism, anti-parliamentarianism, for the parliamentary system corrupted everyone it touched.[116]

What was responsible for this state of affairs? Barrès singled out Lemaître as the prime mover of the anti-ministerial turn of nationalism. By uniting with the Mélinists, Lemaître had brought the triumph of *Progressistes* instead of nationalists. The old Opportunists had called themselves *Progressistes* when Opportunism was no longer popular and had posed as nationalists when even *Progressisme* became bankrupt. While their conversion appeared to strengthen nationalism, they had only weakened it by taking it over and watering it down. Had the nationalists adhered to their principles, not as many would have been elected, but "we would have a group conscious of itself, inspired with its work, doctrine, and future." They would be a group willing to speak forcefully for the anti-parliamentary principles of nationalism instead of becoming part of an amorphous band of flabby anti-ministerials.[117]

Throughout the year Barrès continued this line of attack in *La Patrie*, the only major nationalist newspaper open to him since the demise of *Le Drapeau*. Nor was he alone in his position. The groups around Syveton, now virtually in control of the League of the Patrie Française, Rochefort, the League of Patriots, and Millevoye were of this opinion. By June, Syveton could conclude, "We worked for our adversaries."[118] The League of the Patrie Française's abundant purse had elected only anti-ministerial *Progressistes*, although its program had called for constitutional revision, stricter naturalization laws, two-year conscription law with the army's approval, and some attempt to link up with the workers through mutualism and pensions.[119] By May the league's stand in favor of "free association" instead of clericalism drove out Coppée and with him many of the league's clericals and conservatives.[120] By July the Patrie Française was becoming more republican, more plebiscitary, more willing to engage in street action; it held a unity rally with the League of Patriots, its first real support for the Déroulèdists—an action Barrès applauded.[121] These leaguers were ardent enough even to want a counter-demonstration on the day of Zola's funeral in October, but they were over-ruled by the nationalist deputies.[122]

On November 13 Lemaître finally fell under the sway of Syveton's plebiscitary politics and came out for the presidential republic in a speech which split the League of the Patrie Française.[123] Déroulède was ecstatic over the conversion, and Emile Massard, the director of *La Patrie*, praised it for bringing the Patrie Française "to the program of the League of Patriots in what is the most essential."[124] Barrès welcomed the League of the Patrie Française's adherence to the principle of a popularly elected president and only wished that Lemaître's conversion would remove any fears of caesarism by also supporting his decentralization program.[125] However, the Lemaître speech was not received with undivided approval by the nationalist bloc. When it was opposed by the groups surrounding Paul Cassagnac, Cavaignac, and George Grosjean, *Le Temps* rejoiced that the Patrie Française had become a "tower of Babel," but police reports show little tapering off of membership.[126]

The sharpening of the League of the Patrie Française and Barrès' renewed political vigor thrust him into a new electoral campaign for a Chamber seat. It came with the death in December, 1902, of Daniel Cloutier, a Rochefortist leader in both the League of Patriots and the League of the Patrie Française and Deputy for Paris' fourth *arrondissement*. The district was part of the traditionally artisan and leftist Faubourg St. Antoine, and included Paris' most concentrated Jewish quarter. The census classified the district as "well-off," third on a scale of six from "very poor" to "very rich," a category consistent with the district's vote, regularly divided between nationalists of the Arsenal and socialists in St. Gervais.[127]

Because of his nationalist and "socialist" past and the fact that he was the only nationalist candidate, an advantage Cloutier had not had, Barrès' prospects for victory were good. He got letters of endorsement from Lemaître, Rochefort, Drumont, and Déroulède and the groups they represented, principally the Patrie Française, the Nationalist and Socialist

Republican Committee of the district, and the League of Patriots. Only a little over a year before he had abandoned all the leagues. Now he was the candidate of nationalist unity to bring victory for what, with Lemaître's speech, seemed to be the near fusion of the League of Patriots and the League of the Patrie Française. The latter's enormous treasury was thrown into his campaign. He saw Galli daily at the League of Patriots' office. Syveton was "constantly with him," and his "devoted comrade."[128] Barrès had been chosen because he was the only candidate able to unite the diverse nationalist leagues.[129] This unity was reflected in the various rallies for Barrès, chaired by leaders of the various nationalist wings —Lemaître, Dausset, General Mercier, and Cavaignac—with speeches by them and Galli; Edmond Archdeacon, the nationalist deputy from the neighboring first *arrondissement*; Ernest Roche, the lieutenant of Rochefort; Paulin-Méry, an old Boulangist and socialist; Syveton; Millevoye; and Maurice Spronck, a Progressiste-nationalist.

In these rallies and his campaign program, Barrès politically activated the doctrine he had developed in the "novel of national energy" and *Scènes et doctrines du nationalisme*. In doing so, he more closely approached fascism than he had in any earlier campaign or period. If fascism claims to be the revolutionary opposition to liberalism, socialism, positivism, and conservatism to bring individualism without alienation, social reform without collectivist destruction of property, authority without abandonment of popular rule, and democracy without the indirection and drift of parliamentarianism through an irrational reconstruction of national and traditional vigor on a mass base, Barrès' 1903 program was more fascist than any of his earlier or later campaigns.

In no earlier period could Barrès be called a fascist or a proto-fascist. Certainly he had shown isolated elements which might be construed as fascist—the leadership principle and anti-parliamentarianism of Boulangism, the federalistic and socially radical anti-parliamentarianism of *La Cocarde*, and the socially radical nationalism of "rootedness" of the Nancy campaign of 1898. In each of these periods, however, he had abandoned the fascistic element held in the preceding period, and each period had looked to something other than fascism. Barrès' Boulangism resembled left-wing Gaullism far more than it did fascism. *La Cocarde* lacked the leadership principle and was more the handmaiden of anarchism or socialism than the precursor of fascism. There was neither the leadership principle nor anti-parliamentarianism in the 1898 Nancy program of left-wing nationalism. Those formerly isolated elements of Barrès' thought which resembled fascism came together into a single doctrine only in the "novels of national energy" and *Scènes et doctrines du nationalisme*. In the campaign of 1903 he converted the doctrine into political action.

Needless to say this new doctrine became action because of the Dreyfus affair and Barrès' experience with the nationalist leagues. Another reason was the nature of the opposition in 1903. No longer was he running against the candidates of the Center and Right which formerly put him against liberalism and conservatism. Nor was he running, as in 1896, as one socialist against another socialist. Now, in 1903, he added to anti-liberalism and anti-conservatism that other fundamental ingredient of fascism, anti-socialism, because the opponent was Gabriel Deville. In the general election of 1902 Deville, the one-time Guesdist translator of Marx's *Capital* and presently an intimate of Jean Jaurès, had barely lost to Cloutier in a district having a socialist majority. In this campaign, unlike the one at Neuilly in 1896, Barrès would not try to run as the better socialist. Instead, he ran as an anti-socialist nationalist.

In 1903 Barrès combined into a single program all the formerly isolated fascistic elements of his thought: the Boulangist presidential republic and leadership principle, federalism, and social radicalism. All those elements were expressed with the shrill rhetoric of the "soil and the dead":

> Given the general anarchy for conducting our private lives and the need for remedying the mortal weaknesses of France, we must seek our guiding principle in our hereditary reserves and feed on them. This tradition, found in our consciences and in the dead of our soil, is not merely a set of emaciated affirmations which can be cataloged or enumerated. Nor is it merely

207

a way of perceiving things. Rather, it is a way to react in common in all circumstances with men of the same formation.[130]

A party and a program were merely devices working to that end. Politically, as the candidate of the League of Patriots and League of the Patrie Française, he would replace the parliamentary republic with a plebiscitary one, tempered by his federalism. "At the summit of the State, Authority; on the soil and in groups, Decentralization."[131] Socially, unlike the internationalist collectivists, "nationalists resolve, more simply to assure the economic security of each Frenchman. Of each Frenchman, and not . . . each of the men who populate the universe. . . . To desert the cause of the disinherited would be to betray the cause of the nation itself." Social radicalism, then, was only another device for the expansion of nationalism:

> A man is commanded by the soil where he is born, through the milieu where his forefathers lived. . . . We are obliged to protect the more humble of our compatriots, because we recognize in him the eminent dignity of being a Frenchman. . . . The nation has a debt toward the more poor of Frenchmen and, at the same time, it is interested in ennobling him (that is to say, to create for him well-being and leisure).[132]

Such nationalistic social radicalism was not completely bogus, either, especially in Barrès' electoral district. In many parts of Paris, workers had not yet been preempted by the socialists. Cloutier, whom Barrès hoped to replace, had held the district's workers with socially radical nationalism. In other districts so did the followers of Rochefort's *Parti republicain socialist français* or Paulin-Méry's *Comité d'action socialiste patriotique* in the twelfth *arrondisement*, often in cooperation with the other leagues. Regularly such groups coupled nationalism with separation of Church and State, plebiscitary politics, anti-Semitism, "war against capital," nationalization of basic industry, pensions, decentralization of capital, and worker participation in management decisions.[133] Barrès might not go as far as they in program, but he could echo their charges against his socialist opponent. He portrayed Deville as a member of a party which was unable to deliver meaningful reforms even though Jaurès was vice-president of the Chamber, whose faith was misplaced in the utopias of collectivism and universal peace, which had disavowed Alsace-Lorraine, which supported the statement of Jaurès that the Triple Alliance was "the necessary counter-balance to our chauvinism and Franco-Russian fantasies," and which had refused to disown the anti-militarist statements of Gustave Hervé.[134]

In spite of the all-out efforts of the leagues, their purse, and speakers, the results of the first balloting on March 22 gave Barrès only 3,974 votes to the 3,826 of Deville. Another 2,000 were scattered among two other socialists and a *Progressiste*. The total socialist vote was 5,333, a clear majority.[135] By the second ballot most of the republican committees endorsed Deville.[136] In the run-off election of April 5, Deville won with 5,062 votes to the 4,836 of Barrès, who obviously picked up some of the votes which had gone on the first ballot to the socialist rivals of Deville.[137] *Le Temps* attributed the defeat to voter apathy: with 1500 fewer voters in 1903 than in 1902, the better-disciplined forces of Deville lost only 500 voters while the nationalists lost 1000.[138] Publicly the League of the Patrie Française blamed the loss on the failure of the first-round voters for the *Progressiste* and a nationalist socialist, who had sought league help, to "do their duty" on the second round. Privately they accused *La Libre Parole*, *La Patrie*, and Rochefort's *Intransigéant* of inadequate support. Those, in turn, blamed Barrès for alienating too many voters by his strong advocacy of an anti-parliamentary presidential republic. "What the devil," said Millevoye of *La Patrie*, "when you are going to violate a woman you do not tell her your intentions ahead of time and above all you do not take down your trousers."[139] Barrès merely blamed the defeat on the government for bringing in its own men to vote the ballots of a great number of dead or moved-away voters.[140]

To some nationalist observers the defeat may have appeared to be but a temporary setback to the progress of the nationalist cause. Yet, as the next months and years unfolded, Barrès' failure in the fourth *arrondissement* marked the beginning of an irreversible decline of nationalist power. The day of the nationalist leagues was almost over. Before long, the weakness Barrès sensed in them made them even less a threat to the parliamentary republic than Boulangism had been. The leagues, like Boulangism, had been only a "fever." If Barrès ever had ambitions to shape them into a real force and vehicle for his ideas, that opportunity also was lost with his defeat in Paris.

Even so, the fever of the Dreyfus affair and its leagues had brought yet another stage in Barrès' thought. The fascist-like doctrine expressed with such great literary power in the "novel of national energy" trilogy and *Scènes et doctrines du nationalisme* would continue to inspire right-wing Frenchmen in later times of trouble. Its political expression in turn-of-the-century politics, however, did not sell any more than the nationalist leagues did. Their decline would be accompanied by Barrès' rapid abandonment of his proto-fascist doctrine.

CHAPTER EIGHT

FROM THE DEATH OF NATIONALISM
TO THE NATIONALIST REVIVAL, 1903–1914

"I was at the baptism of nationalism,"
Barrès told Paul Acker right after the
1903 by-election. "Now I am at its burial. You see, a nationalist
program was not applied to nationalism. I know what nationalism is, but I do not know what a Nationalist Party is. I have
never been shown anything but an anti-ministerial party."[1]
His judgment was certainly correct, for after 1903 the deputies whom the leagues elected were nothing more than anti-
ministerials, and the leagues fell into such a decline that they
could not hope to elect even anti-ministerials, let alone real
nationalists. While Barrès may have been premature by a few
years in this obituary for the nationalist movement, certainly
by 1910 the anti-Dreyfusard leagues were dead, and France no
longer had any stomach for either their politics or their doctrine. Moreover, the Barrésian doctrine of the "novel of national energy" and *Scènes et doctrines du nationalisme*, at least in its
1903 electoral expression, was so irrelevant that he virtually
gave it up in favor of a traditional conservative nationalism.
As he did, oddly enough, he reached a conjunction with that
establishment he had fought all his adult life. By 1914 France
was in the midst of what historians have called a "nationalist
revival" where establishment politicians, who had opposed
Barrès and his ideas for years, were doing just about everything he wanted.

As early as 1903 Barrès' judgment of the ineffectiveness of
the leagues was already apparent. Split between Anglophobes

and supporters of the emerging Entente Cordiale, they even disagreed on how to react to the visit of Edward VII in 1903.[2] A 1903 congress of the League of the Patrie Française misfired, with its Paris militants quarreling with its wavering provincial conservatives. By summer it could only reissue its vague call for constitutional revision instead of demanding a popularly-elected president, local politicking instead of newspaper propaganda, and a social program encouraging cooperatives instead of supporting pensions, income tax, and real government intervention.[3] Increasingly, police reports indicate that both the League of Patriots and League of the Patrie Française experienced greater and greater money and membership problems, as members and contributions fled into the seemingly more effective moderate Action Liberale of Piou. League leadership grasped at every straw to find some issue more dynamic than the Church-State problem to restore the vigor of the leagues.[4]

Hope for revival came in late 1904 with the *affaire des fiches*, the discovery by Gabriel Syveton that the War Office of General André had enlisted the services of the Masonic Grand Orient in getting royalist and clerical information on army officers. By publicly striking the general, Syveton was guaranteed a trial in which he could tell all. Before he could make a full revelation of the affair, however, the government revealed that he had been embezzling funds from the League of the Patrie Française since 1902 and had had sexual relations with his nineteen-year-old ward.[5] His suicide in the face of these charges left the Patrie Française rudderless. Through his dispensing of the league's funds and his position on the great nationalist daily newspaper, *L'Echo de Paris*, he had been the league's and nationalism's most effective organizer. He was almost the only nationalist with support in all the leagues, and he had almost single-handedly brought Lemaître and the League of the Patrie Française to support of the presidential republic and a conjunction with the League of Patriots. Barrès greatly admired Syveton, but recognized that he, by breaking the power of all his rivals in the nationalist movement—Coppée, Lemaître, Déroulède, Cavaignac, and Dausset—had made it impossible for the nationalist movement to survive his death. By April, 1905, Dausset and Lemaître resigned their offices in the league, and the new vice-president, Admiral Bienaimé, had to admit that the disclosure and suicide had brought "sadness, discouragement . . . [and] some trouble to our ranks."[6] That was putting it mildly. The league promptly abandoned the Lemaître-Syveton position on the presidential republic and underwent depoliticalization to the further benefit of the Action Liberale; by 1910 its lingering death was complete.

The League of Patriots suffered a similar decline. Plagued by the same money and membership problems as the Patrie Française, the League of Patriots hoped that the return of the amnestied Déroulède in November, 1905, would revive it. While it could bring out one hundred thousand demonstrators for the return, it was able to sign up only one thousand new members. Its candidates in the 1906 legislative elections did so badly that Galli lamented, "There is nothing to do." The formidable Déroulède could not even win in his old stronghold, Charente. Barrès advised, "The present role of the [nationalist] opposition is that of a doctor in a duel. Let us watch our adversaries exchange blows: they will appeal to our devotion and ideas to dress their wounds."[7]

Indeed, the 1906 election, and its aftermath, was a disaster for all the leagues. In 1906 the nationalist vote in Paris fell from 37 percent to 25 percent, and the nationalist bloc in the Chamber fell from fifty-five to thirty-seven deputies. Both leagues were now in such trouble that in June, 1907, at Barrès' house, their long-time seemingly inevitable fusion almost took place. Officers, with Barrès as a vice-president, had already been chosen, but when Bienaimé demanded the suppression of the League of Patriots' plank for the return of Alsace-Lorraine, "Déroulède became as white as a sheet" and walked out.[8]

The League of Patriots continued, but its militancy was gone. Déroulède's return to literature destroyed the hopes revived by his return; the league became merely a non-political patriotic society conducting annual pilgrimages to battle sites and leaving street action to the rising Action Française. Barrès was virtually alone in his unsuccessful bid in 1909 to get the leaguers to make patriotic and republican demonstrations against the Sorbonne lectures of François Thalamas, who had given some anti-Jeanne d'Arc lectures a few years earlier. The object was to undercut the Action Français's royalist street action against the professor by both acclaiming Jeanne d'Arc and crying *Vive la République*! After that, league militants increasingly rushed into the Action Française, while the League of Patriots became more and more moderate, held together by money-raising rallies and financial angels such as Barrès. On one occasion police reported that Barrès raised fifteen hundred francs at a rally in which he was the principal speaker. On Déroulède's death in 1914, Barrès took over the leadership of the league after the failure of a Barrès-Galli-Habert troika. By this time, however, the league's only issue was Alsace-Lorraine, and in politics it had so abandoned anti-parliamentary presidential republicanism that its affairs were now even attended by that some-time socialist Alexandre Millerand, who became president of the league on Barrès' death in 1923.[9]

As it turned out, then, the "new Boulangism" of the nationalist movement, like that of the old, remained only a "fever" and never became the "national conscience" Barrès wished. Yet, how can one account for the mercurial success and failure of these nationalist leagues born in 1898 and 1899, climaxed in the 1902 legislative elections, and buried in the 1906 legislative elections? The best explanation has come from D. R. Watson.[10] He combined electoral results of six elections in Paris between 1896 and 1906 and electoral statements of the candidates with sociological data for each constituency provided by the 1891 census, the last census which analyzed Paris socially, down to the *quartier* level. Although he did not use them, his analysis is confirmed by police reports and a reading of the press of the nationalist leagues. Unlike their Boulangist predecessors, nationalist candidates won in the middling to wealthy first through tenth *arrondissements* in the center of the city, none of which had been Boulangist. Only the poor to very poor twelfth, seventeenth, and eighteenth *arrondissements* voted both for Boulangism and nationalism. In the prosperous areas, nationalists won because the Dreyfus affair had temporarily made the nationalist movement the party of order instead of discredited *Progressistes* and conservatives or Dreyfusard Radicals. With the end of the Dreyfus affair by 1906, the voters returned to their origins, particularly to the revived conservatism of the Action Libérale and the Radicals, the latter by that time having been shorn of their Dreyfusard socialist allies. Police reports would indicate that Watson's analysis of the lower middle-class nature of nationalism is even stronger than he would make it. The only poor *arrondissements* voting nationalist were those where Rochefortists had withstood being replaced by socialists. But even here they had become weakened enough that they needed middle-class League of Patriots or League of the Patrie Française allies to win against socialist candidates. Away from Paris the forces of nationalism were even more establishmentarian and even more willing to return to establishment parties when the Dreyfus crisis was past.

In other words the Dreyfus affair brought a marriage of convenience between league militants and moderate to conservative politicians. No league had a comprehensive program able to attract wide support. The League of the Patrie Française was against the Dreyfusard ministry; the Anti-Semitic League hated Jews; the League of Patriots championed the presidential republic and the lost provinces. None had a social program. Each was Parisian and small. There were perhaps no more than one thousand militants in the entire movement. This is difficult to document, but when one reads countless accounts by newspaper reporters and police agents, one reaches the conclusion that the same people were attending all the meetings and rallies, regardless of which league was the sponsor. The meetings of all the leagues were about the same size, and the same slogans were shouted at every meeting. The anti-Semites, for example, distributed confetti printed with anti-Semitic epithets which filled the air of meetings of all the leagues. Likewise, as Watson says, one gets the feeling that during the Dreyfus affair the Dreyfusard ministry seemed to a large minority to be the "party of disorder." For that reason nationalism was, in Raoul Girardet's phrase, "a movement of defense."[11] By 1906 that relationship was reversed: Radical ministries were

215

the party of order which broke strikes, made separation of Church and State work, and solidified the Triple Entente against Germany. Ministries were to become increasingly firm in each of those areas, so dear to the hearts of moderates and conservatives, by the eve of the World War.

While Barrès came to a similar analysis of the nationalist movement and leagues, for awhile it appeared to him that a "new Boulangism" might arise out of the Dreyfus Affair. Although Raoul Girardet argues that Barrès' nationalism was "fundamentally educative and moral" while Maurras' "decisive preoccupation was the political order,"[12] the Dreyfus affair actually caused Barrès to be both "educative" and "political." Momentarily the Affair seemed to have created a revolutionary or, if you prefer, a counter-revolutionary situation. With it Barrès briefly became, in contrast to the days of *La Cocarde* and socialism, a "realist" with "dirty hands," up to his elbows in the abortive Reuilly coup of Déroulède, the editorship of *Le Drapeau*, and the work of the nationalist leagues. To be sure, he resigned from *Le Drapeau* and the League of the Patrie Française executive committee in 1901 and became disillusioned with the Action Française. Yet, in spite of that kind of disillusionment he could still enter the 1903 Paris by-election. The fact that he could enter at all, let alone with such a fascistic platform, shows that he was indeed politically *engagé* so long as the political movement would do what he wanted.

What Barrès demanded in a political movement was either that it believe in his ideas or that it have a real chance of victory. When one or both were improbable he hedged, trimmed his sails, and would not get dirty hands. Had the Action Française only remained republican would not Barrès have been its pillar just as he had remained at Déroulède's side at Reuilly until it was clear that the army was not a fellow conspirator? The "burial of nationalism" for Barrès occurred not merely because nationalists would not be Barrésians; they could not win. The Dreyfus affair had neither rallied enough troops nor found an "expedient" or *homme national* to unite the disparate leagues into a "new Boulangism." Barrès, like later fascists, wanted a revolution of the spirit and would participate in po-

litical or social revolutionary action to get it. The trouble for
him was that he was not in a revolutionary or counter-revolutionary situation. He mistakenly considered the Dreyfus affair
to be one, however, when at best it had created a *pre*-revolu-
tionary or *pre*-counter-revolutionary situation. When he discovered this, he turned away from his 1903 fascistic political
formula and became convinced that nationalism and its
leagues, like Boulangism, had been only a "fever" when it
should have been a national conscience. Then, indeed, Barresianism became exclusively "educative and moral" and not political.

This impending collapse of the nationalist movement and
Barrès' abandonment of his 1903 program were all too evident
when he again was thrust into a political campaign in 1906.
With the death of Edmond Archdeacon, the Federation of Republican, Liberal, and Patriotic Committees of the first *arrondissement* of Paris chose Barrès to run for his seat, as the only candidate capable of uniting the district's rival nationalist factions.
Barrès promised to follow Archdeacon's program, which had
opposed everything threatening French unity.[13] This district had
been offered Barrès in 1902 and was such a nationalist stronghold that Archdeacon had been swept to office on the first ballot.
It was still nationalist enough for Barrès to go in on the first
ballot against a *Progressiste* and Radical with as big a margin
as Archdeacon had received.[14] Although Barrès had the endorsement of Déroulède, Rochefort, and all four municipal councilors of the *arrondissement*, his victory was not a party one.[15] For the
first time, he ran in a prosperous district and as the candidate
of no party or movement. His party now, in the words of Déroulède, was that "of the Republic of honest men against the republic of *coquins*."[16]

Although victory was almost certain, Barrès did conduct a
vigorous campaign in 1906 in which he spelled out his mature,
but personal, political views. He held numerous rallies in
every quarter, usually chaired by the quarter's municipal councilor, with speeches by the councilors, Coppée, and Georges
Gachet, the president of the League of the Patrie Française. At
these rallies, in great contrast to the fascistic quality of the

217

1903 campaign, he was merely applauded for his "patriotic and social" or "patriotic and liberal" program. His name was described as "synonymous with patriotism and liberty of conscience," and the crowds greeted his remarks with, "Down with the [governmental] Bloc! Down with the sectarians! Long live France! and liberties!"[17]

His program was a far cry from the fascistic one of 1903. Now it was stock conservative nationalism, little distinguishable from that of the Action Liberale. According to Paul Acker, Barrès still believed in the nationalism of "the soil and the dead" speech. He told Acker that all questions should be solved from the "French point of view." "Each time that a measure is proposed, I ask myself: will it serve France or not?" He believed, for example, that because the anticlerical legislation of Emile Combes created civil war, it would weaken France, and should be opposed on nationalistic grounds. Nor had he completely forgotten social reforms, so long as they fit a nationalist framework. He told Acker:

> It is necessary to recall that a way to reunite the poor classes with the idea of the fatherland, is to make the fatherland charitable to them. There is no reason at all to leave the initiative for social reforms with the revolutionaries: on the contrary, only the men of order are able to be men of progress. It is to conservatives, who are worthy of the name, to bring to a good end great reforms, merely as a way to look after defense and the foreign interests of the country.[18]

Such a program was just what his middling, conservative voters wanted in an electoral district comprising, according to census evaluation, two "very comfortable" quarters, one "rich" one, and one "very rich" one.

Even parliamentary victory did not destroy Barrès' disillusionment with the nationalists. Since they now stood for nothing more than anti-ministerialism, he refused to join their Nationalist Republican bloc in the Chamber, a bloc whose members included Gauthier de Clagny, Ernest Roche, Cavaignac, and Georges Berry. Instead, he remained an Independent along with other nationalists like Millevoye and Andrieux who felt that even the Nationalist Republicans had sold out to anti-ministerialism.

218

Ironically, then, 1906 saw Barrès crowned with personal laurels, since he was elected to both the French Academy and to the Chamber of Deputies from a district he would represent until his death in 1923. Yet, 1906 also saw the defeat of the great ambition which had driven him since 1889: the formation of a political movement capable of bringing constitutional revision, social reconciliation, and a nationalistic France. As both deputy and writer, after 1906 he ceased these endeavors. He reverted to his role as educator. Between 1906 and the outbreak of the war both his writing and his political activity, such as it was, were dominated by the questions of Church-State relations and the loss of Alsace-Lorraine. Aside from those causes, he increasingly became little more than a typical right-wing deputy on social and political issues. Remarkably, then, by 1906 his ideas and action were cast in a conservative nationalism rather than the fascistic variety of the period of the nationalist leagues.

The exceptional feature of Barrès' career between 1906 and the outbreak of the war is that he increasingly became a part of the political establishment rather than its enemy. From the beginning, from the *Culte du moi*, he had been anti-establishment. By 1914 he was a part of it. His association with the League of the Patrie Française and election to the Academy had already made him a fixture of the literary establishment he had once attacked. His conjunction with the political establishment after 1906 can be seen in three aspects of his career: his voting record on those social and political issues which divided Left and Right, his campaign on behalf of the churches, and his continued efforts on Alsace-Lorraine which contributed to the "nationalist revival" on the eve of the war.

In stark contrast to his voting record in the 1889 Chamber of Deputies and in his electoral pronouncements thereafter, Barrès joined the 1906 Chamber as a thoroughgoing old-fashioned conservative on social and political issues. By 1914 little separated him from the governmental parties on these, but initially such issues put him against them. There was, for example, the income tax. As an earlier campaigner, Barrès had consistently supported the progressive income tax. Charged by socialist opponents with being a millionaire, he had in those days always volunteered to have the tax start with him. When the Caillaux income tax proposal of 1907 came before the Chamber in 1909, however, it was a different story. Barrès joined the Right to vote for almost every effort to gut the measure and, when that failed, to vote against the passage of the bill on March 9, 1909.[19] The same was true regarding nationalization of railroads. At least as late as his 1898 campaign in Nancy he had supported that principle, but when the Clemenceau government nationalized the near-defunct Western railroad by a vote of 364 to 187 on December 7, 1906, Barrès was found with the rightist minority.[20]

While these matters divided Barrès and other rightists from the establishment, other significant political and social issues drew them together. Least significant of these was the issue of pensions. Barrès had supported old age pensions since his original campaign in Nancy. A pensions bill, based on employee and employer contributions and introduced in the early 1890s, finally passed the Chamber of Deputies over rightist objections just before his election to that body in 1906. Barrès' first chance to express himself on the issue came only when the Senate modified the bill and returned it to the Chamber in 1910. By that time pensions had won such wide support in both France and neighboring nations that only three deputies could be found to vote against them. The bill's overwhelming majority of 531 included even a reluctant, by his admission, Barrès.[21]

Much more significant was Barrès' attitude toward government actions on strikes and labor unrest. This issue, perhaps beyond any other, did more to bring together the old anti-Dreyfusard Right and the old Dreyfusard Center. The Dreyfus affair had brought about a coalition of Radicals, moderates and socialists supposedly determined to bring justice for Dreyfus, to republicanize and democratize the army, to complete the program of anti-clericalism, and to usher in social reforms. Under the Waldeck-Rousseau, Combes, and Rouvier ministries of 1899–1905, all but the last aim had been achieved. Until the end of the Combes ministry, Jean Jaurès had convinced his fellow socialists that their Radical and moderate allies would have to turn to social reform after the other goals had been

220

won. Jaurès' loyalty to the governmental bloc had even extended to his support of its spying on officers in the *affaire des fiches*. By 1905, however, the socialists had had enough of the coalition and had broken with Combes' successor, Rouvier.

Although the period after Combes did see some mild social reforms, it was more characterized by frequent, severe, and bitter labor unrest, and governments hardly responded sympathetically with that aspect of the social question. The spring of 1906 saw Clemenceau, as the Sarrien government's minister of interior and "number one cop of France," send in troops to break a miners strike and fire striking postmen. In June the Chamber was treated to a celebrated several day debate between Jaurès and Clemenceau on the government's behavior.[22] Barrès, newly arrived at the Chamber, was fascinated with it. As a nationalist he should have had no use for either side, but his several page description of the debate in his *Cahiers* shows his obvious sympathy for Jaurès: "What a speaker. How he inspires enthusiasm. Ah! if he were only a patriot."[23] The debate ended with Clemenceau winning an overwhelming vote of confidence from the Chamber, but Barrès, along with but a handful of rightists, voted with the socialists against him.[24] With a similarly small group of rightists, he joined the socialists in unsuccessfully trying to strengthen an amnesty bill requiring the government to hire back all fired striking postmen.[25]

As time went on, however, Barrès had less enthusiasm for this kind of thing and increasingly supported a government concerned with law and order. In 1907 he still could be found to oppose the government when it fired government workers to keep schoolteachers from organizing and affiliating with the syndicalist and—to the government—revolutionary *Confédération générale du travail*. At the end of another long debate over government strikebreaking, Barrès and a few rightists joined the Left in favor of a defeated motion asking the government to show "benevolence" toward the workers and against the victorious motion expressing confidence in the government's action.[26] The debate, mainly between Jaurès and Aristide Briand, Clemenceau's ex-socialist minister of education, occasioned another long entry in Barrès' journal, an entry in opposition to his public vote. Publicly Barrès had continued to side with the Left, as he had after the Jaurès-Clemenceau debate. Privately in his journal, however, Briand was the hero. To be sure, Briand's refusal to let government employees be syndicalist reminded Barrès of Bismarck and Rouher, Napoleon III's policeman, but now that was all right because Briand merely "wishes to defend society." Jaurès, on the other hand, stood for revolutions. Even though such revolutions are made "in the name of Justice," they "leave only ruins." "If you put limits on this justice, you are a traitor, you are Briand."[27]

The same entry contains two other comments which indicate even more sharply that Barrès, after 1906, was rapidly becoming a man of the Center. In one he admitted that his "sensibility" was still attracted by both the Right's concern with ethics and the socialist interest in "knowing the universe." In contrast, the Center was "commonplace." Yet, "my spirit tells me to resign myself to the commonplace in a parliament, to the possible, to compromise."[28] If Barrès was really beginning to consider himself a man of the Center, he could not yet let that cat out of the bag. His comments on the attractiveness of the Center were immediately followed by this:

> Gauthier de Clagny [Barrès' fellow nationalist who, like him, had just voted for the workers on the strikebreaking issue] recalls that when the Charles Dupuy ministry closed the Bourse du Travail, he voted against the ministry while his colleague from Versailles, M. Haussmann, *more honestly and conscientiously* voted for the ministry's actions. When the next elections came around Haussmann was fought by a governmental candidate strongly backed by the prefect who said: "Vote against that Haussmann who sold out the rights of the workers." And, Haussmann was beaten while the prefect had to apologize to the government that "we can do nothing against Gauthier. He supported the Bourse du Travail."[29]

How many members of the right wing must have voted with the Left on social questions for just that reason? Barrès *honestly and conscientiously* supported Briand's anti-labor stance, but the government neither needed nor would appreciate his vote. Unless rightwing opponents of the government were in safe districts, there was no point in needlessly antagonizing working-class voters. If Barrès were not careful, that vote could just as easily be mobilized by the chief opposition in his constituency, the governmental candidate.

Yet, a change was coming. In 1909 he merely abstained, instead of voting against the Chamber's support of Clemenceau's firm handling of a postman's strike.[30] His margin of victory in his first-round re-election in 1910 as a "liberal republican," however, was so comfortable that he could take off his pro-labor mask permanently. From then on he regularly voted for government repression of trade union activity. The first occasion was the 1910 railroad strike. The new government of Briand broke it by threatening to conscript striking railroad workers into the army, and the Chamber, with Barrès, approved the action.[31] When the schoolteacher union was dissolved in 1912 for being anti-patriotic, Barrès supported the Poincaré government like almost every other deputy of the Right and Center.[32] On these occasions Barrès not only voted in favor of governmental "union busting" as such, but he supported a more determined variety of it under Briand and Poincaré after he had opposed the milder Clemenceau type. Nor did he now agonize over his votes as he had on the earlier occasions. On measures of social control he had come to line himself up with the establishment without regret.

If there was one issue which should have prevented Barrès from being reconciled with the establishment, it surely would have been Church-State relations. Here, too, Barrès reached a conjunction with the moderate political establishment by the eve of the war as the Dreyfusard revolution ran out of gas. Among their other accomplishments the victorious Dreyfusards had revived anti-clericalism. Convinced that Dreyfus had been convicted by a veritable clerico-military conspiracy, they had resolved to democratize both army and church. The republicanization of the army was accomplished by reducing the military obligation from three to two years and by the methods of the *affaire des fiches*; that of the church began with the Waldeck-Rousseau government's Associations Law of 1901 which required parliamentary authorization for all religious orders or congregations. Aimed primarily against those vicious anti-Semitic and anti-Dreyfusard orders such as the Assumptionists, the law was applied almost universally by Waldeck-Rousseau's successor, Emile Combes. By refusing authorization to well over one hundred religious orders, the Combes ministry succeeded in closing several thousand Catholic schools and driving into exile many more priests, brothers, and nuns. That paved the way for the separation of Church and State, pushed into law by Briand in 1905. Separation ended the state salaries to clergymen of all faiths. While the government retained ownership of church buildings and property, they were to be administered by committees of laymen. By 1907 Briand, as Minister of Cults, modified that arrangement by allowing Catholic groups to lease their buildings from municipal governments, which retained responsibility for maintaining the structures.

That, in brief, was the Church-State situation when Barrès first took an active interest in it. The nationalist leagues had, of course, opposed the Waldeck-Combes-Briand legislation every step of the way. Initially, the question had been secondary for Barrès, but by 1910 he had become the Church's champion. This work for the Church, along with his campaign on behalf of Alsace-Lorraine, would constitute his principal "educative and moral" effort after 1906.

For Barrès even to be interested in the Church, let alone be its champion, marked a sharp turn in his career. As late as the beginnings of the Dreyfus affair, his statements, writings, and thought are eminently secular. The *porte-paroles* of his *Culte du moi* and "novel of national energy"—Philippe, Maltère, and Sturel—put their faith in the secular world of "self," other men, and worldly ideologies. While they can admire the religious faith of, say Bérénice and Saint-Phlin, they cannot adopt it. While Barrès could admire Loyola, he did so, not for the saint's Catholicism, but for his ability to excite energy and magnify the ego. Often accused by his political enemies of being a clerical, Barrès always denied it with considerable credibility. In 1889 he adhered only to the Boulangist "open republic" and opposed the clerical candidates in Nancy; in the Neuilly campaigns he supported separation of Church and State; at Nancy in 1898 the clericals were aware enough of his position to vote for the victorious Gervaize; in the nationalist leagues he regularly identified with the anti-clerical wing. At most, writes Pierre de Boisdeffre, "he retained from the Church only its liturgy, the art with which it made all the powers of the earth poetic, and what he called 'the baptism of Cybele': he loved 'Catholic sensibility' without adhering to its dogmas."[33]

After 1910, however, Barrès projected an altogether different image. By that time he had become convinced that the ending of State financial support to the Church had caused church structures to decay and fall into ruins. With that conviction he started a campaign to preserve them, beginning with an open letter and petition to Briand on January 4, 1910, followed by two interviews with the Minister in March and November.[34] While Briand remained convinced that the plight of the village churches was exaggerated, he was quite sympathetic to their survival—a position completely in keeping with his speech at Périgueux the previous October in which he promised the "appeasement" of all Frenchmen, clerical and anti-clerical alike. By Fall, 1910, Barrès launched the campaign in newspaper articles, and in January, 1911, he took it to the floor of the Chamber of Deputies.[35] He circulated a new petition in 1912 which, like the earlier one, called for state and local financial intervention to preserve church buildings built before 1800 as historical monuments. By this time the project had won the support of politicians as varied as Henri Buisson, Albert Thomas, P. E. Flandin, Jules Siegfried, Joseph Reinach, and Louis Barthou. Théodore Steeg, the minister of interior, opposed forcing municipalities to repair church buildings, and such a bill was voted on November 28, 1912.[36] By March, 1913, under a new Briand ministry, a more comprehensive bill passed which established two repair funds, one for historic buildings and another for non-historic ones.[37] Barrès, rightly convinced that anti-clerical municipal officials would never repair "non-historic" churches, tried to have all pre-1800 buildings declared historic, but his amendment was not even considered.

Increasingly the Church-State issue became another point of accord between Barrès and the political establishment he formerly opposed. While he continued his public campaign for the churches, publishing his speeches and newspaper articles on the issue as *La Grande Pitié des eglises de France* (1914) and the religious novel, *La Colline inspirée* (1913), privately he found it increasingly difficult to be against a government which appropriated money to repair churches. On this issue as on social peace, Briand and most of his successors more and more were doing what he wanted. Briand, especially, was hard to figure out. Barrès had merely abstained rather than following his fellow rightists in opposition when Briand reorganized his ministry in November, 1910. Barrès admitted he liked the handling of the railroad strike, but he still had reservations on the Church-State issue.[38] By the following year, after their conversations, he remained utterly baffled as to whether Briand, the separator of Church and State, was now the church's friend or foe.[39] By 1912–1913, however, there no longer were any doubts. Briand's "appeasement" had become the order of the day. Not only did he and most of his successors halt social change and maintain labor peace, they also were in process of reconciling clericals and anti-clericals. Little wonder that by 1914 Barrès could send Briand a copy of *La Grande Pitié des eglises de France* with a surprisingly warm inscription.[40]

There remains the problem, however, of how the anti-clerical Barrès became a pillar of the Church. Several reasons account for this shift, not the least being a religious experience. Needless to say, it was no Damascus road conversion. How early it came is difficult to say, but certainly it was complete by 1907. "Comes a shock," Barrès wrote in his *Cahiers* in that year. "Political defeat. Death of my mother. After such shocks, one accepts the Catholic thesis. We have seen that we are not absolute masters of ourselves. We accept our fatalisms."[41] "For my part," he wrote about the same time, "I find it odious being Maurice Barrès after forty-four years of life."[42] And, for the first time, a genuine prayer, a typical prayer of the middle-aged convert who had sought success and on finding it remained unfulfilled:

> 17 July 1907. - Ah! Savior, give me the courage to contemplate my heart without disgust. In my relations with others I judge

myself imperfect, and it makes me sad. That is the principal cause of my feeling of isolation.

More and more I am not satisfied with my political and social conduct, and no party that I try to serve accepts me . . .

Forty five years of age is time to make our conversion. Yes, Catholicism surrounds and sustains life.[43]

Two years later he indicated how his conversion could be activated:

I defend Catholicism because it teaches those truths and laws which are just, conformed to eternal conditions of the soul and the human conscience. I love it because it responds to my deep, hereditary needs, to my very structure.

Leading a Christian life.

Having faith.

Frequenting the sacraments.[44]

At the same time there were more typically Barrésian reasons for becoming the Church's paladin: the French Church was an integral part of the doctrine of the "soil and dead." Although he could write that "for me religion is not simply a means for public order,"[45] it did contain that element as well as the personal religious experience. "In defending the churches," he told a reporter at the opening of his campaign on behalf of the churches, "I defend our civilization and our hereditary formation." Just the same, "nothing disgusts me more than the idea of considering Catholicism as a kind of spiritual gendarmerie." Rather, "I will defend the Church in the name of everyone's spiritual life."[46] In other words, France had both Catholics and anti-clericals. It needed both, and both were part of France's heritage. Barrès accepted the Church, just as he accepted the Revolution and the Republic, because it was rooted in the soil and dead. "The resistance of the State against the Church is a legitimate work, historically," he admitted. "But it must be stopped before it leaves some vanquished. That would be bad not only for the vanquished. It would be bad even for the vanquisher."[47] France needed all of its past, and the anti-clericals sought to wipe out a part of it. "Above all," he wrote, "religion is the bond which unites the living with the dead . . . The soil and the dead, that is what there is in religion."[48]

Despite his disclaimers to the contrary, another reason for Barrès' championing of the Church was its power as a source of discipline and authority. Statements to that effect are scattered throughout his *Cahiers* after 1907. Such a view was, of course, tied to his own religious experience. His faith did discipline and temper him. Moreover, as he had in his move toward nationalism, he universalized on his own personal insight: religion could do the same for all Frenchmen.

Nowhere did Barrès put this more strongly than in what was, with *Les Déracinés*, his greatest novel—*La Colline inspirée* (1913)—which traces the career of a Lorraine priest and another *porte-parole* of the mature Barrès, Leopold Baillard. In the 1840s Baillard's vision and the organizational ability of his two brothers finance and restore the decaying Lorraine religious shrines of Flavigny, Mattaincourt, Sainte-Odile, and Sion-Vaudémont. The Bishop of Nancy, fearful of the implications of this overly nationalistic and mystical religious movement, smashes it in 1850 and leaves the brothers in control only of the chapel at Sion-Vaudémont, an isolated "sacred hill" commanding magnificent views of the Lorraine countryside and bearing today both the chapel and an ugly monument to Barrès. Leopold then falls in with a Norman mystic, Vintras, and turns Sion into a Vintras-inspired shrine run by the Baillards and their devoted nuns. The movement combines Celtic paganism and soil-and-dead Lorrainianism with mystical Christianity. Indeed, Sion is as much the protagonist of the novel as is Baillard. In the hill resides the very life force of Lorraine and the instinctual drives of mankind. The hill had been so sacred to pre-Christian Celts, as well as to Christians, that Our Lady of Sion merely replaced the Celtic Rosmertha.

In his vision and cause Leopold is a religious *homme libre*, but his outcome is markedly different from the *homme libre* of the *Culte du moi*. Leopold's religion drives him to find fulfillment against the "barbarians" of the established Church. In the first half of the novel both author and reader identify with Leopold and his heroic struggle. Then the author turns against him, for he goes too far. Suddenly the Church and the formerly vicious villagers at the foot of the hill become the heroes. In the end, however, the dying Leopold mellows and submits to the Church, reconciled through the love of the young priest sent by the Church to crush the heresy. And that, says Barrès in the celebrated dialogue between the chapel and the meadow which concluded the novel, is what we all must do. Like Leopold we must have enthusiasm, instinctual drives for individual fulfillment rooted in the soil and dead, but all of these must be tempered, channeled, and directed into meaningfully realistic practice. That was the role of the Church, the Latin and Roman foreigner imposing its "barbarian" direction on the Celtic and Gallic soil.

While social peace and Church-State reconciliation were certainly significant Barrésian themes after 1903, the most important was the question of Alsace-Lorraine. Here, too, Barrès served as "educator." Here he also found himself increasingly at one with the political establishment he formerly rejected as it got caught up in what Eugen Weber calls the "nationalist revival."[49] In this cause as in his others, Barrès' forum remained his speeches before the dying nationalist leagues, newspaper articles in journals remaining open to him like the *bien-pensant* and conservative *Echo de Paris*, and in the two novels of the "bastions of the East" cycle. The kindest thing which can be said about these two incredibly maudlin pieces, *Au service de l'Allemagne* (1905) and *Colette Baudoche* (1909), is that they were, to use Pierre de Boisdeffre's phrase, "works of war." As such they were part of an entire genre of novels and essays which revived the Alsace-Lorraine issue in the decade preceding the war. They are no better and no worse than other similar works of that period such as Paul Acker's *Les Exiles* (1911), René Bazin's *Oberlé* (1901), L. Dumont-Wilden's *La Victoire des vaincus* (1911), Jeanne Regamy's *Jeune Alsace* (1909), André Lichtenberger's *Juste Lobel alsacien* (1911), Hansi's *Professor Knatsche* (1910) and *Mon village* (1913), Georges Ducrocq's *Les Provinces inébranables* (1913) and *Adrienne* (1914), Etienne Rey's *La Renaissance de l'orgueil française* (1912), and Robert Baldy's *L'Alsace-Lorraine et l'Empire allemand* (1912).[50] Moreover, Barrès wrote for one of the journals this revival spawned, Henri Albert's *Messager d'Alsace-Lorraine*, and co-founded with Georges

Ducrocq *Les Marches de l'Est* (1903–1914), which dealt with all those suffering under the "oppression of Germanism"—Alsatians and Lorrainers, Schleswig Danes, Poles, Czechs, and Slovaks.[51] While there is no way empirically to measure the influence of these books and journals,[52] their very numbers indicate that there must have been a good market for such literature. Nor could they have appealed merely to the basically Parisian clientele of the old nationalist leagues. One of their numbers, Etienne Rey, could trumpet nationalism while commenting that "the cult of the dead of which [Barrès] has made himself the high priest has little influence upon souls who love life."[53]

If any one of these writers on Alsace-Lorraine had a direct influence on Barrès, it was René Bazin.[54] Unlike his Jean Oberlé, Barrès' Paul Ehrmann stayed behind in Alsace to be drafted into the Prussian army in *Au service de l'Allemagne*. Another *homme libre*, he remains in Alsace and resists the attempts of the German "barbarians" to determine his French soul. The same theme dominates Colette Baudoche in Metz. Her grandmother's boarder, Francophile German professor Asmus, falls in love with her, gives up his German fiancée, and proposes marriage to her and, in effect, to French culture. Considering the shortage of eligible males in Metz and the material prospects of Herr Asmus, Colette is certainly tempted. Just before she gives her final assent, however, she attends a commemorative mass in the cathedral of Metz for the French war dead of 1870, and that makes all the difference. She rejects her suitor to remain loyal to her civilization in spite of thirty-five years of German rule. She cannot betray those who died for her freedom.

With these two novels, coupled with his campaign on behalf of the churches in an effort to reconcile the two Frances, Barrès shifted away from attacking the domestic enemies of France, which he had done in the days of the nationalist leagues. He turned now to the foreign enemy, Germany. In doing so, according to some scholars, his Germanophobia took on a more racist tone. As Robert Soucy points out, every German character in these novels is portrayed as a banal, vulgar, ignoble being, incapable of truly understanding reality because of his lack of emotional depth. It was the fictional stereotype Barrès presented in the *Mercure de France* in 1902: "The German student has no personal idea, no view of the whole, no perception of the intimate sense of things. He does not *feel* beauty, he *learns by rote* the rules and regulations of its elements. Facts, dates, laws, formulas, scaffolding, never the life of things livingly felt."[55]

Rather than being racist, this was Barrès' customary way of attacking his enemies. He had said the same thing about Charles Martin, the "adversary" in the *Jardin de Bérénice*. He fought Zola and the naturalists in the same way for being too "scientific." Barrès' treatment of Asmus, the German schoolmaster in Colette Baudoche, is no different. The reader can only feel that Asmus has been victimized by his German background and culture. Determinism, not racism, is the culprit. The Asmus who comes to the Baudoche household is coarse, ill-mannered, and smells of stale beer and cigar smoke. He is also a Francophile, however, and that sets him apart from the other German conquerors. One of the major themes of the novel is Asmus' conversion to superior French culture and manners. His conversion, stumbling at first, is portrayed favorably. In becoming French, he is such a sympathetic character that some French nationalists criticized Barrès for not having Colette marry him and turn him into a good Rheno-Frenchman. Years later Barrès admitted that exactly such a process had created one of the leaders of the Rhenish autonomy movement. His final conversion, however, was achieved by the force of French arms in World War I, rather than by the love of a wife brought up in Metz.[56]

The fact that Barrès shared his racism toward Jews and non-Western peoples with most members of his class in *fin de siècle* France does not excuse it, of course. He did not extend it to foreigners, however. His *Au service de l'Allemagne* and *Colette Baudoche* were not racist tracts. Operationally they were in the service of French nationalism, literary pleas to retain faith in a revanche. "In politics," he wrote to the editor of *Le Matin* in 1908, "I have held profoundly to but one thing: the recapture of Metz and Strasbourg."[57] In this sense the "bastions of the East" novels were but a means to that end, a means similar to the other works of propaganda in the revival of the Alsace-Lorraine issue before the war. Indeed, a change of the character and place names could have made it a part of an entire international genre. *Colette Baudoche. A Maid of Metz*, for example, could just as easily have become a *Coleen O'Boyle. A Maid of Londonderry*. It was no accident that Colette was one of only two of Barrès' novels to be translated into English for the American reader, and its publication date was, appropriately enough, 1917. For Barrès, then, these novels, articles, and speeches of the entire campaign were directed to the specific end of "serving France and defending a Latin culture whose extreme bastion we are."[58] "Our honor is Alsace-Lorraine; our security is in the Rhine frontier."[59] Their real purpose was to strengthen the national defense and determination of a diminished France, a recurrent theme in the nationalism of a France successively weakened by the loss of Alsace-Lorraine, the resurgence of Nazi Germany, or the rise of cold war bi-polarity.

Nor was this part of Barrès' post-1903 action unsuccessful. By the eve of the war the political establishment and nation were also becoming more nationalistic and taking an increasingly hostile stand against Germany. By 1913 Barrès could say:

> It is certain that first Boulangism, then nationalism, have failed, but it is equally certain that all their content and goodness have survived them. Our terminology can be rejected, our doctrines are being realized. We find them in the work of Millerand, in the speeches of Poincaré, in the noble transports of those very men who, only yesterday opposed us and who today work to realize what we wanted. What does it matter to us that the nationalist party fades away if, at the same time, we see the opposing parties being nationalized![60]

In the same year, Clemenceau's newspaper, *L'Homme libre*, "published a large cartoon entitled 'Neo-Nationalism,' which showed Barrès talking before a bust of Barthou to a great concourse of priests, bishops, and choirboys assembled under the banners of the Sacré Coeur and the Ligue des Patriotes: 'Qu'importe le nom, si nous avons la chose!' "[61]

With Raymond Poincaré, Barrès found the first prime minister he could support. While almost all the Right abstained in the vote establishing the Poincaré ministry on January 12, 1912, Barrès voted for the ministry, even though it supported laicization.[62] By October, 1913, after Poincaré became president, Barrès wrote him, saying, "I am immensely grateful to you for wanting to restore and for knowing how to restore the pride [les fiertés] of the country."[63] His gratitude was not misplaced. In a speech to the Alliance Républicaine Democratique as early as July, 1911, before the Agadir crisis had heightened nationalistic fervors, Poincaré had sounded completely Barrésian: "We should undertake a crusade in this *troubled and disoriented country*—to remind it that a great nation has reasons for its existence other than material interests; to reawaken wherever they have languished, *individual energies*."[64] "Patriotism," he said on another occasion, "rather than being in contradiction with our duties toward humanity, is a necessary condition for it . . . The fatherland is the material and moral patrimony which our ancestors bequeathed to us . . . It is not only our soil; it is also our soul."[65]

If Barrésianism only recently had found itself in accord with establishment politicians, it continued to beat strongly in the hearts of French youth. A number of surveys of student attitudes were conducted between 1910 and 1914, such as *L'Esprit de la nouvelle Sorbonne* and *Les Jeunes Gens d'aujourd'hui* of Agathon [Henri Massis and Alfred de Tarde], Gaston Riou's *Aux écoutes de la France qui vient*, and Emile Henriot's *A quoi rêvent les jeunes gens*, which left Barrès "enchanted with the sympathy that they generally show for me."[66] While he remained for one of these compilers, Henri Massis, "the *maître* of youth and its thought,"[67] he had developed considerable competition from Henri Bergson and Charles Péguy.[68] This youth, doubtlessly all too carefully selected by the surveyors to evoke the appropriate responses, indicated that they were nationalistic, caught up in the activism of sport and in the speed of the new automobile and airplane, and unalterably opposed to the scientific and positivistic spirit of the university. Repelled by its mediocrity and by its preoccupation with the scientific method, so obviously inspired by the Germany Barrès had decried in *Les Déracinés*, the students still found sustenance in the sensitivity of Barrès' doctrine of selfhood, as reinforced by Bergsonianism. Not for nothing did the students, in their year-end satiric revue of 1910, entitle the act which "showed the leadership of the Sorbonne scheming to ruin classical humanities, confound the literary spirit, and open the *Ecole normale* to all comers" *Sous l'oeil des barbares.*[69]

While these surveys indicated that students were generally apolitical and not attracted by the positivistic Action Française, they were somewhat activated by Catholicism and certainly by nationalism, both of which were Barrésian concerns of this period. "That the renaissance of patriotic sentiment appears with a particular sharpness in certain sectors of intellectual youth is testified to by all the numerous inquests devoted to youth on the eve of the war," writes Raoul Girardet, and the one "particularly characteristic" student response he quotes mentions *Bérénice*, Alsace-Lorraine, and virtually all Barrésian concerns.[70] Massis concluded from his and Tarde's survey that "patriotic faith, the taste for heroism, the moral and Catholic renewal, the cult of classical tradition and political realism are the principal elements of what can be called a French renaissance," and what he meant by "political realism" was "a Republic founded on a central non-illusory authority, a reduced parliamentarianism, solidarity of professional groupings, an elected Chamber of Labor, and a large decentralization"—thoroughgoing Barrésian nationalism.[71]

It needs to be remembered, however, that the Barresianism which was in accord with the political establishment and youth, generally, was not Barrès' nationalism of the Dreyfus affair and the fascistic campaign of 1903. Rather, it was the sensibility of the *Culte du moi*, the appeasement of clericals and anti-clericals, a strong France against menacing German power and control of Alsace-Lorraine, and the maintenance of social control by the powers-that-be. All of those, not just the fear of Germany inspired by the second Moroccan crisis of 1911, went to create the "French nationalist revival." Etienne Rey, writing in 1912, gave a similar list—"resistance

to Germany, resistance to revolutionary socialism, appeasement of civil struggles, restoration of the principle of authority, concern for honor"—and pointed out that the first
French leaders to sense these were Clemenceau in foreign
policy and Briand in domestic affairs.[72] Rey's insight has been
more fully substantiated by David E. Sumler.[73] According to
him, "the nationalist revival appears to have been less a
reaction to German pressure than an integral part of a conservative resurgence, a product of the domestic struggle for
power between the Center-Right and Center-Left." That
struggle was to undo the reforms inaugurated by the Dreyfusard ministries. It began with Briand's policy of "appeasement" and his support of proportional representation. It
continued with the successful effort to replace Caillaux and
his income tax with Poincaré, whose policy of "national pride
[fierté]" included supporting a patriotic holiday honoring
Jeanne d'Arc, crushing the schoolteachers union, and restoring
his war minister's military reviews. "The passage of the
Three Years Law [i.e. the law passed in 1913 requiring draftees
to serve three years instead of two] was the culmination of
the conservative resurgency which had begun in 1910." This
domestic policy was also accompanied by an ever more
hostile policy toward aggressive Germany.

As it occurred, Barrès found it completely to his liking and
supported all these domestic and foreign policy moves. He
had been won over by Briand's appeasement policy, and he
voted for the ministries of Poincaré and his conservative and
nationalistic successors. Barrès confessed that Briand's policy
had made him a man of the Center, even though it was
"commonplace." He found himself there, against his will,
because it did his work. "I am not a party man in the Chamber," he wrote in 1913. "Rather, I collaborate with all those
who serve the national interest, all who unify and who
eliminate those who conspire against the genius of the nation."[74] That might work operationally, but it did not completely
convert him:

> This country wants neither king, nor emperor, nor parlia-
> mentary republic, nor socialism.

What does it want? I do not know. Something unknown, new, plainly made of eternal materials, but with form.
Boulangism was an attempt. A national ministry? It is worth a try, but toward what?[75]

Plainly, then, his loyalty to his new found friends of the Center was conditioned on their willingness to perform the essentials of his program. If they did not? In 1914, after a series of rightist governments which he supported, he could still write:

I have put aside the political ideas of Déroulède, but not because they are unimportant. His conception of the presidential republic, which he sensibly renounced, is a way out when the nation becomes far too much confused.[76]

France, however, no longer was "far too much confused." It was now hard to describe as "uprooted, disunified, and drifting" a France whose government stood up to Germany, reconciled Church and State, and kept law and order. What Barrès and the nationalists had considered the party of disorder had become the party of order. As it did, Barrès had been forced to seek a new "axiom, religion, or prince of men" to satisfy his search for selfhood. Boulangism, socialism, the "national-socialism" of the 1898 campaign at Nancy, and the fascist-like program he developed for the nationalist leagues had all successively failed either to take power or to analyze his world. There had been no new "prince of men" since Boulanger. In this sorry state of affairs, sorry in terms of his previous stances, Barrès had reached a conjunction with the establishment and had adopted a traditional conservatism as his "axiom." Poincaré, even, had become his "prince of men."

CHAPTER NINE

THE LAST YEARS

The last ten years of Barrès' life showed that his change was permanent. If he had become reconciled to the establishment by 1914, the outbreak of the World War made him one of its pillars. From then until his death in 1923, he remained, in the words of one of his admirers, "the all but official champion of all the great French causes."[1] Initially, at least, the common enemy united Frenchmen of all political stripes into the *race* Barrès had yearned for in *Scènes et doctrines du nationalisme*. The *Union sacrée*, as it was called, created a war cabinet extending from Marxist Jules Guesde to Barrès' conservative colleague Denys Cochin. In the wartime Chamber of Deputies, Barrès was now able to push for his desires and get them: improvement of military medical services, the establishment of the *croix de guerre*, the adoption of the steel helmet, aid to war widows and orphans, protection of art treasures, and the final winning of an annual *fête* celebrating Jeanne d'Arc.

If those causes were not so "great," another activity of Barrès perhaps was. Throughout the war he contributed an almost daily column to *l'Echo de Paris*, the great 100,000 circulation daily, long devoted to the army and Catholicism. Collected after the war as *La Chronique de la Grande Guerre*, the well over a thousand articles ran to fourteen volumes.[2] This enormous and well-placed output, plus its nature, made Barrès a kind of national cheerleader, indeed, almost an unofficial minister of morale and, in Victor Giraud's term, "ministre de la parole."[3] In addition to using the articles to publicize the causes he championed in the Chamber, Barrès lent his considerable literary talent to

237

writing what must have been effective propaganda. Yet, his exaltation of sacrifice and dying for one's country in a kind of holy war for the defense of Latin values and the French fatherland can seem but sentimental to a modern reader conditioned by the writings of Henri Barbousse, Erich Maria Remarque, and Wilfred Owen. Jeanne d'Arc became a new "professor of energy" for Barrès and France. He described his frequent visits to the front. He was the first to label the single supply route into Verdun as *la voie sacrée*. His reputation as a spokesman for French patriotism won him invitations to visit the Italian front and Great Britain, where he spoke to the Royal Society and was received by David Lloyd-George. The English translation of that speech, which made extensive use of letters written by soldiers killed in action, appeared in the United States under the imprimateur of Yale University Press and with an introduction approvingly pointing out the similarities between Barrès' doctrine of "selfhood" and Theodore Roosevelt's "strenuous life." An article along similar lines (but, appropriately, containing letters from French *Protestant* soldiers) reached the readers of the equally establishmentarian *Atlantic Monthly*.[4]

Inspired by the spirit of the *Union sacrée*, Barrès virtually abandoned his former attacks on France's internal enemies in favor of denouncing the German invader. Almost, but not quite. Nowhere in his war writings is this ambivalence toward the internal enemies more clear than in his *Diverses Familles spirituelles de France* (1917). While he claimed that he did not favor any single one of the families of a France bound together by the *Union sacrée*, the "traditionalist" one came off best. "Regionalism and tradition, which is the life of the soul, sustains our armies in the most thorough way."[5] Another family, the Catholics, ran a close second, even though their battle was primarily to preserve Catholicism from pernicious German influences of Kantianism, higher criticism, and modernism.[6] While "the real tradition of the Reformation is in France" just as "the most beautiful and healthy" Catholic tradition of Pascal and Saint Vincent de Paul are French, Protestants did not come off as well. "The calm and moderate spirits" of the fighting sons of his old Protestant enemies of the Dreyfus affair just did not stand up to the "violent states of consciousness and joyous frenzy" of the "Catholic heroes" he described.[7] If he was still sceptical toward Protestants, he distrusted Jews even more. Their patriotism was not the "irrational, quasi-animal" "love of country (as in our attachment to our mother)" which real Frenchmen had. Patriotism for them was "only an association freely consented to," "an act of will, decision, a mental choice."[8] Nor could he pass up this occasion to take one more swipe at the socialists. He lectured them that a German victory would be a triumph for Metternich or Marx and the destruction of that proper French socialist tradition which "seeks forms of harmony with Fourier and forms of justice with Proudhon."[9]

While the war could almost reconcile Barrès to these former enemies, at least if they died in the trenches, others remained beyond the pale. Of course his anti-parliamentary railings continued, directed now principally against the Chamber's lack of war preparedness and its refusal to hand over direction of the war to a wartime dictatorship. He reserved his sharpest barbs, however, for the pacifist left wing. Although Barrès did not bring to the stake in 1917 the editors of the *Bonnet Rouge*, whose defeatist propaganda was paid by Germany, or Jean-Louis Malvy, the minister of interior who protected and subsidized them, or Joseph Caillaux, who sought a negotiated peace, he helped stoke the fire.[10] "When are you going to arrest the *canaille* of the *Bonnet Rouge*?" he cried to the government in the July 7, 1917, issue of the *Echo de Paris*,[11] and he continued through the autumn with heavy attacks on Malvy. The real leaders in this business against the defeatists were Léon Daudet of the Action Française and Georges Clemenceau, who profited by becoming prime minister in November and who brought Malvy to trial. They, like Barrès, had bigger fish to fry. For all three the "ball-master" (in Barrès' words) of Malvy had been his political mentor, Caillaux, and they got him as well. For Barrès, still the Barrès of *Leurs figures* on this point, "Caillaux invented a new kind of treason. It is not that of Judas . . . The appetite for power alone moves him, and the method he chose for the past three years to regain the prime ministership comes from a loss of faith in his country. He played on defeat because he did not believe in France. He is a man who does not believe in the virtue of his mother. He is a case of parricide."[12] In joining the establishment, the old dog had had to learn new tricks, but Barrès knew that the old tricks still worked, too.

This wartime writing did as much if not more than his nationalism of the Dreyfus affair to ruin Barrès' reputation among the literary community. As one scholar recently has pointed out:

> The élite of the young men called to arms in 1914 were nourished on Barrès. But many among this élite were killed, including "Barrésiens" who might have continued the master's tradition and enhanced his reputation. The "Barrésiens" who survived had experienced trench warfare while Barrès had merely written about it. They felt that, in this domain at least, action spoke louder than words . . . The sentimental patriotism of Barrès' war propaganda aroused their ironic contempt. The difference between propaganda literature and "Littérature engagée" appeared obvious to them. From then on, any committed literature that was not authenticated by a parallel commitment in life would be suspect.[13]

As early as 1916 the 5,402 votes of Barrès came immediately behind the 5,653 of ex-pacifist and militarist Gustave Hervé in the poll of the satirical weekly, *Le Canard enchaîné*, to determine "The big chief of the tribe of humbugs [*bourreurs de crâne*]."[14] In 1923 André Breton and other surrealists cooked up a "trial" of Barrès, accused of "crime against the safety of the mind." The trial was visually surreal in its wild dress, a wooden dummy substituting for the absent Barrès, and a goose-stepping "unknown soldier" speaking German. Yet, when Breton asked "how was the author of *Un Homme libre* able to become the propagandist of *l'Echo de Paris*," he spoke for the generation of Barrésians—including Louis Aragon, his fellow surrealist and one of the "defense lawyers"—who had turned away from their early admiration for the author of the *Culte de moi*.[15] Politically the young Barrésians had already turned away into either socialism or the Action Française. Now the systematic literary denigration of Barrès had begun. Before long, the attacks of André Gide and Jean Paul Sartre would virtually destroy his literary standing.

If the war damaged Barrès' literary reputation, it further en-
hanced his position with the political establishment. He accompanied General Pétain to the liberation ceremonies at
Metz, General Castelnau to those at Colmar, and both to a Te
Deum in the cathedral of Strasbourg. He was among the
French delegation for the signing of the Treaty of Versailles,
and he reluctantly voted for its ratification in the Chamber.
With the death or retirement of other rightist leaders like Albert de Mun, Denys Cochin, and Jacques Piou, he emerged as
the foremost leader of the French right wing in the negotia-
tions with Millerand to form the Bloc National. This electoral
coalition of the Right and Center swept the parliamentary
elections of 1919, with Millerand and Barrès heading the Social and National Republican Union ticket for one of the three
multi-member constituencies of Paris. The only problem
for this unlikely match had been the Church-State issue, settled by declaring the neutrality of the state.[16]

Although one would have expected Barrès, as co-author of
the Bloc National and leader by default of the Right, to be a
major figure or minister in governments after 1919, he chose
neither to lead nor to engage himself in more than a few issues.
One was his campaign in the Chamber and in *Pour la haute intelligence française* (1925) to disperse higher education throughout France rather than keeping it focused on Paris. One device
for doing that would be to endow chairs which could attract
great teachers to the provincial universities. He likewise continued a journalistic campaign against the evils of socialism
and the Soviet threat.

His over-riding postwar concern, however, was the question
of the Rhineland. In a series of conferences at the University of
Strasbourg (published as *Le Génie du Rhin* in 1921), newspaper
articles, and speeches in the Chamber, he served as the chief
civilian spokesman for Marshall Foch's Rhineland policy.[17]
What Barrès wanted was a Rhineland free of Prussia but still
tied to Germany. While one gets the feeling that he would have
preferred a France at its "natural frontier" on the Rhine or an
independent Rhineland, neither was realistic any longer. It was
still possible, he believed, to establish an autonomous Rhine-

241

land or, if even that failed, to use a long French military occupation to Gallicize the Rhinelanders. The Rhineland was to be tied to France economically, like the Saar, and serve as a cultural bridge between Latin and Teutonic culture and as a political and military barrier against German revanchism. A nation of Colette Baudoches would Gallicize a state of Asmuses. At any rate, the occupation or autonomy were to be used to infuse French culture and values to balance off the German ones and thereby to insure the safety of France. On his death in December, 1923, during the French occupation of the Ruhr, it all seemed to be working out as he hoped. At a massive funeral held in the cathedral of Notre Dame de Paris, the establishment and the nation paid their respects to their servant.

"I never wrote but one book," Barrès regularly insisted in what could serve as his intellectual and political epitaph, "and with it I indicated at the age of twenty-four everything that I have developed since."[18] To some extent his continued claim that *Un Homme libre* was "the book which became my central expression"[19] was true. In it he set forth his need for a new faith. The old value system was bankrupt and brought only collective decadence because it could not nourish individual fulfillment. Recognition of that fact set him off on a quest for new certainties, a new faith in which his "self" could fulfill itself. The path of that quest was a life of action to find outside himself the energy and force to exalt his sense of selfhood, for it had been beaten down by the "barbarians" as had been the "soil and dead" of his native Lorraine. Only by the turn of the century would the new faith reveal itself to him. It did so with his recognition that nationalism and the "soil and the dead" of Lorraine provided the energy to promote, rather than stifle, the individual fulfillment he had sought for so long. That discovery came to constitute the political doctrine his disciples have always associated with him.

In this search, the political career of Barrès was life as art. It provided the action called for in *Un Homme libre*, an action which led to the new faith. The quest for a new faith took Barrès into one political movement after another, because of the times, his motivations, and his way of knowing through instinct and sensibility rather than through rational analysis.

Boulangism came along just at the time Barrès needed the action outside himself which *Un Homme libre* demanded. It was also just the right movement at the right time because its enemies—the "barbarians"—were his enemies, its strong leader intervened on behalf of the individual, and its mass enthusiasm provided energy for the helpless individual to reach up out of his rootlessness. In turn, and thanks to its being played out among Alfred Gabriel's Nancian working class, Barrès' Boulangism quite by accident led him leftward into socialism. Because socialism had an "ideal," as Barrès put it in *La Cocarde*, and the appropriate establishment enemies, it temporarily appeared to be the new faith every bit as much as the failing irrationalist leadership principle of Boulangism had been.

In socialism, however, Barrès' way of knowing got in the way for the first time. The yearnings of his soul, his sensibility, and his need for self-fulfillment could make him grasp at the socialist faith, but that ideal cost too much. He had the good heartedness of the young to want the better life for both the proletariat and the "proletariat of graduates" plus the conviction that helping the workers' lot could magnify the rootless bourgeois intellectual's soul. Nonetheless, he came to believe, socialism likewise required him to abandon his instinctual way of knowing for a rationalistic one. Moreover, he was too much the anarchist and too "unrealistic" to accept the substitution of collectivism for bourgeois plutocracy and internationalism for nationalism. As early as 1896 he could complain of that "*ex cathedra*" socialism which demanded that he be a collectivist and internationalist, but he was ten years premature. Even Millerand, the future conservative nationalist and eventual president of the League of Patriots, could be considered a good socialist until 1905. In essence, as Eugen Weber has perceived, Barrès' socialism merely "proposed a rich boy's philosophy:"

> to seek without hope of finding, to take pleasure in experiments not in results, to amuse oneself with means careless of the end—these are not recipes for proletarian action or satisfaction, let alone class war. The war that Barrès fought was therefore scarcely in the socialist tradition.[20]

243

Not only that. One cannot but suspect that Barrès also feared that socialist politics would cost him the financial and literary success, respectability, and seat in the Academy he craved so much and which were so often denied writers of the Left. As it turned out, the only lasting contribution of the "socialist stage" for him was federalism and decentralization.

The break with socialism indeed found Barrès at the cross-roads. From then on he moved farther and farther down the road to the political Right. Man wants to reassert his lost individuality, Barrès believed, but he needs to do it in a non-chaotic way. The anarchism implied by the *Culte du moi* is chaos. From the beginning Barrès saw, as George Mosse points out,[21] that this individual revolt must be tamed. For that reason *homme libre* Philippe had borrowed the practicality of Charles Martin to tame the instincts of Bérénice. Barrès had concluded very early on, then, that man can regain his individuality when he comes together in a mass with other alienated men. There needs to be somebody or some idea to join together the fragmented pieces of society. Boulanger had done it by drawing together the "disgusted." Socialism had an "ideal" which united the proletariat with that well-born "proletariat of graduates," but its collectivism and internationalism raised doubts. The only bond which all the alienated, regardless of class, had was the nation. What was true for Barrès and the seven Lorrainers of *Les Déracinés*, alienated in Paris, was true for all Frenchmen. Nationalism was the social glue to bind individual to individual and class to class into a new community. Nationalism was an "ideal" and revolt for inspiring action to regain Alsace-Lorraine, throw out the parliamentarians, and usher in social reform. At the same time, it contained the taming qualities of roots, tradition, and eternity. Best of all, it was a cheap revolution of the "spirit," costing nothing in respectability, unlike the expensive socialist revolution of the material and real.

This realization, with the Dreyfus affair's creation of a crisis which further polarized the disunified segments of French life, took Barrès into the new Boulangism of the "novel of national energy," *Scènes et doctrines du nationalisme*, and the action of the

nationalist and anti-Dreyfusard leagues. France, as he saw it in
this period, was so utterly *déracinée, dissociée,* and *décérébrée*—
uprooted, disunified, and adrift—that it had to be rebuilt from
the ground up. But how? Should the crisis be seized upon with
real and immediate action to institutionalize the building
blocks of reconstruction: anti-parliamentarianism, "authority
at the top," decentralization, and retention of the republic if it
be "armed, glorious, and organized?" Instead, should he work
first to develop a new spirit rooted in the French soil and dead
and uproot the un-French influences of masons, Jews, foreigners, and German idealism à la Kant before the people could be
trusted? Should he at last get "dirty hands"—or not? As it
turned out, of course, he did both. On the one hand he became
a "realist" willing for militant action in accompanying Déroulède in the abortive coup at Reuilly, editing *Le Drapeau,* founding and participating in the League of the Patrie Française and
Action Française. At the same time, however, he bailed out of
Le Drapeau and the Patrie Française in 1901 to coach from the
sidelines, almost as if to "build character" rather than to
bring victory. Then, with the same ambivalence, he returned
to the electoral arena in his remarkably proto-fascist 1903
campaign.

The themes of this action and thought of Barrès, because of
their extraordinary similarities to French fascism of the
1920s–1940s, made this corpus future fascist bibles for some
Frenchmen. Saying that, however, raises countless problems.
Barrès, for example, never called himself a fascist nor lived
long enough to adhere to a movement which did. He specifically rejected the one movement of his time, the Action Française,
which Ernst Nolte among others has called fascist.[22] Others
were not as certain. For French fascists of the 1930s like Pierre
Drieu La Rochelle, Robert Brasillach, Jacques Debu-Bridel,
and the troops of the Action Française, as well as anti-fascists
like André Gide, Barrès was either a fascist or an inventor of
fascism. Barrès' works and action of 1897–1902 convinced
them of it. Generally, on the other hand, the scholars have seen
him not as a fascist but as a conservative nationalist. This is
true for as varied a lot as René Remond, Ernst Nolte, Jean

Plumyène and Raymond Lasierra, Pierre de Boisdeffre, Jacques Madaule, and J. S. McClelland. Yet, Robert Soucy convincingly has discovered fascist themes in much of Barrès' work.[23]

The most that can be said is that Barrès' actionist politics and ideas *prepared* fascists, but at the same time they prepared Gaullists, Pétainists, and Resistance existentialists. The student polls of Agathon and many testimonials witness to the fact that students from 1890 to 1914, at least, drank so deeply of Barrès that his ideas must have been indelibly imprinted on them. Of course, it all depended on which Barrès they read for inspiration. The Barrès of the *Culte du moi*, with or without its attendant socialism of *l'Ennemi des lois* and *La Cocarde*, could easily prepare existentialists of the Left. The testimonials of French intellectuals in Boisdeffre's *Barrès parmi nous* as supplemented by the work of Frederic Grover leave little doubt that this was true for men of the Left like André Malraux, Albert Camus, Jean Guéhenno, Louis Aragon, and even Jean Paul Sartre.[24] Malraux is a prime example of how one could move on to the Barrès of "the novel of national energy" and "bastions of the East" as preparation for Gaullism, and one must remember that Charles de Gaulle, himself, was a student in those same prewar years. Read differently, that same Barrès could prepare fascists, Pétainists, and the backers of *Algérie française*.

Perhaps a better term for Barrès from this period to the end of his career is counterrevolutionary as Arno Mayer uses it. Counterrevolution, he writes, "is a sectarian *levée en masse within* unstable but legitimate authority systems," such as the troops mobilized by the nationalist leagues under a Third French Republic beset by the Dreyfus affair; "*with* the complicity of frightened reactionaries and conservatives" who flocked into the League of the Patrie Française and winked at Déroulède's shenanigans; "*against* massive enemies at home and abroad," such as Jews, Dreyfusards, socialists, and Germans; "and *for* the monopolistic control of state and government by a *new political elite*," namely the advocates of a neo-Boulangist presidential republic.

Any such *levée en masse* requires a supreme leader; needs stirring propaganda appeals; is regimented by new cadres; develops an internal camaraderie with equalitarian overtones; and displays an élan that is characteristic of embattled communities of either old or new believers.[25]

Certainly Barrès and the nationalist leagues fit that definition, but whether one wants to call Barrès a counterrevolutionary or a proto-fascist during the heyday of the leagues, he never really had a chance. The Dreyfus affair simply did not create the necessary crisis strata to bring about any kind of counterrevolution. Socialism was not yet a big enough threat to propertied classes. Relative prosperity had returned after the end of the Long Depression. Economic growth remained slow enough but steady enough to prevent the dysfunctions brought on by either depression or rapid economic change. No potential *fuehrer, duce, chef,* or *homme national* emerged to mobilize what discontent there was. Moreover, that discontent remained basically political, so much so that even Barrès' allies would have been satisfied merely with a change of ministers. Nor did the moderates like Waldeck-Rousseau, Rouvier, and Combes lose either their nerve or their fear of caesarism. Society had not yet been militarized by World War I nor threatened by the very real Russian Revolution. Jaurès and Guesde were not even Lenin and Trotsky, let alone Stalin. Neither conservatives, who remained with such groups as the Action Liberale, nor army sprang to the support of nationalism. The positivism Barrès had challenged in the 1880s without offering a replacement now competed against established rivals like Bergsonianism. Nationalism was basically Parisian and urban, although Barrès' thought remained rural-oriented and never came to grips with the urban social problem. The "novel of national energy," notably the section on the Moselle valley, gave no indication that Barrès ever ran in a working-class district. The figures of speech in *Scènes et doctrines du nationalisme* are almost always rural, such as "our race of foresters, farmers and winegrowers," with labor as an afterthought and working-class notions relegated to an appendix.

Because he never had a chance for fascism, one can only conclude that Barrès was at most a proto-fascist fellow-traveler, not a true believer. He might gladly have been one only if victory had been certain in this period. Had there been a real crisis which caused anxious conservatives and petit bourgeois to turn to an *homme national*, Barrès doubtless would have been perfectly willing to be his Alfred Rosenberg or, for that matter, an André Malraux to an earlier de Gaulle. Had the opportunity arisen, however, which ministry would he have chosen: culture, information, education, or *cultes*?

Yet, he never got the chance. After 1903 it was a different world, and he moved from proto-fascism to conservatism. Certainly Barrès continued some of his earlier themes, but in a muted fashion. Reconciliation remained, but oriented toward the ebbing Church-State problem. Only Alsace-Lorraine and nationalism, which were there in his Boulangism but not in his socialism, remained strident and became the central issues. Most of all, these aims, along with social control, were coming about in the nationalist revival through the moderate ministries of Briand, Poincaré, and their fellows. How could Barrès, increasingly socialized by the Chamber of Deputies he once despised, argue with that? Earlier he had always identified with Antigone, whose struggle against "barbarians" epitomized the doctrine of selfhood. By his *Voyage de Sparte* in 1906 he had shifted his loyalties to Creon, and by the eve of the war Creon had become Poincaré.

The last years of Barrès' life put him still farther down that road. If proto-fascism had once made sense to him, it certainly no longer did so under the circumstances of the *Union sacrée* and the Bloc National. With them traditional conservatism served well enough. There was no need for an *homme national* when one had Poincaré, Millerand, and Clemenceau, that one-time *bête noire* of *Leurs figures*. They could and did regain Alsace-Lorraine, break strikes, keep social peace, reconcile Church and State, and conduct a forceful foreign policy. Barrès even found himself seeing eye to eye politically with his fellow conservative Joseph Reinach, the formerly detestable Jewish Dreyfusard.[26] Little wonder that many of his post-war troops in the League of Patriots broke with him for his refusal to move the league toward fascism.[27] This record makes one wonder whether ideas or crises make for fascism.

Barrès' career had taken him from cultural to political rebellion and on into the arms of the establishment, if not the counter-revolution. Circumstances of art and politics had made the *homme libre* come to terms with the "barbarians" and the Charles Martins of his world. Throughout his life that conjunction had posed his chief dilemma, and nothing expressed it better than the closing passage in his *Colline inspirée* of 1913, the dialogue between the meadow and the chapel of Sion-Vaudémont:

"I am," says the meadow, "the spirit of earth and of the most distant ancestors. I am liberty, inspiration."

And the chapel replies:

"I am order, authority, the link between man and man; I am a body of fixed ideas and the city appointed for the soul."

"I shall move your heart," continues the meadow. "Those who breathe me begin to wonder, to question. The workman climbs here from the plain on his day of leisure, when he desires to meditate. An instinct brings him to me. I am a primitive site, a perennial spring of emotions."

But the chapel tells us:

"Visitors to the meadow, bring me your dreams that I may refine them, and your impulses that I may direct them. It is for me you are seeking, for me you are longing unconsciously. What do you feel, if not a homesick desire for my shelter? I continue the meadow, even when it denies me. It was through dreams in the meadow that I came to be constructed. Whoever you may be, there is nothing good within you that keeps you from accepting my aid. I will put you in harmony with life. Your liberty, you ask? But how can my guidance fail to satisfy you? We have been prepared, you and I, by your fathers. Like you, I am their incarnation. I am the lasting stone, the experience of the ages, the vaults in which are stored the treasures of your race. House of your childhood, home of your parents, I am in conformity with your deepest tendencies, with the very ones that you ignore; and it is here you will find, for every circumstance of your life, the mysterious word that was formed by you when you did not exist. Come to me if you hope to find the stone of solidity, the slab on which to rest your days and inscribe your epitaph."

Eternal dialogue of the two forces! Which shall we obey?

249

And must we choose between them? Ah! rather let these two antagonists strive with each other eternally; let neither be the victor, and let both of them grow through their very struggle! Neither can be great without the other. What is an order that has ceased to be animated by enthusiasm? From the meadow the church was born, and from it the church is eternally nourished—to save us from the meadow.[28]

If asked today, the average Frenchman probably would respond to Barrès' work as these two did. "My *father* has a whole shelf of his books," said a well brought-up young matron, but those books obviously did not speak to her. Or, a young father of Metz, doubtless a man of the Left, when asked on that same Lorraine hill of Sion-Vaudémont if he had come to visit the monument to Barrès, "the poet of your region." "No," he replied, "he is the *crapule* of my region." He had come to collect a different kind of fossil. Barrès lived his life supporting both the meadow and the chapel at different times and appealed as a result to both and to neither. Because the chapel came to have such a hold on him, he is remembered for that, unfortunately, by both his friends and enemies. For some, he ends up being only of their father's time or the *crapule* of his region. For those many Frenchmen from the 1880s to today whose classrooms and shelves were filled with millions of copies of the *Culte du moi*, the "novel of national energy," and the "bastions of the East," however, it was different. For them, whether because of Barrès' literary or ideological power, he remains the father of French fascism, the Vichy "national revolution," Gaullism, and *Algérie française*, much as they differ from each other.

NOTES

The following abbreviations are used in these footnotes:

ADS   Archives du Département de la Seine
AMM   Archives de Meurthe-et-Moselle (Nancy)
AN   Archives Nationales
APP   Archives de la Prefecture de Police (Paris)
JOC   *Journal officiel de la République française. Débats. Chambre.*

INTRODUCTION

1. Julien Green, *Journal, 1950–1954* (Paris, 1955), pp. 33–34.
2. Claude Sarraute, "Maurice Barrès et Solange Lusanger acquittés," *Le Monde*, January 18, 1974, p. 21.
3. Geoffrey Barraclough, "Mandarins and Nazis: Part I," *New York Review of Books*, October 19, 1972, pp. 39-40.
4. F. Grover, "The Inheritors of Maurice Barrès," *Modern Language Review*, LXIV (July, 1969), pp. 529-545 and Pierre de Boisdeffre, *Barrès parmi nous* (Paris, 1969).

CHAPTER ONE

1. For an analysis of the forces which shaped French education in the 1870s, see: John A. Scott, *Republican Ideas and the Liberal Tradition in France, 1870–1914* (New York, 1951), *passim*; Claude Digeon, *La Crise allemande de la pensée française, 1870-1914* (Paris, 1959), *passim*; Georges Weill, *L'Histoire de l'enseignement secondaire en France (1802–1920)* (Paris, 1921), pp. 154–169; and Antoine Prost, *L'Histoire de l'enseignement en France 1800–1967* (Paris, 1968), pp. 122, 184–185, 192–203, 246–247, 325–340, 384–385, and 396–397.
2. Maurice Barrès, *Mes Cahiers* (Paris, 1929–1957), XIV, 278–279.
3. Louis Marin, *Regards sur la Lorraine* (Paris, 1966), pp. 112–115.
4. The author wishes to thank Professor George S. Craft Jr. of California State College at Sacramento for this information on Lorraine nationalism in the 1870s. See also his unpublished dissertation: "The Emergence of National Sentiment in French Lorraine, 1871–1889" (Stanford University, 1971).
5. Although Barrès wrote frequently on Renan and Taine, his most celebrated passages are *Huit jours chez Monsieur Renan* (Paris, 1888) and a section entitled, "L'Arbre de M. Taine," from *Les Déracinés* (Paris, 1961), I, 202–231.

251

6. Jean Dietz, *Maurice Barrès* (Paris, 1927), p. 23.

7. Barrès, "Au quartier des étudiants," *Le Voltaire*, November 2, 1887.

8. Barrès, *Le Depart pour la vie* (Paris, 1961), *passim*.

9. *Ibid.*, p. 223.

10. Barrès, "Psychologie contemporaine," *Les Taches d'encre*, November 5, 1884, pp. 1–2.

11. *Les Taches d'encre*, January 1885, p. 48.

12. Digeon, *La Crise allemande*, p. 404.

13. Barrès, "Un Mauvais Français: M. Victor Tissot," *Les Taches d'encre*, November 5, 1884, pp. 32–33. Oddly enough virtually every scholar has changed "Midi" in this passage to "Metz." Doing so certainly simplifies matters, making it easier to harmonize the internationalism of the young Barrès with the nationalism of the mature Barrès. Zeev Sternhell has observed the same error in his *Maurice Barrès et le nationalisme français* (Paris, 1972), pp. 28–29.

14. Digeon, *La Crise allemande*, p. 406. See also: Pierre Georges Castex, "Barrès collaborateur du *Voltaire*," *Annales de l'Est*, mémoire no. 24, 1963, p. 53.

15. Barrès, "Un Mauvais Français," pp. 32–33.

16. Barrès, "En Allemagne," *Le Voltaire*, October 19, 1887.

17. Barrès, "Un Entretien de Bonaparte," *ibid.*, October 5, 1887.

18. Barrès, "Un Salon fermé," *ibid.*, September 7, 1886.

19. Barrès, "Dostoiewski," *ibid.*, July 10, 1886.

20. Barrès, "Les Historiens en 1887," *ibid.*, December 16, 1887.

21. Barrès, "Heine et Tourgueniev," *ibid.*, January 6, 1888.

22. Barrès, "Les Chansons du 14 juillet," *ibid.*, July 14, 1886.

23. Barrès, "La Chanson en province," *ibid.*, October 19, 1887.

24. Barrès, *Mes Cahiers*, I, 39.

25. Auguste Marcade in *Le Figaro*'s literary supplement, September 8, 1888. Quoted in Kenneth Cornell, *The Symbolist Movement* (New Haven, 1951), p. 73.

26. Barrès, *Le Depart pour la vie*, p. 279.

27. Pierre de Boisdeffre, *Barrès parmi nous* (Paris, nouvelle edition, 1969), p. 38.

28. Barrès, *Examen des trois romans idéologiques* in *Le Culte du moi* (Paris: Le Livre de Poche, 1966), p. 472. In this essay, originally published as a pamphlet in 1892, Barrès explains the trilogy's message to a wider public. It was then published as a preface to both the 1892 and 1896 editions of *Sous l'oeil des barbares* and is included as an appendix in this edition of all three novels.

29. *Ibid.*, p. 467.

30. Barrès, *Sous l'oeil des barbares* in *Le Culte du moi*, p. 81.

31. Barrès, *Examen*, p. 470.

32. Barrès, *Sous l'oeil des barbares*, p. 115.

33. Barrès, *Examen*, p. 481.

34. *Ibid.*, p. 468.

35. Barrès, *Sous l'oeil des barbares*, pp. 134–135.

36. Barrès, *Examen*, p. 481.

37. Barrès, *Un Homme libre* in *Le Culte du moi*, p. 209.

38. *Ibid.*, p. 236.

39. *Ibid.*, p. 236.

40. *Ibid.*, p. 228. Barrès' description of the impact of Lorraine on his being is so far from being a paean to nationalism that his adversaries in later political campaigns used his words against him to show that he denigrated Lorraine and was, himself, an outsider there.

41. *Ibid.*, p. 271.

42. *Ibid.*, p. 278.

43. Barrès, *Examen*, p. 476.

44. Barrès, *Un Homme libre*, p. 317.

45. *Ibid.*, p. 324.

46. Barrès, *Le Jardin de Bérénice* in *Le Culte du moi*, p. 406.

47. *Ibid.*, p. 405.

48. *Ibid.*, p. 406.

49. *Ibid.*, pp. 365, 373, and 381.

50. *Ibid.*, pp. 377–378.

51. *Ibid.*, p. 381.

52. Quoted in Adrien Dansette, *Le Boulangisme* (Paris, 1946), p. 28. Unless otherwise indicated the account of Boulangism which follows is based on Dansette; Alexandre Zévaès, *Au temps du Boulangisme* (Paris, 1930); Jacques Chastenet, *La République des républicains* (Paris, 1954); "Notes sur boulangisme," *Le Figaro*, November 18 and December 4 and 11, 1889; and Pierre Denis, *Le Mémorial de Sainte-Brelade* (Paris, 1894). Two recent studies, Frederic H. Seager, *The Boulanger Affair* (Ithaca, 1969) and Fresnette Pisani-Ferry, *Le Général Boulanger* (Paris, 1969), update Dansette's recent work by using archival materials. Seager's study, published after this study's research on Boulangism was completed, also points out the leftist nature of the Boulangist movement.

53. Barrès, *L'Appel au soldat* (Paris, 1920), p. 45.

54. Barrès, "Les Français malgré eux," *Le Voltaire*, May 25, 1887.

55. Chastenet, p. 191.

56. Dansette, p. 96 and *passim*.

57. Barrès, "M. le général Boulanger et la nouvelle génération," *La Revue indépendante*, April, 1888, pp. 55–56.

58. *Ibid.*, p. 57.

59. *Ibid.*, p. 59.

60. *Ibid.*, p. 56.

61. Barrès, "La Jeunesse boulangiste," *Le Figaro*, May 19, 1888. This article was a rewriting of "M. le général Boulanger et la nouvelle génération" for a wider public.

62. Barrès, "M. le général Boulanger et la nouvelle génération," p. 59.

63. *Ibid.*, p. 60.

64. Barrès, *L'Appel au soldat*, p. 53.

65. *Ibid.*, p. 59.

66. *Ibid.*, p. 205.

67. Dansette, p. 139.

68. Sybil, "Croquis parlementaires: M. Maurice Barrès," *La Revue bleue*, November 23, 1889, p. 644.

69. Camile Mauclair, *Paul Adam (1862–1920)* (Paris, n.d.), *passim*; and Digéon, *La Crise allemande*, pp. 399–400.

70. Francis Magnard, "M. Maurice Barrès," *Le Figaro*, May 11, 1888. Barrès later used the story to show Sturel's Boulangism in *L'Appel au soldat*, p. 155.

71. Maurice de Fleury, "L'Opinion politique des artistes et des savants," *Le Figaro*, January 20, 1889.

72. *Le Figaro*, April 22 and 23, 1888.

73. Barrès, "La Jeunesse boulangiste."

74. Dansette, *Le Boulangisme*, pp. 328–329.

CHAPTER TWO

1. *AMM*, wM/757bis, Parti boulangiste, December 26, 1888; and wM/762ter, Comité revisionniste, March 15, 1889.

2. *AMM*, wM/757bis, March 20, 1888.

3. *Ibid.*, April 28 and 29, 1888; and *Le Figaro*, April 27 and 28, 1888.

4. *AN*, F⁷12450, La Ligue des Patriotes, report of April 18, 1888.

5. *Ibid.*, *passim*; and *AMM*, wM/757bis.

6. *AMM*, wM/762ter, March 15, 1889.

7. *Ibid.*, *passim*; *AMM*, wM/757bis, *passim*; Alphonse Bertrand, *La Chambre de 1889* (Paris, 1889), p. 309; Gabriel Richard, "Le Boulangisme à Nancy. L'Election au Conseil général de Nancy ouest. La région nancienne vers 1888," *Le Pays Lorrain* (1962), I, 14 and "Les Elections de 1889 en Meurthe-et-Moselle," *ibid.*, II, 47–48; and Jean Jolly, *Dictionnaire des parlementaires français* (Paris, 1960–Present), V, 1755.

8. "Réunion révisionniste à Frouard," *Le Courrier de l'Est*, February 26, 1889.

9. "Les Réunions révisionnistes," *ibid.*, September 1, 1889.

10. Alfred Gabriel, "La République nouvelle," *ibid.*, April 7, 1889.

11. Adam's views appear in his preface-introduction to Francis Laur, *Epoque boulangiste* (Paris, 1914), reprinted as an appendix to Camile Mauclair, *Paul Adam (1862–1920)* (Paris, n.d.), pp. 259–284 and, especially, p. 276.

12. Friedrich Engels and Paul and Laura Lafargue, *Correspondence*, trans., Yvonne Kapp (3 vols.; Moscow, 1959), II, *passim*.

13. "Meurthe-et-Moselle," *La Grande Encyclopédie* (Paris, 1886–1902), XXIII, 828–845; E. Eisenmenger, *La Lorraine au travail* (Paris, 1925), pp. 68, 78, 108, 117, 133–164, 170–190; and Richard, "Le Boulangisme a Nancy," pp. 10–12.

14. *AMM*, wM/655, Syndicalisme: rapports de police (1880–1938), Rapports sur les syndicats professionnels existant en Meurthe-et-Moselle au 31 décembre 1889 et 5 décembre 1890.

15. Richard, "Le Boulangisme à Nancy," pp. 11–12.

16. *AMM*, wM/757bis.

17. Various issues of *Le Courrier de Meurthe-et-Moselle*, November 11–December 11, 1888.

18. *AMM*, wM/757bis.

19. Paul Adam, *Le Mystère des foules* (2 vols., Paris, 1895), I, 101–105.

20. *AMM*, wM/757bis, report of Jan. 5, 1889; *Le Courrier de la Meurthe-et-Moselle*, Jan. 6–7, 9, and 20–21, 1889; *Le Figaro*, Jan. 9, 1889; Maurice Barrès, "A un ami politique de la première heure," *Le Courrier de l'Est*, Aug. 18, 1889; and *Le Courrier de l'Est*, Nov. 9, 1890.

21. *Le Courrier de l'Est*, February 1, 1889.

22. *Ibid.*, February 15, 1889; and "Les Réunions révisionnistes," *ibid.*, September 1, 1889.

23. Barrès, "Sommes-nous prêts?," *ibid.*, February 2, 1889.

24. "Réunion révisionniste à Frouard," *ibid.*, February 26, 1889.

25. "Lettre d'un Opportuniste," *ibid.*, March 7, 1889.

26. Barrès, "Combien sommes-nous," *ibid.*, January 22, 1889.

27. Barrès, "Les Travailleurs décideront," *ibid.*, January 26, 1889.

28. Barrès, "Quels sont nos alliés," *ibid.*, March 10, 1889.

29. Adam, "Le Comité révisionniste," *ibid.*, January 30, 1889; and *AMM*, wM/762ter. Estimates of rally audiences by the opposition press and police usually cut the *Courrier's* estimate in half.

30. Barrès, "Autorité et démocratie," *La Presse*, February 4, 1890.
31. Barrès, *Le Jardin de Bérénice* in *Le Culte du moi* (Paris, 1966), p. 335.
32. *Ibid.*, p. 353.
33. *Ibid.*, p. 417.
34. *Ibid.*, p. 405.
35. *AMM*, wM/757bis.
36. *AMM*, wM/762ter.
37. "Résponse aux alliançards," *Le Courrier de l'Est*, February 19, 1889.
38. Gabriel, "La République nouvelle," *ibid.*, April 7, 1889.
39. Gabriel, "Les Caisses de retraite," *ibid.*, April 16, 1889.
40. "Les Réunions révisionnistes," *ibid.*, September 1, 1889.
41. *AMM*, wM/762ter.
42. Barrès, "Nos contradicteurs," *Le Courrier de l'Est*, February 27, 1889.
43. "Le Punch du 20 juin," *ibid.*, June 23, 1889.
44. "Les Réunions révisionnistes." This article contains the *compte rendu* of several rallies held by Barrès, Gabriel, and Adam at the end of August, 1889.
45. Barrès, "Quels sont nos alliés," *ibid.*, March 10, 1889.
46. This analysis of the Boulangist constitution and the quotations which follow are from: "Le Programme du parti national boulangiste," *ibid.*, February 28 and March 1, 2, and 6, 1889; and "La Prochaine constitution," *ibid.*, February 21, 1889.
47. Barrès, "Un Camouflet à l'Alliance," *ibid.*, March 13, 1889.
48. Barrès, "Leurs efforts inutiles," *ibid.*, March 2, 1889.
49. Barrès, "Nos grotesques," *ibid.*, January 25, 1889.
50. Barrès, "Pour les filles du peuple," *ibid.*, February 16, 1889.
51. Barrès, "Misérables occupations," *ibid.*, February 13, 1889.
52. *Le Courrier de l'Est*, February 12, 1889.
53. Barrès, "Le Juif dans l'Est," *ibid.*, July 14, 1889.
54. Robert F. Byrnes, *Anti-Semitism in Modern France* (New Brunswick, 1950), *passim*; and Frederic H. Seager, *The Boulanger Affair* (Ithaca, 1969), pp. 174–181.
55. Barrès, "Les Bélisaires," *Le Courrier de l'Est*, January 31, 1889.
56. Barrès, "Bonne nouvelle," *ibid.*, February 14, 1889.
57. Barrès, "On demande des policiers," *ibid.*, March 5, 1889.
58. *Le Courrier de l'Est*, April 7, 1889. Italics in the original.
59. Barrès, "Leur bétise fait notre malice," *ibid.*, April 7, 1889.
60. Barrès, "La République en exil," *ibid.*, April 28, 1889.
61. Richard, "Boulangisme à Nancy," pp. 12–13.
62. *Ibid.*, pp. 13–14; and Alfred Gabriel, "Sur la sellette," *Le Courrier de l'Est*, July 7, 1889.
63. Patrick H. Hutton, "The Impact of the Boulangist Crisis upon the Guesdist Party at Bordeaux," *French Historical Studies*, VII (Fall, 1971), 226–244.
64. *Le Courrier de l'Est*, July 28, 1889.
65. Mauclair, *Paul Adam*, p. 276; Dieudonné Terrail-Mermeix, "Coulisses du boulangisme," *Le Figaro*, October 1, 1890; and *AN*, F[7] 12445, "Note sur mon role dans le mouvement Boulangiste" by Maurice Vergoin, December 10, 1890, p. 133. The latter is cited hereafter as Vergoin. Emilien Carassus, "Maurice Barrès feuilletoniste," *La Revue d'histoire littéraire*, LXX, No. 1 (January-February, 1970), 90-97.
66. Seager, *The Boulanger Affair*, pp. 217–218.

67. Barrès, "La République ouverte," *Le Courrier de l'Est*, March 24, 1889.
68. Barrès, "Le Flot qui monte," *ibid.*, May 26, 1889.
69. Barrès, "La Noce empoisonnée," *ibid.*, June 30, 1889.
70. "Le Punch du 20 juin," *ibid.*, June 23, 1889.
71. Gabriel, "La République triomphante," *ibid.*, June 30, 1889.
72. *AMM*, wM/762ter, report of July 23, 1889; and wM/805, Renouvellement du Conseil Général dans différents cantons dont celui de Saint-Nicolas de Port, prefect to Interior, July 24, 1889.
73. Barrès, "L'Opportunisme. Parti des juifs," *Le Courrier de l'Est*, July 21, 1889.
74. Barrès, "L'Attitude de M. Larcher en face des concussionnaires," *ibid.*, July 21, 1889.
75. *AMM*, wM/805, prefect to Interior, July 24, 1889.
76. Gabriel, "Les Ouvriers étrangers," *Le Courrier de l'Est*, July 21, 1889. See also Maurice Barrès, "Comment on se déconsidère," *ibid.*, July 28, 1889.
77. Barrès, "L'Opportuniste ou le Révisionniste;" and Alfred Gabriel, "Avant tout, révision," *ibid.*, August 4, 1889.
78. Vergoin, p. 73; and Richard, "Elections législatives," pp. 52–53.
79. *Le Figaro*, September 7, 1889.
80. "Trop d'habilité nuit," *Le Courrier de l'Est*, September 29, 1889.
81. Barrès, "Les Masques," *ibid.*, September 1, 1889. See also the last manifesto of Barrès before the run-off elections: "Aux électeurs de la 3e circonscription," *ibid.*, September 29, 1889.
82. *AMM*, wM/785, Elections législatives de 1889, prefect report of September 9, 1889.
83. Barrès, "Une Lettre," *Le Courrier de l'Est*, August 25, 1889. This letter contains both the comments of Buquet and the reply of Barrès.
84. "Les Réunions révisionnistes," *ibid.*, September 1, 1889.
85. Louis Dumont-Wilden, *Le Crépuscule des maîtres* (Brussels, 1947), p. 100.
86. *AMM*, wM/785, Procès verbal du recensement général des votes émis dans les collèges électoraux de la 3eme circonscription de Nancy.
87. *Le Figaro*, October 3, 1889; and Richard, "Elections legislatives," pp. 62–63.
88. *AMM*, wM/785, "Procès verbal . . ."
89. *Le Courrier de l'Est*, October 20, 1889. After the years had cooled his passions and he had become a Millerand socialist, Adam attributed his defeat to a coalition of Radicals and reactionaries. See Mauclair, *Paul Adam*, p. 276.
90. Barrès, "Aux ouvriers," *Le Courrier de l'Est*, October 20, 1889.
91. For the following analysis of the defeat of Boulangism, see: "Notes sur boulangism," *Le Figaro*, November 18 and December 4 and 11, 1889; Dansette, pp. 312–337; Pierre Denis, *Le Mémorial de Sainte-Brélade* (Paris, 1894), pp. 147–169; Alexandre Zévaès, *Au temps du boulangisme* (Paris, 1930), pp. 144–192; Dieudonné Terrail-Mermiex, "Les Coulisses de boulangisme," *Le Figaro*, August 20 and 27, September 3, 10, 17 and 24, October 1 and 22, 1890. Seager, *The Boulanger Affair*, pp. 229–238 comes to similar conclusions.
92. Gaston Jollivet, "Au petit bonheur!," *Le Figaro*, October 14, 1889.

CHAPTER THREE

1. Jules Lemaître, "Donec eris felix," *Le Figaro*, October 12, 1889.
2. For the following backgrounds and programs of the Boulangist deputies,

see: Alphonse Bertrand, *La Chambre de 1889, biographies des 576 deputés* (Paris, 1889), *passim*; Adrien Dansette, *Le Boulangisme* (Paris, 1946), *passim*; Jean Jolly, *Dictionnaire des parlementaires francais* (Several vols. in progress; Paris, 1960–present, I–V, *passim*, Henry Fouquier, "Quelques élus," *Le Figaro*, October 9, 1889.

3. Friedrich Engels and Paul and Laura Lafargue, *Correspondence*, trans., Yvonne Kapp (Moscow, 1960), II, 296, 328, and 333.

4. For the attendance at the Jersey meeting, see "Hors Paris," *Le Figaro*, November 8, 1889.

5. "Les Élections législatives," *Le Temps*, October 7, 1889.

6. Jacques Bertillon, *Résultats statistiques du dénombrement de 1891 pour la ville de Paris* (Paris, 1891), pp. xcix–civ and especially p. civ.

7. In addition to *ibid.*, Dansette, pp. 312–337, and Alexandre Zévaès, *Au temps du boulangisme* (Paris, 1930), pp. 144–192, see: "Notes sur boulangisme," *Le Figaro*, November 18 and December 4 and 11, 1889; Pierre Denis, *Le Mémorial de Sainte-Brélade* (Paris, 1894), pp. 147–169.

8. "Le Punch du 20 juin," *Le Courrier de l'Est*, June 23, 1889.

9. Maurice Barrès, "Les Enseignements d'une année de boulangisme," *Le Figaro*, February 2, 1890. The quotations which follow immediately also come from this article.

10. Barrès, "Notes d'un nouvel élu," *ibid.*, October 27, 1889.

11. Barrès, "Autorité et démocratie," *La Presse*, February 4, 1890.

12. Barrès, "Du Recrutement d'un personnel révolutionaire," *Le Figaro*, April 2, 1890. See also his "Coup d'oeil sur la session parlementaire qui vient de finir," *Le Courrier de l'Est*, March 3, 1890.

13. Barrès, "Le Rôle de la politique s'amoindrit chaque jour," *Le Courrier de l'Est*, April 13, 1890. Italics in original. By this Barrès meant that his own victory had been the first indication of the socialist nature of the electorate.

14. X., "La Politique socialiste," *Le Courrier de l'Est*, February 16, 1890.

15. *Le Figaro* and *La Presse*, November 19, 1889.

16. "La Réunion d'hier," *La Presse*, February 4, 1890.

17. *Le Temps*, January 5, 1890.

18. *Le Figaro*, March 19, 1890.

19. Quoted in Jacques Chastenet, *La République triomphante, 1893–1906* (Paris, 1955), p. 30.

20. "Le Scrutin de samedi," *La Presse*, May 13, 1890.

21. Albert Millaud, "Le Premier discours de M. Barrès à la Chambre," *Le Figaro*, November 5, 1889.

22 *JOC*, May 14, 1890, pp. 789–791 and 799–800.

23. *Ibid.*, July 27, 1890, pp. 1649 and 1656–1657.

24. Besides Barrès, these were Aimel, Argeliès, de Belleval, Borie, Boudeau, Castelin, Chiché, Dumonteil, Farcy, Gabriel, Goussot, Jourde, Laguerre, Laisant, Laur, Le Hérissé, Le Senne, Le Veillé, Millevoye, Naquet, Paulin-Méry, Pontois, Revest, P. Richard, Saint-Martin, Terrail-Mermeix, and Turigny.

25. The following analysis is based on that procedure.

26. In these votes, a bloc of 45 to 50 generally indicates Boulangist, Radical-Socialist, and socialist cooperation; 60 to 75 adds the left-wing Radicals; 90 to 115 adds the Radicals and perhaps the social Catholics of de Mun.

27. *JOC.*, November 24, 1889, p. 146.

28. *Ibid.*, November 26, 1889, pp. 153–157 and 169–170.

29. *Ibid.*, March 29, 1890, pp. 693–694 and 696 and 697.

30. *Ibid.*, May 14, 1890, pp. 797 and 803–804.

31. *Ibid.*, May 20, 1890, pp. 823–843 and 848–849.

32. *Ibid.*, July 7–9, 1890, pp. 1320–1328, 1335–1338, 1342–1346, 1354–1361, 1363–1364, 1379–1386, and 1395–1398.

33. X., "La Politique socialiste."

34. *JOC*, November 20, 1889, pp. 87 and 97.

35. *Ibid.*, February 25 and June 6, 1890, pp. 331–333, 351, 959, and 975–976.

36. *Ibid.*, June 15, 1890, pp. 1062–1064 and 1076–1077.

37. *Ibid.*, January 26, 1890, pp. 98-99.

38. *Ibid.*, February 11, 1890, pp. 254–255.

39. As quoted in *Le Figaro*, February 9, 1890.

40. *JOC*, March 26, 1890, pp. 641–644.

41. *Ibid.*, June 17, 1890, pp. 1083–1087 and 1091–1092.

42. Denis, p. 178.

43. *APP*, Ba/1032, report of November 19, 1889.

44. Quoted in *Le Temps*, April 1, 1890.

45. *APP*, Ba/1032, report of November 19, 1889.

46. Barrès, "L'Infaillibilité du suffrage universal," *La Presse*, December 8, 1889.

47. *Ibid.*, March 11, 1890; *Le Figaro*, January 14, 18, 19, 22, and ff., 1890.

48. *Ibid.*, January 20, 1890.

49. *Ibid.*, January 28, 1890; and *Le Temps*, January 22, 1890.

50. Barrès, "La Formule antijuive," *Le Figaro*, February 22, 1890.

51. Barrès, "Les Adhésions démocratiques," *Le Courrier de l'Est*, March 28, 1891.

52. Robert Soucy, *Fascism in France: The Case of Maurice Barrès* (Berkeley, 1972), pp. 62–63.

53. *Le Temps*, March 25 and April 6, 1890; and *Le Figaro*, April 3, 1890.

54. *Le Temps*, April 18 and April 24, 1890.

55. *Le Figaro*, April 13, 1890.

56. As shown by the election results in *Le Temps*, April 29, 1890.

57. *Le Figaro*, April 29, 1890.

58. Denis, pp. 189–195 and 210–211.

59. X. [Dieudonné Terrail-Mermeix], "Coulisses du Boulangisme," *Le Figaro*, August 20 and 27, September 3, 10, 17 and 24, October 1 and 22, 1890.

60. Barrès, "La Voie du peuple et le proscrit," *Le Courrier de l'Est*, August 31, 1890. See also: Maurice Barrès, "Impressions de rentrée," *ibid.*, November 9, 1890.

61. *Le Temps*, September 2, 1890.

62. *Ibid.*, September 6, 1890.

63. *Ibid.*, September 30, 1890.

64. "Bien joue Laguerre!," *Le Figaro*, November 1, 1890. Laguerre's quotations which follow in the next paragraph are from this article.

65. *Le Temps*, November 10, 1890.

66. *JOC*, November 5, 1890, pp. 1873 and 1889–1890.

67. *Ibid.*, November 9, 1890, pp. 1958 and 1964–1965.

68. *Ibid.*, December 10, 1890, pp. 2522–2523 and 2530–2531.

69. *Ibid.*, December 11, 1890, pp. 2536–2537 and 2556–2558.

70. *Ibid.*, December 11, 1890, pp. 2550–2551 and 2559–2560.

71. *Le Courrier de l'Est*, April 18, 1890.

72. *JOC*, December 23, 1890, pp. 2614–2617 and 2621–2622.

73. *JOC*, January 27, 1891, pp. 105 and 117–118.

74. *Ibid.*, January 28, February 3, 4, 6 and 8, 1891, pp. 124–125, 131–138, 182–184, 192–193, 199–202, 207–215, 219–220, 226–227, 240–241, 247–248, and 266.

75. *Ibid.*, June 4, 1891, pp. 1112–1121 and 1126–1127.

76. *APP*, Ba/1032; Jerôme and Jean Tharaud, *La Vie et la mort de Déroulède* (Paris, 1925), pp. 74–77; Denis, *passim*; Dansette, *Boulangisme*, pp. 350–358.

77. *Le Figaro*, January 13, 1891.

78. *Ibid.*, October 3, 1891; *Le Courrier de l'Est*, October 3, 1891; Maurice Barrès, "Devant le cercueil," *ibid.*, October 3, 1891; and Charles Chincholle, "Les Obsèques du général Boulanger," *Le Figaro*, October 4, 1891. According to Chincholle, the list of Boulangists attending the funeral included Le Hérissé, Rochefort, Déroulède, Laur, Barrès, Gabriel, Boudeau, Ernest Roche, du Saussay, Pierre Richard, Le Senne, Laisant, Paulin-Méry, Dumonteil, Castelin, Elié May, Goussot, Revest, Madame Séverine, Léouzon Leduc, Vergoin, Pierre Denis, and lesser lights, including a delegation from Nancy.

79. Barrès, "Impressions de Rentrée," *ibid.*, October 16, 1891. The carnation was Boulanger's favorite flower and the badge of his followers.

80. Quoted in *ibid.*, October 4, 1891.

81. Francis Magnard, "Echos," *ibid.*, October 5, 1891.

82. Barrès, "Impressions de rentrée," This article reprints exerpts of letters to Barrès from Laur, Laguerre, and Laisant.

83. Barrès, "Impressions du cimetière d'Ixelles," *Le Courrier de l'Est*, October 10, 1891.

84. "Une Lettre de M. Laisant," *ibid.*, October 17, 1891.

85. "Reunion du Comité révisionniste-socialiste," *ibid.*, October 17, 1891; and Maurice Barrès, "Deux mots en courant," *ibid.*, November 7, 1891.

86. Barrès, "Renaissance de l'opposition," *ibid.*, November 14, 1891.

87. *JOC*, December 9, 1891, p. 2489.

88. Barrès, "Attitude nette," *Le Courrier de l'Est*, December 12, 1891.

89. Barrès, "Les Meneurs," *Le Figaro*, December 8, 1891.

90. *JOC*, December 16, 1891, pp. 2712–2713.

91. *JOC*, February 17, 1892 and October 21, 1892, pp. 104–106, 118–119, 1275–1283, 1290–1291.

92. *Ibid.*, May 22, 1892 and July 3, 1892, pp. 593–600, 608–609, 1011, and 1025–1026.

93. *Ibid.*, July 5, 1892, pp. 1031 and 1055-1056.

94. *Ibid.*, November 7, 1890, pp. 1915–1916, October 27, 1891, p. 1971, and January 20, 1893, p. 133.

95. *Ibid.*, October 30 and December 13, 1891, pp 2011–2013, 2017–2018, 2626–2627, and 2604–2624.

96. *APP*, Ba/1032, report of December 17, 1891.

97. "Déclaration des députés socialistes et révisionnistes," *Le Courrier de l'Est*, March 5, 1892. Other Boulangist adherents were Aimel, Argeliès, Dumonteil, Farcy, Gabriel, Goussot, Granger, Jourde, Laisant, Paulin-Méry, Revest, Saint-Martin, and the some-time Boulangists Borie, Laporte, and

Le Hérissé. A text of the declaration, along with a list of the signers, also appears in the Engels-Lafargue *Correspondence*, III, 160–161.

98. *Le Temps*, July 5, 1892; and *Le Figaro*, July 4, 1892.

99. Francis Magnard, "Echos," *ibid.*, July 5, 1892.

100. Engels-Lafargue, *Correspondence*, III, 160–161, 164–165 and 168–169.

101. *JOC*, November 20, 1892, pp. 1638–1640.

102. *Ibid.*, November 22, 1892, pp. 1645–1655.

103. *Ibid.*, December 24, 1892, pp. 1944–1953 and especially 1951–1953.

104. Goncourt, XIX, 52.

105. *APP*, Ba/1032.

106. *JOC*, June 23, 1893, pp. 1787–1795.

107. "L'Union socialiste," *Le Figaro*, January 15, 1893; "Le Meeting de Tivoli-Waux-Hall," *L'Intransigéant*, January 16, 1893; *La Revue socialiste*, XVII, 239–240; Alexandre Zévaès, *Histoire du socialisme et communisme en France, 1871–1947* (Paris, n.d.), pp. 226–227; and Aaron Noland, *The Founding of the French Socialist Party (1893–1905)* (Cambridge, 1956), pp. 30–31.

108. *JOC*, January 13, 1893, pp. 12–17 and especially p. 14.

109. *La Revue socialiste*, XVII (May, 1893), 351.

110. See *ibid.*, XV (May, 1892), 567–589 and XVII (February, 1893), 167.

111. *Ibid.*, XVIII (November, 1893), 602–603.

112. Victor Jaclard, "Tactique socialiste," *ibid.*, XVII (April, 1893), 385–401 and Hugues Thiercellet in *L'Ere nouvelle*, I (August, 1893), 202.

113. Paul Lafargue, "Les Dernières Élections législatives," *ibid.*, II (August, 1894), 367 ff.

114. *La Revue socialiste*, XVII (July, 1893), 84.

115. *Le Temps*, May 3, 1892.

116. Eugen Weber, "Nationalism, Socialism, and National-Socialism in France," *French Historical Studies*, II (1961–1962), 273–307 and especially 290–291.

CHAPTER FOUR

1. "Le Comité socialiste révisionniste," *Le Courrier de l'Est*, October 27, 1889.

2. *Ibid.*, April 13 and 20, 1890; and "Chronique de l'Est," *L'Impartial de l'Est*, April 29, 1890.

3. *Le Courrier de l'Est*, April 27, 1890.

4. Maurice Barrès, "Lettre ouverte à des amis de Saint-Nicolas et de Dombasle", "Seconde lettre ouverte à des amis de Saint-Nicolas et de Dombasle," *ibid.*, July 27 and August 3, 1890; and *AMM*, wM/762ter, reports of May 23, May 24, May 30, June 22, and July 4, 1890.

5. *AMM*, wM/655, reports of December 5, 1890 and February 3, 1891; *L'Impartial de l'Est*, January 20, February 3, April 21, and April 23, 1891; Maurice Barrès, "A des amis de Saint-Nicolas et de Dombasle," *Le Courrier de l'Est*, July 27, 1890; and "Réunions de M. Barrès," *ibid.*, October 18, 1890.

6. "Conférence publique sur le loi et l'avenir des syndicats," *ibid.*, April 25, 1891; and "Chronique de l'Est: la réunion de la salle Poirel," *L'Impartial*, April 21, 1891.

7. "Chronique de l'Est," *L'Impartial*, April 29, May 3, and May 4, 1890.

8. "Le 1er Mai à Nancy," *Ibid.*, May 2, 1891.

9. H. S., "Au *Progrès de l'Est*," *Le Courrier de l'Est*, August 31, 1890; Maurice

Barrès, "Les Vraies 'Coulisses,'" *ibid.*, October 5, 1890; "Démenti de M. Gabriel à *l'Est Républicain*," *ibid.*, October 18, 1890; "Démenti," *ibid.*, October 18, 1890; Maurice Barrès, "Les Pharisiens," *Le Figaro*, November 1, 1890.

10. Barrès, "Les Vraies 'Coulisses;'" "Comité républicain revisionniste de Nancy," *Le Courrier de l'Est*, September 28, 1890; "La Reunion du Gymnase" and "Réunions de M. Barrès," *ibid.*, October 18, 1890; "La Réunion du gymnase," *Le Progrès de l'Est*, October 14, 1890; "Chronique de l'Est: La Réunion de la salle du Gymnase," *l'Impartial de l'Est*, October 14, 1890; "Chronique de l'Est; la réunion de Saint-Nicolas," *ibid.*, October 16, 1890.

11. Barrès, "A nos amis de Dombasle," *Le Courrier de l'Est*, October 12, 1890.

12. Barrès, "Au raseur satisfait," *Le Courrier de l'Est*, September 21, 1890.

13. Alphonse Bertrand, *La Chambre de 1889, biographies des 576 deputés* (Paris, 1889), p. 310.

14. Alfred Gabriel, "Leur programme," *Le Courrier de l'Est*, July 23, 1892; and *Le Progrès de l'Est*, September 27 and October 3, 1890.

15. Gabriel, "Le Papelierisme," *ibid.*, January 31, 1891.

16. Barrès, "Le Mauvais Quart d'heure," *ibid.*, June 13, 1891.

17. *JOC*, February 3 and 8, 1891, pp. 184, 192–193, and 247–248.

18. X., "Contradictions opportunistes," *Le Courrier de l'Est*, February 7, 1891.

19. A. S., "Les Amies des syndicates," *ibid.*, April 11, 1891.

20. "Réunion de la salle Poirel," *ibid.*, April 18, 1891; and "Chronique de l'Est, M. Gabriel et Barrès à Nancy," *L'Impartial de l'Est*, April 14, 1891.

21. "Conférence publique sur la loi et l'avenir des syndicats," *Le Courrier de l'Est*, April 25, 1891.

22. *AMM*, wM/748, Monthly prefect report of March 31, 1896.

23. *AMM*, wM/655, Monthly prefect report of April 8, 1898.

24. *AMM*, wM/762ter and various issues of *l'Impartial de l'Est, Le Progrès de l'Est*, and *Le Courrier de l'Est*.

25. Barrès, "L'Etape socialiste," *Le Courrier de l'Est*, April 18, 1891.

26. Barrès, "La Dernière Semaine," *ibid.*, April 23, 1892.

27. Gabriel, "Le Prochain Premier Mai," *ibid.*, April 16, 1892.

28. Gabriel, "Répresentation proportionnelle," *ibid.*, April 23, 1892.

29. *Ibid.*, April 30, 1892; *l'Impartial de l'Est*, March 27, April 2, April 26, April 28, and April 30, 1892; and *AMM*, wM/924, prefect to Interior, April 28, 1892.

30. "Comité républicain socialiste de Nancy: Programme municipal," *Le Courrier de l'Est*, April 23, 1892.

31. *Le Temps*, April 6, 1892; and "Scandale à la cathédrale, "*L'Impartial de l'Est*, April 5, 1892.

32. Barrès, "A la cathédrale," and Alfred Gabriel, "Troubles de cathédrale," *Le Courrier de l'Est*, April 7, 1892.

33. *Le Temps*, May 3, 1892.

34. "Chronique de l'Est: Conférence de M. Papelier", *L'Impartial de l'Est*, May 1, 1892.

35. "Les Mensonges de M. Goulette," "Mauvais Foi," "Maurice Barrès à Saint-Nicolas," and "Analyse du discours prononcé à Saint-Nicholas," *Le Courrier de l'Est*, February 20, 1892; *Le Temps*, February 17 and 23, 1892; and "Chronique de l'Est: Réunion à Saint Nicolas," *L'Impartial de l'Est*, February 16, 1892. Maurice Barrès, "Le Tarif des douanes et mes votes," *Le Courrier de l'Est*, February 27, 1892.

36. *Le Temps*, June 7, 1892.

37. Various issues of *Le Courrier de l'Est* and *L'Impartial de l'Est* for June, July, and August, 1892; and *AMM*, wM/806, prefect to Interior.

38. "L'Election de Saint-Nicolas," *Le Courrier de l'Est*, August 6, 1892; and "Bulletin," *L'Impartial de l'Est*, August 2, 1892.

39. Barrès, "Premier article," *Le Courrier de l'Est*, April 10, 1898, and "Les Elections législatives," *Le Figaro*, August 10, 1893.

40. *Le Temps*, May 3, 1892.

41. Barrès, "Ouverture générale," *Le Journal*, July 28, 1893.

42. Jules Huret, "Les Littérateurs à la Chambre: M. Maurice Barrès," *Le Figaro*, July 31, 1893.

43. *JOC*, May 7, 1893, pp. 1360–1361 and 1363–1365.

44. Barrès, *Contre les étrangers*, reprinted in his *Scènes et doctrines du nationalisme* (Paris, 1925), II, 186–207.

45. *Le Figaro*, August 19, 1893, and Maurice Barrès, "Moeurs nouvelles," *Le Journal*, September 1, 1893.

46. Edmond de Goncourt, *Journal: mémoires de la vie littéraire [par] Edmond et Jules de Goncourt* (Monaco, 1956–1958), XIX, 201.

47. *Le Figaro*, September 5, 1893.

48. *La Gazette de Boùlogne*, various issues of July and August, 1893.

49. *ADS*, D²M², Carton 32.

50. *Le Figaro*, September 2, 1893. See the same newspaper for August 28, 1893; and Charles Chincholle, "Les Elections législatives," *ibid.*, September 3, 1893.

51. "Nos candidats," *Intransigéant*, August 20 and August 30, 1893; and "Chronique électorale," *ibid.*, August 29.

52. *La Petite République*, various issues of August, 1893.

53. *ADS*, D²M², Carton 32.

54. *JOC*, July 10, 1893, p. 2062.

55. *Ibid.*, October 24, 1890, pp. 1745–1748.

56. *Ibid.*, January 30, 1891, p. 155.

57. *Ibid.*, March 18, 1892, pp. 285–286.

58. *Ibid.*, March 7, 1893, pp. 859–860.

59. For example, the *Progrès de l'Est* took great delight that the Barrès speech on Naas, the deported Boulangist, had been received with "a glacial silence." See *Le Courrier de l'Est*, April 2, 1892. The *Courrier* probably would not have replied to the charge had not Barrès' ineffectiveness as a deputy been used by the opposition.

60. *JOC*, March 18, 1892, pp. 295–296.

61. Barrès, "L'Invalideur," *La Presse*, December 10, 1889.

62. Barrès, "Huit jours à la Chambre," *ibid.*, November 25, 1889.

63. Barrès, "Le Tour d'esprit de M. Floquet," *ibid.*, December 24, 1889.

64. Henri Beranger, "De Chateaubriand à Barrès," *La Revue bleue*, XXXIV, part 1 (January 30, 1897), 134.

65. Goncourt, XX (January 20, 1895), 208.

66. Huret, "Les Littérateurs à la Chambre."

67. Barrès, "Entre deux réunions," *Le Journal*, August 11, 1893. See also Maurice Barrès, "De l'Utilitée des injures," *Le Figaro*, August 12, 1890.

68. Biblioteque nationale, N.A.F. 24511, pp. 50–51.

CHAPTER FIVE

1. Joseph Paul-Boncour, *Recollections of the Third Republic*, trans., George Marion Jr. (New York, 1957), I, 62.

2. Aaron Noland, *The Founding of the French Socialist Party (1893–1905)* (Cambridge, 1956), p. 40; Alexandre Zévaès, *Histoire du socialisme et communisme en France, 1891–1947* (Paris, n.d.), p. 237. These Boulangists were Argeliès, Goussot, Jourde, Paulin-Méry, P. Richard, E. Roche, and Turigny. Missing were Castelin, Le Senne, and Laporte.

3. Victor Jaclard, "Tactique socialiste," *La Revue socialiste*, XVII (April, 1893), 385–401.

4. Maurice Barrès, "M. Jean Jaurès," *Le Journal*, January 20, 1893.

5. *Ibid.*

6. "La Nouvelle 'Cocarde'," *La Cocarde*, September 5, 1894.

7. Edmond de Goncourt, *Journal: Mémoires de la vie littéraire [par] Edmond et Jules de Goncourt* (Monaco, 1956–1958), XX, 145 (entry for November 1, 1894). Goncourt was convinced that this journalistic venture showed that literature for Barrès was "only a contrivance [*moyen*] and that he has above all a political ambition." *Ibid.*, XX, 119–120 (entry for September 2, 1894).

8. Henri Clouard, "La 'Cocarde' de Barrès," *La Revue critique des idées et des livres*, VIII (February 10 and 25 and March 10, 1910), 205–230, 332–358, and 397–419. This was published in book form under the same title and date.

9. Barrès, *Mes Cahiers*, III, 365.

10. Zeev Sternhell, *Maurice Barrés et le nationalisme français* (Paris, 1972).

11. Eugen Weber, *Action Française* (Stanford, 1962), p. 69.

12. Pierre de Boisdeffre, *Barrès parmi nous* (Paris, 1969), p. 82.

13. Robert Soucy, *Fascism in France: The Case of Maurice Barrès* (Berkeley, 1972), pp. 236-241.

14. Eugène Fournière, "Encore des cooperatives," *La Cocarde*, September 24, 1894.

15. Gabriel, "Pour et contre le collectivisme," *ibid.*, December 14, 1894.

16. Gabriel, "Preparation révolutionnaire," *ibid.*, November 7, 1894.

17. Pierre Denis, "La Loin d'airain," *ibid.*, January 27, 1895.

18. Fournière, "Socialiste tout simplement," *ibid.*, February 4, 1895.

19. *Le Figaro*, July 4, 1893. Although Barrès did circulate among the rioters, he limited his remarks, in the parliamentary debate of July 9 on the riot, to calling Prime Minister Dupuy the "parrot of the police." *JOC*, July 10, 1893, p. 2062.

20. Alexandre Zévaès, *Notes et souvenirs d'un militant* (Paris, 1913), pp. 26–31.

21. Paul-Boncour, *Recollections*, I, 62.

22. Léon Blum, *Souvenirs sur l'Affaire* (Paris, 1935), p. 86.

23. Barrès, "Sur l'éducation nationale," *La Presse*, December 31, 1889; "Du Recrutement d'un personnel révolutionnaire," *Le Figaro*, April 2, 1890; "L'Enrégimentement de la jeunesse," *ibid.*, May 26, 1890.

24. From a speech by Barrès quoted in Paul Lagarde, "A la Maison du Peuple," *La Cocarde*, December 11, 1894. Italics in the original.

25. Barrès, "La Question des 'intellectuels,' " *ibid.*, September 20, 1894.

26. Barrès, "L'Histoire intérieure d'un journal," *La Revue encyclopédique*, November 15, 1895, p. 417.

27. Barrès, "Individualisme et solidarité," *La Cocarde*, September 6, 1894.

28. Barrès, "Le Problème est double," *ibid.*, September 8, 1894, and "Opprimés et humilités," *ibid.*, September 14, 1894.

29. Barrès, "La Classe capitaliste," *Le Courrier de l'Est*, September 21, 1890, and "La Lutte entre capitalistes et travailleurs," *ibid.*, September 28, 1890. Except for his notions on Proudhon, Barrès appears to have gotten his Marxism and other socialist ideas at second hand from commentaries such as this one.

30. "La Fête du 22 septembre," *La Cocarde*, September 24, 1894, and "Conférence de Maurice Barrès," *ibid.*, October 3, 1894.

31. Barrès, "Conversation de Goblet et Jaurès," *De Hegel aux cantines du Nord* (Paris, 1904), pp. 29–42 (Originally in *La Cocarde*, September 13, 1894).

32. Barrès, "Il faut un idéal," *ibid.*, pp. 43–47 (Originally in *La Cocarde*, September 13, 1894).

33. Barrès, "La Foi en sociologie," *ibid.*, p. 94 (Originally in *La Cocarde*, October 26, 1894).

34. For Jaurès' views in this period, see: Harvey Goldberg, *The Life of Jean Jaurès* (Madison, 1962), pp. 110–115 and 134–136. Barrès seemed especially influenced by the Jaurès debate with Paul Lafarge on January 12, 1894.

35. Barrès, "Pas de dictature," *De Hegel*, pp. 75–76 (Originally in *La Cocarde*, December 30, 1894).

36. Barrès, "L'Arbre de vie d'une idée," *ibid.*, p. 25 (Originally in *Le Journal*, December 7, 1894).

37. Barrès, "L'Idéal et les premières étapes," *ibid.*, pp. 56–57 (Originally in *La Cocarde*, September 18, 1894).

38. Barrès, "La Fédération donne à tous une patrie," *ibid.*, pp. 29–33 (Originally in *Le Journal*, December 14, 1894).

39. Barrès, "Partisans de la décentralisation," *La Cocarde*, October 27, 1894; "Les Bénéfices de la décentralisation," *ibid.*, October 20, 1894; and "Assainissement et fédéralisme," *Le Journal*, June 30, 1895.

40. Barrès, "L'Histoire intérieure d'un journal," pp. 417–419.

41. Barrès, "Assainissement et fédéralisme."

42. Barrès, "Commune et région," *Le Journal*, October 2, 1895.

43. *Ibid.*; Barrès, "La Fédération donne à tous une patrie;" and "L'Histoire intérieure d'un journal."

44. Barrès, "L'Association libre c'est de la décentralisation," *De Hegel*, pp. 77–78 (Originally in *La Cocarde*, February 13, 1895). See also Barrès, "Les Bénéfices de la décentralisation."

45. Barrès, "Le Point de vue historique," *La Cocarde*, February 16, 1895.

46. Barrès, "Fédération non uniformiste dans le socialisme," *La Cocarde*, October 28, 1894.

47. Barrès, "Commune et région."

48. Barrès, "Un Canton laboratoire de réformes sociales," *De Hegel*, pp. 68–74.

49. Barrès, "Encore l'ingérence du pouvoir central," *ibid.*, pp. 63–67.

50. Barrès, "Les Bénéfices de la décentralisation."

51. For Proudhon's ideas, see: G. D. H. Cole, *Socialist Thought: The Forerunners, 1789–1850* (London, 1955) pp. 201–218.

52. Matthew H. Elbow, *French Corporative Theory, 1789–1948* (New York,

1953), pp. 53–121. Elbow, who lists most corporative thinkers, does not mention Barrès as a theorist or follower, although he does discuss Charles Maurras and the Action Française, to whom Barrès is often linked.

53. "Mais qu'aurait dit Le Play?," *La Cocarde*, January 11, 1895.

54. Barrès, "Les Masques de mercredi prochain," *ibid.*, January 9, 1895; "Leroy-Gigot-Picot," *ibid.*, January 10, 1895; "Les Opportunistes au Quartier," *ibid.*, January 11, 1895; and "Conférences socialistes au Quartier Latin," *ibid.*, January 11, 1895.

55. Barrès, "Sur Brisson," *ibid.*, December 26, 1894.

56. Barrès, "La Chambre cherche un alibi," *ibid.*, February 2, 1895.

57. Barrès, "Quel couteau tuera l'élu de ce soir?," *ibid.*, January 18, 1895.

58. *La Cocarde*, January 17, 1895. Quoted in Clouard, p. 222.

59. Barrès, "Une enquête extraparlementaire," *La Cocarde*, February 9, 1895; "La Journée d'hier au parlement," *ibid.*, February 14, 1895; "Des Dreyfus, pas de Canivet," *ibid.*, February 19, 1895.

60. Barrès, "Premier mot de l'année," *ibid.*, January 1, 1895.

61. Barrès, "L'Assainissement, voilà la tactique," *ibid.*, February 6, 1895, and "27 Janvier," *ibid.*, January 27, 1895.

62. Barrès, "L'Assainissement, voilà la tactique."

63. Barrès, "Premier mot de l'année."

64. Barrès, "Philosophes et politiciens," *ibid.*, September 9, 1894.

65. Barrès, "Déroulède à Paris," *ibid.*, November 24, 1894.

66. Barrès, "C'est peut-être une idée," *ibid.*, December 23, 1894.

67. Barrès, "A la gare du Nord!," *ibid.*, February 3, 1895, and "La Fin d'un régime," *ibid.*, February 5, 1895.

68. "Le Retour de Breton," *ibid.*, February 6, 1895; and "Le Retour d'Edouard Drumont," *ibid.*, February 7, 1895. Barrès and *La Cocarde* consistently asserted that they did not support Drumont's anti-Semitism, only his anti-parliamentarianism. See: Pierre Denis, "Pourquoi parler; de corde," and Paul Pascal, "Au Radical," *ibid.*, February 6 and 7, 1895.

69. Gabriel, "L'Opposition socialiste au XIIIme," *ibid.*, December 29, 1894, and "L'Exil et le prisonnier," *ibid.*, February 16, 1895; Maurice Barrès, "Violence! Violence!," *ibid.*, January 8, 1895.

70. "Le Fédéralisme de Maurice Barrès," *La Nouvelle Revue*, XCV (July 15, 1895), 383–384.

71. *La Revue socialiste*, XXII (July, 1895), 106–107.

72. *Ibid.*, XXII (September, 1895), 384.

73. Charles Maurras, *Maîtres et témoins de ma vie d'esprit* (Paris, 1954), pp. 27–28 and 108.

74. *La Revue socialiste*, XXII (November, 1895), 631.

75. Charles Maurras, "L'Idée de la décentralisation," *La Revue encyclopédique*, December 25, 1897, reprinted in Maurice Barrès, *Scènes et doctrines du nationalisme* (Paris, 1925), II, 212. See also the view of Barrès, *ibid.*, II, 220.

76. Léon de Seilac, "L'Organisation socialiste," *La Revue bleue*, XXXIII, part 1 (January 25, 1896), 108.

77. Jean Paul Sartre, *Dirty Hands* in *No Exit and Three Other Plays* (New York: Vintage Books, 1946), p. 166.

78. *Ibid.*, pp. 223–225.

79. Alasdair MacIntyre, "On Marcuse," *New York Review of Books*, October 23, 1969, p. 38.

NOTES

80. Barrès, *L'Ennemi des lois* (Paris, 1893), p. 8.
81. *Ibid.*, pp. 9–10.
82. *Ibid.*, p. vi.
83. *Ibid.*, pp. 12-14.
84. *Ibid.*, pp. 122–123.
85. *Ibid.*, p. 126.
86. *Ibid.*, p. 141.
87. Georges Diamondy, "L'Ennemi des lois," *L'Ere nouvelle*, November, 1893, pp. 440–441.
88. Barrès, "L'Histoire intérieure d'un journal."
89. Barrès, "Assainissement et fédéralisme" and "Commune et région."
90. Barrès, "Exploitation du sentiment nationaliste," *La Cocarde*, October 24, 1894.
91. Barrès, "Evolution nationaliste et contre la guerre," *La Cocarde*, October 25, 1894.
92. Barrès, "Assainissement et fédéralisme."
93. Barrès, "Contre l'extension du pouvoir parlementaire," *La Cocarde*, October 21, 1894, and "Avant la rentrée," *ibid.*, October 23, 1894.
94. Barrès, "La Glorification de l'énergie," *La Cocarde*, December 19, 1894.
95. Barrès, "L'Utilité des héros," *ibid.*, December 20, 1894.
96. Barrès, "Napoléon, professeur d'énergie," *Le Journal*, April 14, 1893.
97. Barrès, "Un philosophe du 'moi'," *La Cocarde*, January 20, 1895.
98. Barrès, "Napoleon, professeur d'énergie," "L'Utilité des héros," and "Et pourtant l'auteur n'est pas 'clerical'," *La Cocarde*, December 29, 1894.
99. Barrès, "Tous les exaltants sont bons," *Ibid.*, January 13, 1895.
100. Georges Renard, "Politique et littéraire: Maurice Barrès d'après son dernier livre," *La Petite République*, January 20, 1895.
101. Eugène Fournière, "La Problème," *ibid.*, January 15, 1895.
102. *APP*, Ba/651, reports of January 3, January 13, and February 12, 1896.
103. *Ibid.*, Various police reports and press clippings from otherwise unavailable Neuilly-Boulogne newspapers.
104. *Ibid.*
105. *Ibid.*
106. *ADS*, D²M², Carton 32. Procès verbaux des elections législatives.
107. Barrès, *Mes Cahiers*, I, 62.
108. "Elections législatives du 8 mars," *Le Temps*, March 10, 1896.
109. "Banquet offert au citoyen Louis Sautumier, par les comités de Boulogne," *Le Reveil de Neuilly-Boulogne*, March 28–April 4, 1896.
110. Barrès, *Mes Cahiers*, I, 61.
111. *Ibid.*, I, 99.
112. Noland, pp. 49–50; "Tous collectivistes," *Le Temps*, June 1, 1896.
113. *La Cocarde*, October 13, 1894.
114. *APP*, Ba/1194, various reports.
115. *Ibid.*, report of July 20, 1896; and *La Petite République*, July 21, 1896.
116. Barrès, *Scènes*, II, 52–53.
117. *Ibid.*, II, 168-174 (Originally in *Le Journal*, January 22, 1897).
118. Barrès, *Mes Cahiers*, I, 108–109. This passage runs to p. 117, one of the longest passages on one subject in *Mes Cahiers*.
119. *Ibid.*, I, 110. According to the police, Sautumier's suicide resulted from depression following his getting a young actress pregnant and refusing

her demands for marriage. *AN*, F⁷12888, item 12, November 19, 1896. The evidence seems to indicate, however, that Sautumier's route to socialism both paralleled and was as flimsy as Barrès' socialism of the *moi*. The difference was that Sautumier's brought success, and that got the better of him. That would also explain Barrès' obvious empathy toward him.

120. *Ibid.*, I, 112.

121. *Ibid.*, I, 114–115.

122. *Ibid.*, I, 113–115; "Chronique electorale," *Le Temps*, December 11, 1896; *AN*, F⁷ 12885, item 33, police report of November 30, 1896; *APP*, Ba/650, various police reports and press clippings.

123. Clipping from *l'Estrafette*, December 10, 1896, in *APP*, Ba/650.

124. "L'Election de dimanche," *Le Reveil de Neuilly*, December 12-18, 1896.

125. Barrès, *Mes Cahiers*, I, 122.

126. *Ibid.*, I, 124.

127. *Ibid.*, I, 231.

128. Jean Jaurès, *Oeuvres* (9 vol., Paris, 1931–1939), II, 104.

CHAPTER SIX

1. Jean Touchard, "Le Nationalisme de Barrès," in *Maurice Barrès: Actes du colloque organisé par la Faculté des lettres et des sciences humaines de l'Université de Nancy (Nancy, 22–25 octobre 1962)* (Nancy, 1962), pp. 161–173.

2. Barrès' letters to Charles Maurras, April 9 and July 15, 1894, in Maurice Barrès and Charles Maurras, *La République ou le roi* (Paris, 1970), pp. 76–77 and 80.

3. Barrès, *Mes Cahiers* (Paris, 1929-1957), II, 90 and 93–94.

4. Barrès, *Scènes et doctrines du nationalisme* (Paris, 1945), II, 52.

5. Barrès, *Les Déracinés (Paris, 1961)*, I, 25.

6. *Ibid.*, I, 21.

7. *Ibid.*, I, 41.

8. *Ibid.*, I, 126–127.

9. *Ibid.*, I, 258.

10. *Ibid.*, I, 252.

11. *Ibid.*, II, 215 and 245.

12. *Ibid.*, I, 255–258.

13. *Ibid.*, I, 262.

14. Léon Blum in *La Revue blanche* of November 15, 1897, as quoted in Barrès, *Scènes*, I, 93.

15. Jean Jaurès, *Oeuvres* (Paris, 1931), II, 103–104.

16. A.M., "Les Déracinés," *La Revue socialiste*, XXVII (June, 1898), p. 762. In an otherwise excellent analysis of *Les Déracinés*, Robert Soucy commits the same error in his *Fascism in France: The Case of Maurice Barrès* (Berkeley, 1972), pp. 258–259. The novel's characters, Mouchefrin and Racadot, do not "come to bad ends" because they betrayed their "lower-class backgrounds." Rather, Racadot's fortune from a livestock speculator father made him probably the richest of the seven Lorrainers in the novel, and five of them were certainly from well-to-do agricultural or business families. Mouchefrin, son of a photographer, had been poor enough to be a scholarship student at the Nancy lycée, but the other petit bourgeois scholarship student enjoyed a "harmonious evo-

lution" to success in journalism by being always on the outlook for the main chance. Mouchefrin's social criticism derived not from his nonexistent "lower-class background," but from his bohemianism, a bohemian criticism of society shared by the well-born Racadot. The other scholarship student and an additional bourgeois son also came to "bad ends," even though they found successful careers. As Barrès portrayed the seven young Lorrainers, success or failure did not come from their social origins, but from their uprootedness.

17. Barrès, "Les Trahisseurs," *La Cocarde*, November 4, 1894; "Dreyfus sera décoré," *ibid.*, December 1, 1894; "Ecoutons l'accusé," *ibid.*, December 8, 1894; "Le Motif de sa trahison," *ibid.*, December 24, 1894; and "La Parade de Judas," *ibid.*, January 6, 1895.

18. An analysis of the Dreyfus Affair is beyond the scope of this essay. For more recent interpretations, consult: Guy Chapman, *The Dreyfus Case* (London, 1955); Marcel Thomas, *L'Affaire sans Dreyfus* (Paris, 1961); Nicholas Halasz, *Captain Dreyfus: The Story of Mass Hysteria* (New York, 1955); and Douglas Johnson, *France and the Dreyfus Affair* (London, 1967).

19. Barrès, *Scènes*, I, 25–31 (Originally: "La Foi dans l'Armée," *Le Journal*, November 20, 1897).

20. Barrès, "L'Education nouvelle," *Le Journal*, December 4, 1897.

21. Barrès, *Mes Cahiers*, I, 223–224 and 230.

22. Léon Blum, *Souvenirs sur l'Affaire* (Paris, 1935), pp. 87–88.

23. Barrès, *Scènes*, I, 47–51 (Originally: "La Protestation des intellectuels," *Le Journal*, February 1, 1898). Victor Brombert, in his "Toward a Portrait of the French Intellectual" (*Partisan Review*, XXVII, Part III [Summer, 1960], 480–502), argues that the use of "intellectual" in its derogatory sense began with Barrès. However, Barrès himself had been described as an intellectual in that very sense. See: G. Bernard–Kahler, "La Littérature dans la politique," *L'Ermitage* (1891), pp. 513–519.

24. Blum, *Souvenirs*, pp. 88–89.

25. Barrès, *Scènes*, I, 32.

26. Lucien Herr, "A. M. Maurice Barrès," *La Revue blanche*, XV (February 15, 1898), 244.

27. Barrès, *Mes Cahiers*, II, 7.

28. *AN*, F⁷12449, prefect report of February 4, 1893, and telegram of February 25, 1897; *AMM*, wM/762ter, various reports of 1894 and 1895; *ibid.*, wM/7, police reports of March 17, 20, 23, and 24, 1898; various issues in March, 1898, of "Chronique électorale," *Le Progrès de l'Est*; Maurice Barrès, "Premier article," *Le Courrier de l'Est*, April 10, 1898; "Nos réunions" and "Opinions et votes imposés par le Congrès au candidat opportuniste de la 3e circonscription," *ibid.*, April 17, 1898.

29. "Un Ordre du jour du comité," *ibid.*, April 10, 1898.

30. "Nos reunions," *ibid.*, April 24, 1898.

31. *AMM*, wM/748, monthly prefect report of March 31, 1896.

32. *AMM*, wM/655, prefect reports of April 8, 1898, and December, 1898.

33. *AMM*, wM/787, various reports of March, April, and May, 1898.

34. George Mosse has observed a similar phenomenon in the appeal of the Jaune movement. See his "The French Right and the Working Classes: Les Jaunes," *Journal of Contemporary History* (July–October, 1972).

35. Unless otherwise noted, the following analysis of the program comes from the reprint of it in *Scènes*, II, 160–168. An English translation of the pro-

gram is in David Thomson (ed.), *France: Empire and Republic, 1850–1940* (New York, 1968), pp. 268-273.

36. *Ibid.*, Maurice Barrès, "La Féodalité financière," *Le Courrier de l'Est*, April 10, 1898; "Les Grands magasins et le petit commerce," *ibid.*, April 10, 1898; Maurice Barrès, "Discours du Congrès," *ibid.*, April 24, 1898; "La Réferendum municipal," *ibid.*, April 24, 1898; Maurice Barrès, "Réponse à M. Gavet sur les Syndicats et les Impòts," *ibid.*, May 1, 1898; "Sur les bouilleurs de cru," *ibid.*, May 1, 1898; Alfred Gabriel, "Le Progrès s'accentue," *ibid.*, May 5, 1898; and Maurice Barrès, "Que faut-il faire?," *ibid.*, May 12, 1898.

37. *AMM*, wM/787, undated police report no. 2541.

38. "Chronique électorale," *Le Temps*, April 10 and 19, 1898; and "Chronique électorale," *Le Progrès de l'Est*, April 18, 1898.

39. "Chronique électorale," *ibid.*, April 24, 1898; and *AMM*, wM/787, police report of April 24, 1898.

40. Various articles in *Le Courrier de l'Est* and *Le Progrès de l'Est* and reports in *AMM*, wM/787.

41. "Chronique électorale," *Le Progrès de l'Est*, May 6, 1898.

42. "Discours de Maurice Barrès à la réunion publique du 23 avril, á Nancy," *Le Courrier de l'Est*, April 28, 1898; "Ce que disent les prolétaires," *ibid.*, April 10, 1898.

43. "Nos réunions," *ibid.*, April 17, 1898.

44. "Chronique électorale," *Le Progrès de l'Est*, May 7 and April 27, 1898.

45. Various articles in *Le Progrès de l'Est* and *Le Courrier de l'Est*.

46. *AMM*, wM/787, various police reports.

47. "Nos réunions" and "Pour les électeurs de Dombasle," *Le Courrier de l'Est*, April 17, 1898.

48. *AMM*, wM/787, police report of April 24, 1898.

49. "Chronique électorale," *Le Temps*, May 8, 1898; Maurice Barrès, "Guetapens de Champenoux," *Le Courrier de l'Est*, May 5, 1898; "La bagarre de Champenoux," *ibid.*, May 8, 1898; Barrès, *Mes Cahiers*, II, 9–10; and "Chronique électorale," *Le Progrès de l'Est*, May 4 and May 5, 1898.

50. Barrès, *Mes Cahiers*, II, 19–20.

51. Gaston Save, "Le Triomphe de 'La Croix'," *Le Courrier de l'Est*, May 12, 1898; B., "Les Ballotages," *Le Progrès de l'Est*, May 11, 1898; J. Cordier, "Le Retour offensif," *ibid.*, May 19, 1898.

52. Letter of Houdaille to Philippe Barrès (December 10, 1929), *Mes Cahiers*, II, 309; "M. Barrès et les clericaux;" *Le Progrès de l'Est*, May 20, 1898; *AMM*, wM/787, reports of March 20 and April 3, 1898.

53. *AMM*, wM/787.

54. *Ibid.*, police reports of April 21 and 25, 1898.

55. Jean Cordier, "Ce qu'il faut faire," *Le Progrès de l'Est*, May 17, 1898.

56. Barrès, "Avis aux républicains, aux democrates et aux patriotes," Alfred Gabriel, "Dernières réflexions," and Gaston Save, "Le Désistement de M. Nicolas," *Le Courrier de l'Est*, May 19, 1898.

57. Barrès, "Que faut-il faire?," *ibid.*, May 12, 1898, and "Reproches absurdes," *ibid.*, May 19, 1898.

58. Barrès, "Citoyens," *ibid.*, May 17, 1898, and Barrès, "Que faut-il faire?"

59. Save, "Le Triomphe de 'La Croix'."

60. "Antisémitisme et antisémitisme," *ibid.*, May 19, 1898.

61. *Le Courrier de l'Est*, May 19, 1898.

62. Barrès, "Sauvons la République," *ibid.*, May 17, 1898.

63. "Gervaize désavoué" and "Paul Déroulède dans la 3e circonscription," *ibid.*, May 17, 1898.

64. *AMM*, wM/787, "Procès verbal du resensement général des votes émis dans les collèges électoraux de la 3e circonscription de Nancy. 2e tour."

65. Barrès, *Mes Cahiers*, II, 22; and "Un Temoignage à rectifier," *Le Journal*, December 22, 1899.

66. *Indépendant*, May 22, 1898.

CHAPTER SEVEN

1. Maurice Barrès, *Scènes et doctrines du nationalisme* (Paris, 1945), I, 32–42 (Originally: "L'Etat de la question," *Le Journal*, October 4, 1898; and "La raison nationale," *Le Journal*, December 9, 1898).

2. Joseph Reinach, *Histoire de l'affaire Dreyfus* (Paris, 1901), IV, 442.

3. Barrès, "La Seizième audience," "La Vingtième audience," and "La Vingt-troisième audience," *Le Journal*, August 26, September 1 and 5, 1899.

4. Barrès, "Le Cas de Georges Grosjean," *ibid.*, March 17, 1899, and exchange of letters between Barrès and Reinach, *ibid.*, March 19, 1899.

5. Barrès, *Mes Cahiers* (Paris, 1929–1957), II, 117–121, 141–142. See also Jules Soury, *Une Campagne nationaliste* (Paris, 1902), passim.

6. "Interview de Maurice Barrès," *La Liberté*, December 2, 1903, reprinted in Barrès, *Mes Cahiers*, III, 155-159, and "Maurice Barrès et l'affaire Dreyfus," *L'Avant-garde*, December 6, 1903.

7. Barrès, *Mes Cahiers*, IV, 185.

8. *APP*, Ba/1032, *AN*, F⁷12449, and Jérôme and Jean Tharaud, *La Vie et la mort de Déroulède* (Paris, 1925), pp. 100–103; Barrès, *Mes Cahiers*, I, 260.

9. "La Manifestation populaire," *Le Gaulois*, October 26, 1898; Reinach, IV, 300–302, 309–310, 330-334.

10. Barrès, *Scènes*, I, 231–242 (Originally: "L'Anarchie de l'estrade," *Le Journal*, December 23, 1898); Henri Galli, "La Politique," *Le Drapeau*, June 17, 1901; "Les Manifestations d'hier," *Le Gaulois*, December 11, 1898; and *AN*, F⁷12449, undated report c. end of 1898.

11. Barrès, "Les Trois Étapes," *Le Journal*, February 10, 1899.

12. Barrès, *Scènes*, I, 69-71 (Originally: "La Patrie Française," *Le Journal*, January 2, 1899); Reinach, IV, 500–505; *AN*, F⁷13229, undated Prefecture de Police report c. February, 1899.

13. See, especially, the position of Coppee in Arthur Meyer, *Ce que je peux dire* (Paris, 1912), pp. 246–247.

14. "La Ligue de la Patrie Française," *Le Gaulois*, January 4, 1899.

15. Barrès, *Scènes*, I, 72 (Originally: "La Première Manifestation de la 'Patrie Française,' " *Le Journal*, January 20, 1899).

16. *Ibid.*, I, 75 (Originally: "Ce que nous entendons par conciliation," *Le Journal*, February 3, 1899).

17. "La Conférence de M. Jules Lemaître," *Le Gaulois*, January 20, 1899.

18. *Ibid.*, and "La Ligue de la Patrie Français," *Le Temps*, January 21, 1899.

19. Barrès, *Mes Cahiers*, II, 91–92.

20. Barrès, "A demain la Politique," *Le Journal*, February 17, 1899.

21. Barrès, "Ce qu'on attend," *ibid.*, February 18, 1899, and "Commentaire sur une déclaration de la 'Patrie Française,' " *ibid.*, February 20, 1899.

22. "Les Cérémonies d'hier," *Le Gaulois*, January 23, 1899.

23. *APP*, Ba/1032, reports of October 16 and November 19, 1898; and *AN*, F⁷12876, dossiers of March 1 and 4, 1901. Tharaud, pp. 114–117; Barrès, *Scènes*, I, 242–262; "Les Manifestations d'hier," *Le Temps*, February 25, 1899. In *Mes Cahiers*, II, 96, Barrès presented at the time and without comment this list of real or imagined plotters: "[General] Chanoine (60,000). (Formellement) [General] Pellieux. (Détourné par Cavaignac) [General] Roget. [General] Jamont, [Paul] Deschanel, [ex-war minister Godefroy] Cavaignac, Déroulède."

24. Barrès, *Scènes*, I, 259.

25. Barrès, *Mes Cahiers*, II, 147–148.

26. Jacques Chastenet, *La République triomphante, 1893–1906* (Paris, 1955), p. 162.

27. Barrès, *Scènes*, I, 249.

28. *Le Temps*, February 25, 1899.

29. Barrès, *Scènes*, I, 106–107. This is a combination of two articles in *Le Journal*: "Les deux ligues" of July 29, 1899, and "L'Oeuvre des ligues" of December 8, 1899.

30. Barrès, *Mes Cahiers*, II, 92.

31. Maurice Barrès, *L'Appel au soldat* (Paris, 1920), I, 205 and II, 49.

32. Jean Touchard, "Le Nationalisme de Barres," in *Maurice Barres: Actes du colloque organsé par la Faculté des lettres et des sciences humaines de l'Université de Nancy (Nancy, 22–25 octobre 1962)* (Nancy, 1962) suggests this regarding *Appel au soldat*, but it is also true for *Leurs figures*.

33. Barrès, *Appel*, I, 118, 59, 207, 141, and 155.

34. *Ibid.*, I, 105.

35. Barrès, *Leurs figures* (Paris, 1932), p. 2.

36. *Ibid.*, p. 120.

37. Barrès, *Appel*, I, 26–27.

38. *Ibid.*, I, 246–247.

39. *Ibid.*, II, 146.

40. *Ibid.*, II, 162.

41. Barrès, *Scènes*, I, 99.

42. *Ibid.*, I, 83.

43. *Ibid.*, I, 83 and 85.

44. *Ibid.*, I, 36.

45. *Ibid.*, I, 40 and 59.

46. *Ibid.*, I, 11, 17, 12, 11, 90, and 13.

47. *Ibid.*, I, 8.

48. *Ibid.*, 8, 86.

49. *Ibid.*, I, 71–99. This is an altered form of an article, "Ce que nous entendons par conciliation", *Le Journal*, February 3, 1899, and a speech Barrès had intended to deliver to the Patrie Française on March 10, 1899.

50. *Ibid.*, I, 20–21 and 85.

51. *Ibid.*, I, 94 and 87.

52. Barrès, *Mes Cahiers*, II, 160.

53. Barrès, *Scènes*, I, 67–68.

54. Barrès, *Leurs figures*, p. 208.

55. Barrès, *Scènes*, II, 3–29; and Tallemont, "Conférence de Maurice Barrès à la 'Patrie Française'," *Le Journal*, December 12, 1899; *APP*, Ba/1336. For a brief summary of Barrès' views, see: "L'Actualité, Alsace-Lorraine," *Le Drapeau*, July 12, 1901.

56. "Une Conférence de M. Jules Lemaître," *Le Temps*, November 15, 1899;

"Le Banquet de la Patrie Française," *ibid.*, January 16, 1900; Henry Jarzuel, "L'Anniversaire de la Patrie Française," *Le Gaulois*, January 15, 1900; Jules Lemaître, "Les Elections municipales," *Annales de la Patrie française*, May 1, 1900, pp. 1–3.

57. APP, Ba/1336, report of "Vétiver," October 12, 1900; AN, F⁷ 12719, report of June 8, 1900.

58. AN, F⁷13230, reports of July 28, 1900; APP, Ba/1336, report of "Vétiver," February 14, 1900.

59. APP, Ba/1336, report of "Vétiver," April 25, 1900; and AN, F⁷13230, reports of May 21, 1900, and June 8, 1902.

60. AN, F⁷ 13230, report of July 28, 1900; APP, Ba/1336, reports of "Vétiver," May 30, 1900, and "Malaga", August 15, 1900, and January 16, 1901.

61. APP, Ba/1336, "Règlement intérieur des comités" forwarded by "Chatenet" on September 8, 1900.

62. AN, F⁷ 12721, reports of the Sûreté générale of May 14, 1900; and "L'Organisation de la Patrie française," *Annales de la Patrie française*, September 1, 1901, pp. 277-278.

63. Barrès, *Mes Cahiers*, II, 164–165; "En Province: La 'Patrie Française' en Lorraine," *Le Gaulois*, January 30, 1900; Maurice Barrès, "Une Nouvelle Étape de la 'Patrie Française,'" *Le Journal*, February 1, 1900; "En Lorraine," *L'Echo de Paris*, April 4, 1900; AMM, wM/757, police reports of January 29 and April 1, 1900; "Courrier des comités," *Annales de la Patrie française*, December 15, 1900, pp. 503–504.

64. APP, Ba/1336, report of "Chatenet," May 19, 1900, and "Vétiver," May 12, 1900; AN, F⁷ 13230, report of "Moscou," July 11, 1900; "Le mouvement nationaliste," *Annales de la Patrie française*, I (1900), p. 83.

65. Barrès, *Mes Cahiers*, II, 207–208.

66. *Ibid.*, II, 200 and 250.

67. AN, F⁷13230, reports of July 28, 1900; APP, Ba/1336, report of "Vétiver," February 14, 1900; APP, Ba/1336, reports of February 25, March 7, March 9, and March 11, 1899.

68. Barrès letter to Charles Maurras of March 9, 1899, in Maurice Barrès and Charles Maurras, *La République ou le roi* (Paris, 1970), pp. 223–224.

69. AN, F⁷13230, report of "Moscou," March 21, 1899.

70. *Ibid.* and APP, Ba/1336, report of "Moscou," February 25, 1899.

71. APP, Ba/1336, reports of "Vétiver," March 13 and May 21, 1899, and various Barrès-Maurras letters in 1899 in *La République ou le roi*.

72. Eugen Weber, *Action Française: Royalism and Reaction in Twentieth Century France* (Stanford, 1962), pp. 18–23; "L'Action française," *Le Gaulois*, June 21, 1899; *Le Temps*, June 23, 1899; AN, F⁷12862, reports of "Alger," June 21, 1899, and "Moscou," June 22, 1899; APP, Ba/1341, reports of Controle générale and 2nd Brigade, June 21, 1899.

73. Barrès, *Scènes*, I, 101–103 (Originally: "L'Education nationaliste," *Le Journal*, October 30, 1899).

74. *Ibid.*, I, 103–105. A reprint from *La Revue de l'Action française*, November 15, 1899.

75. AN, F⁷12720, report of "Naples," April 6, 1900; APP, Ba/1341, various reports of February and March, 1900; "Le Mouvement nationalist," *Annales de la Patrie française*, May 15, 1900, p. 57.

76. Barrès, *Scènes*, I, 109 and 126. For a brief account of the association of

Barrès with the Action Française, see W. M. Frohock, "Maurice Barrès' Collaboration with the Action Française," *Romanic Review*, XXIX (1938), 167–169.

77. Weber, pp. 26–30 and Maurras-Barrès letters of 1899 in *La République ou le roi*, especially the letters of November 18–19 and December 25, 1899, pp. 249–257.

78. Barrès, *Mes Cahiers*, II, 159–160 and 162.

79. *Ibid.*, II, 177–178; and "Discours de Maurice Barrès pour l'anniversaire de l'Action française," *Scènes*, I, 131.

80. Barrès, *Mes Cahiers*, II, 291–293.

81. *Ibid.*, II, 251.

82. *AN*, F⁷ 12870, No. 3, report of "Naples," February 7, 1901; "Le Mouvement nationaliste," *Annales de la Patrie française*, February 15, March 1 and 15, 1901, pp. 626–627 and 659.

83. *APP*, Ba/1314, reports of June 11 and 13, 1901.

84. *Le République ou le roi*, letters of 1901–1902, *passim*.

85. Barrès, *Mes Cahiers*, III, 136.

86. "L'Affaire Déroulède et Marcel Habert," *Le Gaulois*, May 31 and June 1, 1899; Maurice Barrès, "Ah! les braves gens," *Le Journal*, June 2, 1899.

87. Barrès, "Une Oeuvre de haine," *Le Journal*, September 18, 1899.

88. Barrès, "La Haute Sagesse d'un Paul Déroulède," *ibid.*, March 8, 1900; Barrès, *Mes Cahiers*, II, 147–148 and 200–201.

89. *AN*, F⁷ 12719, *passim*.

90. *APP*, Ba/1336, reports of "Malaga," February 15, 18, and 20, 1901.

91. Barrès, *Mes Cahiers*, II, 202.

92. Tharaud, pp. 144–145; and Barrès, *Mes Cahiers*, II, 338.

93. *APP*, Ba/1336, report of "Malaga," March 20, 1901, and Ba/1033, report of "Malaga," February 21, 1906.

94. Barrès, " 'Le Drapeau,' " *Le Drapeau*, May 16, 1901.

95. "Réunion des patriotes," *ibid.*, May 24, 1901; and Barrès, *Scènes*, I, 286–288.

96. Andre Blondet, "Contre le déracinement," *Le Drapeau*, May 16, 1901.

97. See especially the speech of Barrès at the rally of the League of Patriots on July 14, 1901, reprinted in Barrès, *Scènes*, I, 286–288.

98. "La Réunion des patriotes," *Le Drapeau*, May 24, 1901.

99. *AN*, F⁷ 12870, report of "Rennes," April 2, 1903.

100. *Ibid.*, report of "Bruxelles," July 30, 1900; *APP*, Ba/1336, reports of "Malaga," April 4 and 17, 1901; *AN*, F⁷ 13230, report of "Seine," April 18, 1901.

101. Tharaud, pp. 144–145.

102. "Menus propos: A la statue de Strasbourg," *Le Temps*, July 14, 1901.

103. *AN*, F⁷ 12870, No. 4, report of "Seine," December 9, 1902.

104. *Ibid.*, report of "Seine," April 10, 1905.

105. Barrès, *Scènes*, I, 126. Comment in his second *"Appel au soldat"* dinner (February 7, 1901).

106. Various articles, *Le Drapeau*, June 13 and 14, 1901.

107. "La Réunion de la rue d'Athènes," *ibid.*, July 12, 1901.

108. Barrès, "Les Patriots haissent l'equivoque," *ibid.*, July 24, 1901.

109. Georges Thiébaud, "Le 'Plebiscite filtré,' " *ibid.*, July 24, 1901.

110. André Maurel, "Retraite de Maurice Barrès," *Le Figaro*, September 13, 1901.

111. Paul Déroulède, "Lettre de Paul Déroulède à Maurice Barrès," *Le Drapeau*, September 15, 1901.

112. Marcel Habert, "Tribune des Proscrits," *ibid.*, September 18, 1901.

113. See, for example, "La Retraîte de Maurice Barrès," *Annales de la Patrie Française*, October 1, 1901, pp. 327–328.

114. Barrès, *Mes Cahiers*, II, 227 and 228. See also 221–228.

115. Barrès, *Scènes*, I, 100–101. This was written in January, 1902.

116. Barrès, "Ne changeons point notre drapeau," *La Patrie*, June 13, 1902.

117. Barrès, "Il faut 'décoller,' " *ibid.*, June 27, 1902. See also: Maurice Barrès, "Il y a une littérature nationaliste," *Le Gaulois*, July 16, 1902.

118. *AN*, F⁷ 12719, report of M1180, June 2, 1902.

119. "Le Mouvement nationaliste," *Annales de la Patrie franaise*, September 1, 1901, pp. 276–278; and Jules Briard, "La Verité sur le nationalisme," *Ibid.*, May 1, 1902, pp. 7–11.

120. *AN*, F⁷ 13230, report of "Paris," May 26, 1902; *AN*, F⁷ 12721, report of M1166, May 31, 1902; *APP*, Ba/1336, report of "Vétiver," May 28, 1902; Jules Lemaître, "Il n'ya rien de change," *Annales de la Patrie Française*, June 16, 1902, pp. 133-135; Barrès, *Mes Cahiers*, III, 12–14.

121. *APP*, Ba/1336, reports of "Vétiver," July 30 and August 3, 1902; *AN*, F⁷ 13230, report of "Rennes," August 1, 1902; "Le Mouvement nationaliste: Au Manège Saint-Paul," *Annales de la Patrie française*, July 15, 1902, pp. 250–251.

122. Barrès, *Mes Cahiers*, III, 50–51.

123. *Annales de la Patrie française*, December 1, 1902, pp. 617–622; and G.P., "Les Assises du nationalisme," *Le Gaulois*, November 13, 1902.

124. Emile Massard, "Bloc contre bloc," *La Patrie*, November 14, 1902; and *AN*, F⁷ 12719, report of "Seine", November 26, 1902.

125. Barrès, "L'Histoire me se recommence pas," *La Patrie*, November 21, 1902, and *Mes Cahiers*, III, 37–38.

126. "Le Parti sans nom," *Le Temps*, November 16, 1902; Charles Demailly, "A travers la presse," *Le Gaulois*, November 14, 1902; various reports in *APP*, Ba/1336 and *AN*, F⁷ 12719.

127. "Les Élections législatives," *Le Temps*, April 29 and May 13, 1902.

128. *AN*, F⁷ 12870, reports of "Rennes," January 26 and March 21, 1903; and F⁷ 13210, report of "Rennes," January 19, 1903.

129. "Maurice Barrès, candidat à Paris," *L'Avant-garde*, January 4 and 25, 1903; "Une Lettre de Maurice Barrès," *ibid.*, February 1, 1903; "La Candidature de Maurice Barrès, *ibid.*, February 1 and 8, 1903. *L'Avant-garde* was a nationalist weekly in Nancy, subsidized by Barrès, which reprinted articles he had written for various newspapers.

130. Barres, "La Tradition," *ibid.*, February 22, 1903.

131. "Maurice Barrès, candidat à Paris."

132. Barrès, "Socialisme et nationalisme," *ibid.*, March 8, 1903.

133. *AN*, F⁷ 12719, F⁷ 12720, F⁷ 12870, No. 5, F⁷ 13229, various reports and *comptes rendus* of various meetings in *Le Drapeau*, 1901. See also: D. R. Watson, "The Nationalist Movement in Paris, 1900–1906," in David Shapiro (ed.), *St. Anthony's Papers, Number 13: The Right In France, 1890–1919* (Carbondale, Ill., 1962), pp. 61–76.

134. Barrès, "Plus dreyfusard que Dreyfus," *L'Avant-garde*, February 15, 1903; "La Candidature de Maurice Barrès," *ibid.*, February 15, 1903; Maurice Barrès, "Nous sommes des usufruitiers," *ibid.*, March 15, 1903; Maurice Barrès,

"D'abord, il faut durer, *ibid.*, March 1, 1903; and Barrès, "Socialisme et nationalisme."

135. *ADS*, D²M², Procès verbaux des élections législatives, Carton 38.

136. "Chronique électorale," *Le Temps*, April 1, 3, and 4, 1903.

137. *ADS*, D²M², Carton 38.

138. "L'Election du IVe arrondissement," *Le Temps*, April 7, 1903.

139. *AN*, F⁷ 12870, reports of March 24 and May 2, 1903; and "L'Election du quatrième," *Annales de la Patrie Française*, April 15, 1903, p. 826.

140. Barrès, "La Révision des listes électorales," *L'Avant-garde*, January 25, 1903; Maurice Barrès, "Les Fraudes électorales," *ibid.*, February 8, 1903; "Chronique électorale," *Le Temps*, March 11, 1903; Paul Acker, *Petites confessions* (Paris, 1903), pp. 209–210.

CHAPTER EIGHT

1. Paul Acker, *Petites confessions* (Paris, 1903), pp. 208–209.

2. *AN*, F⁷ 12870, report of May 2, 1903, and F⁷ 12877, Galli to Déroulède telegram of April 24, 1903, and Déroulède to Galli telegram of April 30, 1903.

3. Various issues of *Les Annales de la Patrie Française*, June 15 to July 15, 1903; and Jules Lemaître, "Le Devoir social," *ibid.*, March 1, 1904, pp. 1309 ff.

4. See, for example: *AN*, F⁷12719, reports of May 21, December 5, and December 16, 1903; F⁷ 12870, report of "Seine," October 18, 1904; and F⁷13230, reports of "Metz," April 6 and April 27, 1904.

5. *APP*, Ba/1276, Syveton dossier, *passim*; and Ba/1336, report of "Vetiver," October 9, 1902; and *AN*, F⁷13230, various reports of January, 1905; and various issues of *Annales de la Patrie Française*.

6. Maurice Barrès, *Mes Cahiers* (Paris, 1929–1957), IV, 34-35; "L'Assemblée générale de la 'Patrie Française,' " *Annales de la Patrie Française*, May 1, 1905, pp. 589 ff. and especially p. 593; and *AN*, F⁷12870, *passim*.

7. *AN*, F⁷13229, clipping from the *Bulletin officiel de la Patrie Française*; F⁷12870, cote numbers 7 and 8, *passim*.

8. *AN*, F⁷12873, reports of "F," May 24, 1907, and "Seine," June 17, 1907.

9. *AN*, F⁷12873, reports of January 1, February 8, March 21, 1908; May 9, May 21, June 21, and July 1, 1909; November 25, 1911; July 15 and November 27, 1912; January 25, and November 26, 1913; and February 22, May 15, and July 11, 1914; F⁷13230, various reports of 1907, and 1908; *APP*, Ba/1033, reports of "Leseur," January 1, 1906, June 2, 1908, January 22, January 25, and July 1, 1909.

10. D. R. Watson, "The Nationalist Movement in Paris, 1900–1906" in David Shapiro (ed.), *St. Anthony Papers. Number 13: The Right in France 1890–1919* (Carbondale, Ill.: 1962), pp. 49–84.

11. Raoul Girardet, *Le Nationalisme française, 1871–1914* (Paris, 1966), p. 18.

12. *Ibid.*, p. 216.

13. *AN*, F⁷12544, reports of February 23, 25, and 26, March 3 and 5, 1906; F⁷12870, cote 8, report of March 23, 1906; F⁷12872, cote 1, reports of March 5, 6, and 10, 1906; "Chronique électorale," *Le Temps*, March 9, 1906; and "Interview-express: M. Maurice Barrès," *Le Gaulois*, March 9, 1906.

14. *ADS*, D²M², Carton 38, Procès verbaux des élections legislatives, May 10, 1906. The vote gave Barrès 6,520, the *progressiste* Alexis Muzet 2,465, the Radical-Socialist Paul Vibert 2,103, and the socialist G. Mesnard 765.

NOTES

15. Barrès, *Mes Cahiers*, IV, 149–156 and 304–309; and "Les Elections de 1906," *Le Gaulois*, April 24, 1906.
16. Barrès, *Mes Cahiers*, IV, 306.
17. "Faits du jour: La Candidature de Maurice Barrès," *Le Gaulois*, March 27, 1906; and "Les Réunions électorales," *ibid.*, March 27, April 25, 26, and 27, and May 4 and 5, 1906.
18. Paul Acker, "La Candidature de Maurice Barrès," *ibid.*, March 24, 1906.
19. *JOC*, March 9, 1909, pp. 700–701; and Malcolm Anderson, "The Right and the Social Question in Parliament, 1905–1919" in Shapiro, pp. 110–114. The issues examined here are those considered key ones by Anderson and by David E. Sumler, "Domestic Influences on the Nationalist Revival in France, 1909–1914," *French Historical Studies*, VI (Fall, 1970), pp. 517–537.
20. *JOC*, December 7, 1906, p. 3016; and Anderson, pp. 106–108.
21. *JOC*, March 31, 1910, pp. 1859–1860; and Barrès, *Mes Cahiers*, VIII, 115–118.
22. Harvey Goldberg, *The Life of Jean Jaurès* (Madison, Wisc: 1962), pp. 354–357.
23. Barrès, *Mes Cahiers*, X, 35.
24. *JOC*, June 21, 1906, pp. 2042–2043.
25. *Ibid.*, July 11, 1906, p. 2281; and Anderson, p. 105.
26. *JOC*, May 14, 1907, pp. 1018–1019; and Goldberg, pp. 364–368.
27. Barrès, *Mes Cahiers*, V, 110 and 114–115.
28. *Ibid.*, p. 119.
29. *Ibid.*, V, 121. My italics.
30. *JOC*, March 19, 1909, pp. 787–788.
31. *Ibid.*, October 30, 1910, p. 2670; and Goldberg, pp. 410–413.
32. *JOC*, December 13, 1912, p. 3198; and Sumler, pp. 530–532.
33. Pierre de Boisdeffre, *Barrès parmi nous* (Paris, 1969), p. 147.
34. Barrès, *Mes Cahiers*, VIII, 111–115 and 266–268.
35. *JOC*, January 17 and 18, 1911, pp. 85–92 and 96–97.
36. *Ibid.*, November 28, 1912, p. 2771.
37. *Ibid.*, March 14, 1913, p. 1028.
38. *Ibid.*, November 9, 1910, pp. 2719 and 2723.
39. Barrès, *Mes Cahiers*, IX, 118.
40. *Ibid.*, X, 297.
41. *Ibid.*, V, 248–249.
42. *Ibid.*, V, 285.
43. *Ibid.*, V, 281. See also: *Ibid.*, VIII, 17–18.
44. *Ibid.*, VII, 239.
45. *Ibid.*, VIII, 67.
46. *Ibid.*, 297–298. A reprint of an interview with *Eclair*, December 17, 1910.
47. *Ibid.*, VIII, 181–182.
48. *Ibid.*, X, 68.
49. Eugen Weber, *The Nationalist Revival in France, 1905–1914* (Berkeley and Los Angeles, 1959).
50. For a brief discussion and excerpts of many of these, see Girardet, pp. 223–250.
51. *Ibid.*, p. 238.
52. See, for example *ibid.*, pp. 19–20; and E. Malcolm Carroll, *French Public Opinion and Foreign Affairs, 1870–1914* (New York, 1931), p. 281.

53. Etienne Rey, *La Renaissance de l'orgueil française* (Paris, 1912) and quoted in Carroll, p. 252.
54. Barrès, *Mes Cahiers*, V, 227.
55. Robert Soucy, "Barrès and Fascism," *French Historical Studies*, V (Spring, 1967), pp. 78–79, quoting Barrès, *Mes Cahiers*, III, 65.
56. Barrès' letter to Maurras of February 22, 1922 in Barrès and Maurras, *La République ou le roi* (Paris, 1970), p. 592.
57. Barrès, *Mes Cahiers*, VI, 264.
58. *Ibid.*, III, 145.
59. *Ibid.*, V, 280.
60. Quoted in Weber, *Nationalist Revival*, pp. 126–127. Weber argues that the nationalist revival was created largely in response to the Agadir crisis of 1911 and, unlike the earlier nationalism of the anti-Dreyfusards, appealed mainly to the respectable parties of the Center and Right.
61. *Ibid.*, p. 127.
62. *JOC*, January 12, 1912, p. 21.
63. Barrès, *Mes Cahiers*, X, 205.
64. Quoted in Sumler, p. 523. My italics.
65. Pierre Miquel, *Poincaré* (Paris, 1961), p. 293.
66. Barrès, *Mes Cahiers*, X, 148.
67. Letter of March, 1914, of Massis to Barrès, printed in Henri Massis, *Barrès et nous* (Paris, 1962), p. 140.
68. For the attitudes of French youth in the 1890–1914 period, see Phyllis H. Stock, "Students versus the University in Pre-World War Paris," *French Historical Studies*, VII (Spring, 1971), 93–110.
69. *Ibid.*, p. 104.
70. Girardet, pp. 227–228.
71. Miquel, pp. 285–286. See also pp. 278–287.
72. Etienne Rey, *La Renaissance*, quoted in Girardet, p. 229.
73. Sumler, "Domestic Influences on the Nationalist Revival;" see also Anderson, "The Right and the Social Question," pp. 123–127.
74. Barrès, *Mes Cahiers*, X, 115.
75. *Ibid.*, IX, 361.
76. *Ibid.*, X, 285.

CHAPTER NINE

1. Victor Giraud, "Equisses contemporaines. - M. Maurice Barrès," *Revue des Deux Mondes* (February 15, 1922), p. 905.
2. A single volume of representative selections, edited and introduced by Guy Dupré with a commentary by Philippe Barrès, was published under the same title by Librairie Plon in 1968.
3. Giraud, p. 882.
4. Maurice Barrès, *The Undying Spirit of France* (New Haven, 1917); and Maurice Barrès, "Young Soldiers of France," *Atlantic Monthly*, CXX (July, 1917), 1–13.
5. Barrès, *Les Diverses familles spirituelles de la France* (Paris, 1917), p. 192.
6. *Ibid.*, pp. 194–198.
7. *Ibid.*, p. 195, 56–60, and 64.
8. *Ibid.*, p. 77.

9. *Ibid.*, pp. 199–201.

10. For the *Bonnet Rouge*-Malvy-Caillaux affair, see: Eugen Weber, *The Action Française* (Stanford, 1962), pp. 103–112; Philippe Erlanger, *Clemenceau* (Paris, 1968), pp. 475–481; and Rudolph Binion, *Defeated Leaders: The Political Fate of Caillaux, Juvenal, and Tardieu* (New York, 1960), pp. 71–89.

11. Barrès, *La Chronique de la Grande Guerre*, edited and introduced by Guy Dupré (Paris, 1968), pp. 429–430.

12. *Ibid.*, pp. 525–26.

13. F. Grover, "The Inheritors of Maurice Barrès," *Modern Language Review,* LXIV (July, 1969), 531.

14. Jean Touchard, "Le Nationalisme de Barrès" in *Actes du colloque "Maurice Barrès," organisé par la Faculté des Lettres de Nancy, 22–25 octobre 1962* (Nancy, 1962), p. 166.

15. Maurice Nadeau, *The History of Surrealism* (New York, 1965), pp. 64–66; André Breton, *Entretiens (1913–1952)* (Paris, 1969), p. 67; and Roger Garaudy, *L'Itinéraire d' Aragon* (Paris, 1961), p. 32.

16. Barrès, *Mes Cahiers* (Paris, 1949), XII, 177–181, 187–194, and 321–338.

17. On Foch's actions, see: Jere King, *Foch versus Clemenceau* (Cambridge, Mass., 1960), *passim.*

18. Barrès, *Scènes et doctrines du nationalisme* (Paris, 1945), I, 15.

19. Paul Acker, *Petites confessions* (Paris, 1903), p. 212.

20. Eugen Weber, "The Secret World of Jean Barois" in John Weiss (ed.), *The Origins of Modern Consciousness* (Detroit, 1965), p. 86.

21. George L. Mosse, "The Genesis of Fascism," *Journal of Contemporary History*, I, No. 1 (1966), 15.

22. Ernst Nolte, *Three Faces of Fascism* (New York, 1966).

23. Nolte, pp. 52–53 and *passim*; René Remond, *The Right Wing in France* (Philadelphia, 1966), pp. 214, 277, 299 and 370; Jean Plumyène and Raymond Lasierra, *Les Fascismes françaises, 1923–1963* (Paris, 1963), *passim*; Pierre de Boisdeffre, *Barrès parmi nous* (Paris, 1969), pp. 128–129; Jacques Madaule, *Le Nationalisme de Maurice Barrès* (Marseilles, 1943), pp. 264–266; J. S. McClelland, *The French Right* (London, 1970), pp. 13–16 and 24–26; and Robert Soucy, *Fascism in France: The Case of Maurice Barrès* (Berkeley, 1972), *passim*.

24. Boisdeffre and Grover, *passim*. Even a Communist, poet Louis Aragon, could find inspiration in Barrès for the France of 1948, faced with the Marshall Plan and the Cold War: "I regret having to say that, limited though it be, the nationalism of Barrès is closer to what I feel and doubtless to what the advance guard of the working class of our country feels today than the internationalism of, say, M. Guéhenno: for, like Barrès, the men of our people are not disposed to sacrifice what is national to a Europe made, for example, by MM. Blum and Churchill and financed by M. Marshall." Quoted by Grover, p. 542.

25. Arno J. Mayer, *Dynamics of Counterrevolution in Europe, 1870–1956* (New York, 1971), p. 115 and *passim*.

26. Bibliotèque nationale, N.A.F.24874, No. 150–154: Letters of Barrès to Joseph Reinach, June 21, September 16 and 17, 1919.

27. *AN*, F⁷12873, police reports of November 25, 1918, February 20, 1919 and February 14 and 24, 1923.

28. Barrès, *The Sacred Hill*, trans., Malcolm Cowley (New York, 1929), pp. 268–269.

BIBLIOGRAPHY

This study consulted almost all the political articles by and about Barrès compiled in Alphonse Zarach, *Bibliographie barrésienne, 1881-1948* (Paris: Presses universitaires de France, 1951). Instead of enumerating them here, I refer the reader to the end notes, where the most useful ones are listed, and to Zarach's exhaustive work. Only in *La Semaine de Paris* did I ever find articles by Barrès, omitted in Zarach. These are: "Jean Jaurès" on April 25, 1895 and "Mouvement des idées" on June 23, 1895.

This study also consulted all the Barrès correspondence held in the manuscript collections of the Bibliotèque Nationale and the Bibliotèque de l'Arsenal. Aside from the letter to Zola, cited in this study, they shed little light on Barrès' politics. Barrès' useful early correspondence appears in Maurice Barrès, *Le Départ pour la vie* (Paris: Plon, 1961). His correspondence with Charles Maurras appears in Barrès and Maurras, *La République ou le roi* (Paris: Plon, 1970). Occasional letters appear in Barrès' journal, *Mes Cahiers*, listed below.

This bibliography will limit itself to books by Barrès, works by Barrès in English, newspapers and periodicals consulted, police reports and parliamentary papers, works on Barrès, and the principal works in French history and politics useful to the study of Barrès.

WORKS BY BARRÈS

Huit jours chez Monsieur Renan. Paris: Perrin, 1890.
Le Culte du moi. (Sous l'oeil des barbares, Un Homme libre, Le Jardin de Bérénice, and *Examen des trois idéologies)*. Paris: Le Livre de poche, 1966.
Trois stations de psychothérapie. Paris: Perrin, 1891.
Toute licence sauf contre l'amour. Paris: Perrin, 1892.
L'Ennemi des lois. Paris: Perrin, 1893.
Une journée parlementaire. Paris: Fayard, 1894.
Du sang, de la volupté et de la mort. Un amateur d'ames. Voyage en Espagne. Voyage en Italie, etc. Paris: Charpentier et Fasquelle, 1910.
Le Roman de l'énergie nationale. I. Les Déracinés. Paris: Plon, 1961.

Le Roman de l'énergie nationale. II. L'Appel au soldat. Paris: Nelson, 1920.
Scènes et doctrines du nationalisme. Paris: Juven, 1902.
Le Roman de l'énergie nationale. III. Leurs figures. Paris: Plon, 1932.
Amori et dolori sacrum. La Mort de Venise. Paris: F. Juven, 1911.
Les Amitiés Françaises. Paris: F. Juven, 1903.
De Hegel aux cantines du Nord. Paris: Sansot, 1904.
Les Bastions de l'Est: Au service de l'Allemagne. Paris: A. Fayard, 1905.
Ce que j'ai vu au temps du Panama. Paris: Sansot, 1906.
Le Voyage de Sparte. Paris: Juven, 1906.
Les Bastions de l'Est: Colette Baudoche. Paris: Juven, 1909.
Greco ou le secret de tolède. Paris: Émile-Paul, 1912.
La Colline inspirée. Paris: Émile-Paul, 1913.
La Grande Pitié des églises de France. Paris: Émile-Paul, 1914.
Dans le cloaque. Paris: Émile-Paul, 1914.
Chronique de la grande guerre. 14 vols. Paris: Plon Nourrit, 1920-1924.
Les Diverses Familles spirituelles de la France. Paris: Émile-Paul, 1917.
Les Bastions de l'Est. Le Génie du Rhin. Paris: Plon-Nourrit, 1921.
Un Jardin sur l'Oronte. Paris: Plon, 1947.
Pour la haute intelligence française. Paris: Plon-Nourrit, 1925.
Notes sur Italie. Paris: Horizons de France, 1929.
Mes Cahiers. Paris: Plon, 1929-1938; 1949.
Les Grands Problèmes du Rhin. Paris: Plon, 1930.

BARRÈS IN ENGLISH

Colette Baudoche. Tr. by Frances Wilson Huard. New York: George H.
    Doran Co., 1918.
"Integral Nationalism: The Nancy Program of Maurice Barrès, 1898,"
    in David Thomson, *France: Empire and Republic, 1850-1940.* New
    York: Walker, 1968, pp. 268-273.
"Maurice Barrès" in J. S. McClelland, *The French Right.* London: Cape,
    1970, pp. 145-211. Contents: "De Hegel aux cantines du Nord"
    (*Le Journal*, November 30 and December 7 and 14, 1894); selec-
    tions from *Scènes et doctrines du nationalisme;* and *The Undying Spirit
    of France.*
"The Panama Scandal," *Cosmopolitan*, XVII (June, 1894), 203-210.
The Sacred Hill. Tr. by Malcolm Cowley. New York: Macaulay Co.,
    1929.
The Soul of France: Visits to Invaded Districts. London: T. F. Unwin, 1915.
The Undying Spirit of France. New Haven: Yale University Press, 1917.
"Young Soldiers of France," *Atlantic Monthly*, CXX (July, 1917), 1-13.

POLICE REPORTS AND PARLIAMENTARY PAPERS

Archives nationales: $F^7$13229-13230 (Ligue de la Patrie française), $F^7$12885 (Partie socialiste); $F^7$12449-12453, $F^7$12717, $F^7$12870-12872, $F^7$12874, $F^7$12877 (Ligue des Patriotes); $F^7$12455-12458 (Surveillance des nationalistes); $F^7$12719-12721 (Nationalistes, Action liberale, and Patrie Française); $F^7$12862 (Action Française); $F^7$12878 (Action Liberale); $F^7$13229-13230 (Ligue de la Patrie Française); $F^7$12445-12448 (Agissements boulangistes); $F^7$12459-12464 (Antisemites); $F^7$12465-12473 (Affaire Dreyfus); $F^7$12882-12883 (Antisemites); $F^7$12544 (Elections legislatives de 1906: Seine); and $F^7$12861 (Royalistes).

Archives de la Seine: D^2M^2, cartons 32 and 38. Procès verbaux des elections legislatives (1893, 1896, 1903, and 1906).

Archives de Meurthe-et-Moselle: wM/785 (Elections législatives de 1889), wM/787 (Elections législatives de 1898), wM/924 (Elections municipales: renouvellement de 1892), wM/806 (Renouvellement du Conseil Général dans différents cantons dont celui de Saint-Nicolas de Port), wM/748 (Rapports mensuels des préfets [1894, mars 1896, octobre-décembre 1906]), wM/1492 (Comptes rendus au préfet sur les réunions politiques, février 1894), wM/1494 (Contrôle politique de la presse locale, 1889-1905), wM/757bis (Parti boulangiste, 1888-1895), wM/757^{quater} (Agitation nationaliste, 1873-1917), wM/762 (Réunions réactionnaires et nationalistes, 1877-1936), wM/762ter (Comité révisionniste, Réunions boulangistes, 1888-1895), wM/762^{quater}(Réunions antisémites), wM/655 (Syndicalisme: rapports de police, 1880-1938).

Archives de la Prefecture de Police (Paris): Ba/1250-1252 (Henri Rochefort); Ba/1032-1034 and Ea/43 (Paul Déroulède); Ba/650 (Elections legislatives des 13-27 decembre 1896 dans la 4e circumscription de Saint Denis); Ba/651 (Elections legislatives des 23 fevrier-8 mars 1896 dans la 4e circumscription de Saint Denis); Ea/49 (Marcel Habert); Ba/1276 and Ea/56 (Gabriel Syveton); Ba/1266 (Louis Sautumier); Ba/1150 (Jules Lemaître); Ba/1337-1340 (Ligue des Patriotes); Ba/1334-1336 (Ligue de la Patrie française); Ba/1341 (Action française); Ba/1194 (Marquis de Morès). A marginal notation on one of these reports indicated that the police once maintained a no longer existing dossier on Barrès.

Journal officiel de la Republique française. Chambre. Débats, 1889-1893 and 1906-1923.

BIBLIOGRAPHY

NEWSPAPERS

L'Avant-Garde. 1903 (Nancy).
La Cocarde. 1894-1895 (Paris).
La Courrier de l'Est. 1889-1892 and 1898 (Nancy).
Le Drapeau. 1901 (Paris).
L'Elair. 1899 (Paris).
Le Figaro. 1888-1898 (Paris).
Le Gaulois. 1898-1906 (Paris).
La Gazette de Boulogne. 1893.
L'Impartial de l'Est. 1888-1892 and 1898 (Nancy).
L'Indépendent. 1898 (Nancy).
L'Intransigéant. 1893-1898 (Paris).
Le Journal. 1893-1895 and 1897-1900 (Paris).
La Libre Parole. 1893-1898 (Paris).
La Patrie. 1902 (Paris).
La Petite République. 1893-1905 (Paris).
La Progrès de l'Est. 1888-1892 and 1898 (Nancy).
Le Reveil de Neuilly Boulogne. 1896.
Le Temps. 1888-1923 (Paris).
Le Voltaire. 1886-1887 (Paris).

PERIODICALS

L'Action Française. 1899-1906.
Les Annales de la Patrie française. 1899-1906.
L'Ere nouvelle. 1893-1894.
Mercure de France. 1890-1906.
La Nouvelle Revue. 1888-1906.
Psst. . . ! 1898-1899. Anti-semitic cartoon weekly by Jean Louis Forain and Caron d'Ache.
La Revue blanche. 1891-1903.
La Revue bleue. 1888-1906.
La Revue de Paris. 1896-1906.
La Revue des Deux Mondes. 1888-1906.
La Revue hebdomadaire. 1892-1906.
La Revue politique et parlementaire. 1894-1906.
La Revue socialiste. 1888-1906.
Le Semaine de Paris. 1894-1895.
Les Taches d'Encre. 1884-1885.

STUDIES OF MAURICE BARRES

Beranger, Henri. "De Chateaubriand à Barrès," *La Revue bleue*, XXXIV, Part 1 (January 30, 1897), 130-135.

Bernard-Kahler, G. "La Littérature dans la politique," *L'Ermitage*, September, 1891, 513-519.

Bibliotheque Nationale. *Exposition Barrès*. Paris: Bibliotheque Nationale, 1962.

Boisdeffre, Pierre de. *Barrès parmi nous*. Paris: Amiot-Dumont, 1969.

Boisdeffre, Pierre de. "Justice pour Barrès," *Etudes*, CCLX (March, 1949), 331-350.

Bourne, Randolph. "Maurice Barrès and the Youth of Today," *Atlantic Monthly*, CXIV (1914), 394-399.

Carassus, Emilien, "Maurice Barrès feuilletoniste," *La Revue d'histoire littéraire*, LXX, No. 1 (January-February, 1970), 90-97.

Castex, Pierre Georges. "Barrès collaborateur du *Voltaire*," *Les Annales de l'Est*, memoire no. 24, 1963.

Clouard, Henri. "La 'Cocarde' de Barrès," *La Revue critique des Idées et des Livres*, VIII (February 10 and 25 and March 10, 1910), 205-230, 332-358, and 397-419.

Diamandy, Georges. "L'Ennemi des lois," *L'Ere nouvelle*, I (November 1, 1893), 421-441.

Dietz, Jean. *Maurice Barrès*. Paris: La Renaissance du Livre, 1927.

———. "Les Débuts de Maurice Barrès," *La Revue de Paris*, XXXV (October, 1928), 616-628.

———. "Les Débuts de Maurice Barrès dans la vie politique (1888-1891)," *La Revue hebdomadaire*, August, 1931, 267-284.

Domenach, Jean Marie. *Barrès par lui-même*. Paris: Editions du Seuill, 1954.

"Le Fédéralisme de Maurice Barrès," *La Nouvelle Revue*, XCV (July 15, 1895), 383-384.

Frohock, W. M. "Maurice Barrès' Collaboration with the Action Française," *Romanic Review*, XXIX (1938), 167-169.

Geodorp, Victor. "Un Episode inconnu de la carrière politique de Barrès," *Le Monde*, May 28, 1949, 4.

Giraud, Victor. "Equisses contemporaines.—M. Maurice Barrès," *Revue des Deux Mondes*, January 1 and 15 and February 15, 1922.

Grover, F. "The Inheritors of Maurice Barrès," *Modern Language Review*. LXIV (July, 1961).

Herr, Lucien. "A M. Maurice Barrès," *La Revue blanche*, XV (February 15, 1898), 241-245.

Houppert, Jean. "La Politique dans l'oeuvre de Maurice Barrès," *La Revue politique et parlementaire*, LXIV (1962), No. 725 (July-August), 50-61 and No. 726 (September), 48-57.

King, Sylvia. *Maurice Barrès: La Pensée allemande et la problème du Rhin.* Paris: H. Champion, 1933.

La Jeunesse, Ernest. "De Maurice Barrès et des électeurs," *La Revue blanche*, X (March 15, 1896), 260-262.

Lalou, René. *Maurice Barrès.* Paris: Hachette, 1950.

Lynch, Hannah. "A Political Writer of France," *Contemporary Review*, XXVIII (1900), 381-388.

M., A. "Les Déracinés," *La Revue socialiste*, XXVII (June, 1898), 762.

Madaule, Jacques. *Le Nationalisme de Maurice Barrès.* Marseille: Editions du Sagittaire, 1943.

Massis, Henri. *Barrès et nous.* Paris: Plon, 1962.

———. "Barrès, c'est une vie," *Revue de Deux Mondes*, June 1, 1962, 334-347.

Maurice Barrès: Actes du colloque organisé par la Faculté des lettres et des sciences humaines de l'Université de Nancy (Nancy, 22-25 octobre 1962). Nancy: Annales de l'Est, memoire no. 24, 1963.

Miéville, Henri L. *La Pensée de Maurice Barrès.* Paris: Nouvelle Revue Critique, 1934.

Montesquieu, Léon de. "Maurice Barrès et la doctrine nationaliste," *La Revue de l'Action Française*, July 1, 1902, 3-31.

Moreau, Pierre. "La Jeunesse de Maurice Barrès," *La Revue des cours et conférences*, XXXVII (January 15, 1936), 199-210.

Parodi, D. "La Doctrine politique et sociale de M. Maurice Barrès," *La Revue du mois*, III (January 1907), 18-36.

Rey, Jean. "Une campagne électorale en 1889: Maurice Barrès, candidat révisioniste," *Candide*, April 30, 1936, 5.

Ross, Flora E. *Goethe in Modern France.* Urbana: University of Illinois Press, 1937.

Soucy, Robert. *Fascism in France: The Case of Maurice Barrès.* Berkeley: University of California Press, 1972.

Sternhell, Zeev. *Maurice Barrès et le nationalisme française.* Paris: Armand Colin, 1972.

Sybil. "Croquis parlementaires: M. Maurice Barrès," *La Revue bleue*, 1889, 641-644.

Tharaud, Jérôme and Jean. *Mes Années chez Barrès.* PARIS: Librairie Plon, 1928.

Thibaudet, Albert. *La Vie de Maurice Barrès.* Paris: Nouvelle Revue Française, 1921.

GENERAL WORKS

Acker, Paul. *Petites confessions (visites et portraits)*. Paris: Albert Fontemoing, 1903.

Adam, Paul. *Le Mystère des foules*. Paris: P. Ollendorff, 1895.

Aimel, Henri. "La Révolution de demain," *La Revue socialiste*, XVII (February, 1893), 167.

Augé-Laribé, Michel. *La Politique agricole de la France de 1880-1940*. Paris: Presses Universitaires de France, 1944.

Bertillon, Jacques. *Résultats statistiques du dénombrement de 1891 pour la ville de Paris*. Paris: G. Masson, 1894.

Bertrand, Alphonse. *La Chambre de 1889: Biographies des 576 députés avec avertissement et documents divers*. Paris: L. Michaud, 1889.

————. *La Chambre de 1893*. Paris: Lib.-Imp. Réunies, 1893)

Binion, Rudolph. *Defeated Leaders*. New York: Columbia University Press, 1960.

Blum, Léon. *L'Oeuvre de Léon Blum*. Vol. 1. Paris: A. Michel, 1954.

————. *Souvenirs sur l'affaire*. Paris: Gallimard, 1935.

Bodley, John Edward Courtenay. *France*. 2 Vols. London: Macmillan, 1898.

Breton, André. *Entretiens (1913-1952)*. Paris: Gallimard, 1969.

Brogan, Denis W. *France Under the Republic*. New York: Harper and Brothers, 1940.

————. *French Personalities and Problems*. New York: Knopf, 1947.

Brombert, Victor. "Toward a Portrait of the French Intellectual," *Partisan Review*, XXVII, No. 3 (Summer, 1960), 480-502.

Byrnes, Robert F. *Antisemitism in Modern France*. New Brunswick: Rutgers University Press, 1950.

Cagniard, Gaston. "Les 'Intellectuels' de la Patrie Française," *La Revue socialiste*, XX (June, 1899), 725-727.

Carroll, Eber Malcolm. *French Public Opinion and Foreign Affairs, 1870-1914*. New York, London: The Century Co., c. 1931.

Cavalluci, Giacomo. *Les Derniers Grands Salons littéraires français*. Naples: R. Pironti, 1952.

Chapman, Guy. *The Dreyfus Case*. London: Rupert Hart-Davis, 1955.

Chastenet, Jacques. *Histoire de la troisième république*. Vol. II: *La République des républicains, 1879-1893*. Vol. III: *La République triomphante, 1893-1906*. Paris: Librairie Hachette, 1954-1955.

Cole, G. D. H. *History of Socialist Thought*. Vol. I: *The Forerunners*. London: Macmillan, 1953.

Cornell, Kenneth. *The Symbolist Movement*. New Haven: Yale University Press, 1951.

Corpechot, Lucien. *Souvenirs d'un journaliste*. 3 vols. Paris: Plon, 1936.

Curtis, Michael. *Three Against the Third Republic: Sorel, Barrès, and Maurras*. Princeton: Princeton University Press, 1959.

Dalbert, Georges. "Fédéralisme et provincialisme," *La Revue blanche*, IX (July 15, 1895), 91-93.

Dansette, Adrien. *Les Affaires de Panama*. Paris: Perrin, 1934.

———. *Le Boulangisme*. Paris: A. Fayard, 1946.

Darmesteter, Mary. "The Social Novel in France," *Contemporary Review*, LXXV (1899), 800-813.

Delhorbe, Cécile. *L'Affaire Dreyfus et les écrivains français*. Paris: Editions Victor Attinger, 1932.

Denis, Pierre. *Le Mémorial de Sainte-Brélade*. Paris: Paul Ollendorff, 1894.

Digeon, Claude. *La Crise allemande de la pensée française, 1870-1914*. Paris: Presses Universitaires de France, 1959.

Dolléans, Edouard. *Histoire du mouvement ouvrier*. Vol. II: 1871-1920. Paris: A. Colin, 1939.

Doukas, Kimon A. `French Railroads and the State*. New York: Columbia University Press, 1945.

Dumont-Wilden, L. *Le Crépuscule des maîtres*. Brussels: La Renaissance du Livres, 1947.

Eisenmenger, E. *La Lorraine au travail*. Paris: Librairie Pierre Roger, 1925.

Elbow, Matthew H. *French Corporative Theory, 1789-1948*. New York: Columbia University Press, 1953.

Engels, Frederick and Lafargue, Paul and Laura. *Correspondence*. Translated by Yvonne Kapp. 3 Vols. Moscow: Foreign Languages Publishing House, 1960.

Erlanger, Philippe. *Clemenceau*. Paris: Grasset, 1968.

Fournière, Eugène. *L'Artifice nationaliste*. Paris: Bibliotèque Charpentier, 1903.

Garaudy, Roger. *L'Itinéraire d'Aragon*. Paris: Gallimard, 1961.

Gide, André. *The Journals of André Gide*. Translated by Justin O'Brien. Vol. I. New York: Knopf, 1947.

———. *Pretexts*. Translated by P. Bertocci and others. New York: Meridian, 1959.

Girardet, Raoul. *Le Nationalisme français, 1871-1914*. Paris: A. Colin, 1966.

———. "Pour une introduction à l'histoire du nationalisme française," *La Revue française de science politique*, VIII (1958), 505-528.

Goguel, François. *Géographie des élections françaises de 1870 à 1951*. Paris: A. Colin, 1951.

――――. *La Politique des partis sous la IIIe république*. Paris: Seuil, 1946.

Goldberg, Harvey. *The Life of Jean Jaurès*. Madison: University of Wisconsin Press, 1962.

Golob, Eugene O. *The Méline Tariff: French Agriculture and Nationalist Economic Policy*. New York: Columbia University Press, 1944.

Goncourt, Edmond de. *Journal: mémoires de la vie littéraire [par] Edmond et Jules de Goncourt*. Vols. XVIII-XXII. Monaco: Imprimerie nationale, 1956-1958.

Gooch, George P. *Regionalism in France*. New York: Century Co., 1931.

――――. *Studies in Modern History*. London: Longmans, Green, 1931.

Halasz, Nicholas. *Captain Dreyfus: The Story of a Mass Hysteria*. New York: Grove Press, 1955.

Hayes, Carlton J. H. *France, a Nation of Patriots*. New York: Columbia University Press, 1930.

――――. *The Historical Evolution of Modern Nationalism*. New York: Smith, 1931.

Huddleston, Sisley, *Paris Salons, Cafes, Studios*. Philadelphia: J. B. Lippincott, 1928.

Hughes, H. Stuart. *Consciousness and Society: The Reorientation of European Social Thought, 1890-1930*. New York: Knopf, 1958.

Hutton, Patrick. "The Impact of the Boulangist Crisis upon the Guesdist Party at Bordeaux," *French Historical Studies*, VII (1971), 226-244.

Jaclard, Victor. "Tactique socialiste," *La Revue socialiste*, XVII (April, 1893), 385-401.

Jaurès, Jean. *Oeuvres de Jean Jaurès: Etudes socialistes*. Vols. II and III. Paris: Les Editions Rieder, 1932.

Johnson, Douglas. *France and the Dreyfus Affair*. London: Blandford, 1967.

Kohn, Hans. *Making of the Modern French Mind*. New York: Van Nostrand, 1955.

King, Jere. *Foch versus Clemenceau*. Cambridge: Harvard University Press, 1960.

Lafargue, Paul. "Les Dernières Élections législatives," *L'Ere nouvelle*, II (August, 1894), 317ff.

Lalou, René. *Contemporary French Literature*. Translated by William Aspenwall Bradley. London: Jonathan Cape, 1925.

Levasseur, Emile. *Questions ouvrières et industrielles en France sous la IIIe République*. Paris: A. Rousseau, 1907.

Liedot, Jean Claude. "Les Elections législatives de Meurthe et Moselle en 1902," *Les Annales de l'Est*, IV, 1961.

Longergan, Walter F. *Forty Years of Paris*. London: T. Fisher, 1907.

287

Lorrain, Jean. "Nouveaux Masques," *Mercure de France*, XXIV (November, 1897), 339-345.

MacIntyre, Alasdair. "On Marcuse," *New York Review of Books*, October 23, 1969, pp. 38-39.

McClelland, J. S. *The French Right*. London: Cape, 1970.

Marin, Louis. *Regards sur la Lorraine*. Paris: Paul Geuthner, 1966.

Mauclair, Camille. *Paul Adam, 1862-1920*. Paris: Ernest Flammarion, n.d.

Maurras, Charles. *Enquête sur la monarchie*. Definitive edition. Paris: Nouvelle Librairie Nationale, 1924.

―――. *Maîtres et témoins de ma vie d'esprit*. Paris: Flammarion, 1954.

Mayer, Arno J. *Dynamics of Counterrevolution in Europe, 1870-1956*. New York: Harper and Row, 1971.

Meyer, Arthur. *Ce que je peux dire*. Paris: Librairie Hachette, 1912.

―――. *Ce que mes yeux ont vu*. Paris: Plon, 1911.

Miquel, Pierre. *Poincaré*. Paris: A. Fayard, 1961.

Mosse, George L. "The Genesis of Fascism," *Journal of Contemporary History*, I, No. 1 (1966).

―――. "The French Right and the Working Classes: Les Jaunes," *Ibid.*, July-October, 1972.

Nadeau, Maurice. *The History of Surrealism*. New York: Macmillan, 1965.

Noland, Aaron. *Founding of the French Socialist Party*. Cambridge: Harvard University Press, 1956.

Nolte, Ernst. *Three Faces of Fascism*. New York: Holt, Rinehart, and Winston, 1966.

Paul-Boncour, Joseph. *Recollections of the Third Republic*. Translated by George Marion, Jr. Vol. I. New York: Robert Speller, 1957.

Pisani-Ferry, Fresnette. *Le Général Boulanger*. Paris: Flammarion, 1969.

Plumyène, Jean and Lasierra, Raymond. *Les Fascismes françaises, 1923-1963*. Paris: Editions du Seuil, 1963.

Pouquet, J. M. *The Last Salon: Anatole France and His Muse*. London: Jonathan Cape, 1927.

Prost, Antoine. *L'Histoire de l'enseignenantdn France 1800-1967*. Paris: A. Colin, 1968.

Reinach, Joseph. *Histoire de l'affaire Dreyfus*. 7 Vols. Paris: Fasquelle, 1901-1908.

Rémond, René. *La Droit en France de 1815 à nos jours*. Paris: Aubier, 1954.

Renard, Jules. *Journal, 1887-1910*. Paris: Editions Gallimard, 1965.

Rey, Etienne. *La Renaissance de l'orgueil française*. Paris: Grasset, 1912.

Richard, Gabriel. "Le Boulangisme à Nancy. L'Election au Conseil générale de Nancy - ouest." *Le Pays Lorrain*, I (1962).

BIBLIOGRAPHY

———. "Les Elections de 1889 en Meurthe et Moselle." *Ibid.*, II (1963).

Ridge, George Ross. *The Hero in French Decadent Literature*. Athens: University of Georgia Press, 1961.

Roberts, John. "General Boulanger," *History Today*, V (1955), 657-669.

Rouanet, Gustave. "Le Parti socialiste français en 1898," *La Revue socialiste*, XXVIII (July, 1898), 91ff.

Sartre, Jean Paul. *No Exit and Three Other Plays*. New York: Vintage Books, 1946.

Schapiro, J. Salwyn. *Liberalism and the Challenge of Fascism: Social Forces in England and France, 1815-1870*. New York: McGraw-Hill, 1949.

Scheikevitch, Marie. *Time Past: Memories of Proust and Others*. New York: Houghton Mifflin, 1935.

Scott, John A. *Republican Ideas and the Liberal Tradition in France, 1870-1914*. New York: Columbia University Press, 1951.

Scott, Jonathan F. *Patriots in the Making*. New York: D. Appelton, 1916.

Seager, Frederic H. *The Boulanger Affair*. Ithaca: Cornell University Press, 1969.

Seilhac, Léon de. "L'Organisation socialiste," *La Revue bleue*, XXXIII, Part I (January 25, 1896), 108-109.

Shapiro, David (ed.). *St. Anthony's Papers. Number 13: The Right in France, 1890-1919*. Carbondale: Southern Illinois University Press, 1962.

Shattuck, Roger. *The Banquet Years: The Arts in France, 1885-1918*. New York: Harcourt, 1958.

Siegfried, André. *France: A Study in Nationality*. New Haven: Yale University Press, 1930.

Soury, Jules. *Campagne nationaliste, 1899-1901*. Paris: Plon-Nourrit, 1902.

Stock, Phyllis H. "Students versus the University in Pre-World War Paris," *French Historical Studies*, VII (1971), 93-110.

Suarez, Andre and Claudel, Paul. *Correspondence, 1904-1938*. Paris: Gallimard, 1951.

Sumler, David E. "Domestic Influences on the Nationalist Revival in France, 1909-1914," *French Historical Studies*, VI (1970), 517-537.

Tannenbaum, Edward R. *The Action Française: Die-Hard Reactionaries in Twentieth Century France*. New York: Wiley, 1962.

Tharaud, Jérôme and Jean. *La Vie et la mort de Déroulède*. Paris: Plon, 1925.

Thomas, Marcel. *L'Affaire sans Dreyfus*. Paris: Librairie Arthème Fayard, 1961.

Tint, Herbert. *The Decline of French Patriotism*. London: Weidenfeld and Nicolson, 1964.

Weber, Eugen. *Action Française: Royalism and Reaction in Twentieth Century France*. Stanford, Stanford University Press, 1962.

———. *The Nationalist Revival in France, 1905-1914*. Berkeley: University of California Press, 1959.

———. "Nationalism, Socialism, and National-Socialism in France," *French Historical Studies*, II (1961-1962), 273-307.

———. "The Secret World of Jean Barois" in Weiss, John. *The Origins of Modern Consciousness*. Detroit: Wayne State University Press, 1965.

Weill, Georges. *Histoire de l'enseignement secondaire en France (1802-1920)*. Paris: Payot, 1921.

Willard, Claude. *Les Guesdistes*. Paris: Editions Sociales, 1965.

Zévaès, Alexandre. *Au temps du boulangisme*. Paris: Gallimard, 1930.

———. *Henri Rochefort le pamphlétaire*. Paris: E. F. E., 1946.

———. *Histoire du socialisme et communisme en France 1871-1947*. Paris: Editions France-Empire, n.d.

———. *Notes et souvenirs d'un militant*. Paris: Marcel Rivière, 1913.

Zevort, Edgar. *Histoire de la troisième république*. 4 Vols. Paris: G. Baillière, 1896-1901.

INDEX

Action Française, 5, 121, 194-197, 211, 213-214, 218, 234, 245

Action Liberale, 5, 212, 215, 218

Adam, Paul, 33, 39, 41, 57, 61, 65, 67-68

Agathon (Henri Massis and Alfred de Tarde), 233-234

Aimel, Henri, 56, 71, 93, 98

Alsace-Lorraine, 22-23, 37, 191, 229-232

Amouretti, Frédéric, 122, 138

Anti-Semitic League, 5, 38, 164, 215

Anti-Semitism and racism, 52-54, 60, 62, 84-87, 123, 141-142, 157, 165-167, 169-174, 190-191, 198, 230-231, 239

Appel au soldat, l', 32-33, 184-186

Aragon, Louis, 240, 246n

Archdeacon, Edmond, 198, 200, 206, 217

Argeliès, Jean Baptiste, 71, 96, 148-149, 167-168

Au service de l'Allemagne, 229-231

Bakunin, Michael, 131

Barodet, Desiré, 98

Barrès, Maurice: World War I contribution, 237-240; views on intellectuals, 127, 161-163, 188, 196; and Bloc National, 5, 241; as counterrevolutionary, 246-247; at *La Cocarde*, 120-139; conversion to Boulangism, 29-33; decentralization and federalism of, 131-135, 137-139, 168, 207-208; influence on French youth, 126-127, 233-234, 240, 246; death of mother, 202-203; on Protestantism, 189-191; on Rhineland question, 241-242; proto-fascism of, 206-210, 216-217, 245-248; social program and socialism, 43-49, 80-81, 90-91, 94, 127-136, 139-152, 166-168, 206-208, 219-223; belief in great men, 22, 144; childhood, 8-12; educational views, 15, 127-128, 241; nationalism, 10-11, 15-18, 115, 143-144, 149-150, 153-158, 165-169, 183-191; political role and effectiveness, 63-64, 111-116; view of Marxism, 120, 128-131, 142-143, 150. See also: Anti-Semitism and racism, Church-State question and religion, electoral campaigns, foreign workers question, Alsace-Lorraine question

Barthou, Louis, 225

Basly, Emile, 73

Bazin, René, 229-230

Beauquier, Charles, 137

Belleval, Louis de, 72, 77, 82, 90, 149

Beranger, Henri, 114

Berry, Georges, 218

Bienaîmé, Admiral, 213

Blanqui, Auguste, 77

Blum, Léon, 126-127, 158, 161-162

Boisdeffre, Pierre de, 6n, 20, 122, 229, 246

Bonnamour, Georges, 123

Bonnet Rouge, Le, 239

Borie, Léon, 72, 90

Boudeau, Jean, 72, 91

Boulanger, Georges, 5, 25-29, 34-35, 54-69, 92-93

Bourget, Paul, 20, 123

Bouttier, Alphonse, 38, 41, 172

Brasillach, Robert, 245

Breton, André, 240

Breton, Jules, 137

Briand, Aristide, 220-226, 235, 248

Brisson, Henri, 177, 225

Brousse, Paul, 94, 138

Caillaux, Joseph, 235, 239

Camus, Albert, 246

Castelin, André, 73, 91, 95, 97

Cavaignac, Godefroy, 177, 192, 194, 205-212, 218
Chiché, Albert, 56, 71, 73-74, 81, 96-98
Church-State question and religion, 52, 57, 94-95, 106, 223-229, 238-239
Clemenceau, Georges, 28, 52, 72, 97, 221-223, 232, 239
Clouard, Henri, 121-123
Cloutier, Daniel, 205, 207-208
Colette Baudoche, 229-232
Colline inspirée, La, 4, 226, 228-229, 249
Colson, Albert, 62, 64-65
Combes, Emile, 218, 224
Constans, Ernest, 54, 58, 60, 66, 78
Coppée, François, 179-180, 191, 197, 199, 204, 212, 217
Couturier, Valentin, 81, 95
Culte du moi, Le, 4, 20, 25, 30-33, 42, 45, 51, 86, 126-127, 139-141, 155-156, 219, 224, 228, 234, 246
Darwin, Charles, 130
Daudet, Léon, 239
Dausset, Louis, 179, 192-194, 206, 212-213
De Hegel aux cantines du Nord, 122, 129
Debu-Bridel, Jacques, 245
Delahaye, Jules, 73, 82, 96, 185
Denis, Pierre, 90-91, 123-125, 149
Déracinés, Les, 154-158, 184, 244
Déroulède, Paul, 15-16, 27, 30, 32, 35, 68, 72, 78, 80, 83-84, 87, 90-92, 96-98, 137, 174, 178-182, 185, 191-194, 197-202, 205, 212-217, 236, 245-246
Deville, Gabriel, 207, 209
Diverses Familles spirituelles de France, 238-239
Dreyfus affair, 5, 158-163, 177-178, 183, 188
Drieu La Rochelle, Pierre, 245
Drumont, Edouard, 53, 84-85, 137, 149, 192-193, 206
Du sang, de la volupté et de la mort, 86-87, 154
Dumay, Jean Baptiste, 80
Dumonteil, Jean Marie, 73, 91, 199
Dupuy, Charles, 112, 136, 177

Duret, Théodore, 114
Electoral campaigns: 1889, 36-69; 1893, 108-111; 1896, 146-148, 151-152; 1898, 163-175; 1903, 205-210; 1906, 217-219
Engels, Friedrich, 39, 95-96
Ennemi des lois, L', 4, 131, 140-142, 154, 185
Failure of anti-Dreyfusard leagues, 214-216
Farcy, Eugène, 71
Faure, Maurice, 137
Ferroul, Joseph, 80-81, 95
Flandin, P. E., 225
Floquet, Charles, 113-114
Forain, Jean Louis, 180
Foreign workers, 37, 40-41, 60-61, 108-110, 147-148, 166-167
Fourier, Charles, 131, 141, 239
Fournière, Eugène, 123-126, 145
France, Anatole, 179
French socialism of the 1890s, 118-120, 148-149
Gabriel, Alfred, 38-42, 47-49, 58-62, 64-65, 67, 74-75, 77, 81, 90, 96, 101-108, 109, 111, 123-125, 134, 193, 243
Galli, Henri, 179, 193, 206, 213
Gallifet, General, 77
Gambetta, Léon, 137
Gauthier de Clagny, Albert, 73, 80, 96, 179, 218, 222
Gervaize, Ludovic, 169-175, 182
Gide, André, 240, 245
Girardet, Raoul, 215-216
Goblet, René, 129-130, 137
Goussot, Emile, 72, 91, 193
Grande Pitié des eglises de France, La, 226
Granger, Ernest, 71, 77, 80-82, 98
Green, Julien, 1
Grosjean, Georges, 205
Grover, Frederic, 240n, 246
Guehenno, Jean, 246
Guérin, Jules, 149, 164, 192
Guesde, Jules, 85, 94, 109
Habert, Marcel, 174, 181-182, 198-200, 202-214
Hamon, Augustin, 122
Henry, Major, 177-178
Herr, Lucien, 162-163

Hervé, Gustave, 209, 240
Herz, Cornelius, 96
Homme libre, L', 22-23, 30, 45, 154,
    162, 242-243
Hugo, Victor, 156-157
Hugues, Clovis, 123, 149
Huret, Jules, 77
Indy, Vincent d', 180
Jaclard, Victor, 98, 119, 138
Jardin de Bérénice, Le, 23-25, 45-46,
    185, 230
Jaurès, Jean, 109, 118, 129-130, 137,
    148, 158, 177, 207, 209, 220-222
Jourde, Antoine, 71-72, 77, 93, 98,
    148
Kantianism, 10, 155, 188
Lafargue, Paul, 39, 72, 93-95, 98
Lagarde, Paul, 123, 138
Laguerre, Georges, 28, 30, 35, 67,
    72, 81, 83-84, 89-92
Laisant, Charles, 28, 41, 58, 72, 76,
    81, 83-85, 91, 93
Lalou, Charles, 73
Laporte, Gaston, 72, 80, 90, 98
Larcher, 59-62
Lassalle, Ferdinand, 141
Laur, Francis, 28, 54, 72, 79-80,
    84, 91-92, 107
Lavisse, Ernest, 180
Le Hérissé, René, 28, 35, 65, 72, 90
    199
Le Play and corporatism, 135-136,
    167
Le Senne, Charles, 72, 182
Le Veillé, Georges, 71, 81, 91-92,
    96
League of Patriots, 5, 16, 37-38, 54,
    66-68, 72, 83, 178-183, 197-202,
    204-207, 212-215, 245
Lefèvre, André, 151
Lemaître, Jules, 179-180, 187,
    191-194, 201, 205-206, 212-213
Lemire, abbé, 149
Leo XIII, 76
Leurs figures, 113, 184-186
Ludwig II, 143
Macintyre, Alasdair, 140
Mackau, baron, 82
Madaule, Jacques, 246
Magalhaes-Lima, Sebastian, 138
Magnard, Francis, 33-34

Mahy, François de, 193, 195
Malon, Benoit, 85, 94
Malraux, André, 246, 248
Marcuse, Herbert, 140
Martin, Marius, 73, 80, 90, 96
Martineau, Alfred, 72
Mauclair, Camille, 122-123, 138
Maurras, Charles, 122-123, 138,
    195-197, 216
Mayer, Arno J., 246-247
McClelland, J. C., 246
Méline, Jules, 203-204
Mercier, General, 206
Meyer, Arthur, 180
Michelet, Jules, 137
Millerand, Alexandre, 98, 118, 137,
    148, 152, 183, 214, 232, 241
Millevoye, Lucien, 73, 91, 95-97,
    149, 179, 182, 193, 203-204, 206,
    209, 218
Minck, Paule, 123-124, 138
Mitchell, Charles, 73
Moreau, Emile, 81
Morès, marquis de, 84, 97, 149,
    151-152, 172, 186
Mosse, George, 244
Mun, comte de, 81, 91, 94
Naquet, Alfred, 28, 30, 67, 72, 82-84,
    88-92
Nicholas, Eugène, 169-171
Nolte, Ernst, 245
Notes sur Italie, 154
Panama scandal, 96-98
Papelier, Pierre Albert, 62, 102-106,
    164-165
Pascal, Paul, 123, 138
Patrie Française, League of the, 5,
    179-180, 182-184, 187, 191-194,
    197-198, 200-201, 203-209,
    212-213, 215-217, 219, 245-246
Paul-Boncour, Joseph, 117, 126-127
Paulin-Méry, César, 72, 80, 90-92,
    96, 149, 179, 193, 206, 208
Pellieux, General, 181-182
Pelloutier, Fernand, 122, 124
Platon, G., 128-129
Plumyène, Jean and Lasierra,
    Raymond, 246
Poincaré, Raymond, 177, 223,
    232-233, 235, 248
Polignac, Edmond de, 41-42, 44

Pontois, Jean, 72, 90
Pressensé, Francis de, 110, 177, 179
Proudhon, Pierre Joseph, 131-135, 137, 141, 239
Pujo, Maurice, 194
Quinet, Edgar, 12, 137
Rebell, Hugues, 123
Reclus, Paul, 179
Reinach, Jacques de, 96, 186
Reinach, Joseph, 160, 177-178, 225, 248
Remond, René, 245
Renan, Ernest, 127
Renard, Georges, 138, 145
Revest, Emile, 71
Rey, Etienne, 229-230, 234-235
Ribot, Alexandre, 203
Richard, Pierre, 73, 91, 94-95, 193
Roche, Ernest, 71, 77, 80-82, 97-98, 137, 193, 206, 218
Rochefort, Henri and Rochefortists, 5, 27-28, 35, 55, 58, 66, 71-72, 83, 91-92, 97, 137, 192-193, 198, 204-209, 215, 217
Roosevelt, Theodore, 238
Saint-Just, Antoine Louis, 76
Saint-Mandé program, 148, 152
Saint-Martin, Jean Baptiste, 28, 67, 72
Saint-Simon, Claude Henri de, 131, 141
Sartre, Jean Paul, 139, 246
Saussay, Raoul de, 73, 80, 90
Sautumier, Louis, 147-148, 150-151
Say, Léon, 109, 143
Scènes et doctrines du nationalisme, 184-185, 187-188, 206-207, 210-211

Sembat, Marcel, 138, 151
Siegfried, Jules, 225
Sorel, Albert, 180
Soucy, Robert, 3, 7, 86-87, 122, 158n, 230-231, 246
Soury, Jules, 178
Sous l'oeil des barbares, 20-22, 30, 45, 153, 162
Sternhell, Zeev, 7, 15n, 122
Sumler, David E., 235
Symbolism and decadence, 11-14, 32-33
Syveton, Gabriel, 179, 192-193, 198, 204-206, 212-213
Taches d'encre, Les, 14-16
Taine, Hippolyte, 127, 129, 134, 155-156
Talmeyr, Maurice, 199
Terrail-Mermeix, Dieudonné, 57, 72, 88-89
Thalamus, François, 214
Thiébaud, Georges, 179, 181, 199, 201
Thomas, Albert, 225
Touchard, Jean, 153-154
Turigny, Jean, 28, 65, 72, 90, 98
Vallès, Jules, 16
Vaugeois, Henri, 179, 194-195
Veber, Adrien, 138, 201
Venice, 23
Vergoin, Maurice, 41, 54, 57, 61, 68
Viviani, René, 137, 148
Waldeck-Rousseau, René, 183-184, 203
Watson, D. R., 214-215
Weber, Eugen, 99, 122, 243
Zévaès, Alexandre, 126-127
Zola, Emile, 66, 112, 115, 160-164